Encountering the
Jewish Future

Encountering the Jewish Future

with

Elie Wiesel
Martin Buber
Abraham Joshua Heschel
Hannah Arendt
Emmanuel Levinas

MARC H. ELLIS

Fortress Press
Minneapolis

ENCOUNTERING THE JEWISH FUTURE
With Wiesel, Buber, Heschel, Arendt, and Levinas

Cover image: *The Talmudists* (oil on canvas) by Jacob Kramer (1892–1962). Leeds Museums and Galleries (City Art Gallery) U.K./ The Bridgeman Art Library
Cover design: Nicole Summers
Book design: PerfecType, Nashville, TN

Interior photos: Elie Wiesel © Sergio Gaudenti/Kipa/Corbis. Martin Buber: Wikimedia Commons. Abraham Joshua Heschel © Bernard Gotfryd / Getty Images. Hannah Arendt © Estate of Fred Stein, FredStein.com (http://FredStein.com). Used by permission. Emmanual Levinas © Bracha L. Ettinger, under the CC-BY-SA 2.5 License. Richard L. Rubenstein: Photo supplied by author.

Library of Congress Cataloging-in-Publication Data
Ellis, Marc H.
    Encountering the Jewish future : with Elie Wiesel, Martin Buber, Abraham Joshua Heschel, Hannah Arendt, and Emmanuel Levinas / Marc H. Ellis.
    p. cm.
    Includes bibliographical references and index.
    ISBN 978-0-8006-9793-8 (alk. paper)
    1. Judaism—Doctrines. 2. Jewish philosophy. 3. Jews—Civilization. 4. Jews—Identity. 5. Holocaust (Jewish theology) 6. Arab-Israeli conflict. I. Title.
    BM602.E55 2011
    296.3—dc22
                            2011009186

"Like the training of a fighter"

For Aaron and Isaiah
loves of my life

and those who saved me

Roger Sanders
Michael West
Rosemary Reuther
Hulitt Gloer
Sara Roy

Contents

Richard Rubenstein
(1924–)

Introduction

In 1963 the great Jewish philosopher Emmanuel Levinas published a collection of his essays on Jewish life. In his fascinating and provocative essays, Levinas sought to counter the drift in Jewish life toward an uncritical assimilation to the culture and violence of the modern world. After the Holocaust and the birth of the state of Israel, Levinas felt that a new chapter of Jewish history was opening.

Levinas was born in Lithuania and became a French citizen in 1930; he was one of the few Jews to survive the Holocaust and continue to live in post-Holocaust Europe. As such, Levinas was an eyewitness to both the Holocaust and the birth of the state of Israel. In those dark times, Levinas wondered if the surviving Jewish world was ready—and able—to persevere. Age-old questions confronted Jews anew, but, once again, these questions presented profound challenges. Jews were deeply wounded and scarred. Now they had reemerged on the world scene. If Jews were to take control of their destiny, Levinas thought they had to return to the traditions of Judaism and the essence of what it means to be Jewish.

But were Judaism and Jewishness the same as they had always been, without change and eternal? Though Levinas thought this to be the case in general, he also realized that different contexts present challenges for ancient principles and understandings. Through the confluence of the ancient and the modern,

Levinas sought to articulate a way for Jews to return and renew their identity in a changing world.

Perhaps unsurprisingly, Levinas held out the Jewish ethical tradition as the medium for modern Jews to re-embrace their vocation in the world. Levinas hoped that the formative challenges would not suppress this ethical tradition. The contemporary challenges for Jews revolved around the systematic murder of six million Jews in the Holocaust and the Jewish assumption of power in the state of Israel. In light of this trauma and hope, Levinas believed ethics were even more defining of Jewish identity and a renewed Jewish commitment.

Levinas was ambivalent about this prospect, as were the other Jewish thinkers I explore in these pages: Elie Wiesel, Martin Buber, Abraham Joshua Heschel, and Hannah Arendt. Each articulated their ambivalence with differing points of view. Their strength is that they dealt with the two formative events in Jewish history. The Holocaust exposed the intense vulnerability of European Jewry. The state of Israel proposed the physical and military empowerment of the survivors of the Holocaust and Jews around the world.

In exploring these Jewish thinkers, the scope of their interest and expertise is so wide as to defy categorization. Their thought moves within and beyond what we know today as academic disciplines. They are philosophers and theologians, biblical exegetes and interpreters, political scientists and sociologists, mystics and realists. They are Jewish "thinkers" who are also "committed."

First and foremost, Wiesel, Buber, Heschel, Arendt, and Levinas explored the difficult, almost impossible questions facing the Jewish people after the Holocaust and the creation of the state of Israel. Their first priority was their Jewishness and how that Jewishness interacted with the broader world: they were committed Jewish thinkers.

Though we might group them together, emphasizing their many similarities, each also displayed a variegated self. Although some aspects of each of these thinkers are well known, because of their complexities there are aspects that neither the thinker nor the world recognize and aspects that it would be difficult for each to affirm. A variegated self is insistent and yet open to interpretation. Profound thinkers, Jewish or otherwise, should be mined for what they thought in their time, as well as unearthed for another time. These twentieth-century Jewish thinkers spoke to their time. They also speak to ours.

Personalities are complex and thinkers no less so in the persona that emerges within and from their work. When the stakes are high, thought takes on an urgency that may lack the self-reflection we presume as normative in ourselves and in others. Although Jewish thinkers are known for their precision and incisiveness, like all thinkers they are limited.

Sometimes limitations come from the urgency of the moment or from a thinker's context. Jewish thought provides an incredibly vibrant and open window onto the world, but sometimes this can block other windows that provide other important vistas. The depth of Jewish thought comes from the preoccupation with what it means to be Jewish. The limitations of Jewish thought come from that same preoccupation.

I frame my exploration around the encounters I had with these Jewish thinkers. Sometimes, as with Abraham Joshua Heschel, these were personal encounters. Other encounters came through the meeting ground provided by my teacher, Richard Rubenstein, whose voice is the thread that weaves through my other encounters. Like these other Jewish thinkers, Rubenstein thinks with a fierce urgency that yields much fruit and few friends.

In one way or another, each of our thinkers met and engaged each other, if not personally then in the interaction of the Jewish world on issues central to its existence. Though global in its reach, the Jewish world is small and personal. Intellectual encounters are often personal encounters. For example, Wiesel met Buber, Arendt, and Heschel; Buber and Heschel were more than acquaintances. Sometimes they held their peers in high esteem. Other times, there were intellectual disagreements that included personal animosity.

Each of our Jewish thinkers was speaking for themselves and on behalf of the Jewish people. Our thinkers were judged by other thinkers and those Jews who were not engaged in the intellectual life. Like Jewish thinkers, ordinary Jews can be incisive and judgmental. Yet as a small minority community with a tremendously high visibility as well as a history of suffering, Jews have a stake in what their fellow Jews say about them. Not unsurprisingly, the followers of our Jewish thinkers are often equaled by those who vehemently disagree with them.

The encounters I recount in this book—highly intellectual, deeply personal, often direct, tangible, and in person—are fraught with historical and personal significance. Some are mutually reinforcing, as when one understanding builds upon another. Others result in clashes that lead to deep fissures that never heal. With so much at stake, how can we expect otherwise?

Encounters are like conversations; they begin and continue in different forms and venues. Genuine encounters mark us for life. Each of our thinkers left an indelible and monumental mark on my life, on Jewish life, and on the world. I benefited from all of these encounters when they initially occurred and continue to do so over time, and now again in this writing.

Today Jewish life stands on the shoulders of intellectual and spiritual giants. In these encounters I witness a past greatness, a willingness to grapple with profound and difficult issues, as well as a way that opens up beyond the encounters themselves. Yet I would not be showing these thinkers the respect they are due by remaining silent about their limitations. In the end I conclude that the future of Jewish life faces still greater peril than even they understood.

What they saw as the potential or possible future we now encounter as our present, our *now*. It may be, as Levinas understood it, that fidelity as a Jew today is our "difficult freedom." For me that has transposed itself into an increasingly "difficult future." It is in that difficult future that the Jewish encounter takes place today.

This book began in an encounter that might, at first glance, seem unusual. During the 1980s I taught at the Maryknoll School of Theology in New York. It was a curious teaching assignment for someone who has been Jewish from birth and is a practicing Jew as well. Even so, the Catholic Foreign Mission Society of America invited me to teach at its school of theology and develop a Master of Arts program in Justice and Peace Studies. Founded in the early twentieth century as the American counterpart of the worldwide Christian mission to convert "pagans" to Christianity, in the 1960s, Maryknoll underwent its own conversion to the poor and the oppressed. During that conversion, it shifted its primary vocation from one of converting others to Christianity to working with indigenous peoples around the world for their own liberation from poverty and oppression. Maryknoll discovered the liberation theology that was then emerging in Latin America. Through its publishing arm, Orbis Books, Maryknoll began to publish liberation theology in English, which made it possible for African theologians to read Latin American theologians and Asian theologians to read and be read by people around the world. Soon liberation theology spread to other parts of the globe.

My program in Justice and Peace Studies had this liberation perspective, and soon students from around the world came to study with me. Most of the students were already pursuing justice and peace in difficult, often violent situations. As a young twenty-six-year-old, my students from Africa, Latin America, and Asia had much to teach me. My world expanded.

What I experienced in travelling to my students' native lands was eye opening. I found grinding poverty and engaged struggle, cultural renaissance and elite powerbrokers. I found that a dominating Christianity was alive and well. I also found resisting Christians seeking economic and political revolution.

Even then, I heard the tired refrains of an interfaith dialogue in which Jews and Christians had finally made their peace with each other in America. In my classroom at Maryknoll a different engagement took place. Here students from around the world encountered me developing a Jewish theology of liberation. At the same time, I encountered their theologies of liberation. The interaction was intense. None of us knew where it would go.

I learned that the environments from which my students came and returned to was dangerous and their work among the poor made their lives precarious. As a Jew, I would soon be venturing into dangerous intellectual and religious territory. Our common danger augured a new interfaith dialogue or, more importantly, a new solidarity among Jews and Christians in the struggle for liberation.

Many of my students had become Christian in their lifetime. Since they lived in parts of the world where there were few Jews, I was the first Jew they encountered. Because of the missionaries' stories about the demise of Judaism in the coming of Jesus the Christ, many of my students were surprised to know that Jews and Judaism still existed. Our first encounters were sometimes awkward, other times amusing. They were also invigorating. On their side, no one they knew had ever met a Jew. On my side, Jews were becoming more and more isolated in America and Israel.

One such student was Mun Kyun Hun, whom I knew at Maryknoll as "Father Mun." Despite his limited English, I realized that there was something different about him. His face brightened as we discussed the Jewish God of liberation. I felt a force emanating from him. Since he said little during the course, I was surprised when he asked me to be his thesis advisor.

Father Mun asked to write on the reunification of the Koreas from a theological perspective, a topic that resonates today. With Korea having been racked for centuries by wars and imperialisms, he thought that a theological justification for a political unification of the Koreas was important.

One day, after his thesis was complete, Father Mun asked to see me. Seated in a chair in my office, Father Mun asked a question that was a decision for action. He was seeking my approval. I thought of Martin Buber's understanding of "meeting"—a time when two persons come together for a decision essential to a person's destiny. The listener needs to focus and discern what is at stake. I listened intently. What was Father Mun saying to me? What was being left unsaid?

Father Mun proposed placing his thesis into action. Having argued for a unified Korea, it was time to enact his thesis by traveling to North Korea and crossing the border into the South. He asked what I thought of his plan. I asked him what the consequences might be if he carried it out. He told me he would be arrested and jailed, probably for years. He awaited my thoughts, even though I knew he had already decided upon his course of action. As a Christian, Father Mun was taking on suffering for the sake of his nation. Should I try to dissuade him?

After Father Mun accomplished his mission, he was arrested, tried, and convicted. His trial gained national and international attention. The publicity surrounding the trial spread the word that many in Korea wanted a reunified country. Father Mun was jailed for more than three years. After being released, Father Mun again crossed into North Korea, and again was jailed.

During his time in prison, Father Mun expanded his thesis into a history of the Catholic Church in Korea. It is a devastating account of the collusion of his own church with powers outside of Korea. Yet it is also a work of great hope. Here a Catholic priest acted on his principles and was jailed for his commitment. In prison he wrote of his own tradition's complicity in the hardship of the Korean people. Father Mun's life is a clarion call to his faith community for introspection and a renewed commitment to repentance and sacrifice on behalf of justice.

After his release from prison, I visited Father Mun in Korea. I also met with many of my former students, also Korean. Seeing my students in their own setting made me understand their quest for knowledge as part of their commitment to a more just society. It made my teaching come alive in another dimension, and it deepened my learning of what I was teaching. How much more learning takes place when the students who come to you are also teachers in their own right.

Then Father Mun and I lost track of each other. Years later I found him again through a Korean professor, Dr. Choong-Koo Park (CK), when we were both teaching at Union Theological Seminary in the Philippines. In the Philippines there was an ongoing insurgency where government-sponsored death squads sought to quell unrest among the civilian population. Peasants were being displaced from the land. Unions were being constrained.

CK and I traveled the countryside. During our travels we met a Protestant minister who had been shot in the legs as a warning. The powers that be weren't pleased with his work among the peasants and the unemployed. We also met with a union president who was on the run, threatened by a multinational corporation. Fearing for his life, he slept in a different house every night. His three predecessors had been assassinated.

During our late night discussions, I mentioned my lost connection with Father Mun, who CK helped me find. The following year I reconnected with Father Mun in Korea. I left this emotional "meeting" with him as when I first encountered him at Maryknoll. Was I Father Mun's teacher or his student?

Before leaving Korea, I was asked to return to participate in the celebration of the six-hundredth issue of the Korean journal *Christian Thought* as their keynote lecturer. When wondering what subject would be relevant to a Korean audience, the journal editor responded immediately, "Abraham Joshua Heschel." They asked if there might be other Jewish thinkers that I could lecture on. Much to my surprise, they had read Jewish thinkers that I felt close to and who were relevant to them as Christians and as Koreans. They admired Jewish thinkers for articulating deep spiritual realities in a complex and difficult world.

When I returned home I began writing about Jews and Judaism through the lenses of the Jews I explore in this book. What unfolds is a story of Jewish life in the twentieth and now twenty-first century. Yet in the background of these encounters is the question of the Jewish future. What will the Jewish future look like decades from now? Or has the Jewish future already arrived? What is that Jewish future? Is the Jewish future in continuity or discontinuity with the past? Or both?

In many ways I had been working on the question of the Jewish future for years, although not necessarily in those terms. I have read many studies on the Jewish future that focus on intermarriage and birth rates, essentially asking about the future of Jewish identity by noting how many Jews there are or will be in the coming years. After the Holocaust and living in open societies, the concern is obvious. If Jews have a chance to be whoever they want to be, will they choose to be Jewish? Other studies focus on the relation between Diaspora Jews and Israel (for example, how many American Jews visit Israel or what Israelis think of American Jews). Still other studies survey the American population and their views of Jews and Israel. What do Americans think of Jews? What do they think of Israel? Do Americans support the state of Israel and do they think that American foreign policy should tilt toward or away from Israel?

Since September 11, Islam has become firmly entrenched on the American and Jewish radar screen. How do non-Jews view Islam and how in their eyes do Jews fare when compared with Muslims? Has September 11 strengthened America's relationship with Israel or has it raised questions about that support? Since increasing parts of the world question America's special relationship with Israel, what do Americans think about that?

My focus has been different, as have the Jews I encounter here. For me, the question has always been the ethics of Judaism and Jewishness and how Jewish ethics can be brought to bear on Jews and the world. In my view, the issues of intermarriage and the Jewish birthrate pale in significance to these questions, as does polling on what others thinks of Jews and Israel. Perhaps it is naïve. I feel that the Jewish future has to do with the Jewish prophetic and how that prophetic comes alive in the world.

I believe that without the prophetic there is little reason to be Jewish. Perhaps this applies to Christianity and Islam as well. Nonetheless, ancient Israel bequeathed the prophetic to the world. The prophetic is indigenous to the Jewish people, our foundational principle. I believe that each Jewish generation faces the daunting task of renewing the prophetic.

I also know as a teacher, writer, and public speaker that Jews can be hard on those who carry the prophetic message in our time. Long ago I realized that although Jews hold the prophetic as our founding principle, we also are the great strugglers against the prophetic. Depending on one's perspective, it is either paradoxical or ironic that Jews embody the prophetic and attempt to limit or destroy it. Perhaps it is both.

All of the Jewish thinkers I encounter were framed by the Holocaust. Elie Wiesel survived Auschwitz and lost his family in the Holocaust. Abraham

Joshua Heschel fled Poland and lost his immediate family there. Martin Buber and Hannah Arendt had to flee Germany. Emmanuel Levinas, born in Lithuania but already in France, was imprisoned during World War II. Though born in America, Richard Rubenstein wrote one of the first and most provocative books on the Holocaust and its meaning for contemporary Jews.

All of the Jewish thinkers I encounter were framed by the birth of the state of Israel. Though differing in some respects, all were Zionists. When Martin Buber fled Germany in the late 1930s, he went to Jerusalem where he lived until his death in 1965. Hannah Arendt, like Buber, as a homeland Zionist, wrote extensively about the possibility of a Jewish homeland in Palestine. Elie Wiesel visited Israel after its birth in 1948 and has been a supporter ever since. Abraham Joshua Heschel wrote a lyrical and analytical book about Israel after the 1967 Arab-Israeli war. Like Richard Rubenstein, Emmanuel Levinas supported Israel throughout his life, though unlike Rubenstein he worried about the challenges Israel brought to Jews and Judaism.

All of our Jewish thinkers were haunted by the prophetic. Especially Martin Buber, Abraham Joshua Heschel, and Emmanuel Levinas wrote innovatively and beautifully about the prophetic tradition. If the prophetic Jewish tradition was alive in the twentieth century, these men defined it. Yet, as was the case with the Holocaust and Israel, they also worried about its survival. If it did survive, they worried what shape the prophetic might take in the future.

Though each of our Jewish thinkers primarily wrote on Jewish themes, they were also extraordinarily important to Christian thinkers and indeed helped shape the future of Christian theology and life. Many were read and perhaps taken even more seriously by Christians than Jews. In the 1950s and 1960s, Martin Buber and Abraham Joshua Heschel featured prominently in the Jewish-Christian dialogue. Often they were written about by Christian theologians who attempted to chart a new path for Christianity after the Holocaust. In the 1980s and 1990s, Elie Wiesel took Buber's and Heschel's place in importance and soon was joined by Emmanuel Levinas. In the twenty-first century, Levinas has become an avatar for Christians searching out a relevant spirituality for our time.

Have I left out God? This may be the most dramatic part of our encounter. All except Hannah Arendt, who was secular, though in a delightfully Jewish way, wrote extensively about God and specifically the Jewish God of history. What Jews can say about God after the Holocaust is the driving question and an intense one as well. No one of our Jewish thinkers pretends to solve the God question, yet their assertions are strong. Perhaps God and the prophetic can be seen by Jewish thinkers only in relation to the Holocaust and birth of the state of Israel. Still, they leave a legacy for the Jewish future. What will we say about God as the Jewish future dawns?

In encountering these Jewish thinkers, I re-encountered my own Jewishness. Although I have lived with these thinkers my entire adult life, they have come to me at distinct times and places and have impacted my life in different ways. All are perennials; they have something to say to us at different times. They are inspirational and more. Indeed, encountering them is often like entering a storm you did not envision, cannot control, and must somehow ride out. In the meantime you are turned upside down and around. Over the years, I have been turned upside down and around by the men and women I write about in these pages. In writing this book, I have been turned upside down and around again.

I cannot relate my encounters without engaging aspects of my own life. I was born in the 1950s to a lower-middle-class Jewish family in North Miami Beach, Florida. While attending public school during the day, I also attended Hebrew School in the afternoons and weekends. Since the area in which I lived was newly developed, there was only one Orthodox synagogue in the neighborhood, which I attended until a Conservative synagogue was built. I received most of my Jewish education there, and in 1965, I became a Bar Mitzvah. Thus, my Jewish education took place before the 1967 Arab-Israeli war.

It was in the aftermath of that war that the state of Israel and the Holocaust became formative for Jewish identity. I grew up in a Jewish community that knew of the Holocaust and Israel but where Rabbinic Judaism was still the guiding force in our training and worship. After the 1967 war the foundations of Jewish identity changed precipitously. No one quite knew where that change would lead us. Entering Florida State University in 1970, I encountered Richard Rubenstein, who had recently arrived there to teach in religious studies. It was through him that I began to understand the centrality of the Holocaust to Jewish life and the tumult that followed.

It may feel like a time warp to imagine that naming Jewish suffering in Europe as the "Holocaust" was controversial, yet this certainly was the case. Rubenstein was exiled to Tallahassee, Florida, because his views were so controversial. Through Rubenstein, I entered the controversy that surrounded him, not knowing then that this would be an omen for my own future. Years later I was forced into exile when I questioned Israel's policies toward Palestinians.

Instead of immediately going on for graduate studies, I travelled to New York City where I lived at the Catholic Worker house for a year. The Catholic Worker movement was founded in the 1930s as an effort to stand by the unemployed of the Great Depression and to witness to a more Christian social order. The movement was thriving when I arrived at their house of hospitality in New York City in 1974. I lived there, serving soup and bread to the homeless. My life among the poor was so difficult for me that I could make sense of it only by writing diaries and poetry. Later my writing was published as a book.

Unbeknownst to me a Maryknoll missionary priest bought the book in a New York bookstore to read as he travelled to Yemen for dialogue with Muslims. While completing my doctorate degree at Marquette University, I received from this priest an aerogram that he wrote in an airport in Saudi Arabia as he waited for his flight to Yemen. The priest recalled his experiences among the poor in Bolivia and how similar he found my experiences among the poor in New York City. I was ambivalent about how to respond. I wanted to teach others but was wary of a traditional academic environment. I wanted to teach people who were committed to those who were suffering in the world but was suspicious of missionaries. I found out that Maryknoll was a place where commitment to the poor was emphasized. I asked him if the Maryknollers might have such a position for me. They did, and I spent the next fifteen years there. My time at Maryknoll significantly expanded my view of the global community. It is unusual for anyone, let alone a Jew, to have the experiences I had.

Looking back, as a post-Holocaust Jew, I encountered suffering in the contemporary world. I also experienced the commitment that accompanied that suffering. During the years at the Catholic Worker and Maryknoll, I met and spent time with Dorothy Day and many of the luminaries of the world of liberation theology. I think especially of my encounters with the Catholic feminist Rosemary Radford Ruether, the Black liberation theologian James Cone, and the Peruvian father of Latin American liberation theology, Gustavo Gutierrez.

While at Maryknoll, two Maryknoll sisters and a lay worker who had trained at Maryknoll were brutally raped and murdered in El Salvador. Commitment is a serious business and many of the students I taught were in harm's way. My encounter at the Catholic Worker and Maryknoll challenged my own commitments as a Jew. What were the challenges ahead for us as Jews?

The Holocaust loomed large in my life and in my community. So did the state of Israel. Yet during the time I was at Maryknoll, Israel became increasingly entangled in building and maintaining settlements in the Palestinian territories it had conquered in the 1967 war. During the early 1980s Israel invaded Lebanon and bombed civilian areas of Beirut. As the decade came to a close, Israel crushed the Palestinian uprising that sought the creation of a Palestinian state. I found it difficult to witness the commitment of Christians to justice and peace without asking myself if I were willing to risk making my own commitment on behalf of the Jewish and, yes, Palestinian people.

For financial reasons, Maryknoll closed the doors of its theological school in 1995. I spent time at Harvard as a Senior Fellow at the Center for the Study of World Religions and then as a Visiting Scholar at the Center for Middle Eastern Studies. In 1998 I was approached by Baylor University to become University Professor of Jewish Studies.

Like Maryknoll, Baylor is also intentionally Christian in its identity. Yet there are significant differences in their Christian background and outlook. Maryknoll is Catholic and quite progressive in its outlook. Baylor is Baptist and moderate, even conservative. Whereas Maryknoll attracted students primarily interested in social justice work and how faith guided the practice of justice, Baylor is more evangelical in its orientation. For many of my Baylor students, practicing Christianity is seeking the conversion of others to Jesus Christ as Lord. Whereas at Maryknoll wealth and power were analyzed critically within the context of the international political and economic world order, at Baylor such wealth and power is often seen as a deserved blessing bestowed by God. Furthermore, the Catholic tradition has undergone a severe revision in light of its history of anti-Semitism, and there is now a recognized and positive status for Jews in Catholic faith and life. In parts of the conservative Protestant tradition, especially in the Bible Belt, much less work has been done in this regard.

When I arrived at Baylor in 1998, I was the first Jew the university had hired in such a prestigious position. Soon I founded a Center for Jewish Studies, which flourishes today. I teach courses on the Holocaust, Jewish Philosophy, Modern Judaism and Liberation Theology, as well as writing and lecturing around the world.

Meanwhile, the ethical behavior of the state of Israel continues to deteriorate. As we enter the second decade of the twenty-first century, the Jewish future is hotly contested. After this long history of suffering and struggle, are Jews destined to become conquerors and oppressors? Or, with our history in mind, can we change direction?

The Jewish future will be determined by our response to these questions. Encountering those in the recent past who have dealt with these questions as they came into being is enlightening. It forces us to think through our own presuppositions, our own point of arrival. Only then can we begin again.

Elie Wiesel
(1928–)

I

Encountering the Holocaust

Elie Wiesel

Elie (Eliezar) Wiesel was born in 1928 in Sighet, Romania. Along with his family, he was deported to Auschwitz in 1944 where he lost his mother and sister. Wiesel and his father were forced to march to Buchenwald, where his father died months before the camp was liberated. After the war, Wiesel lived in France and Israel before settling permanently in the United States. It was at this time that he wrote his autobiographical Night, *which in many ways established the Holocaust as a formative event in the twentieth century. Wiesel is the Andrew Mellon Professor of Humanities at Boston University and founder of the Elie Wiesel Foundation for Humanity. He served as chairman for the Presidential Commission on the Holocaust, which initiated the building of the United States Holocaust Memorial Museum in Washington, D.C. In 1986 Wiesel was awarded the Nobel Peace Prize for bringing to the world's attention the importance of the Holocaust and for speaking out against violence, repression, and discrimination.*

On First Hearing the Holocaust Named

I first encountered Elie Wiesel in 1971 in the classroom of Professor Richard Rubenstein. I arrived at my university in Florida the previous year and, for quite different reasons, so had Rubenstein. I went to Tallahassee for financial reasons and to get away from what I had known growing up. I needed to explore a new geographic and intellectual landscape. But moving from a Jewish neighborhood to the racially segregated Protestant enclave in Tallahassee in 1970 was like entering a different world.

Rubenstein arrived at Florida State having just published his groundbreaking and controversial book *After Auschwitz: Radical Theology and Contemporary Judaism*. This book gained notoriety, not all of it positive. Indeed, as *After Auschwitz* gained a wider readership, Rubenstein was on the run. Travelling from a Hillel appointment at a university in the Northeastern U.S. where Jews abounded, Rubenstein landed in Tallahassee, part of the deep South, where Jews were few in number.[1]

In Tallahassee, Rubenstein was far from the mainstream of American Jewish life. In those days the city center was dominated by established Protestant churches. As in most cities in the deep South, the color divide was noticeable. One of the first bus boycotts in the South was held in Tallahassee, and those in Black leadership positions had been coworkers of Martin Luther King Jr. Though the civil rights movement had moved Tallahassee toward integration, the vestiges of slavery and Jim Crow were very much alive.

Today there are thousands of Jews at the university, and Tallahassee is much more cosmopolitan. Back then there were less than a hundred Jews at the university, and probably not many more in the city itself. Yet the university was on the move, with one of the most interesting religious studies departments in the nation, one that had asked Rubenstein to join their faculty.

During the years I studied with him, Rubenstein named the mass destruction of Europe's Jews during the Nazi period as the *Holocaust* (or in Hebrew, *Shoah*). Though years had passed since the end of World War II, for the most part the Holocaust had remained unnamed. In my childhood, we knew that something terrible had happened to the Jews of Europe—I had Hebrew School teachers in the 1950s who had arrived in America only some years earlier—but could a catastrophe of such magnitude be named?

World War II had claimed so many lives, and many of my friend's fathers had served in the war. Having been part of the American occupying forces in Germany as the war came to a close, for the rest of his life my father harbored deep suspicions about Germany. As many Jews of his generation, he felt that Germany was prone to militarism and, when given the chance, would remilitarize and embark on still more wars of conquest. Yet even as we flipped through my father's army scrapbook and listened to his commentary on where he had been and what he had done, the emphasis was on World War II—not on the particular suffering of Jews.

Naming the Holocaust was just beginning to occur during my teenage years, and Rubenstein was on the cutting edge of that naming. It was during one of Rubenstein's lectures that I heard the term *Holocaust* for the first time. At that moment a deep darkness surfaced within me. I was stunned and somehow energized, but I had no idea where it would lead. His naming of the Holocaust made immediate sense to me and seemed to have significance beyond me. Rubenstein named the Holocaust as a formative experience for the Jewish people, one that, though past, was part of the Jewish future.

Rubenstein became my model of a professor who was willing to state the issues on his mind without regard for the personal consequences. Nothing of importance seemed off limits. He lectured on various themes and personalities, from Max Weber's view of the spirit of capitalism and the Protestant ethic to the existential search of Saint Paul. Not only was his naming of the Holocaust controversial, he also named Paul, seen historically as the great divider of Jews and Christians, as his brother. Both had come to the end of normative Judaism as a religion that could sustain and nourish them.

In naming the Holocaust, Rubenstein saw the end of the Judaism he had inherited and known. This compounded his negative credentials with the Jewish establishment, even as his boldness endeared him to many of his students. I was fascinated by his wide-ranging intellect and his "take no prisoners" approach to the intellectual life.

Rubenstein was prickly and distant, some would say arrogant. Though he allowed everyone their say in class, he announced his conclusions with authority. Even as a freshman I saw that Rubenstein was embattled. In asides during his lectures, other prominent names in Jewish life were discussed and they all, even in Rubenstein's accounting, seemed opposed to his views. There I first glimpsed a battle on the Jewish front, perhaps even a civil war, over thoughts Rubenstein was articulating. Little did I know that years later I would be drawn into a similar struggle.

Over the years, I maintained contact with Rubenstein and, though he has mellowed to some extent, he remains as he was then—defiant. Over the years he has negotiated Jewish life, on the one hand being exiled from the Jewish community and on the other making peace with it. Time has smoothed the rough edges of his thought, and the subversive challenges he posed seem less important now than his overall contribution to Jewish life in naming the Holocaust. As an increasingly conservative political thinker and a strong supporter of the state of Israel, the Jewish community values his holding the line on Israel over his controversial past. It seems that the Jewish community forgives all if Israel is supported uncritically.

Yet unlike some others, Rubenstein's support of Israel and its policies flows from his Machiavellian realpolitik. Though I disagree with aspects of Rubenstein's support for Israeli policies, I admire that he has never sugarcoated them with a liberal gloss. After the Holocaust, in this dog-eat-dog world, Rubenstein believes that Jews need power, pure and simple, and Israel is that power.

Today the Holocaust is mentioned often and evokes a cascade of associations. Back in 1970, the Holocaust was just being named as an event much broader than its parts. There were few images attached to this event other than the sheer horror of the slaughter of innocent Jews. Rubenstein's *After Auschwitz* changed that.

The very naming of the Holocaust was controversial because many Jews did not want the event named at all. They feared that in naming the Holocaust it would become definitive of Jewish identity and the trajectory of Jews and Judaism would change. Where would that change take Jews individually and as a community? It could be a reckoning with Jewish history and with the majority populations surrounding Jews. After the destruction of Europe's Jewish communities, could Jews afford yet another reckoning with history?

Experiences of destruction are horrible beyond words. In the wake of destruction, survivors pick themselves up and try to rebuild their lives. For a minority the process of rebuilding is complicated, especially when the majority population is of the same stock and religion as those who caused the destruction. Jews in America lived among descendants from Europe who are Christian in belief, the same population and religion of Germans and Europeans who were hostile to Jews and had murdered them. It might be better to rebuild what was left of the Jewish world, keep silent so as not to antagonize the majority population, and hope for the best.

Naming the experience of mass death was complex. Jews could name the experience of the Holocaust within the community, keeping the discussions limited and among Jews only. Or Jews could name the event of mass death as important for Jews and others. The first option would be respected by others and contained within. The second option could be seen as intrusive, since the hostility toward Jews that led to the Holocaust had deep religious roots. If Jews named the murder of millions of Jews as the Holocaust, then Jews had to name anti-Semitism as part of Christianity. In doing so, Jews would have to call for revisions in Christianity itself. Throughout their history, Christians had resented Jews precisely because, from their perspective, Jews "intruded" on their beliefs and life of faith. Should Jews intrude once again on Christianity? Could Jews do this without suffering the consequences evident throughout history?

Naming and speaking about the Holocaust are two different matters. If the murder of six million Jews was named but not spoken, the possible consequences would be lessened, the future of Jews less uncertain. To name the Holocaust was to go on the offensive, asserting the value of Jewish life against those who had demeaned it. Though Jewish life in America was far better than it had been in Europe, anti-Semitism existed here as well. In the 1950s and 1960s, there were still quotas for Jewish students in Ivy League universities. Unheard of was the notion of a politically engaged and active Jewish life, with Jewish political candidates and office holders at the national level. When presidential candidate Al Gore chose Senator Joseph Lieberman as his vice-presidential candidate in 2000, the dream of a Jew becoming a high official in the nation was greeted with enthusiasm by many. When I studied with Rubenstein, few Jews had thought of such a possibility. Rubenstein was also troubling to the Jewish establishment because he was an ordained rabbi. Through his studies at Hebrew Union College in Cincinnati, a seminary of the Reform movement, and Jewish Theological Seminary in New York City, a seminary of the Conservative movement, Rubenstein earned his rabbinical degree and subsequently served as a rabbi for several congregations. His writings on the Holocaust made rabbinic service and paid employment in the Jewish community difficult. With criticism of him coming from within the Jewish community, his days with the Jewish establishment were numbered. As a rabbi and a trained theologian, Rubenstein challenged the community from within the Jewish religious tradition. In questioning what it meant to be a Jew after Auschwitz, he directly criticized Jewish leadership, including those who employed him, for their lack of leadership on this most crucial question. Rubenstein accused them of being cowardly and perhaps complicit, as had been other Jewish leaders throughout Jewish history who had not faced the central questions before their people.

Whereas previous Jewish leaders failed to recognize the annihilationist policies of the Nazis before it was too late, contemporary Jewish leaders did not want the Holocaust named. Rubenstein broke the rabbinic wall of silence. He aired the community's dirty laundry in public. Before and after the publication of *After Auschwitz*, Rubenstein's words were broadcast widely. Rubenstein was an "up and coming," "go-to" Jew for the media. From the vantage point of the Jewish establishment, there could only be more trouble ahead.

Published in 1966, *After Auschwitz* was comprised of essays previously published in relatively obscure Jewish publications. The book reached a much broader public, partly because of its timing. After the 1967 Arab-Israeli war, with Israel's swift and decisive victory, Israel was also named as formative for Jewish life. With *After Auschwitz* and in the wake of the 1967 war, Holocaust consciousness was born.[2]

Holocaust consciousness—or in its religious form, Holocaust Theology—is a way of viewing Jewish history through the lens of anti-Semitism, the Nazis, and historic Jewish vulnerability. For many Jews, Jewish survival and flourishing can be insured only through Jewish empowerment. Jewish empowerment is viewed as embracing and defending the state of Israel. It also means arguing against those who criticize Israel and its policies toward Palestinians.

With the passing years, the Holocaust and the state of Israel have come to define what it means to be an authentic Jew. When Rubenstein began writing, the sense of the Holocaust and Israel as central to Jewish identity was foreign.

Today, the only accepted definition of what it means to be Jewish revolves around remembering the Holocaust and support for Israel.

The questions posed by both the Holocaust and the state of Israel were already present in 1970 and remain so today. In the Holocaust, theological questions are as prominent if not more so than political questions. How the Holocaust could be perpetrated on the Jews of Europe is a question addressed externally to the broader European community and to Christianity in particular. Internally, there are questions about Jewish political leadership and how Jews could be so weak and vulnerable that it left the entire the European Jewish community exposed. Yet the further troubling question about God is obvious: Where was God at Auschwitz?

The subject of political culpability and the absence of God in the Holocaust begged for answers retrospectively, partly out of historical curiosity. More important, however, were answers for the future. What did Jews need to do to alter their weak and vulnerable situation? What could Jews say about God after the Holocaust had ended and Israel had been created?

Rubenstein's inquiries about Jewish life and the human predicament after the Holocaust focused on Auschwitz, a major Nazi death camp located in Poland where almost a million European Jews were murdered. Partially because of his book, Auschwitz eventually came to symbolize the killing of six million European Jews. Today, Auschwitz as a signifier of the Holocaust is central to Jewish identity and is a rallying call for Jewish survival—*after*. The word *after* contains layer after layer of soul searching, political queries, and religious examination. What can Jews say about humanity, Christianity, Judaism, the Jewish community, politics, and God *after* Auschwitz?

With the almost complete elimination of Jews and Jewish culture from Europe during the Holocaust, the Jewish place in the world radically shifted. Before the Holocaust the center of Jewish population and learning was in Europe. After the Holocaust, the two largest communities of Jews came to reside in North America and in Israel. After the Holocaust, both America and Israel provided a series of challenges to Jews, indeed to Judaism. In America, Jews live free as citizens and with the respect of the majority non-Jewish population. In Israel, Jews now have a state of their own that is in their ancient homeland. As Jews contemplate the horror of the Holocaust, they also have to deal with the complexities of acceptance in America and Jewish power embodied in a state.

Writing The Other Kingdom

In 1993, the United States Holocaust Memorial Museum in Washington, D.C. opened to the public. The memorial museum represents the culmination of the naming of the Holocaust that began to crystallize with the publication of Rubenstein's book. Yet the museum has two competing visions of what the Holocaust was and what it says to us—*after*. One part of the Holocaust museum comes from Rubenstein, the other from Elie Wiesel.

The issues that Rubenstein and Wiesel began to wrestle with in the 1960s and early 1970s mark the museum's exhibits and remain unresolved. Rubenstein is represented in the timeline of the Holocaust and the emphasis on the methodical and industrial mass murder of Europe's Jews. Wiesel is represented in the evocative, silent, and almost mystical spaces that surround the rendering of the millions murdered. With Rubenstein, we follow the destruction of Europe's Jews step by step. With Wiesel, the murders remain an unsolved—and irresolvable—rupture in the fabric of the universe.

Rubenstein's timeline is historical and earthly. Wiesel evokes an otherworldly nightmare. Over the years, Rubenstein resolved God's absence by orienting his exploration of the Holocaust to the political. Rubenstein began seeing the Holocaust as a paradigm for what happened to a multitude of peoples before and after the Holocaust. For Rubenstein, the Nazis were anti-Semitic to their core. Their ability to execute their nightmare scenario for Jews, however, was dependent on modernity. It was the ability to mobilize the bureaucracy, social organization, and advanced technology of the German state that gave the Nazis the ability to exterminate Europe's Jews.

Rubenstein describes the process by which the Jews of Germany were eliminated from German society and life itself:

> The process was a highly complex series of acts which started simply with the bureaucratic definition of who was a Jew. Once defined as a Jew, by the German state bureaucracy, a person was progressively deprived of all personal property and citizenship rights. The final step in the process came when he was eliminated altogether. The destruction process required the cooperation of every sector of German society. The bureaucrats drew up the decrees; the churches gave evidence of Aryan descent; the postal authorities carried the messages of definition, expropriation, denaturalization, and deportation; business corporations dismissed their Jewish employees and took over "Aryanized" properties; the railroads carried the victims to their place of execution, a place made available to the Gestapo and the SS by the *Wehrmacht*. To repeat, the operation required and received the participation of every major social, political, and religious institution of the German Reich.[3]

Rubenstein seems detached, warning his readers that to see the Holocaust only through the framework of Jews and Judaism is to miss the point. "On the contrary, we are more likely to understand the Holocaust if we regard it as the expression of some of the most profound tendencies of Western civilization in the twentieth century."[4]

For Wiesel, any attempt to explain the Holocaust in light of politics or bureaucracy is to miss the larger meaning of the event itself. Such thinking reduces the Holocaust to manageable proportions. So reduced, the Holocaust can then be compared with other events, which Wiesel believes trivializes the magnitude of Jewish suffering. Even explaining God's role or negligence in the Holocaust attempts to manage and ultimately trivialize the horror of the destruction of Europe's Jews. That is why Wiesel's contribution to the Holocaust Memorial Museum refuses any specific explanation for the Holocaust. Instead, Wiesel evokes an unremitting void.

Rubenstein's political sensibility represented an evolution in his thinking. Though quickly reached, his evolution represents the initial and highly contested first phase of Holocaust Theology. While Rubenstein's *After Auschwitz* set the tone of the Holocaust debate, it was quickly confronted and overcome by Elie Wiesel in his autobiographical memoir of his time in Auschwitz, *Night*. By 1975 Rubenstein published his more political work, *The Cunning of History: Mass Death and the American Future,* where he argues how the Holocaust was dependent on modernity.

The Cunning of History is an edited version of the much longer book *The Age of Triage: Fear and Hope in an Overcrowded World*, in which Rubenstein takes his analysis of the Holocaust out of its singular paradigmatic place and further relativizes the Jewish trauma. Instead of anti-Semitism, Rubenstein places the blame for the Holocaust squarely on the "revolution of rationality." The Holocaust becomes a paradigm for the violence and mass death of the twentieth century. Modern advances in bureaucracy, social organization, and technology, which bring progress, also bring mass death. What happened to the Jews of Europe happened to others before and after the Holocaust. Rubenstein sees the Holocaust of peoples as part of the future of humanity.[5]

Even more disturbing to many Jews, in *The Age of Triage* Rubenstein detailed his theories of superfluous populations in the age of industrialization and the Enlightenment and how those populations were dealt with by emerging political and military authorities. As it turns out, they too were dispatched to ghetto-like conditions and death before and after Europe's Jews during World War II. He views the fate of the Jews as little different than the fate of the peasants in Europe or how the Irish were treated during the famine. In the nineteenth and early part of the twentieth century, Jews had become superfluous to the functioning of modernizing societies, especially in Eastern Europe. When the migration of superfluous Jews became too much, they were "rationalized" out of existence. Anti-Semitism played its part to be sure, but it was not the only reason for the Holocaust.

As I witnessed Rubenstein's encounter with Elie Wiesel and his subsequent movement toward the more political understanding of the Holocaust, I realized how naïve I was about nuanced distinctions in public discussions on volatile issues. In their encounter, Wiesel emerged the victor. Wiesel's victory was partly personal and, more importantly, a sign of where the Jewish community was heading in understanding the Jewish place in the world. It would also leave me torn, since though Rubenstein's teaching was analytically formative for me, Wiesel's sensibility evoked the emotional core of my Jewishness.

I was hardly alone in feeling Wiesel awaken the core of my Jewishness. Most Jews had never heard of Rubenstein and, like me, encountered Wiesel through his writing and lecturing. Soon Rubenstein's public spotlight dimmed. Wiesel and those attached to him, including wealthy Jews who contributed millions to establish programs in Holocaust and Jewish Studies, used his symbolic and their financial power to further distance Rubenstein from mainstream Jewish life.

The Question of God *After*

In *After Auschwitz*, Rubenstein explored the Jewish claims about the God of history. During the Holocaust, where was the God who chose Israel among the nations, guided Israel into the Promised Land, and promised always to be with her? Every Passover, Jews commemorate the Exodus event and are commanded to place themselves there at that saving moment. For Jews the Exodus is past as well as present, for God exists in history then and now. Yet if the God of Israel is in history as a force for good and liberation, what can we say about the presence of God in history when suffering abounds? Why is there suffering, especially the suffering of God's chosen ones?

The traditional explanation for the people of Israel's suffering in the world is that Jews have strayed from God. Typically, Israel's straying had to do with worshipping false Gods and treating the most vulnerable of the community unjustly. Yet the threat of God's punishment was couched in a form of intimate love. As God's special people, more was expected of Israel, and their disappointing God was more significant. Idolatry and injustice distanced Israel from God.

God's punishment was a form of God's love. You see this vividly in the prophets when the judgment on Israel is pronounced. The punishment for failing to hear the prophet's warning is exile from the land and, along the way, abominations beyond belief. Right up to the last moment, God's punishment can be avoided if Israel returns to righteous ways. Even after punishment a return to God is still possible, but again righteousness has to be pledged and then lived out in individual and communal ways.

In light of the Holocaust, Rubenstein asked how such a God could continue to be worshipped. What could Jews have done to merit the extraordinary punishment of six million dead, one million of them children? If God were punishing Israel for its infidelities, what were they? Even if Israel's sins were specified by God, could they merit the indiscriminate destruction of Europe's Jews? If the Holocaust was part of God's punishment for Israel's sins, then in Rubenstein's view, God had become a moral monster. Such a God deserved to be confronted and exiled from Jewish life.

Rubenstein invoked God's covenant as a discussion point since religious Jews believed that the covenant with Israel, originally proposed and accepted at Mount Sinai, was still in place. The Sinai covenant worked two ways. God and Israel had responsibilities and obligations on both sides. Israel promised to follow God's ways. God promised to guide and protect Israel. As a mutually binding pact, God periodically called out Israel for its sins and Israel periodically challenged God for either being too harsh with the people or being absent at a time of great need. God concentrated on the large and small failures of Israel as well as Israel's return to God's way. Israel challenged God's power and attention span with regard to Israel's suffering presence in the world.

The give and take of the covenantal partners provided room for both parties to speak boldly and address each other. This is portrayed vividly in Jewish canonical books as a series of arguments between God and the people. An example is Abraham, who argues with God over the fate of Sodom and Gomorrah. Abraham is mortified that a just and compassionate God would condemn entire cities for the sins of a few. When Abraham challenges God to spare the righteous, God reconsiders his blanket condemnation. Later, Moses argues with God about God's despair regarding Israel and God's desire to jettison Israel for another people. Though God offers to spare Moses, and though Moses also is clearly fed up with the people, Moses lectures God on his responsibilities. In the end Moses sides with the people and offers God an ultimatum—either condemn Israel and Moses together or take a deep breath and reconsider his position. Some arguments with God are lost, while others are won. God overwhelms Abraham with his power and destroys the cities while Moses convinces God to deal with his anger and start again.

Though Rubenstein felt that the covenantal tension between God and Israel broke under the enormity of the Holocaust, he believed that Jews who continued to accept the covenant after the Holocaust had to accept the Holocaust as God's judgment on Israel. Rubenstein knew that those who stayed within the covenant would reconcile the sins of Israel and the Holocaust and ultimately affirm an omnipotent God. Was there any other way for the believing Jew?

Surveying the grounds at Auschwitz, Rubenstein was defiant. Whether God actually existed or not was less important to Rubenstein than his inability to affirm such a God—*after*. For Rubenstein there was no way back. The ancient Jewish covenant was irretrievably broken. Rubenstein understood the reluctance to admit this brokenness, but he also felt that in the end such reluctance was self-defeating. Rubenstein's language is forceful in the opening pages of *After Auschwitz*:

> It would have been better had six million Jews not died but they have. We cannot restore the religious world which preceded their demise nor can we ignore the fact that the catastrophe has had and will continue to have an extraordinary influence on Jewish life. Although Jewish history is replete with disaster, none has been so radical in its total impact as the Holocaust. Our images of God, man, and the moral order have been permanently impaired. No Jewish theology will possess even a remote degree of relevance to contemporary Jewish life if it ignores the question of God and the death camps. This *is the* question for Jewish theology in our time. Regrettably most attempts at formulating a Jewish theology since World War II seem to have been written as if the two decisive events of our time for Jews, the death camps and the birth of Israel, had not taken place.[6]

Rubenstein was hardly alone in his understanding that something in the relationship between God and the Jewish people had gone terribly wrong. As Rubenstein was writing the essays that became *After Auschwitz*, Elie Wiesel was writing his memoir *Night*. In *Night* the Jewish universe is turned upside down and God is brought to trial. Because *Night* is a memoir, it is more evocative than Rubenstein's more analytical writing. Still, reading *After Auschwitz* and *Night* together is an overpowering experience. It is difficult to imagine more powerful challenges to God.

There are profound differences in Rubenstein's and Wiesel's backgrounds and experiences, beginning with their birthplace and early life. Rubenstein was born and educated in America. Wiesel was born and educated in Romania. The war years saw these differences widen considerably. Rubenstein spent the Holocaust years studying to be a rabbi in America. Wiesel lived the same years incarcerated in Auschwitz and Buchenwald. Rubenstein spent the Holocaust years pensive and brooding about the terrible war in Europe. Wiesel lost most of his family at Auschwitz and Buchenwald and barely survived himself.

After the Holocaust, Rubenstein analyzed the Holocaust and its meaning for Jews and the world. Wiesel saw himself as a witness to the Holocaust event itself. Instead of exploring the theological meaning of the Holocaust directly as Rubenstein did, Wiesel sought a remembrance of the victims of the Holocaust as a solemn duty for all Jews and indeed for all peoples of the world. Wiesel felt that without remembrance the victims of the Holocaust would become a black void in the universe. In remembering them, they could be viewed as martyrs and thus become the seed of future Jewish life. Rubenstein opposed Wiesel's view of the Holocaust dead as martyrs; this might reopen the question of God.

The distinction drawn between the Holocaust dead as victims or martyrs is important. Rubenstein believed that the murdered Jews of the Holocaust were victims of the Nazis. Wiesel acknowledged them as martyrs. The victim/martyr distinction became emblematic of their different approaches and conclusions regarding the meaning of the Holocaust for the future of Jewish life. This argument became central to the dispute that emerged between them in the 1970s and illustrated a larger dispute within the Jewish community in America and Israel, now enshrined in the United States Holocaust Memorial Museum.[7]

As a survivor of the Holocaust, Wiesel remained in Europe, with a short stopover in the newly formed state of Israel. Like Rubenstein, Wiesel pondered the meaning of the Holocaust, with his own experience of Auschwitz as the focal point. Yet Wiesel had a problem articulating these memories. It took him years to create a language that described the landscape of Auschwitz. Although Jews in different periods of history have written about suffering, none before had dealt with the experience and magnitude of Holocaust suffering. Wiesel did not oppose Rubenstein's sense that the experience of the Holocaust was a new and different experience of industrial mass death, but he saw it as a *novum* in history visited upon Jews by a hatred that knew no bounds. It took Wiesel years to articulate the Auschwitz experience.

> I knew that the role of the survivor was to testify. Only I did not how. . . . How does one describe the indescribable? How does one use restraint in recreating the fall of mankind and the eclipse of the gods? And, then, how can one be sure that the words, once uttered, will not betray, distort the message they bear? So heavy was my anguish that I made a vow not to speak, not to touch upon the essential for at least ten years. . . . Long enough to unite the language of man with the silence of the dead.[8]

Others writing on the Holocaust experienced a similar conundrum. On the one hand, Holocaust survivors had to create a language that described the Holocaust so that others could understand what no one before in human history had experienced. On the other, they also had a responsibility to be faithful to the dead and to the survivors. To be there at the beginning was a supreme literary challenge surrounded by the reality of mass death. How could the writer describe an experience that was new in human history and be believable to those who had not been there, all the while presenting the story so that survivors could feel that their dead friends and relatives had not been betrayed?

The landscape of the Holocaust is familiar to us now because these writers braved the unknown. What once was a vision of transcendent punishment was now an earthly horror. Holocaust historian, Lucy Dawidowicz, described the transposition this way:

The murder of six million Jews, in its unparalleled scope, devastating effect, and incomprehensible intent, overtook the capacity of man's imagination to conceive of evil . . . eclipsed man's visions of hell. The names of these death factories—and especially the name of Auschwitz—replaced Dante's Nine Circles of Hell as the quintessential epitome of evil, for they were located not in the literary reaches of the medieval religious imagination, but in the political reality of twentieth-century Europe. [9]

Today we are inundated with memoirs and visual images from that time period. Yet if we reflect on the difficulties involved in describing the Holocaust world, we can imagine how daunting it was. Think, for example, of what it was like to live in a concentration camp that was planned and built to dehumanize the Jews brought there. Consider the living conditions that were designed for that express purpose. Then bring thousands of impoverished and dislocated Jews into the camp to live knowing that they are sentenced to die. As thousands around you die, then think of what it is to survive the death of your family members with the knowledge that you too are slated for death. Now tell the story to someone who has never been incarcerated even for a day.

Such a transposition demanded a literary imagination rooted in the reality of mass death. The challenges are clear. Since Auschwitz was unimaginable to those who had never been there, the use of the literary imagination necessarily had to distort the Holocaust experience so the uninitiated could enter the experience the writer was trying to describe. To ease this transition some Holocaust writers began to refer to the Holocaust using inverse metaphors such as "The Holocaust Universe," "The Concentrationary Universe," "Planet Auschwitz," and even as "The Other Kingdom." Transposing what was known with what was unknown helped the writer and reader alike.

The inversion of God's Kingdom in The Other Kingdom might be the most jarring literary illusion in Holocaust literature. Images of God's Kingdom are projections on a human scale; we can only imagine God's Kingdom from our limited human angle. God's Kingdom, however, has never been seen by living human beings. Imagining God's Kingdom then is more or less an exercise in the imagination. So, too, with The Other Kingdom; those who were never there hardly have a clue. Those who dwelled there and survived live in a double bind. They have lived where we haven't. Now they live among us.

The writer on the Holocaust has to be a bridge between the dead and the living. How do you construct such a bridge? Where does that bridge lead to? Having survived leaves a mark on the survivor. Living among the non-survivors also leaves a mark. The survivor who seeks to tell the tale must take both experiences to heart and with a distance from their own experience tell the tale in a way that even the survivor living among non-survivors can relate to.

Writers on the Holocaust faced another haunting problem. Who speaks for the Holocaust dead? What kind of speech honors those who died? Speaking for those who can no longer speak is a moral obligation akin to a religious commandment. Such a commandment must be obeyed. It can also be betrayed. Who would be the judge of what was said and what was left unsaid?

Since the Holocaust dead were all victims of the Nazis, should they be presented only as victims? In a situation of victimization, people act differently. Some are saints who give up their life for others. Others survive as best they can under the circumstances. Few victims are completely innocent in their behavior. In The Other Kingdom should compromising situations be brought to light? If so, would that shift the blame to the victims themselves or introduce a gray area where judgment becomes difficult and the chasm between the victims and perpetrators collapses?

For Wiesel, the survivors took priority. Only those who experienced the death camps could speak in the name of those who perished in the Holocaust. At the same time, the image of the Holocaust dead must not be besmirched.

In the 1950s and early 1960s, few outside of those searching for the meaning of the Holocaust wanted to hear about this other world of death. Citing a need to be silent for some years to absorb the experience of the Holocaust, Wiesel's first and much longer version of Night was published in 1956. The present, shortened, and widely read Night was published two years later but found a readership only a decade later.

As Rubenstein and Wiesel wrote about the Holocaust, there were questions as to whether there would be an audience for their work. Would the survivors want their experiences recounted, and if so would they want to re-experience their travail through the written word? If so, who would they trust to portray their experiences accurately? The experience of each survivor was unique. Could there be a collective portrait of the Holocaust without distorting it? Then there was the question of an audience beyond the survivors. Would people want to read about such horrific experiences? How could the authors make the experience believable to those who were not there? Again the issue of distortion was front and center.

There was also the issue of the hopelessness of the suffering. The memories of the survivors made it difficult for many of them to make their way in the "ordinary" universe of family and employment. Reliving the hopelessness of the Holocaust might make it even more difficult.

Was the public ready to read about a subject that would introduce a sense of despair into their lives? There were few happy endings in the Holocaust and these were shadowed by horror beyond imagining. In tragic literature there are places of redemption, but not in the Holocaust. Could writing on the Holocaust invest itself in literary hope?

In the two versions of *Night*, Wiesel grapples with these issues. While the first, longer version emphasizes Jewish rage at what has happened to the Jews of Europe, the second, shorter version emphasizes the existential crisis of a youthful Jew caught in the Holocaust world. Would a prospective audience identify more with the rage of a Holocaust survivor or with a more introspective exploration of a shattered man?

Wiesel's first version of *Night* is written in Yiddish and was mostly for the survivors of the Holocaust who spoke that language. Whereas the first version emphasized the desire of survivors for revenge, the second version was written in French for a largely non-Jewish audience and sought sympathy from the outside world.

According to the Jewish scholar Naomi Seidman, Wiesel's second version of *Night* deemphasizes an understandable Jewish rage in favor of the values of acceptance and reconciliation that permeate the Christian culture in Europe and America. This resonates more easily with repentant Christians. Christian reception of *Night* was essential to its finding an audience.

How far could such a Christian audience be pushed on their culpability in the Holocaust without demanding that they relinquish their faith and history? If Christian faith remained important to his audience, didn't Wiesel have to leave room for them to repent and affirm their own heritage? The difficult historical relationship between Jews and Christians had just culminated in the Holocaust. Why widen that gap just when many Christians were on the cusp of understanding and rejecting the anti-Semitism of their past?

Writing on the Holocaust actually precipitated a new, more positive encounter of Jews and Christians. It also served as a means for Christian renewal in the post-Holocaust era and secured Jewish life in America to an unprecedented degree. However, the result of many years of interfaith discussion surrounding the Holocaust did not mean that the terrain of the Holocaust was without danger for the Jewish future. The Holocaust was explosive and had to be managed carefully.

Whether Wiesel was conscious of this or not, the final version of *Night* has earned a significant place in the post-Holocaust Christian world. Wiesel may have felt that clearing a way for Holocaust memory by deemphasizing rage was more important to the Jewish future than the rage he and other Jews felt. The harsher version of *Night* might have been rejected by a chastised Christian Europe and Christian America. If Christianity had rejected the Holocaust as a claim on Christian conscience, the Holocaust dead might have vanished from the memory of Western civilization.[10]

The second version of *Night* carries a foreword from the French Catholic novelist Francois Mauriac. Yet in this foreword there is hardly a word about Christian anti-Semitism or about the rage of Holocaust survivors. Instead,

Mauriac writes of Wiesel as a supplicant appealing to the world to recognize the horrors of Jewish suffering. Despite this suffering, Mauriac writes that he retains a traditional belief in the superiority of Christianity and the role of Jews as God's chosen people. Mauriac ends his foreword recalling his encounter with Wiesel and sets it in a framework Christians could hear and embrace:

> And I, who believe that God is love, what answer could I give my young questioner, whose dark eyes still had the reflection of the angelic sadness which had appeared one day upon the face of the hanged child? What did I say to him? Did I speak of that other Jew, his brother, who may have resembled him—the Crucified, whose Cross has conquered the world? Did I affirm that the stumbling block to his faith was the cornerstone of mine, and that the conformity of the Cross and the suffering of men was in my eyes the key to that impenetrable mystery whereon the faith of his childhood had perished? Zion, however, has risen up again from the crematoria and the charnel houses. The Jewish nation has been resurrected from among the thousands of dead. It is through them that it lives again.... If the Eternal is the Eternal, the last word for each one of us belongs to Him. This is what I should have told this Jewish child. But I could only embrace him, weeping.[11]

The Additional Covenant

Wiesel's *Night* languished, as did most writing about the Holocaust, until after the 1967 Arab-Israeli war. In the war's wake, sales of *Night* grew significantly. Soon Wiesel emerged as a major spokesperson for Jews and Judaism. Over the years *Night* has sold millions of copies and become required reading in Holocaust courses around the nation.

Wiesel has become an icon of the Holocaust. In recognition of this iconic status, Wiesel was awarded the Nobel Peace Prize in 1986. Rubenstein's experience has been quite different. Though academically successful, he languished on the periphery of Jewish life. While Wiesel is honored internationally, Rubenstein remains in exile.

Wiesel and the reception of *Night* exist in the realm of paradox, if not irony. On the one hand, Wiesel's evocation of his time in Auschwitz is chilling to the bone. His description of the landscape of Auschwitz is so desolate that there seems to be no way back to his—or our—full humanity. Like Rubenstein, Wiesel's memoir questions God so thoroughly that God's displacement and banishment is obvious. *Night* buries Israel's God of history with a literary force compared to which Rubenstein's theoretical constructs can only hint.

The cadence of Wiesel's initial passage about God sets the stage for the referendum on God:

> Never shall I forget that night, the first night in the camp, that turned my life into one long night seven times sealed.
>
> Never shall I forget that smoke.
>
> Never shall I forget the small faces of the children whose bodies I saw transformed into smoke under a silent blue sky.
>
> Never shall I forget those flames that consumed my faith forever.
>
> Never shall I forget the nocturnal silence that deprived me for all eternity of the desire to live.
>
> Never shall I forget those moments that murdered my God and soul and turned my dreams to ashes.
>
> Never shall I forget these things, even if I were condemned to live as long as God Himself.
>
> Never.[12]

The repeated "never" has become part of the litany of Holocaust literature, a slogan taken up in the wake of the 1967 war as well—but Wiesel's "never" is about what Jews can say about God *after*. "After" is already present in Wiesel's experience that first day in Auschwitz. "Never" is also a confrontation with Israel's God. "After" and "never" is forever—"even if I am condemned to live as long as God Himself."

Rather than an abandonment of God, however, "never" becomes a difficult life with the God of Israel who, though absent, remains. Though Wiesel's confrontation with God in Auschwitz is personal, a broader communal confrontation is implied. Partly through Wiesel's *Night*, this confrontation is accepted by Jews around the world as our "forever." This means that God continues on and Jews continue on, though in a highly contested covenantal relationship.

On that first day of Auschwitz and forever more, the covenantal power equation shifts with Jews gaining authority and boldness to speak their truth to the chastened-though-still-almighty God. God remains capitalized—*Himself*—even as the young Elie Wiesel puts caution to the wind and hurls accusations at God because of God's indifference. The stakes are even higher for the people of Israel, God's chosen. Such a God deserves to be cursed all the way to heaven.

Can God withstand such a challenge? As in other passages of *Night*, there seems no way back to God and no way forward for God. Yet in Wiesel's other writings since *Night*—indeed perhaps within Wiesel's memoir itself—there is a constant search for other ways to relate to God lest God be lost completely.

If the original covenant has to be readjusted as Wiesel suggests, rather than abandoned as Rubenstein had suggested, what can Jews affirm in this new covenantal configuration? If God is absent in Auschwitz while still being able to be confronted, how does this frame the future of Jewish discourse about God?

Michael Berenbaum also encountered Wiesel through Rubenstein in the same years I did. Berenbaum wrote that Wiesel was suggesting an "additional" covenant to Israel's original one. This covenant was forged at Auschwitz so that, even though the original covenant was radically chastened in Auschwitz, it still remained a covenant, albeit in an altered form—*after*.[13]

With this additional covenant, though on many levels Wiesel agrees with Rubenstein about God, he also parts company with him. The additional covenant demands that Jews survive and flourish after the Holocaust by means of memory and witness. These replace God's presence or are a way of lamenting God's absence. Memory and witness defy God's presence that was so ineffectual at Auschwitz, such that after Auschwitz God can be remembered only in Israel's past.

For Berenbaum, the additional covenant allows Wiesel partially to resolve the tension between God and the Jewish people in the post-Holocaust world. The additional covenant is "no longer between humanity and God or God and Israel but rather between Israel and its memories of pain and death, God and meaning," Berenbaum writes. "God has proved an unreliable partner in the covenantal bondedness. Therefore, if we are to continue as Jews, our self-affirmation must be based on our choice to remain Jews and to assure the past of Jewish history as our own and in some way implicated in our future." The result is a covenant that speaks of God in the past tense only, as if the mourning that surrounds God can also comfort a mourning people.[14]

Wiesel is daring in his assertion of the additional covenant, perhaps more daring than if he left God behind completely. After all, if God was absent then and pretends to be present now, why not send the absent God away? In Jewish spirituality God can be absent and still present. Wiesel assumes this paradoxical dichotomy of absence and presence.

If God was really somewhere else or nowhere, the tension in addressing God would dissipate. Only the proximity of God makes defying God possible. It is the very presence of God throughout *Night* that makes Wiesel's memoir so striking. If there were no additional covenant, or no covenant at all, struggling with God would make little sense.

Embedded in the additional covenant is solidarity, witness, and the sanctification of life as seen through the prism of the Holocaust. Solidarity is first and foremost to be with the Jews who died in the Holocaust and with Jews who are alive today. Also, solidarity with the non-Jewish victims flows from the memory of the Jewish Holocaust dead.

Solidarity in the present is a form of witness to the dead. Through memory and witness the unmarked graves of the Holocaust dead resist becoming a further scandal. The memory of the Holocaust dead in the present is the Jewish—and human—anchor for the drive to sanctify life *after*.

Pervading all of Wiesel's writing is the sense that forgetting the Holocaust dead is worse than a sacrilege. Forgetting would rend the universe in two. Or it would continue and further the tearing that began in the Holocaust. The only way to mend the universe is through remembering the Holocaust dead. Though nothing can bring back their lives or their sacrifice, through memory we can rescue the dead from oblivion. To refuse to remember is to become a bystander again, perhaps even an enabler.

Throughout the additional covenant, the touchstone for Wiesel remains the Holocaust. The rupture of the Holocaust makes speech impossible—and necessary. It is from the memory of the Holocaust that action on behalf of Jews and non-Jews is authentic. Forgetting the Holocaust dead, comparing them to the dead of other atrocities, or living without their memory is abandoning the definitive and ongoing Jewish stake in the world.

Wiesel's concentration on the Jewish dead of the Holocaust is the key to all of Holocaust Theology and the Jewish preoccupation with the Holocaust. Many millions of non-Jews were killed during World War II and millions of non-Jews were killed in the violence that had little or nothing to do with warfare. Jews were not the only ones murdered in the camps either. Yet for Wiesel and for most Holocaust thinkers, the way Jews were singled out for destruction is crucial. This destruction had the longest history in Europe and was tied to Christianity, the major religion of the West. For most Jews, the Holocaust has a religious significance that was lacking in the persecution of other nationalities.

While Wiesel's solidarity with the Holocaust dead is speaking on their behalf to Jews and the world, it also is a continuing argument with God. This reaches its apex in *The Gates of the Forest*, a novel Wiesel published in 1966. Here, Wiesel replicates a trial he witnessed among the inmates of Auschwitz as a trial of God for abandoning the Jewish people during their time of greatest need. A survivor of the camps confronts the traditional interpretations of God by demanding that a Hasidic *rebbe* acknowledge that there were such trials with the obvious verdict. The survivor told the *rebbe* a story from his recent past:

> In a concentration camp, one evening after work, a rabbi called together three of his colleagues and convoked a special court. Standing with his head held high before them, he spoke as follows: "I intend to convict God of murder, for He is destroying His people and the Law He gave them from Mount Sinai. I have irrefutable proof in my hands. Judge without fear or sorrow or prejudice. . . ." The trial proceeded in due legal form,

with witnesses for both sides with pleas and deliberations. The unanimous verdict: "Guilty."

. . . After all, He had the last word. On the day after the trial, He turned the sentence against His judges and accusers. They, too, were taken off to the slaughter.[15]

Wiesel later summarized his argument with God and pointed to what a Jew should be: "To be a Jew means to serve God by espousing man's cause, to plead for man while recognizing his need for God. And to opt for the creator *and* His creation, refusing to pit one against the other. Of course man must interrogate God . . . [but] only the Jew knows that he may oppose God as long as he does so in defense of His creation.[16]

Wiesel's unannounced assertion is that the Holocaust represents a contemporary form of Jewish chosenness. As in ancient times, Jews were singled out as witnesses among the nations. During the Holocaust they were again singled out, but for death rather than liberation.

What can this peculiar sense of election mean? Emil Fackenheim, a Jewish philosopher and compatriot of Wiesel, asserts that while the Commanding Voice of Sinai was not heard at Auschwitz, the Commanding Voice of Auschwitz is now heard by post-Holocaust Jews. Fackenheim believes that this makes possible a new 614th commandment of Jewish Law: "The authentic Jew of today is forbidden to hand Hitler yet another posthumous victory."[17]

If the original covenant with God is now in the past, the memory of the time when God was with the people lives on. Seeing God only through the prism of memory might lead to nostalgia or a paralysis. However, because of the precarious situation of post-Holocaust Jewry, paralysis is not an option. In fact, Fackenheim believes that Jews refused paralysis and actively accepted their responsibility for their own destiny by surviving and banding together for self-defense in the 1967 Arab-Israeli war.

Although neither Wiesel nor Fackenheim speculate about God in the future, the question of God's absence or presence cannot be determined in advance. It is only by keeping the Jewish community alive that a further consideration about God might occur in the future.

Perhaps placing God on trial in the death camps was a way of baiting God into reappearing. Wiesel's writing about the trial keeps the question of God in the forefront. Perhaps Wiesel, and also Fackenheim, find the future of Jewish life impossible without God. In the meantime, only by keeping Jews alive can there come a time when the Commanding Voice of Sinai might be heard again.

There is also the possibility that the Commanding Voice of Auschwitz, while coaxing God to reappear, is also God's stand-in, God's voice, as it were, without God. The Commanding Voice of Auschwitz might be the prophetic voice appearing at a time when the argument against God is irrefutable. Here the prophetic voice is the voice of the people crying out against the injustice of God and humanity. Rather than be bereft and unable to continue, the prophetic voice of the people carries this complaint with strength and fortitude. It could be that Jews cannot endure the loss of God, especially if it means the loss of the prophetic voice that is nourished by God. In the case of the Holocaust, the prophetic voice is in solidarity with the Jewish people over against God. Even if God has become a memory, Jews will not allow the prophetic voice to be stilled. Yet it is important to note that the prophetic voice here is truncated; it speaks almost exclusively of the empowerment of the Jewish people. What happens to others is less important.

Throughout *Night* there is a mixture of religious affirmation and defiance. At the beginning of Wiesel's deportation, his entire village is in shock. Nonetheless, the people keep falling back on their tradition, imploring God and uttering prayers. Even in Auschwitz this continues for a time until the situation becomes impossible. In person after person, God becomes more and more distant. In the end there is no discussion at all. Even God's memory seems to have disappeared.

When the question becomes the future, Wiesel, with Fackenheim's aid, seeks an authentic expression to justify the continuance of Jewish life *after*. Both look to the God who was with Israel into a future where God cannot be affirmed as God was in the past. It is here that Jews can survive and sort out a new way of life.

Rubenstein, Wiesel, and Fackenheim all affirm that the covenant is shattered. At stake is the future of the Jewish people. Wiesel and Fackenheim affirm the Jewish future as a form of fidelity to the Holocaust dead that, in turn, is also understood as a form of fidelity to all of Jewish history. Rubenstein sees it another way. There can be no retroactive solidarity with the dead of the Holocaust. They died within the void of God's absence. For Rubenstein, no Commanding Voice of Auschwitz can rescue them.

Though the Jewish understanding of God and the covenant as Jews knew it is past, for Wiesel and Fackenheim the covenant remains, now controlled by Jews themselves. Just as Wiesel sees the covenant as memory and mourning for what was, Fackenheim sees the contemporary response of Jews and the state of Israel to continue Jewish life as a testament to the fact that Jews, with every reason to give up and transfer their loyalties to other communities and ideologies, remain steadfast. Fackenheim uses language with which Wiesel would agree:

> Jews are forbidden to hand Hitler posthumous victories. They are commanded to survive, lest the Jewish people perish . . . to remember the victims of Auschwitz lest their memory perish. They are forbidden to despair

of man and his world, and to escape either into cynicism of otherworld-liness, lest they cooperate in delivering the world over to the forces of Auschwitz. Finally they are forbidden to despair of the God of Israel, lest Judaism perish. . . . A Jew may not respond to Hitler's attempt to destroy Judaism by himself cooperating in its destruction. In ancient times, the unthinkable Jewish sin was idolatry. Today, it is to respond to Hitler by doing his work.[18]

If the memory of God and the ability of Jews to take present responsibility for Jewish life were abandoned, then the Holocaust dead and the whole of Jewish history would be rendered null and void. It is the Jewish refusal to accept this void that so impresses Wiesel and Fackenheim and allows them to articulate a post-Holocaust future for the Jewish people.

Perhaps defiantly, this Jewish refusal asserts that out of the incredible darkness there is the light of Jewish survival. Without Jewish survival the Holocaust dead, indeed all of Jewish history, is consigned to oblivion. If Jews loose even the memory of God's presence, then Hitler wins as well. In banishing the Jews from the world, Hitler sought to rule over others without suffering the bad conscience that he thought Jews evoked. In some sense, Jews operated for Hitler in the same way Jews operated for Christians, as a brake on their claims of empire and truth. In Wiesel and Fackenheim there is a sense that both Hitler and Christianity were correct in their assumptions that without Jews in the world injustice could more easily prevail. For Wiesel and Fackenheim the Jewish presence in the world is less a negation of others than a powerful and sustaining force in the universe for conscience and justice. Severely wounded and almost annihilated, Jewish leaders must first take care of Jewish survival before once again assuming their place in saving others. The Commanding Voice of Auschwitz is one necessary stop on this way to recovery.

Holocaust Martyrdom and the 1967 War

The term *Holocaust dead* refers to an argument in 1970 between Wiesel and Rubenstein, a decisive, intensely personal moment in their relationship. It also has deeply influenced public policy.

In their exchange, Rubenstein spoke about Jews who historically accepted martyrdom when confronted with the demand to convert to another faith. In the Holocaust, however, Jews were killed simply because they were Jews. No conversion was demanded or accepted. Because he could not affirm the covenant after the Holocaust, Rubenstein felt that there was no Jewish future other than the need for defense and security. Why then raise martyrdom as an issue for the future? Wiesel took offense at Rubenstein's closure of the Jewish future.

Instead, Wiesel affirmed the Holocaust dead as martyrs, thus as the seeds of a Jewish future. This confrontation was decisive. Was Jewish life worth continuing? Was the Holocaust the terminus of Jewish life or a clarion call for yet another beginning? If a future was affirmed, what would be the content of Jewish life *after*?

The apprehension was palpable on both sides of the argument. Each man had an anxiety about the other, as if Rubenstein needed Wiesel to make his argument and vice versa. It could be that they were so distant from the other that only one could be relevant. I am sure that both viewed it that that way. Still, I feel there is a meeting ground between them. Each man articulates part of the post-Holocaust Jewish experience, and both parts are necessary for a more complete picture of the Jewish future.

In a famous and defining year-long conference on the Holocaust held in 1974 at St. John the Divine Episcopal Cathedral in New York City, Wiesel and Fackenheim were present, but not Rubenstein. Wiesel would not speak at the ongoing conference if Rubenstein spoke at any time during the year. The dispute was bitter and foretold the later Jewish civil war on the question of Israel.

The initial setting for their confrontation was the first International Scholars' Conference on the German Church Struggle and the Holocaust, held in 1970 at Wayne State University. Rubenstein presented his paper "Some Perspectives on Religious Faith after Auschwitz," and that evening Wiesel was scheduled to deliver his "The Literature of the Holocaust." However, Wiesel was so angry with Rubenstein's presentation that he changed his subject and proceeded to rebut Rubenstein's main assertions, under what was later published as "Talking and Writing and Keeping Silent."[19]

At the Scholar's Conference, Rubenstein was in full stride. He began with his own intellectual journey toward the rejection of God's covenant with Israel:

> If the God of the Covenant exists, at Auschwitz my people stood under the most fearsome curse that God has ever inflicted. If the God of history does not exist, then the Cosmos is ultimately absurd in origin and meaningless in purpose. . . . I have had to decide whether to affirm the existence of a God who inflicts Auschwitz on his guilty people or to insist that nothing the Jews did made them more deserving of Auschwitz than any other people, that Auschwitz was in no sense a punishment, and that a God who would or could inflict such punishment does not exist. In other words, I have elected to accept what Camus rightly called the courage of the absurd, the courage to live in a meaningless, purposeless Cosmos rather than believe in a God who inflicts Auschwitz on his people.[20]

After making his decisions about God after the Holocaust, Rubenstein continued his journey for meaning mostly outside Jewish theology. When he accepts Camus' courage of the absurd his language is strong. Yet there is a difference between questioning the presence of God at Auschwitz and arguing that God inflicted Auschwitz on the Jewish people.

Rubenstein addressed the historic options Jews faced with regard to Christian anti-Semitism. Though initially anti-Semitism might seem a deflection from the question at hand, part of Rubenstein's argument was that despite the rejection of God and the covenant, being singled out as Jews remained an important issue in the post-Holocaust world. The world continued to be dangerous for Jews. Hence, Rubenstein saw Jewish empowerment, especially in the state of Israel, as crucial for the Jewish future.

Rubenstein's argument about Jewish chosenness was also controversial. In *After Auschwitz*, Rubenstein argued that part of the problem non-Jews had with Jews was exactly the assertion by Jews that they were God's chosen. Asserting chosenness set Jews up for invectives hurled against them and physical assaults on their being. For Rubenstein, the Holocaust spoke clearly about the impossibility of belief in a God of history, and yet at the same time it cautioned Jews to jettison this belief in chosenness. Without the God of history, there was no longer any basis for such a claim. Besides, it set the Jewish people up for a genocidal attack in the future. If Christians had to take responsibility for their anti-Semitism, Jews had to take responsibility for how their claims functioned in the world against them.

What Rubenstein did not understand was that Jewish theologians would try to preserve the Jewish sense of election even without a clear sense of what could be said about God after the Holocaust. Ironically, the sense of chosenness became even more important for Jews without God. Was this part of the defiance that Wiesel and others showed, asserting a chosenness without God?

Having refused God and chosenness, Rubenstein argued strongly for the importance of the state of Israel. Yet he also argued against a sense that the state of Israel was innocent or a moral cause. As with his language about the covenant, Rubenstein's words grated many, including Wiesel:

It might be argued that the same God who delivered the Jews to the ovens also gave them Jerusalem in 1967. When I stood at the Wall for the first time during the summer of 1967, people who knew me came up and asked,

"What do you think now? God has given us all of Jerusalem!"

"God is not on the side of the Jews," I replied, "nor is he against the Arabs. The Jews and the Arabs both love this place and consider it their own. We have a terrible conflict. But, to treat the Arab as *villian* rather than *enemy* is to misconceive the nature of the conflict. I refuse to say *Gott mit uns* under any circumstances.

The Six Day War, tentative as its conclusions may have been, is no royal road back to the God of History.[21]

Rubenstein's view on Israel and Israel's victory in the 1967 war contrasted sharply with Wiesel's. While Wiesel agreed that the 1967 war was not a return to God or redemption from the Holocaust, he saw the 1967 war as a vindication for the martyrs of the Holocaust and for the entirety of Jewish history.

Wiesel's writing on the 1967 war has the immediacy of one who has entered into an experience and is almost overwhelmed by it. Wiesel begins with a confession: as war became imminent, he did not believe Israel would win. On the contrary, he thought Israel would lose the war and that this would be the last war of the Jewish people, "the end of our march to eternity." For Wiesel the Israeli experience was much too beautiful to last, but could he live, could the Jewish people continue if Israel disappeared?

Thinking this to be the end, Wiesel flew to Israel on the second day of the war as an act of defiance and solidarity. On the plane to Israel, he met an old friend who was motivated by the same conviction: that Jews were heading toward a reenactment of what happened in the Warsaw Ghetto and, like Wiesel, he wanted to be on the inside. "But the tragedy did not occur. We have all been saved. Had Israel lost the war, we would all have been doomed. . . . The Jewish people would have survived for centuries to come, even if Israel had not been established in 1948. But now that Israel does exist, our people is so linked to it that we could not survive its disappearance."[22]

Holocaust imagery is ever present in how Wiesel depicts Israel. Wiesel records in his diary that in the moment of anguish Israel was alone, as before in Europe "during its night." The indifference of friendly or neutral governments was also the same. The Vatican again remained silent, and the invocation of total war, this time by the Arab governments, was familiar. Israel was a ghetto again, and the war recalled the uprising of the Jewish survivors in Warsaw. "The inhabitants would resist until the end, and the so-called Christian nations, civilized and progressive, faithful to their tradition, would watch and do nothing." And for the Jewish people everything would have to begin again, "except that no longer would we have the strength or desire to begin again.[23] Thus, Israel's victory is seen as a miracle. "The people plunged suddenly into the unreal, outside the realm of time and thought. . . . At times, they seemed to be reliving the trials and triumphs of the Bible; the names and battles had a familiar ring. At other times, they felt themselves thrust into a far away messianic future."[24]

The scene as Wiesel describes it could hardly be more different than Rubenstein's proclamations of the end of God in the Holocaust and that the

1967 war was no royal road back to the God of history. Instead, the entire Jewish community, past and present, is united in Jerusalem, this time to forestall destruction and to experience the miraculous. The enemy is defeated by the sum total of Jewish history. Two thousand years of suffering, longing, and hope are mobilized for the battle, "just as the million of martyrs of the Holocaust were enlisted in the ranks." Like the Biblical pillars of fire, the martyrs of the Holocaust came and shielded their spiritual heirs. And the possibility of Israel's defeat is reversed, for what enemy could ever conquer them?[25]

The passion of Wiesel's writing makes it clear that for him, as for Jews around the world, everything changed with the war. Wiesel describes this period as a watershed: "I became a child again, astonished and vulnerable, threatened by nightmare. . . . Suddenly all Jews had again become children of the Holocaust." The watershed involves a military victory and a religious manifestation to be interpreted, in Wiesel's words, by poets and Kabbalists. Indeed, the details of the war, if they are known in their totality, can hardly describe "the great mystery in which we are encloaked, as if by the command of the Almighty." Religious and secular Jews alike interpret the experience of victory as a religious one, compelling each Jew to "confront his people, his past, and his God." The war was a matter of the survival of the Jewish people. A unity emerged that Wiesel describes movingly: "University students flooded embassies to enlist for the fight; the Hasidim of Williamsburg declared days of fast and prayer; youngsters from assimilated homes organized fund raising drives and joined in protests; millionaires cast aside their businesses and took off for Jerusalem; community leaders went sleepless night after night because of their great efforts and profound anxiety. Never was the Jewish people so united, never so moved and anxious, never so ready and prepared to offer and sacrifice everything it had, its 'might, heart, and soul.'"[26]

For Wiesel, there is another miracle involved in the Israeli victory, and that is the humanity of the Jewish soldiers, who fought without hate. Despite the "poisonous incitement" over Arab radio, the Israeli soldiers exhibited no cruelty toward Arab prisoners of war or toward civilians. "I have seen many armies; none more humble, more humane in its victories. I have seen Israeli paratroopers crying before the Wall. They were sad rather than proud." For Wiesel those soldiers sum up his sense of Israel as a moral victory:

> In the Jewish tradition a victory is never linked to defeat . . . one can be victorious without defeating the enemy. Judaism recognizes only victory over oneself. . . . My pride is that Israel has remained human because it has remained so deeply Jewish. During the Six-Day War the Jewish fighters did not become cruel. They became sad. They acquired a certain maturity, a very moving maturity, which I simply cannot forget. And if

I feel something towards them, the child-soldier in Israel, it is profound respect.[27]

Though Wiesel is less a systematic thinker than a storyteller, by 1967 he had enunciated the major themes foundational to the Holocaust. First, after the Holocaust, Jews and Jewish history exist in a dialectical tension between the suffering of the Jewish people in Europe and the miracle of empowerment in Israel. Second, the innocence of the Jewish people and the redemptive aspects of Israel are affirmed. Both are tied together in a narrative that ultimately becomes a liturgical rendering of Jewish history and the Jewish future.

For Wiesel, Jews were innocent in the suffering of the Holocaust and innocent in the empowerment of the state of Israel after the Holocaust. This innocence could be seen in the martyrdom of the Holocaust dead and in the creation of Israel in response to their martyrdom. All of Jewish history was at the crossroads after the Holocaust and in the creation of the state of Israel. Who then could oppose any part of this narrative except those who want to tear at the edges of, or even destroy, Jewish history? The answer for Wiesel is simple. Only those who hate Jews—anti-Semites—or hate themselves—dispute this miracle of Jewish renaissance.

What is important is that Wiesel is able to articulate these themes in a pre-ideological and pre-theological manner, appealing to the emotive aspects of the experience of the Jewish people and gathering all Jews, regardless of their individual stories, into a collective history. The Holocaust and Israel become vantage points from which a perspective on Jewish singularity and continuity can take shape, and the historical mission of the Jewish people becomes articulate. Wiesel's genius is that this terrain is less definable as a political or religious program than as a formative platform from which Jewish thought and action emanates. Thus the dialectical tension allows Jewish suffering to point to the miracle of Israel's victory without being consumed by it; the redemptive aspects of Israel continually evoke Jewish innocence because of the absolutely unjustified suffering of Jews in Europe. In a sense, Wiesel recreates the rhythms of contemporary Jewish life almost as a liturgy and suggests avenues of Jewish commitment within those rhythms. In Wiesel's world, and by extension in the Jewish world, Jews remain in the throes of suffering even as they are empowered, an innocent people haunted by isolation and abandonment even as redemption beckons.

Remaining in suffering, with its possible return, even as Israel wins its mighty victory, is crucial to Wiesel's narrative arc. Rather than assuming that power and victory in war forecloses suffering once and for all, the opposite is the case. Over the years, as Israel counters threats and deals decisively with them, Wiesel and other Jews are consumed with the vision of another Holocaust. Paradoxically, Israel's military prowess becomes a sign of Jewish vulnerability.

In Wiesel's evocative Jerusalem scene, Jews are once again alone, another Holocaust lurking in the future. Jewish history is replete with reversals, a golden age of peace and flourishing followed by eras where Jews are rejected and have to flee and find safe harbor. Was Israel's victory just another turn of the tables, awaiting yet another turning?

Part of the somberness in Wiesel's rendering of the 1967 war is its liturgical quality. For Wiesel, Israel's victory is more a spiritual than military one. It is seen within the context of the suffering of Jewish history, as a gathering point of Jewish martyrs. Though the martyrs powerfully propelled Israel to victory in 1967, what if the martyrs, like God, become absent? What if the militaries of those who would like to see the state of Israel defeated conduct a surprise attack that catches the martyrs off guard? It seems that such a force to guard the state is limited. Is it therefore to be expected that one day, despite this victory, that Israel will be defeated and another Holocaust will take place?

In contrast, for Rubenstein the concentration on Jewish suffering should end with Israel's military victory in the 1967 war. Though he counsels that Israel's victory is less than definitive, the only way to maintain that power is to think militarily and politically; the liturgy of suffering and innocence is misplaced and dangerous. Even if the victims of the Holocaust are considered martyrs, martyrs in history cannot protect the state. If in the state of Israel, Jews have returned as a power to be reckoned with, those with just grievances will seek to limits Israel's power or displace it altogether. Even if Jewish empowerment must take precedence, Jews cannot expect that the Palestinian Arabs and surrounding Arab governments will celebrate or permanently accept their defeat. They have their own reasons for rejecting Israel, only some of which may be based on their feelings toward Jews.

Rubenstein associates both the end of Judaism and Jewish life and its continuance with anti-Semitism. Jews have a profoundly human need to identify with a community whose symbols, calendar, and rites ground them. Therefore Rubenstein argues strongly for Israel as a place for the protection of those who positively identify themselves as Jews as well as for those who have been identified as Jews and vilified.

For Rubenstein any religious content to Jewishness disappeared after Auschwitz and therefore there is no content-oriented future for the Jewish people. Yet that does not mean that Jews would or should disappear from history. Jews can find contentment in being Jewish simply as Jews who are familiar with Jewishness and are therefore grounded by it. At the same time, the world will not forget the Jewishness of Jews. Rubenstein argues for the assimilation of Jewishness in the world, but he also does not believe that it is possible. Anti-Semitism is too deep in the cultures and religions of the world to allow that.

After citing the example of anti-Semitism in Ferdinand and Isabella's Spain and the three options then presented to Jews—to convert to Christianity, flee, or stay and die as martyrs—Rubenstein expresses his respect for those who accepted martyrdom. However, Rubenstein insists that the Holocaust dead are not comparable:

> By his decision such a man elected martyrdom. His death was freely chosen. It served as a witness both to his love of place and his Jewish faith. This is in stark contrast to what took place in the Nazi death camps. One of Hitler's greatest victories was that he deprived the Jews of *all* opportunity to be martyrs. . . . All Jews were slaughtered without distinction. It must be sadly noted that the pathetic attempts of the Jewish community to see the six million as martyrs is a tragic albeit understandable misperception.[28]

Rubenstein closes his argument about martyrdom with an even more provocative statement: "Unfortunately, Auschwitz can be seen as the first triumph of technological civilization in dealing with what may become a persistent human problem, the problem of the waste disposal of superfluous human beings in an overpopulated world."[29]

Hearing these words, Wiesel was beside himself. It was one matter to attack or even denigrate God. Wiesel's *Night* is full of such commentary. But when Rubenstein refers to the attempts of the Jewish community to designate the Holocaust dead as martyrs as "pathetic," since they were done away with like "waste disposal," Wiesel saw where Rubenstein was going with his argument. He was disposing of the Holocaust dead as meaningless victims devoid of testimony. Thus Jewish history could be seen as meaningless as well. This challenged the Jewish sense of chosenness and Israel as a miraculous response to the Holocaust. If the Holocaust dead were not Jewish martyrs then the state of Israel could be criticized on political terms. The establishment of such a state could be justified only in relation to suffering in Jewish history. If Israel were criticized on strictly political terms, then charges of colonialism and military interventionism would have full play. Besides, if there were no martyrdom that could justify the existence of the state of Israel, and if God's presence could not be affirmed in the present, what reason would there be for continuing on as Jews and sacrificing for a Jewish state?

Sensing this downward spiral of commitment to a Jewish future, Wiesel changed how he presented his Holocaust experience. In ways quite different than in *Night*, Wiesel began to emphasize the remarkable commitment of Jewish leaders to their people and the essential dignity of Jews in the face of death. By doing this Wiesel hoped to retrieve the meaning found within and after the

Holocaust. Wiesel's language was as strong as Rubenstein's. It was Wiesel's turn to lecture Rubenstein:

> You say, Dick, that Hitler deprived the Jews of martyrdom. That is not true. Many Jews, especially the rabbis, could have saved their lives . . . and do you know who wanted to save them? The priests. It's not the first time in history that they wanted alibis. The priests came to our rabbis—we had some thirty of them in our center—offering them refuge in a monastery. But, of course, what rabbi would choose it? I think there were two who chose to escape individually, out of at least fifty thousand rabbis in Eastern Europe. . . . All the others preferred voluntarily, knowingly, to go with their Jews. How did these rabbis maintain their Jewishness and their humanity? That is the wonder! [30]

Wiesel continued that the Nazis wanted to exterminate Jews "spiritually" and substitute themselves for God. In spite of this, there were many Jews "who remained human and who remained Jewish and went on praying to God." Once again Wiesel admonished Rubenstein. "And here I will tell you, Dick, that you don't understand *them* when you say that it is more difficult to live today in a world without God," Wiesel continued. "NO! If you want difficulties, choose to live *with* God. Can you compare the tragedy of the believer to that of the nonbeliever? The real tragedy, the real drama, is the drama of the believer."[31]

Night is about the drama of the unraveling believer. Wiesel's memoir is full of stories of those religious Jews, including himself, who increasingly find it difficult to pray and then lose their ability altogether. Wiesel records that in Auschwitz even Talmudic scholars and rabbis ultimately gave up on their faith. If there are heroes in *Night,* they are those who first lose their piety and then lose their faith. Indeed, the heroes of *Night* have either lost their faith or are seen as mentally disturbed by their fellow Jews.

One thinks here of Mrs. Schachter, a woman in her fifties whose husband and two older sons had been deported before her. Wiesel knew the family. Mrs. Schachter's husband was a pious Jew who spent his days studying Jewish texts while she supported the family. Taken in the same railroad car, Wiesel describes her as having "lost her mind," when on the third day of the transport she began to shout out her visions of a fire without end, a terrible fire with huge flames. Confronted with these horrifying outbursts, her railroad car companions sought to calm her down. When despite their entreaties she continued shouting, they bound and gagged her. When she broke free from her constraints and once again cried out, she was beaten. Finally, as they pulled up to Auschwitz, a place none had heard of before, she shouted, "The fire, over there!" The fire she envisioned was real. It is the burning bodies that occasions Wiesel's confrontation with God.[32]

An earlier version of Mrs. Schachter is Moishe the Beadle, who initiated the young Wiesel into the study of the Jewish mystical tradition of the Kabbalah. As a foreigner, Moishe was expelled by the Nazis. There he witnessed the mass killings of Jews across the border in Poland. Moishe was slated for death but was only wounded. Having survived, he found his way back to the village and warned Wiesel and his fellow Jews of what was going to happen to them. "Jews listen to me! That's all I ask of you. No money. No pity. Just listen to me!" He kept shouting in synagogue, between the prayers at dusk and the evening prayer.[33]

The heroes in *Night* are not typical martyrs at all. Mrs. Schachter, wife of a pious husband, is thought to be mad. Moishe, always an outsider, is thought to want money or pity. In each case their vision and knowledge remains hidden from the population or, if there in plain sight, their vision is beaten down or ignored. Were the Jews who beat Mrs. Schachter and ignored Moishe soon to be victims or later to be lamented as martyrs?

Only a cynic could see the early Wiesel as manipulating the Holocaust to his own advantage. Remember as well that Wiesel's early writing on the Holocaust occurred well before he or the Holocaust had become an icon in Jewish life. During the writing of *Night*, Wiesel dwelled in obscurity, as did Rubenstein when he began writing articles that would later be included in *After Auschwitz*. Even at the time of their exchange in 1970, the future of the Holocaust narrative was uncertain. Would such evocations of Jewish suffering and innocence continue to gain ground in the Jewish community and the non-Jewish world? The state of Israel had its detractors as well. It was impossible to know in advance how the story of Israel would play in the decades ahead.

So while there was something primal in Wiesel's discussion of the Holocaust and Israel, there was also something primal in Wiesel's address to Rubenstein. When he is confronted with Rubenstein's disdain for Jewish martyrdom in the Holocaust, Wiesel shifts the balance of his argument as a defiant attempt to keep alive the world he lived through. If that world finally and irrevocably died, what would become of the memories of his father, sister, and mother who perished? What would become of the life he knew before deportation? The full and wholesome Jewish world that Wiesel evoked in the opening pages of *Night* still lives on somewhere in Wiesel, the survivor. Would he be able to go on living if his own beginnings were also seen as an illusion?

Holocaust Icon

Though incisive and deep, Rubenstein recognized that the Jewish people as a whole would not recognize their voice in his. Early on, Rubenstein realized that it was Wiesel who spoke for the community.

At a 1991 symposium honoring the pioneering Holocaust historian Raul Hilberg, Rubenstein recalled his first meeting with Wiesel: "I first met Elie Wiesel on October 3, 1968, when he came to Pittsburg to lecture.... I had been deeply moved by reading *Night*, but what struck me most was the enormous spiritual authority he conveyed by his presence.... Few if any other Holocaust survivors seemed to convey a comparable authority." Reflecting back on their encounter in Detroit several years later, Rubenstein affirmed the fundamental difference between Wiesel's anguish about God and his own conclusion that the "idea of a God who chooses Israel lacks credibility. Those Jews who come to the latter conclusion are no longer troubled or agonized about God and the Holocaust. They do not demand that God stand in judgment for what he had done to Israel nor do they feel the slightest sense of revolt against God. Rebellion is, after all, an indirect statement of belief. They believe the world is the way it is. They also believe the Jewish problem is how to survive in the world the way it is." In Rubenstein's retrospective view, Wiesel was correct in Detroit and later in his speech accepting the Nobel Peace Prize: "Of course he was right about the tragedy of the believer in Detroit and in Oslo. I had ceased to believe in the traditional God because I could not stand the incessant inner psychic warfare between what I was expected to believe and preach and what I learned about the Holocaust and the world in which a Holocaust could take place."[34]

Rubenstein's anger had been softened by time. As Rubenstein experienced exile, Wiesel was showered with invitations and honors. By the 1980s, Wiesel was courted by world leaders as the spokesman for the Holocaust martyrs and others who suffer in the present. Though Wiesel is careful to reserve martyrdom for the Holocaust dead, over time he began to speak out for others, from the boat people of Vietnam to the crisis in Darfur. Wiesel assumed the moral leadership ascribed to him. Indeed, as one biographer noted, his message is to all humanity. Still his primal roots remained Jewish.[35]

Rubenstein's voice had been vanquished as too strong and critical. Realizing this, a month after their encounter in Detroit, Rubenstein left the active service of the rabbinate and began his academic career. A few years later he was on the road again, the road that led him to Tallahassee and our encounter. At the symposium on Raul Hilberg, Rubenstein commented on this transition: "I had made the journey from a religious career within the Jewish community to a scientific career in a publicly supported state university. Judaism and Jewish history continued to be of fundamental interest to me, but it was now my vocation to investigate religion as a humanly produced phenomenon. Insofar as my profession was concerned, my personal belief and practice were now strictly private matters." He went on: "In this new environment, I went through a period of impatience with Wiesel's writings. Why, I asked myself, does he go to such convoluted and torturous efforts to maintain some kind of relationship with his God when he, of all people, knows about Auschwitz."[36]

To most of the students who came Rubenstein's way, he was an unknown, a teacher who taught the Holocaust at their university. Wiesel's *Night* had led them to the study of the Holocaust. What was Rubenstein to say to them?

One can imagine the inner psychic conflict that Rubenstein experienced when the rejection he expected and acknowledged—the one that sent him into a permanent exile—reached his doorstep there with students who admired his adversary.

I encountered Wiesel through Rubenstein before the adoration had reached its apex. I also encountered Wiesel in person after the adoration was firmly in place. The first time was at a conference on the Holocaust at Oxford University in 1988. Rubenstein was there, in fact we spoke together at a session that featured a discussion of interfaith relations in the post-Holocaust world. True to form, Rubenstein scolded the Christian contingent, some of whom were Germans, for their romantized repentance of anti-Semitism. The repentant Christian delegation was shocked when Rubenstein regaled them about the logic of Pope Pius XII's reluctance to speak clearly and directly about the suffering of the Jews during the Holocaust. Though the Christians lamented the Pope's silence, Rubenstein counseled them on the logic of the Pope's reluctance. After all, the Pope's constituency was Catholic, not Jewish. Why should he risk the future of the Catholic Church for Jews? The Christians were mortified. I was brought back to Rubenstein's classroom where romanticism was outlawed. I smiled inside as the Christians cringed.

There were other awkward, though telling, moments at the Oxford conference. The non-violent Palestinian uprising had begun in 1987 and the brutal repression of the Palestinians by Israeli armed forces was underway. I was becoming known for speaking out against such abuses, and people began to ask if I had anything newly written on the subject that I could offer them. Indeed I had, and while sitting next to Rubenstein I passed one copy to the person who first asked me. Soon I was surrounded by others wanting my essay.

I felt shy about this attention, especially with Rubenstein sitting right next to me. I was also hoping that he wouldn't ask me for a copy of my essay. Rubenstein was like a father to me, and with his Freudian perspective it was obvious that the son, me, was trying to supplant him, the father. At least he would interpret it that way. Eventually he did ask me, and even though I told him it was unimportant and he shouldn't bother with it, he insisted. I remember him reading the title and mouthing the words—"The Occupation Is Over: The Palestinian Uprising and the Future of the Jewish People." He wasn't pleased.

When I encountered Wiesel, I did so from a distance. He was constantly surrounded by admirers, and when he spoke it was as the featured speaker.

Since only members of the conference were in attendance, there were perhaps a hundred people or so standing as Wiesel spoke.

Wiesel looked a bit uncomfortable as he began to speak. Perhaps it was the lengthy introduction provided by the billionaire businessman Robert Maxwell. Maxwell bankrolled the conference. Judging by the surroundings and through second-hand information, the cost of the conference was well over a million dollars. Just three years later in 1991, with his business empire in freefall, Maxwell died under mysterious circumstances. His body was flown directly to Israel for immediate burial—without an autopsy. This fed speculation that Maxwell had been an Israeli spy who under the duress of financial collapse threatened to reveal his sources and Israel's undercover operations in the United Kingdom and beyond. The rumor was that he had been murdered by Israel's intelligence unit, the Mossad.

Whatever the circumstances of his death, it was soon revealed that Maxwell had stolen money from pension plans and beyond. His sons later stood trial in a case that drew international attention. Though they were eventually acquitted of wrongdoing, Maxwell's reputation was sullied.

Well before Maxwell's death, I felt something had gone terribly wrong with his sponsoring such an important Holocaust conference. In his introductory remarks at the conference, Maxwell spoke at great length about his important work of Holocaust commemoration. Midway through, he broke down and started to weep. As a person who fled Czechoslovakia in 1939 and lost most of his family in the Holocaust, Maxwell had succeeded beyond the imagination in the United Kingdom, his adopted homeland. Yet behind the scenes, Maxwell had been known as being ruthless. When he arrived in the United Kingdom, it was rumored that he had even converted to the Anglican faith. Theatre it was. Then I asked myself if theatre had invaded the memory of the Holocaust.

Wiesel stood off by the side as Maxwell spoke and wept. Whether it was intended or not, Wiesel showed no emotion. He did not move to comfort Maxwell. Nor did anyone else come to his aid. When Wiesel was finally accorded his say, he was brief, speaking for ten minutes or less. He spoke as he wrote. The cadences were familiar, evocative, but considering the setting, a bit worn, as if he had delivered more or less the same talk for some years. Then it was over and he was ushered out by friends and officials of the conference. Having heard of Wiesel for so many years, it was interesting to see him in person. His effect on me was limited, however, and even a bit negative. The entire scene depressed me.

Several years later at another Holocaust conference at Oxford University, I heard Wiesel again. This time he addressed the widely rumored publication of Norman Finkelstein's book on the Holocaust industry, which singled out Wiesel for approbation. Yet as with Rubenstein years earlier, Wiesel never mentioned Finkelstein's name or the title of his book. It was all about the one who was absent. This, of course, made Finkelstein even more vividly present. It made me wonder whether Finkelstein was the new Rubenstein, cutting at the edges of Holocaust orthodoxy.

In the opening pages of his book *The Holocaust Industry: Reflections on the Exploitation of Jewish Suffering,* Finkelstein names Wiesel as one of the primary culprits in the public relations aspect of exploiting Jewish suffering. Finkelstein is harsh, overly so, but his insistence points to the debate over how the Holocaust functions in Jewish life today.

Finkelstein argues that "The Holocaust" is an ideological representation of the Nazi attempt to destroy European Jewry. By representing the destruction of European Jewry in this light, Finkelstein believes Wiesel and other Jews intentionally misrepresent Jewish suffering as a leverage point for Jewish empowerment in America and Israel. With the Holocaust as an ideology, the Jewish community and the policies it supports become off-limits for critical appraisal. Finkelstein writes boldly:

> Like most ideologies, it bears a connection, if tenuous, with reality. The Holocaust is not an arbitrary but rather an internally coherent construct. Its central dogmas sustain significant political and class interests. Indeed, the Holocaust has proven to be an indispensable ideological weapon. Throughout its deployment, one of the world's most formidable military powers, with a horrendous human rights record, has cast itself as a victim state, and the most successful ethnic group in the United States has likewise acquired victim status. Considerable dividends accrue from this specious victimhood—in particular, immunity to criticism, however justified. Those enjoying immunity, I might add, have not escaped the moral corruption that typically attends it. From this perspective, Elie Wiesel's performance as official interpreter of "The Holocaust" is not happenstance. Plainly he did not come to this position on account of his humanitarian commitments or literary talents. Rather, Wiesel plays this leading role because he unerringly articulates a dogma of, and accordingly sustains the interests underpinning, "The Holocaust."[37]

Despite this criticism, Wiesel's words continue to be prized and trumpeted. Today he is feted as a contemporary Jewish mystic whose liturgical cadences provide an element of hope within the ultimate tragedy of the Holocaust. In a difficult and still suffering world, Wiesel's evocation of tragedy and hope was and remains appealing to Jews and non-Jews alike. Yet Finkelstein is only the most well known of Wiesel's public critics; in private there are many others, others who have remarked about Wiesel's propensity for honors and wealth. I blushed when I even heard one important rabbi sing: "There's no business like Shoah business."

Over the years the power of Wiesel's words and images created a Holocaust narrative in the West that others are cautioned against ignoring or criticizing. The Holocaust, which once was a subversive memory of suffering that even many Jews found difficult to affirm, has become a mantra. Wiesel's rage toward Germans in the original *Night* and toward those like Rubenstein who, from his point of view misinterpreted the meaning of the Holocaust, have turned outward toward critics of Israeli policies toward Palestinians. Many critics of Israeli policies toward the Palestinians have been threatened with the Holocaust images and constructs that Wiesel created and keeps reciting.

Perhaps Wiesel, like Rubenstein, became less provocative over time because of the acceptance of the Holocaust as a formative event and because of the repetition of Holocaust writing and imagery. It may also have to do with the changing image of the state of Israel that Wiesel, like Rubenstein, defends unabashedly.

Over the years, Israel's standing in the world and among some Jews has become increasingly tarnished because of its policies toward the Palestinians. For Wiesel, however, the state of Israel remains a dream and a miraculous response to the Holocaust. Because of Israel's relationship to the Holocaust, Wiesel still believes that Israel like the Holocaust should be off limits for normal discussion and debate.

The next decades saw little change in the views of either man. In the beginning, the naming of the Holocaust was dramatic and subversive. As Wiesel noted after writing *Night*, the world, including Jewry, wanted little to do with Holocaust survivors per se even if the Holocaust had become useful as a public relations tool for American Jews and as political leverage for the state of Israel. The Holocaust as a public relations tool troubled Wiesel. Yet the haunting question facing Wiesel is whether he has consciously or unconsciously contributed to that which he criticizes. Too, the question is whether Wiesel has become a prisoner to his own narrative.

From a different perspective, and some years earlier, the Jewish essayist Phillip Lopate also criticized what to him had become "the Holocaust." Once the Holocaust is introduced there are problems: "One instantly saw that the term was part of a polemic . . . the Holocaustians used it like a club to smash back their opponents. . . . In my own mind I continue to distinguish, ever so slightly, between the disaster visited upon the Jews and 'the Holocaust.' Sometimes it almost feels that 'the Holocaust' is a corporation headed by Elie Wiesel, who defends his patents with articles in the Arts and Leisure section of the Sunday *Times*." Lopate continued: "The Hitler/Holocaust analogy dead-ends all intelligent discourse by intruding a stridently shrill note that forces the mind to withdraw. To challenge the demagogic minefield of pure self-righteousness from an ironic distance almost ensures being misunderstood. The image of the

Holocaust is too overbearing, too hot to tolerate distinctions. In its life as rhetorical figure, the Holocaust is a bully."[38]

Avishai Margalit, an Israeli philosopher, also complains about the constant evocation of the Holocaust. In an article titled "The Kitsch of Israel," Margalit worried that turning Israel into *the* response to the Holocaust, especially for Jews and others who live outside Israel, had the danger of turning flesh and blood Israelis—and Palestinians—into simplified symbolic representations of reality.

Margalit applied this analysis to the new children's room at Yad VaShem, the Israeli Holocaust museum, which features tape-recorded voices of children crying out to their mothers in Yiddish. Margalit remarks that even a "kitschman of genius" like Elie Wiesel would find this hard to surpass. For the tourist to Israel who visits the museum, as well as the mandatory visits by heads of state, this manipulation has the effect of picturing Israelis as perpetual victims and Palestinians as the new Nazis. As Margalit sees it, speaking of the Palestinians in the "same tone" as one talks of Auschwitz is an "important element of turning the Holocaust into kitsch." More than fifty years after the publication of *Night*, has the Holocaust degenerated into an industry, a bully, and kitsch?[39]

I encountered Wiesel through Rubenstein more than forty years ago. Today I teach a course on the Holocaust where my students read *Night*, but, perhaps surprisingly, most of the students have already read *Night* by their high school years in Holocaust courses that are often mandated by the state as part of its core curriculum. Moreover, though the building of the United Sates Holocaust Memorial Museum was financed by private funds, its yearly financing is provided by the United States government. The Holocaust museum is visited by millions of people from around the world and has become one of the most popular museums, a major tourist site.

Over the years, I have noticed that the students in my Holocaust course are disturbed by the content I teach, especially my discussion of anti-Semitism in the Christian tradition. This makes the Holocaust disturbing to them in a way they had yet to experience. While this might seem an anomaly—how could the Holocaust not be disturbing?—for many young people the Holocaust is a safe harbor where emotions can be vented and hope secured. After all, Jews survived the Holocaust and Israel stands strong and proud among the nations.

As a Jew who believes that Israeli policies toward Palestinians are wrong, I am constantly confronted with "The Holocaust" being used as a political weapon by officials in national Jewish organizations and by local Jewish communities. Often they use Elie Wiesel as their not-so-hidden weapon to deflect or delegitimize criticisms of Israeli policies. Of course, they don't ask Wiesel's permission to use his good name. But on the other hand, Wiesel's virtual silence over the years on the Palestinian issue encourages this use. As a Holocaust icon,

Wiesel has used his power, and others use it as well, to silence criticism on Israel. Has Wiesel himself become kitsch?

Sometimes it is difficult to recognize the primary impetus for speech and what becomes of it over the years. The Holocaust was real and Elie Wiesel's experience of it was as well. Yet clearly there are issues to be sorted out. One of the major differences between Rubenstein and Wiesel was over the moral character of the state of Israel: Rubenstein opts for a realpolitik of power for power's sake, while Wiesel sees Israel as a moral drama of Jewish renewal. This mirrors their differences over the Holocaust dead as victims or martyrs.

After Rubenstein and Wiesel it is hard to separate the Holocaust and Israel, but perhaps we should. Yet this separation often is seen as the same kind of blasphemy that once both Rubenstein and Wiesel were accused of, when they demanded that the Holocaust be recognized for the sake of the future of Jewish life.

Still, Wiesel commands center stage in the discussion of the Holocaust. When President Obama traveled to Cairo to promote his opening to the Muslim world in 2009, Wiesel was with him. Traveling from Cairo to Buchenwald, where Wiesel spent the last days of the war and his father died, Wiesel spoke about the Holocaust to a worldwide audience. Perhaps this is the summation of Wiesel's life:

> Mr. President, Chancellor Merkel, Bertrand, ladies and gentlemen. As I came here today it was actually a way of coming and visit my father's grave—but he had no grave. His grave is somewhere in the sky. This has become in those years the largest cemetery of the Jewish people.
>
> The day he died was one of the darkest in my life. He became sick, weak, and I was there. I was there when he suffered. I was there when he asked for help, for water. I was there to receive his last words. But I was not there when he called for me, although we were in the same block; he on the upper bed and I on the lower bed. He called my name, and I was too afraid to move. All of us were. And then he died. I was there, but I was not there. . . .
>
> What can I tell him that the world has learned? . . . But the world hasn't learned. When I was liberated in 1945, April 11, by the American army, somehow many of us were convinced that at least one lesson will have been learned—that never again will there be war; that hatred is not an option, that racism is stupid; and the will to conquer other people's minds or territories or aspirations, that will is meaningless.
>
> Paradoxically, I was so hopeful then. Many of us were, although we had the right to give up on humanity, to give up on culture, to give up on

education, to give up on the possibility of living one's life with dignity in a world that has no place for dignity.

We rejected that possibility and we said, no, we must continue believing in a future, because the world has learned. But again, the world hasn't. Had the world learned, there would have been no Cambodia and no Rwanda and no Darfur and no Bosnia.

Will the world ever learn? I think that is why Buchenwald is so important—as important, of course, but differently as Auschwitz. It's important because here the large—the big camp was a kind of international community. People came there from all horizons—political, economic, culture. The first globalization experiments were made in Buchenwald. And all that was meant to diminish the humanity of human beings.

It's enough—enough to go to cemeteries, enough to weep for oceans. It's enough. There must come a moment—a moment of bringing people together. And therefore we say anyone who comes here should go back with that resolution. Memory must bring people together rather than set them apart. Memories here not to sow anger in our hearts, but on the contrary, a sense of solidarity that all those who need us. What else can we do except invoke that memory so that people everywhere who say the twenty-first century is a century of new beginnings, filled with promise and infinite hope, and at times profound gratitude to all those who believe in our task, which is to improve the human condition.[40]

Now in his eighties, Weisel's words were more or less what they were over four decades ago. The world has changed considerably in that time. The Jewish community and the state of Israel have changed as well. Is Wiesel's message about Jewish martyrdom and hope like a perennial philosophy, always the same despite the changing context? Or is something new in the offing? When I saw Wiesel speak those words on television, I couldn't help but think that I had heard them before. And that they were no longer enough.

Martin Buber
(1878–1965)

2

Encountering the Bible

Martin Buber

Martin Buber was born in Vienna, Austria, in 1878. Buber spent much of his child-hood with a grandfather who was a scholar of the Jewish tradition and literature. As a young man, Buber studied in Vienna, Leipzig, Berlin, and Zurich and soon entered the Zionist Movement, as much for religious and cultural as for political reasons. In 1923 he published his now classic book, I and Thou. *He lectured in Jewish religion and philosophy at the University of Frankfurt from 1924 to 1933. During that time, he worked together with Franz Rosenzweig on Jewish philosophy and spirituality as well as a groundbreaking translation of the Hebrew Bible into German. During the early years of Hitler's rule, Buber stayed in Germany, laying the groundwork for Jewish renewal in a time of crisis. Buber left Germany in 1938 and settled in Jerusalem, where he was Professor of Social Philosophy at the Hebrew University. While writing and publishing major works in Jewish spirituality, Buber also sought common ground between Jews and Arabs in Palestine and later in Israel. At the same time, Buber traveled to Germany to begin a postwar dialogue between Jews and Germans. Buber died in 1965.*

My encounter with Martin Buber began prior to my hearing Richard Rubenstein or reading Elie Wiesel, in other words, before the Holocaust was named for me. My encounter with Buber marked me deeply then and continues to do so today. I entered Buber's world as the Holocaust and Israel were being recognized as formative to Jewish life but before they had been named decisively in mine. Growing up in what was then a Jewish hinterland saved me from knowing too much about what was normative in the centers of Jewish life like New York City and Los Angeles. This allowed me a relatively unformed inner Jewish space to explore my own Jewishness.

Today it is difficult to appreciate this freedom and how little pressure there was to conform to an already established Jewish identity. Before Jewish identity was mobilized, and even militarized on behalf of the Holocaust and Israel, there was little sense of urgency. Young Jews of my generation went off in many directions, searching here and there for meaning. Most often the search began in Hebrew School, yet for many of us that atmosphere felt foreign and stifling. We explored spiritualities outside the Jewish world, Zen being the most popular. We did not have a sense of betraying Jewish history or leaving behind our Jewish responsibilities. This was the 1960s, when Jewish identity was in flux. What we had inherited wasn't enough for us. We didn't know where we were going. Did we have to have a destination?

The world in general is very different now, and the Jewish world a very different place. When I reflect back, I ask whether the openness of Jewish identity in these years was a romanticized fantasy, a reality that didn't exist, or one to which I now seek to escape. Although there is no return, I think that those days have something to say to the Jewish future.

My encounter with Buber brings me back to those years. Each time I read Buber, I feel like I am returning to the beginning. He has become even more significant in my journey as a Jew and even more important now to the Jewish future than when I first encountered him.

Buber traversed so many fields of study that he cannot be pigeonholed in any one of them. He was, among other things, a linguist, a researcher of Asian religions, a translator and interpreter of the Bible, a sociologist, a philosopher, and a theologian. His influences extend far beyond religion to philosophy, education, and psychology. It is hard to find a Jewish writer who has had more influence on thoughtful discourse in the world than has Buber. With him we are in the company of one of the great spiritual seekers in history.

Since my first encounter with Buber, the Jewish world has changed precipitously, and in some ways so have I. Much of Buber is pre-Holocaust and pre-Israel, though he did live during and in the aftermath of both events. While Buber can be glimpsed only in fragments and through a historical lens, there is something peculiarly present about his writing. Buber's voice allows us to encounter Jewish life from a different vantage point. If we listen to his voice, we might see ourselves clear of the narrow confines of Jewishness as it presents itself today.

I begin with some of the major philosophical and theological themes that Buber explored in his book *I and Thou* (1923), as well as some of his essays in *Israel and the World: Essays in a Time of Crisis*, written in the 1930s in Germany as the Nazi era dawned. These writings predate both Richard Rubenstein and Elie Wiesel by decades.[1]

The Jewish world is small in population and intense by way of shared experience. After the Holocaust the Jewish world shrunk significantly as entire areas of Jewish life in Europe and elsewhere were eliminated or abandoned. The rise of the state of Israel became a magnet for Jews fleeing persecution or seeking new hope in a land that they could call their own. Rather than dissipating the intensity of the Jewish world, it increased it. Surviving Jews huddled together.

Having survived the Holocaust and then living in France, Elie Wiesel recalls several encounters with Buber. Though Buber fled Germany in the 1930s and spent the rest of his life living in Jerusalem, he was in great demand as a lecturer around the world. Wiesel recalls his first encounter with Buber at the Sorbonne shortly after the end of World War II:

> The hall was packed, the audience enthusiastic. Buber was treated like a prophet. His listeners were elated, conquered in advance, ready to savor every word. There was just one problem. Had Buber spoken in Hebrew, Yiddish, English or German, there would have been some people in the hall able to follow him. But he opted for French, and his accent was so thick no one understood him. Everyone applauded just the same. No matter they would read the text when it was published. But I was delighted to have seen the handsome face and heard the searching voice of the author of *I and Thou*, one of the great Jewish spiritual thinkers of our time.[2]

Toward the end of the 1960s, Wiesel encountered Buber again through a telling anecdote:

> Addressing an audience of priests, he said something like this: "What is the difference between Jews and Christians? We all await the messiah. You believe He has already come and gone, while we do not. I therefore propose that we await Him together. And when He appears, we can ask Him: Were You here before?" Then he paused and added: "And I hope that at that moment I will be close enough to whisper in his ear, 'For the love of heaven, don't answer.'"[3]

Wiesel perceived Buber very much as did others. In 1953 Aubrey Hodes was a troubled young South African living on a kibbutz in Israel. He heard of Buber and one day sought to meet him. After multiple visits, Hodes recalled what drew him and others to Buber:

> Whatever Buber did was done intensely. . . . He laughed often . . . [and] intensely. When he drank a cup of tea . . . [he] enjoyed it intensely. To see him read a letter that had just arrived in the post was an education; the

eyes, the mind, the memory, the entire acute person responding to the new situation, to the stimulus of the unexpected question. I knew that Buber's intense projection of himself was totally unselfconscious and sincere. When I sat opposite him, trying to put a fugitive idea into words of everyday speech, and felt his eyes on me, burning and searching, I responded with a similar intensity, saying things I had not consciously thought out and had not realized were buried so close beneath the surface. It was Buber's concentration on what I was about to say, his commitment to my not-yet-spoken words, which made them come alive.[4]

One day Hodes escorted Anthony Benn, a young man already quite active in British politics, who later wrote to Hodes of his encounter with Buber:

The thing I remember most about Buber was the very quiet way in which he received us and his habit of giving his entire attention to the person to whom he was speaking.

I also remember that one woman from New York made a suggestion to him about some educational work that might be undertaken in the kibbutz. "Are you prepared to do this work yourself?" he asked her. She said that she was not thinking of doing it herself but thought that it might be a good idea if it was done. In the kindest way possible he explained that he did not think that ideas were worth pursuing unless the people who advocated them were prepared to put them into practice themselves. Though I'm sure he didn't intend it as a rebuke, it was a very testing comment and it made one feel that he was interested more in people than ideas and wanted to know how far people were prepared to sacrifice themselves in order to make real the ideas which, otherwise, it would be so easy to throw off in conversation in the expectation that others would take them up.[5]

Phyllis Anderson, herself a spiritual seeker, described her meeting with Martin Buber in his home in Jerusalem:

It was hot but the stone house had tiled floors, high ceilings, and window blinds that let the breeze through, but moderated the sunlight. Every room was lined, ceiling to floor, with books and large library ladders on rollers, even the dining room. There was a very young child playing with a kitty. After tea we stood around the dining room and in came a frail, fragile looking, old man in house shoes. The child crawled into his lap and he spoke briefly, then told us we could ask questions. We were all awed by the situation but there were questions. Finally, he indicated that he was tired, so only one more question. Someone asked, "Dr. Buber, who do you think has been the greatest man in history?" Buber paused a moment, almost as if surprised and said quietly: "Why, there are *no* great men, only useful ones." Then he rose, smiled a gentle smile, bowed slightly, and shuffled out to the kitchen where women were preparing a meal. Our group exited in total silence.[6]

In the academic world after the end of World War II, Buber was held in awe and honored on a regular basis. He was also a paradox. How did you squeeze Buber into an academic discipline? In a volume to honor Buber we see this paradox in full bloom. Charles Hartshorne tried to describe Buber's metaphysics:

> Buber has no metaphysics; Buber is one of the greatest metaphysicians.... He does not, formally speaking, have a metaphysics, a general system of ultimate categories, carefully defined against rival systems. He is, I imagine, little interested in such things.... Yet there are some pages in *Ich und Du* that seem to be me among the most inspired ever written on the relation of creation and the creator. True, they are couched in the language of piety, of existential response, rather than that of theory and rational evidence. It could be called a kind of ... great poetry.... In Buber there is an austere simplicity and centrality, with just polemical indications to mark off the point of view of some of its most important rivals, and there is no assemblage of arguments or evidences. One feels the sheer force of actual experience, from which, in one way or another, all evidence must come.[7]

Decades after first reading Buber, I encountered him through this very force of actual experience that Hartshorne describes. Once when visiting Germany to meet with the German theologian Dorothee Soelle, I was invited to stay at her home. I arrived just after the accident at the Soviet nuclear plant Chernobyl. There was great fear of the aftereffects of this disaster. However, the reason for my visit was to meet Germans in their contemporary life. Were the Germans Nazis through and through, or was there a new and different side of German nationality and German individuality? I wanted to see for myself.

Soelle had invited me to visit here in Hamburg for this express reason, but I ended up spending most of my time with her husband, Fulbert Steffensky. Steffensky grew up Catholic in Bavaria and was a child during the Nazi time. He was born in 1933, the year that Hitler assumed power in Germany. Steffensky became a Benedictine monk and, though he left his community some years later, he told me a fascinating story of his encounter with Buber in the 1960s in Jerusalem.

Steffensky came to Buber's home where they discussed theology and Jewish-Christian relations for hours. Steffensky went away elated. Unexpectedly, the next day Buber's secretary called him and said that Buber wanted to meet with him a few hours hence. Steffensky was delighted, expecting another afternoon of dialogue, but this meeting turned out to be quite short. It seems that Buber had misspoke on a theological question and wanted to correct his error. When his error was corrected, the meeting was over.

Some years ago, I had another encounter with someone who had known Buber. I was in Zurich to deliver a lecture at a theological institution that had just hosted Soelle. Over six hundred people had come to her lecture. Only three people beside the director came to hear me. At first, I was disappointed at the turn out, but it provided the ability to enter into some dialogue. One of the three was an older man, a European Jew who had survived the Holocaust and gone to live in Palestine after the war. There he met with Buber and became a member of Buber's group that argued for a binational polity of Jews and Arabs in Palestine. Afterward, I was able to talk with him about Buber and the atmosphere in Palestine after the Holocaust and the difficulties Buber's group had in translating their message of peaceful coexistence during that time. My inability to attract a crowd worked to my advantage.

Teaching as a Prophetic Encounter

During my college days, I often went to the library to listen to tape recordings my religious studies teacher made, exploring more of Buber than we could cover in class sessions. I was mesmerized. I couldn't get enough of Buber.

I first encountered Buber through my teacher, a former fundamentalist Christian from Oklahoma who had joined the counter-culture. As a religious seeker, he bracketed his Christianity and traveled to Asia to study and experience Asian spirituality, placing his Christianity aside for the time being in order to explore Buddhism. I wondered if one's Jewishness could be so placed. Still, his search allowed him to entertain Buber in his depth and to enter Buber's world as would a foreigner. Because of our differences in age and location, I too entered the world of Buber as a foreigner. Yet I recognized immediately that Buber's world was also deeply my own.

Why foreign? Synagogue training had introduced me to the essential elements of Judaism. For most Jews of my generation that was the end of their Jewish search. Growing up in the 1950s and 1960s in America, young Jews had difficulty identifying with the cultural trappings of a Judaism we felt to be foreign. We needed distance from our afternoon and weekend Hebrew School so we could feel fully American. We remained Jewish. We also hoped to chart our own destiny in American culture. Could our parents or our Hebrew School teachers really tell us what would become of Jewish life?

As young Jews we thought that much of Hebrew School and synagogue life was hypocritical. Our parents pretended that our Jewishness set us apart, while in real life Jews tried desperately to be the same as our non-Jewish neighbors. In our minds, the distinctions of being Jewish weren't distinctive enough.

Because of this disjunction, rebellion during the time at Hebrew School was almost epidemic. Our rebellions were minor and sometimes humorous. Still there was a serious side to all of it. Things had changed in Jewish life. There were revolutions to come. In what directions they would take us was unknown. What we did know is that the tradition we inherited made little sense to our parents and less to us.

We attended synagogue and observed the major Jewish holy days. Our minds were elsewhere. Why keep up appearances if we rarely discussed God and if the Hebrew prayers were recited by rote? Now I know that Jews inherit a deep skepticism from the Jewish tradition about "religious" claims and "religious" places. As a child this was simply an intuition, perhaps an inborn struggle against assimilation. It was a jumble. We didn't know where to turn.

Usually assimilation is defined by Jews as mixing with non-Jews and giving up the ways of old. Perhaps we saw in our parents another kind of assimilation, to America and the modern world. Without being able to articulate the reasons, we were suspicious of dressing up for synagogue and learning Hebrew. The formalities of the synagogue were strange to us. The Hebrew we prayed in was strange to us. Neither felt natural to our identity. Part of this was due to our youth. Part related to the as-yet-unnamed changes in Jewish life.

I became a Bar Mitzvah in 1965, before the two formative events of contemporary Jewish life—naming the Holocaust and the 1967 Arab-Israeli war—had reached full force. It made a huge difference whether we were formed before or after the naming of the Holocaust and Israel as central to Jewish identity. As well, we understood intuitively that religion as spoken about and practiced in modern society is what seems to be *essential* Judaism, Christianity, or Islam. We somehow knew that organized religion covers over the "real" essentials with "practical" essentials that conform us to the world. As young Jews, we knew this conforming quality intimately. I certainly felt it deeply.

I rebelled against these conforming essentials. True, I was conforming to the secular world in many ways, with long hair, listening to popular music, and playing sports from dawn to dusk. Yet especially in the popular music of our day—from the Beatles to Simon and Garfunkel to Bob Dylan—I embraced the spiritual aspect of the secular world. Perhaps this was my way of rejecting the conformism of contemporary Judaism and carving out a place of particularity within the larger world. I thought that this might create a space for my particularity as a Jew that I could not find in organized Jewish life.

Buber was my first encounter with a Jewish author who spoke to me in a spiritual way. He introduced me to the broader dimensions of Judaism and faith beyond what I was experiencing in American Jewish life. He also opened me to the universe beyond Judaism that was within me. What is the encounter that Buber refers to? Buber's encounter is less definable as an experience than it is an opening that turns us around. Or rather it is an experience that moves us beyond the experiential. In the encounter we are fully present to a reality that is within and beyond us.

Buber thought education to be about encounter, in this case between teacher and student. To create a true encounter the teacher had to be open to the student and the student open to the teacher. Today, education has an industrial feel where "fact" knowledge is prized over the teacher-student encounter.

We see this in how the classroom is arranged, how teachers acquire the credentials to teach, how course schedules are compiled, what is necessary for graduation, what students are being prepared for as they enter the world. Paulo Freire, the great Brazilian educator, called this the "banking" model of education. The teacher gives the students the "facts," which the students learn and then recite back when they are evaluated. Friere's alternative education technique focused on *conscientization*. Rather than rote facts, teachers help students surface the questions within them and the reality that surrounds them.

Ivan Illich, the Austrian Jew who became an influential Catholic priest and lived much of his life in Mexico, was so fed up with modern education that he called for the end of the education industry and the "deschooling" of the individual and society. Like Friere, Illich emphasized a more direct approach of educational encounter, once again around what is important and meaningful for the person and the community.

Buber was before both Freire and Illich and no doubt influenced both. Still, there was another level to Buber's understanding of the education process. Buber believed that the encounter had to be seen and experienced by the student as a possibility in their life. Buber saw the teacher as one who lived fully and brought the fullness of life to the student. This could happen only if the teacher first experienced this fullness in her own life.

I think of how far we are from Buber's vision each year as I prepare to teach my course on the Holocaust. First, I have to prepare my syllabus and reading list. Then, I decide which writings to assign and when they will be due. Finally, I find dates for the exams, then grade them and record the grades.

Many years ago a student named Maria came into my office and told me she was unable to read the books I assigned. The suffering she encountered was too horrific. Maria could not fathom the possibility that human beings could do what was done to other human beings in the Holocaust. The incredible hatred of Jews devastated her. She could not and did not want to absorb it. She felt that if she resisted absorbing it, perhaps the Holocaust would cease to exist.

This almost mystical side to Maria's resistance to the Holocaust brought to mind the prophet Ezekiel. God commands Ezekiel to take a scroll and eat it, thereby internalizing the message God called Ezekiel to proclaim. The message presumed Israel's rejection of the message and therefore sealed Ezekiel's doom.

Ezekiel ate the scroll as commanded and found to his surprise that it tasted sweet, like honey. Maria refused the Holocaust scroll I assigned her to eat. She refused to internalize the bitterness of the Holocaust.

As her professor what was my responsibility in relation to Maria's "problem?" Should I tell her to lay her emotions aside and simply read the material so she wouldn't fall further behind? Should I give her a pep talk about the difficulties we need to transcend so we can move on in life? She was encountering the Holocaust and being turned upside down and around. But could she—or I—afford to encounter the Holocaust?

How different it is to "study" the Holocaust in the safe confines of university life. I sometimes wonder if "teaching" the Holocaust is possible or whether the structure of the university makes this nearly impossible.

How the Holocaust functions today in Jewish and American life makes teaching the Holocaust even more difficult. As a Jewish teacher, I am expected to teach the Holocaust in a certain way. This includes the accusations of historic anti-Semitism against Christianity, while precluding the criticisms that some Jews have about how the Holocaust functions today to silence Palestinians and their quest for freedom. It is difficult to have a true encounter with my students if I emphasize one aspect of the Holocaust and keep silent about the suffering of others.

Some years ago I invited a Palestinian to my class to speak on her view of the Holocaust. She started her lecture by recalling her family's dispossession from Palestine during the 1948 war for Israeli independence. While for many Jews the war for Israel's independence is celebrated, my Palestinian guest saw it as the beginning of the *Nakba*, her family and her people's "catastrophe." As a child she had read the diaries of Anne Frank. As a Palestinian, she asked my class what Anne Frank might think about her dispossession.

If Anne Frank were here today, would she be eloquent or dumfounded? What would she want us to do with the Holocaust? I wonder what Anne Frank would make of her own legacy.

Jews in the community were none too pleased with the thought of a Palestinian addressing my Holocaust class. Though she had been respectful of Jewish suffering in the Holocaust throughout her lecture, she raised some important and critical issues about teaching the Holocaust in a changing global context. My students loved her honesty and challenge. For them, instead of minimizing Jewish suffering, our Palestinian interlocutor raised the stakes of learning from a past event to our present commitments and fidelity.

When we read *Night* and think of my Palestinian lecturer, I think of how far we have travelled from Auschwitz to the American classroom. Can we even touch the outlines of the Holocaust through this academic method? Can we encounter the Holocaust world by pretending that Jews are innocent in the death camps and innocent in the creation and maintenance of a nation-state? Everyone knows that dwelling in Auschwitz and managing the state of Israel are quite different. The Holocaust shouldn't shield Jews from the criticism due for displacing another people. Should I shield Jewish and non-Jewish students from the fact that when Jews have power we do almost everything that has been done to us?

The movies I show in the Holocaust course bring to life the horror of the Holocaust. Yet the constant replay of these images can inure teachers and students alike to its horror. Annual and "popular" courses on the Holocaust can also trivialize the event itself. After we watch the movies, there is lunch to eat, another class to attend, or a faculty meeting to endure. Under these conditions it is difficult to say that we truly encounter the Holocaust. Sometimes I wonder how Buber would "teach" the Holocaust.

For Buber, education is crucial to the spiritual life. He reimagines what teaching is and how we define a teacher, a student, and learning. For Buber, learning is less the mastery of the objective world than it is entry into the subjective reality of the known and unknown. The Buberian twist is that the "objective" world isn't always the "real" world. What is described as "subjective" is often more real than what is known as objective.

For Buber, the secondary task of a teacher is to introduce the student to new information. The teacher's primary task is to participate with the student in the gathering of what is already within her into a new and articulate configuration. Teaching and thus learning is becoming aware and articulate of what is deep inside of us. A teacher passes on to the student the depth of his or her own engagement in the world. Students who are trying to grasp what their own engagement in the world will be are ready to receive the teacher's wisdom. Just signing up to be "taught" is not enough. A teacher is more than a fount of facts.

For Buber, education is the encounter of the whole person, the teacher with the student, the person in formation. Rather than the teacher imparting knowledge as a separate and quantifiable entity, the encounter is between two persons at different stages of their journey. In a 1934 address delivered in Germany, "Teaching and Deed," Buber described education in the following ways:

> In these recurring encounters between a generation which has reached its full development and one which is still developing, the ultimate aim is not to submit a separable something. What matters is that time and again an older generation, staking its entire existence on that act, comes to a younger with the desire to teach, waken, and shape it; then the holy spark leaps across the gap.
>
> [T]eaching is inseparably bound up with doing . . . it is impossible to teach or learn without living. . . . Either the teachings live in the life of a

responsible human being or they are not alive at all. The teachings do not center in themselves; they do not exist for their own sake. They refer to, they are directed toward, the deed . . . "deed" does not, of course, connote "activism," but life that realizes the teachings in the changing potentialities of every hour.

The teachings do not rely on the hope that he who knows them will observe them. Socratic man believes that all virtue is cognition, and that all that is needed to do what is right is to know what is right. This does not hold for the Mosaic man who is informed with the profound experience that cognition is never enough, that the deepest part of him must be seized by the teachings, that for realization to take place his elemental totality must submit to the spirit as clay to the potter.

The influence of the teacher upon the pupil . . . [is] set on a par with divine works which are linked with the human, maternal act of giving birth. The inner turning of the prophet is an actual rebirth, and the educator, who brings the precious ore in the soul of his pupil to light and frees it from dross, affords him a second birth, birth into a loftier life.[8]

A student is seized by the teachings. A teacher who isn't so seized can hardly communicate those teachings. The teachings are not taught to be observed as a "separable something." Rather than being observed, the teachings are life that realizes itself in the "changing potentialities of every hour." It is difficult to see how such teaching can be organized in the form of a course, with assigned readings and due dates determined in advance even before the encounter begins.

There is an existential urgency in Buber. Often he is referred to as a "religious existentialist." Because of his emphasis on the multidimensionality of the person, he is also linked with the Personalist school of thought. Buber was both, and more. For Buber education was about the person in the moment of encounter, yet all that was being brought to that moment came from somewhere else, from the deep past that is more than historical facts and figures. Buber's teachings are bound up with everything known that has gone before and everything that has ceased to be known. That which has been lost is the buried treasure that the teacher embodies and attempts to bring to life. It is the buried treasure that often is the key to awakening the student to encounter. This is what I return to each year when I teach, or more appropriately, share Buber with my students.

Though the Socratic method has its importance, for Buber the grasping of depth rather than simply learning how to ask the right questions is central. Without depth, our questions skim the surface. With depth, our questions take on a new trajectory. Depth can be accessed only through commitment. That is why Buber values the Mosaic over the Socratic.

Buber believed that the answers to our questions are neither the means nor ends of our existence. They are part of our context and important within that framework. Yet context is only the beginning. Though we are defined largely by the circumstances of our birth and our economic and political stations in life, there are parts of us that cannot be so defined or limited:

> The individual can most certainly think, and know, and express himself only on the basis of his own particular being. Certainly, we are dependent in manifold ways both on the social stratum in which we move, and on the psychic strata within ourselves. But the strangest thing about us human beings is that our life is interspersed with volcanic hours in which all is topsy-turvy and outburst takes place. We suddenly find it intolerable to be hedged about by the conditional; we break out and reach into the darkness with both hands in search of unconditional truth, of a truth which is not conditioned by our character and our environment. We court this truth; we struggle for it.[9]

For Buber, the Mosaic understanding is different than the Socratic because questions that have answers respond to our conditionality, whereas the truth that suddenly invades our lives cannot be analyzed or categorized. Though conditionality remains, we are now in a different place. Truth breaks through our conditionality and shakes us to our very bones. Then we are like Moses who has left the palace. We are face to face with God.

Buber believes that truth is a call that remains within our conditioned lives. Rather than taking us out of time, truth deepens our sense of time, adding the unconditioned to the conditioned. Truth has ramifications for the individual and for others, even for history. Being able to name the unconditioned within the conditioned is how the world is renewed:

> Certainly . . . we cannot rid ourselves of the conditional which is our destiny. And yet . . . something unconditional has invaded our conditional state and pervaded it. Something which we were unable to think up to this point has become both thinkable and sayable, and this "something" belongs to that series of unpredictable things which renew the world. That which leads to decisions and alters directions is the encounter with truth. It is the soul's continual rebirth both in the individual man and in mankind.[10]

Buber continues: "Human truth becomes real when one tries to translate one's relationship to truth into the reality of one's life. And human truth can be communicated only if one throws one's self into the process and answers for it with one's self."[11]

Encounter in education has to deal with our conditionality, even the conditionality of what is taught. It also must reach beyond that conditionality. The unconditioned can be taught in such a way that it becomes part of our ongoing "conditioned" living. In that way even the unconditioned becomes part of our conditionality. Life expands. Where we were once stuck, now we are free.

The teacher is the one who touches the unconditioned and transmits that possibility through her being. That possibility, rather than the experience itself, is the "spark that leaps across the gap." The spark is what Buber means by the "teachings," which allow the student to turn away from what is known and toward what is beneath and around the known. When Buber writes that the "influence of the teacher upon the pupil, of the right teacher upon the right pupil, is not merely compared to, but even set on a par with, divine works which are linked with the human, maternal act of giving birth," he is thinking of an "inner turning" that the student must do, knowing now that such a turning is necessary and possible. Teachings are able to "turn" when freed from the constraints of religion, ideologies, and academics.

Buber views this turning as the hallmark of the prophet. With the prophet, "something which we were unable to think up to this point has become both thinkable and sayable, and this 'something' belongs to that series of unpredictable things which renew the world." In Buber's mind the teacher and the prophet are one. Buber sees turning as an "actual rebirth" that the teacher helps the student to find and embrace in the depth of her own being—a "second birth." Through this second birth the student takes hold of her singular destiny. This comes through an opening to depth within the self and in the world.

For Buber, the prophet is one who turns herself and others toward relation and a deep experience of being both free and bound. The solitude experienced when one is only living on the surface, where everything seems set out in advance, is transformed when the primal source is accessed. Instead of solitude, a bond with others and the universe is experienced. The prophet experiences this most directly and at a depth that many might find frightening, especially when viewed only from the perspective of the conditioned life. Once the person is opened to the primal source, the prophetic is close rather than far away. Such are the volcanic moments that combine a deep anxiety with a foretaste of freedom.

That is how it is with an encounter. No matter how old and experienced, we are always beginning. So it is in history. For Buber, a linear accounting of history or of our individual lives mistakes the historical context as the only reality. This is the most superficial aspect of history. Real history, found in encounter, is in prophetic turning. Transmitting this other history allows the holy spark to leap across the gap.

For Buber, the beginning is to ponder once again the beauty of the origins of life, history, community, ourselves, and the source of all being. For this we have to penetrate the superficial history we are taught and clear away the internalized debris we have accumulated over the years. The accumulation of the superficial makes it more and more difficult to access the deeper meaning of our individual lives. This accumulation also obscures the deeper meaning of history. Turning in our encounter, we recover both.

To turn is to return to the beginning and move beyond what Buber calls the proliferating *It*—the object world run amok. By penetrating the proliferating *It* we rediscover the *Thou* of existence—the spiritual center of life itself. The accumulated objects that are created in history block our vision and our path. For Buber, *Thou* is the raw and unfiltered primal sensibility that exists within the *It* world.

We discover and rediscover the *Thou* by seeing within and through the world of objects. As individuals we are made up of diverse parts—history, community and self. The object world is crucial for our existence. We need to separate and use objects for our physical existence. But we also need continually to grasp and encounter the more holistic sense of life, as if for the first time, when the world was young and so were we. The teacher is the one who continues to turn and brings that turning to the student who needs to turn in her own life. The teacher is the turning presented to the next generation so they can continue to encounter the deeper aspects of the human and history. In contrast to our industrialized sense of education, Buber believes that teachings resist being treated as collections of knowable material. If teaching and the teachings themselves are not lived out, they become dead facts. If teachers are not turning, they cannot be a spark. If teachings are not lived, they cannot leap across the gap.

The teacher shakes up the "truth" by presenting the end as just the beginning of the journey. What is outer, even the word of God spoken in synagogue or church, is the superficial level, which contains more depth than it seems at first hearing. The teacher unsettles all that is received as central to truth. By turning, the settled truth is experienced as a provisional outer wrapping of an encounter that we are called to have and name for ourselves.

The Prophetic Community

Buber was born and raised between the two worlds of Eastern and Western Europe. Through this he experienced the diverse and vibrant worlds of Judaism of his day. Aspects of the rabbinic legalistic mind predominated in Western Europe, while the charismatic joyful heart found its way in Eastern Europe.

The diversity of Jewish life mirrored the diversity of modern European life. When Buber was in Western Europe, he experienced advanced modernity with its promise and struggle. When Buber was in Eastern Europe, he experienced a more traditional society on the brink of modernity. In general, while Western European Jews were more assimilated and more Enlightenment oriented, Eastern European Jews were less assimilated and less Enlightenment oriented.

Buber probed the European Jewish landscape and subverted both orientations. In crossing boundaries, he fashioned another way of being Jewish without announcing it as such. Ultimately, Buber's form of Jewishness harkens back to the origins of the people of Israel, which he felt had been lost in the layering of tradition and religious authority. By peeling away the outer layers of tradition, Buber sought the primal roots of Jewishness, which is pre-Sinai yet permeated with the prophetic.

In some ways, Rabbinic Judaism kept the pre-Sinai and prophetic traditions alive through the reading and studying of sacred texts. At the same time, like all religions, Judaism tried to bury the primal, which represented too strong a challenge to its religious structure. With this taming, Buber felt that the Jewish spirit atrophied and entered the sphere of religion.

For Buber, all religion involves the death of the primal and the taming of the prophetic. Religion seeks to orient and explain the encounters of those who have gone before us. Often though we become observers of the very encounters we are called to have ourselves. For Buber, the essence of Judaism, seen and lived through Jewish law, is a death sentence for the spirit. Jews practice Judaism to be sure, but is that the encounter Jews are called to have? Jewish law can become a protection, a conditioned reality that saves us from those volcanic hours when everything is up for grabs. Yet it is in these volcanic hours that we face our destiny.

Buber debunks the myth that normative Judaism represents the whole of Jewishness. He sees Jewish legalism instead as a latecomer that exists primarily to keep Jews from returning to their primal location, the prophetic. Buber seeks to get back behind Judaism as it was known in his time to the more authentic Jewish spirit. In a 1930 address in Stuttgart, Buber spoke about his understanding that Jewish law and his differentiation of the teaching of Judaism as a religion that comes from Moses and the pre-Sinai soul of Judaism:

> For the teaching of Judaism comes from Sinai; it is Moses' teaching. But the *soul* of Judaism is pre-Sinaitic; it is the soul which approached Sinai, and there received what it did receive; it is older than Moses; it is patriarchal, Abraham's soul, or more truly, since it concerns the *product* of a primordial age, it is Jacob's soul. The Law put on the soul and the soul can never again be understood outside of the Law; yet the soul itself is not the Law. If one wishes to speak of the soul of Judaism, one must consider all the transformation it underwent through the ages till this very day; but

one must never forget that in every one of its stages the soul has remained the same, and gone on in the same way.[12]

Buber treads lightly here. He is speaking to Christian missionaries who used the dichotomy of legalism and love to separate Jews and Christians. Still, Buber presses the point that Jewish law is an outer garment, whereas the soul of Judaism is inner. Unlike Christians, the question for Jews has never been about God's existence but rather of trusting God: "The crucial word which God himself spoke of this rediscovery of his presence was spoken to Moses from the midst of the burning bush: 'I shall be there as I shall be there' (Exod. 3:14). He is ever present to his creature, but always in the form peculiar to that moment, so that the spirit of man cannot foretell in the garment of what existence and what situation God will manifest himself. It is for man to recognize him in each of his garments." Law is one garment, as indeed is Christianity a garment, but God's garments should never be mistaken for God. Even the word *God* has become a garment. That is why Buber believes that the word must be emptied of its accumulated and acquired meanings lest the conditioned God be mistaken for *Thou*.[13]

Buber seeks a method to find the lost treasure beneath the accumulation of tradition. For Buber, no matter how beautiful tradition is, it remains a block to authentic encounter. In fact, religion substitutes itself for the encounter we need for ourselves.

In religion, we observe the encounter of others from a safe remove. We already know the story, for example, the fear and trembling of Abraham. Yet our own encounter and its outcome are unknown. We alone must face this unknown. If we only observe the encounter of others, and are not tested, how are we to fulfill our destiny firsthand?

The encounters we read about in the Bible were unknown as they were unfolding. Take the Exodus story that Jews recite each year and that we are commanded to experience as if we are there. This experience is mediated by history; we are placing ourselves in an encounter that has already happened. Not only are we pretending, but we are shielded from the Exodus experience unless we, too, undergo the trials and tribulations of a desert experience. Only then can we taste the jubilation that such an encounter offers.

Describing the encounter is always difficult and, for Buber, almost impossible. The description we have of the Exodus is just that, an attempt to describe the overwhelming power of the encounter of the Israelites with God, the power of Egypt and the struggle for liberation. Though our encounter may have similar underlying qualities, it is impossible for us to describe such an encounter in the same way. If we take the Exodus description of the encounter literally and as a substitute for our own, it dwarfs our own. We have an excuse to participate vicariously in the encounter.

Judaism privileges the encounters in the Bible as if they are more important. Positing a once-and-for-all encounter is typical of religion but also its limitation. The primal quality of the biblical encounter is significant for Buber since the layers of sophistication and distance that we often apply to reality were less developed in ancient times. Primitive humankind was less reticent in describing their encounter. It was raw and without the filter of centuries of "progress." Knowing what will happen in the Exodus is quite different than being there in the first place, wondering if the promised destination will be reached or, if so, what will be found there.

Reading biblical encounters through our layers of religious and societal development distorts their primal quality and at the same time spares us from a similarly raw encounter in our life. If we do embark on an encounter, this allows us to enter into history as did the biblical characters. For Buber, encounters in the Bible demonstrate the possibility of breakthroughs in personal lives and in history. But if we read the Bible as the encounters *par excellence*, this makes encounter less possible in our lives and history.

In Rabbinic Judaism there is palpable fear of the ultimate encounter, the prophetic. From the first centuries of the Common Era, the rabbis sought to orient Judaism toward a framework of study, prayer, and good deeds. According to Buber, the prophetic threatened to break through the rabbi's cautionary system and signal the end of the existing religious institutional establishments that kept their form of Judaism intact. This is true of Christianity as well. If Christians had the encounter that Jesus had in their own time and in their own way, Christianity would explode. Instead, Christians tend to see Jesus as a one-time encounter that ultimately is removed from ongoing history. Who Jesus was and what he meant in history becomes codified, and the encounter that Jesus had with God and others is declared off-limits, to be observed and perhaps emulated from a distant observation point. For Buber, this remove is essential for the Christian religion and yet distorts Jesus, whom Buber encounters as a brother. Disentangling Jesus from Christianity, for Buber, is essential to understanding him as a model of encounter. It is similar to the difficulty of disentangling the Jewish soul from Judaism.[14]

Applying the prophetic to Rabbinic Judaism today would challenge the existing social and political order buttressed by post-Holocaust Jewry. Actually, Rabbinic Judaism has ceased to exist as it was first envisioned. It was built on a Diaspora sensibility, and even with more than half of all Jews living outside the state of Israel, the political orientation of the Jewish community is hardly traditional. It is more accurate to think today of Rabbinic Judaism as an ancillary movement within the more rigorous focus on the Holocaust and Israel. In some ways, Jewish sacred texts are wrapped around the contemporary formative events of the Holocaust and Israel. The sacred texts are read in light of these events. Perhaps Emil Fackenheim was right in proposing the 614th commandment, to which much of normative Judaism responds today.

In Buber's time the rabbis were anxious to address the internal workings of the Jewish community and the political structures of the surrounding world. They had good reason to be wary because the surrounding non-Jewish population was often hostile to Jews, even before the rise of Hitler. Since Jews were minorities in the countries they lived in, internal disturbances or direct challenges to non-Jewish powers could bring disaster upon the Jewish community. They had to remain alert, work on the internal development and safety of the community, and keep Judaism and Jews quiet.

This caution emboldened Buber. To reintroduce the prophetic, Buber used Eastern religions, especially Taoism and Buddhism, Hasidic stories, new and revolutionary biblical interpretations, contemporary Jewish and Christian philosophers and theologians, and radical secular and spiritual socialists. Buber gathered resources from everywhere.

During the early decades of the twentieth century, Buber saw that the situation of European Jews was improving and feared that the outside world would captivate individual Jews who then would be lost to Judaism. The old Jewish strictures would no longer hold. If Jewish life were to continue, new ways of communicating the ancient tradition were necessary. In the 1930s, Buber feared that Jews lacked the spiritual resources to resist the degrading aspects of Nazism and strove to keep intact their dignity as Jews. At first, Buber emphasized a global spirituality, then a distinctly Jewish one.

Especially in *I and Thou,* Buber evoked a mysticism that borrowed from many sources and seemed to have no particular origin or communal home. In his essays in the 1930s, he evoked a specific though wide ranging perspective on what the future of Jewish life might look like. In the 1940s and beyond, Buber argued for a concrete embodiment of Jewish life in Palestine, later Israel. Since Buber's range of spirituality was wide, there were elements of Jewish and non-Jewish spirituality throughout each period. Though Buber's Jewish home became more and more distinct and pronounced as time went on, he never withdrew into an isolated Jewish sensibility.

Buber's universality raises questions about Jewish particularity. Yet as with Elie Wiesel, whose *Night* was introduced to the wider world and who has thrived in a mostly Christian culture of America, the boundaries of Jewishness are flexible. This has always been the case with all religions, whose borrowings are usually disguised. Judaism is no exception. With the coming of modern culture this borrowing has increased and, with the freedom of Jews during and after the Enlightenment, the boundaries between Jews and non-Jews have lessened.

The road to a more open world has not been without setbacks and even devastating results, the Holocaust being the supreme negative example. Regardless,

Jews have chosen a life with others as a positive aspect of individual and communal life. Buber foresaw this choice and, in each phase of his life, tried to navigate it. In doing so, Buber takes his place in a broader tradition that he with others of different faiths began to develop in the twentieth century.

Buber can be placed historically as a Jewish theological and philosophical revolutionary. He is also part of the rebirth of the prophetic voice in the twentieth century. This prophetic community was comprised by such luminaries as the Indian Hindu Mahatma Gandhi, the founder of modern day struggles for justice and independence by nonviolent means, the American Catholic Dorothy Day, the founder of the Catholic Worker movement that combined living with the poor and a radical critique of the social order that creates poverty, and the French Jew, Simone Weil, who thought through the critical social and political issues of her day by developing a spirituality of waiting for God. Others include the African-American civil rights leader, Martin Luther King Jr. and Oscar Romero, the Roman Catholic archbishop of El Salvador. Both were assassinated because of their work among the people they represented and for their message to those that oppressed them. At the same time, their message transcended the particularity within which they lived and died.

Though an agnostic, the French novelist and commentator Albert Camus, should also be included among the prophetic community of the twentieth century. His critique of religion is especially important here. All of these figures carried some form of spirituality forward. They also resisted other aspects of spirituality as they had been practiced. The main reason for their inclusion in the prophetic community is their commitment to the world and to the vexing questions of our time.

Like Buber's life, the contemporary prophetic community can be divided into time periods. In the early part of the twentieth century, the trajectory of modern life was becoming clear. Some worried that in the mad scramble for material abundance the spiritual, indeed even the human dimension would be lost. These thinkers were concerned with the effects of urbanism, industrialism, and modern armaments.

After World War II, the contemporary prophetic community thought critically about the reconstruction of a shattered world. How could the social, political, and economic order be constructed so as to serve our common humanity rather than destroy it? Even as the Holocaust was becoming known, the world embarked on another perilous adventure, and the nuclear age was upon us. Had the world entered a terminal phase or was there still time for the world to turn again?

In probing the deepest dimensions of spiritual and communal life, Buber finds his place in that community. Though each of these savants worked toward and envisioned a decentralized, regional-oriented, ecologically friendly community with spirituality at its core, Buber carried a distinctly Jewish contribution that opened toward the universal. Of all the Jews of the twentieth century, Buber's Jewish voice spoke to the largest audience and in cadences that could be understood and amplified in other communities as well.[15]

The connection of spirituality and how we live in the world continues to be explored, and spiritual seekers like Buber have much to add to the contemporary discussion. Living as he did on the cusp of modernity, Buber saw a dark future of technology and consumerism that now defines us. As a warning, Buber stands back behind us. Looked at from our vantage point, there is a freshness of insight and an incisive hope. Buber believed that there have always been breakthroughs that allow us to see through the present impasse if we refuse to accept the world at face value.

Along with these other prophetic thinkers, Buber saw the modern age as involved in a desperate search for progress and material advance. Bureaucracy, technology, urbanization, and industrialism were the lead organizational tools of modern progress. Progress was being achieved, yet beneath and around that progress was great loss. The human face was being submerged and questions were emerging as to whether the social order was really serving human beings. Buber and others made the point that the world we humans create is for us. When it ceases to serve us it must be changed. The challenge of modern life is that the social order we have created has taken on a life of its own that, paradoxically, uses and sometimes devours us.

Buber believed that when the social, political, and economic world we created makes its own demands, we can only be its victims. In the end, we live for it, with every resource, even our lifeblood dedicated to its service. The outside world therefore becomes a God, demanding everything from us, even our very life. In such an all-encompassing system, it is difficult to hold on to our humanity, focus on the human face, and call the social order back to its true purpose.

If the system we created has become a god that demands worship, and we ourselves are so consumed with that system that we begin willingly to worship it, what kind of spirituality can be developed that will throw everything, including our devotion, into question? Once questioned, what kind of spirituality can lead us back to some kind of sanity? Such a spirtuality needs to have a social, economic, and political connection as well as a way to recover the human face of the world.

Buber felt that the power of the observable and manipulative world was binding us to a path that also limited our ability to change course. The sheer force of the modern world tended to bury the spiritual side of the human journey. Being bound and losing access to the spiritual made the notion of progress dubious. Human destiny was not only about improving our material lot in life.

Buber's sense of the human loss within progress grew over the years. The Holocaust simply reinforced Buber's understandings, crystallizing this loss of the human in a desperate move to overcome the fragility of life through ideological and material security. Buber asked where in progress the human spirit was and how those aware of the dead end we were approaching could alert humanity before it was too late. For Buber, the Holocaust was a wake-up call of unparalleled dimensions.

Within this prophetic sensibility, Buber addressed Jews as to the meaning of Jewishness in their lives. He also addressed Christians about the place of Jews and Judaism in their lives. Buber understood that Judaism had to be relevant to the modern world if it were to be relevant to Jews and felt this to be the case for Christianity as well. In a world where boundaries and borders were collapsing, the spirituality of both Jews and Christians had to be relevant to each other. Buber understood that the era of religion against religion and the competition for particular truths at the expense of a broader truth was coming to an end. Although we now know that this era has continued into the twenty-first century, Buber and others were right in how costly this trajectory would be.

Defensively guarding boundaries made the ancient religions into appendages of the more powerful, alluring religion of modernity. In accenting their ancient qualities and rites as a form of modern identity, Buber felt that religion was becoming strikingly irrelevant in the larger world. To survive in that form, religion would also have to mobilize and militarize its identity as strong and beneficial to the modern world. Religion's understanding of God would also have to become on the one hand more ancient and exclusive, and on the other more sure and militant. Yet whose God was in control? And which religion had the upper hand?

How far things have gone in this world that Buber and others foresaw was illustrated in the aftermath of September 11. Islam and its God had been mobilized through the use of modern technology as weapons. How else could the hijackers of the planes that crashed into the World Trade Center have justified their actions? Yet the response of the United States was also telling in this regard. Not only did the United States respond militarily, the response was couched in the language of a crusade against evil. Though the post-September 11 crusade has a particular Christian flavor, Jews also joined in with alacrity.

The great fear beyond terror and war was the collapse of the economy. So instead of calling for days of reflection, President Bush counseled American citizens to go about their daily business and especially to shop lest the economy, already taking a hit, collapse. Modern society could not afford the time to reflect and, if necessary, change course. The course had already been set and demanded daily feeding. If Americans withdrew from their shopping even for a week, the fear was that the entire American economy would grind to a halt.

While Buber's writing is specifically aimed at Jews, it is also aimed at Christians. And since Jews and Christians live in the modern world, Buber also writes about and for the modern world. As is often the case with Jewish writers, in the end Buber's audience was as much Christian as it was Jewish. Buber believed that Jews and Christians could only hear their own voices within, rather than over against, their modern setting.

On the spiritual level, Buber tried to find the place where Judaism and Christianity could meet. Perhaps psychologically he was attempting to secure the place of Jews in the changing Christian world. This strategic component is understandable because of the animus that Christians have exhibited to Jews. At the same time, Buber was trying to reclaim spirituality's rightful place in the modern world.

If Jews and Christians truly encountered each other, could the animosity that had characterized Jewish-Christians relations continue? Perhaps it was the ossification of the biblical encounters in both traditions that perpetually pitted Judaism and Christianity against the other. A true encounter of Jews and Christians might break through this ossification. This was needed for peace between those who were defined by these religions. It would also benefit the world that was so much in need of a renewed spirituality.

Perhaps this is why Buber assessed Jesus to be "my great brother" and as the person who was always fully present to others and to the situation he was in. For Buber, this was the essence of being Jewish, and his understanding of Jesus as profoundly Jewish and human served as a bridge between Jews and Christians. At the same time, Buber thought this might release Jesus and perhaps other aspects of Christianity to serve humanity in the difficult quest to reclaim the human. The split between Judaism and Christianity had occurred in the realm of religion rather than over the life of Jesus himself.

Buber felt that the messianic aspect of Jesus and Christianity derived from Paul rather than Jesus. There is a sense in Buber that the split between Judaism and Christianity was a mistake. Yet Buber was not aiming to collapse Christianity into Judaism. Instead, reclaiming Jesus as a brother could open both Jews and Christians to the encounter that was prior to either religion. In *I and Thou*, Buber wrote of Jesus:

> . . . how powerful, even to being overpowering, and how legitimate, even to being self-evident, is the saying of *I* by Jesus! For it is the *I* of the unconditional relation in which the man calls his *Thou* Father in such a way that he himself is simply Son, and nothing else but Son. Whenever he says *I* he can only mean the *I* of the holy primary word that has been raised for him into unconditional being. If separation ever touches him, his solidarity of relation is the greater; he speaks to others only out of this solidarity. It is

useless to seek to limit this *I* to a power in itself or this *Thou* to something dwelling in ourselves, and once again to empty the real, the present relation, of reality. *I* and *Thou* abide; every man can say *Thou* and is then *I*, every man can say Father and is then Son: reality abides.[16]

Buber views Buddha in a similar way. Though the question of Asian religions was not a European pre-occupation at the time, Buber foretells a more global sensibility by also stressing Buddha as a man of pure encounter: "The Buddha knows the saying of the *Thou* to men—witness his intercourse with his pupils, in which, though high above them, he speaks very directly—but he does not teach it; for simple confrontation of being while being alien to this love where 'all that has become illimitably comprised in the breast.' He certainly knows too, in the silent depths of his being, the saying of *Thou* to the primal cause—away beyond all those "gods" that are treated by him like pupils. This act of his springs from a relational event that has taken on substance; this act, too, is a response to the *Thou*: but also about this response he preserves silence." There are problems with Buddha's followers, who create a tradition around Buddha himself and have "contradicted him magnificently." They "have addressed the eternal human *Thou* under the name of Buddha himself. And it awaits, as the Buddha that is to come, the last of the age, him by whom love is to be fulfilled." Thus, Buber cautions against confusing the encounter with the messenger who then is divinized and emulated rather than being seen as a guide to encourage our own encounter within which there is no guide or external aid.[17]

Buber explored the depths of Judaism as the twentieth century dawned and at a time when Christianity and Judaism had to evolve lest they become irrelevant to Jews and Christians in particular and to the modern world in general. If he argued for the role of spirituality in the modern world, Buber first analyzed the past and present failures of religion itself. At the same time, Buber addressed modernity and its almost unbridled power as a religion itself, perhaps the most powerful global religion. Even in Buber's time every knee was beginning to bow before the materialism of modernity.

Yet it is doubtful that Buber or the others of the prophetic community had any idea how far this materialism would go. All of them lived before the computer age and the exponentially expanding technological capabilities that make human interaction even more complex and distant. Think back to Buber's understanding of education and then factor in the increasing inability to concentrate for long periods of time, then the challenges are even more daunting.

By the 1930s fascism was erupting in the very heart of Europe with all the trappings of a new religion. Buber attempted to make aspects of the Jewish tradition plausible in a time when the Jewish world was experiencing great change in outlook and would soon be under an annihilationist assault. From

Buber's perspective, Rabbinic Judaism could not survive the modern period. A Judaism that was once seen as a given, and sometimes imposed from inside by Jewish authorities and enforced from outside by Christian and feudal authorities, could not continue in the modern world. In the modern world, Judaism would be voluntarily embraced by Jews or Jews would be lost to the Jewish community. If the modern world opened up to Jews, many Jews would leave Judaism and Jewishness altogether. With Nazism, another even more urgent problem was forced upon Rabbinic Judaism. Rabbinic Judaism had little to say about modernity. Did it have anything to say to Hitler?

For Judaism to survive, it had to be attractive and meaningful to Jews within the larger context of the modern world. Rather than be accepted as received wisdom, the Jewish tradition had to be deconstructed and then reconstructed in light of science and modern studies of society and religion. To Jews eager to participate in and benefit from the modern world, Judaism appeared outdated. Modern life was posing questions to Judaism and Jewish authority structures that were difficult to respond to.

The configuration of Judaism had to change if it hoped to speak meaningfully to the times. This led to the development of the three denominational strands of Judaism we know today: Orthodox, Conservative, and Reform. Yet Buber felt that these were only adjustments to modernity rather than reconsiderations. He felt this would ultimately lead to the assimilation of Jews to modern society. Instead, a deeper probing of modernity and Judaism was essential. Buber felt that layers of tradition needed to be uncovered so that the later and less relevant strands of tradition would give way to the primal impetus for Jewishness in the world. All of this was necessary before the rise of the Nazi scourge, which only made this more urgent.

Speaking in 1937 in Prague, Czechoslovakia, just a year before he was forced to leave Germany, Buber's voice was clear, though by necessity his words were coded. The hour was indeed late; the world had become quite ominous. The spirit of religion, often now found in ideology, had been misused so that people, especially Jewish youth, had fled from the spiritual:

> I am deeply distressed to find a great number of our young people sharing a prejudice against spirituality—even though I quite understand how this came about. It is not difficult to comprehend why many now guard themselves against having faith or confidence in the spirit. For during the past decades the race of man has not, by and large, fared well at the hands of the spirit. For the spirit was not simply silent; it spoke falsely at junctures when it should have been an important voice in history, when it should have told the truth about what was being done or not being done to those who were making or seemed to be making history. On frequent occasions

the spirit consented to be a tool when it should have acted on its own in the capacity of judge and censor. Then again, it has repeatedly retired to a magnificent kingdom of its own, poised high above the world in the realm of circling ideas. Whenever the spirit has done so, it has sacrificed the very factor which makes it legitimate, particularly in crises: its readiness to expose itself to reality, to prove and express itself in reality.[18]

Buber was unable to tell his audience how the spirit could subvert the Nazis and bring Jews and others to safety. In essence, Buber could not lay out a plan whereby the re-visioning of the spirit would lead to an effective resistance against the Nazi juggernaut. Speaking openly against the Nazis was already too dangerous.

Perhaps Buber viewed the misuse of the spirit as part of a cycle that involved militant political ideologies and religious authorities who had "retired to the magnificent kingdom of its own." As his lecture continued, Buber makes more explicit the prejudice against faith and the prejudice against God:

[R]eligious institutions and procedures . . . have become stumbling blocks in the path of the true believer; they have placed themselves in opposition to his humble life, and on the side of whatever happens to be powerful and accepted as valid in the world. This error, which is in the foreground of our time, has affected the souls of the generations which grew up in a time of crisis; it has invalidated their faith. . . . Real faith . . . means holding ourselves open to the unconditional mystery which we encounter in every sphere of our life and which cannot be comprised in any formula. It means that, from the very roots of our being, we should always be prepared to live with this mystery as one being lives with another. Real faith means the ability to endure life in the face of this mystery.[19]

[W]hat we really mean when we say that a God is dead is that the images of God vanish, and that therefore an image which up to now was regarded and worshipped as God, can no longer be so regarded and so worshipped. For what we call gods are nothing but images of God and must suffer the fate of such images [20]

Regarding faith, Buber is clear: For to believe means to engage oneself, and regarding God: "The images topple, but the voice is never silenced." This leads him directly to Judaism:

Judaism is also a mixture of the false and the genuine, but as regards its genuine character, we find a great unity of everything genuine and original and pure which we need to overcome our unjustified prejudices; the meaningfulness of history, the sovereignty of spirit, the verifiability of truth, the power of decision ensuing from personal responsibility, the spontaneity between men and—finally—faith as the engagement of one's entire life to the Lord of the one voice, who wishes to be recognized in each of his manifestations. All of this is the original tidings of Judaism, and the openness of the Jewish people, of Jewish youth, should consist in trying to understand these tidings by tracing them back to their origins.[21]

History as a Mysterious Approach to Closeness

Though Buber was necessarily conditioned by the world in which he lived, he also has an ability to speak to Jews of different generations. Buber critiqued and affirmed Judaism at the same time. He spoke outside of normative Judaism to a Jewishness that Jews felt but had never heard articulated. The power of decision and deed as the Jewish way, the trust that trust itself is possible, the voice that is never silenced even as the images topple, the search that never ends—all of this is relevant over time. Yet do Jews today experience this in organized Jewish life?

I wonder, too, if Buber is even more relevant to Christians than he has been in the past. If any tradition had images that needed to be toppled, it is Christianity. First and foremost to be toppled is the image of Christianity as righteous and the carrier of *the* truth, and also the image of Jesus as the only way to salvation for everyone, through a certain way of belief. The dogmas and doctrines of Christianity—have they not become idolatrous?

By collapsing religion as a flawed and sometimes fatal carrier of the spirit, Buber opens up another way for Jews and Christians to be faithful and free. Buber recognized that religions often offer an image that is exclusive, even violent. Can salvation come at the expense of the Other and still be considered salvation?

Buber reversed the known assumptions of Judaism and Christianity by offering a Jewishness before Sinai, and Judaism and a Christianity before Jesus was thought of as the messiah and God incarnate. In essence, Buber counseled Jews and Christians not to get stuck in the prior definitions of faith. Indeed, the primal encounters weren't stuck anywhere except in the imagination of the religions that followed. If Judaism and Christianity are stuck in their own images, Buber advises to break away, to keep our eyes on the prize that is life lived fully. If we propagate our encounter as the new orthodoxy, we repeat the same cycle. This happened with Buddha, Moses, and Jesus, no doubt against their will.

When reading Buber against the current thrust of Jewish life, I become dismayed—there are too many images that need to topple. When images are imbued with material power as well as symbolic power, it becomes even more difficult. Sometimes I feel that Judaism has changed places with Christianity. In many respects, Christianity has been humbled by history and has lost much of its power while Jewish life is now on the upswing. It has never been more assured of itself or more powerful. Where once we tried to humble Christianity's "truth" and rightfully so, who is there to humble Jewish "truths" today?

Buber has always spoken to me. Perhaps this is because I encountered Buber as I was coming of age spiritually. There are so many levels to *I and Thou*. Especially striking is Buber's *It-Thou* dichotomy. *It* is the objective world that we treat as such. When we live only in the *It* world we turn away from the *Thou*, the subjective world that resides within the *It* world. The *It* world is a world of use and abuse. The *Thou* world is one of relation and encounter.

In the *It* world objects are objectified, and division and separation is necessary and inevitable. Though in its extreme the *It* world is one where violence triumphs, the *It* world also contains objects we use to survive. Yet if we only live in the *It* world, we use objects to such an extent that the *I* also becomes an object. By only using objects and not recognizing the deeper realm of their beauty, we are just one step away of becoming an object as well. Or at least seeing ourselves and being seen as an object.

Buber believed that by objectifying our relationship to the world we lose our core relationship to *Thou*. Instead of reverence for the life of the world and our own interior life we enter a cycle of violence and atrocity. In the end the objectified world and the objectified *I* becomes part of a pattern of violating and being violated.

Living in and for the *It* world, we enter a world of otherness. Depending on the situation, the Other—the Korean, the Mormon, the African, the Muslim, or the Jew—is liable to be defined as an object and debased freely. Nature also can become an Other and thus seen primarily as an object to be used without concern or care. Buber believes that living as if there is only an *It* world is ignorance. It may also represent a longing for but fear of *Thou*.

Here the Other embodies what we have already lost. Buber believes that the very definition of otherness is a projection of what the definer wants to explore but cannot have. We may possess the object; the *Thou* within it can never be possessed. Possessing *Thou* is an illusion. *Thou* can be hidden and buried. Nonetheless, it awaits the encounter.

With Buber, "cannot" is never *the* reality. *Thou*, which is relation and encounter, remains open if we place ourselves here. Why would we deride another's path if we hadn't already derided our own? Why would we demean another person if we hadn't already demeaned ourselves? We cannot enter into relation by denying the possibility of others and their path of relation.

This is true with nature as well. If we only see the natural world as a place for our use, we see nature as Other. In doing this we inevitably position ourselves as objects to be used by nature or other people. However, in "othering" nature, we "other" ourselves. By affirming *Thou* in nature, we also affirm *Thou* within us. Or recognizing *Thou* within us we recognize *Thou* within nature.

For Buber, relation is mutuality. Mutual relation is the essence of encounter. In the encounter what we understand to be the divisions between object and subject collapse. Ultimately, both sides of nature and our humanity have their place as does the relation between them. We cannot only see the tree for its use; we cannot only see our relation to the tree.

At different times, we have various ways of being with nature and with ourselves. The modern understanding emphasizes one way to the exclusion of the other. Buber knows that objectification and violence are not new. However, the modern split between object and subject is intensifying. This robs nature and humanity of dimensions of experience that are healthy and necessary.

Buber does not sugarcoat the *Thou* that is within the *It* world. Buber believes that sometimes we objectify the world in order to avoid the passion of the encounter, which is both human and cosmic without offering any guarantees. To the question of whether there was an experience of paradise in the earlier encounters of humanity, Buber responds: "Even if it was hell—and certainly that time to which I can go back in historical thought was full of fury and anguish and torment and cruelty—at any rate it was not unreal. The relational experiences of man in earliest days were certainly not tame of pleasant. But rather force exercised on being that is really lived than shadowy solicitude for faceless numbers! From the former, a way leads to God, from the latter only one to nothingness."[22]

We can see this "advance" with the technology of war. In Buber's day the Nazis were the most advanced purveyors of death. In mass death they were innovators in extraordinary ways, modeling the death camps on Henry Ford's pioneering concept of mass production of the automobile. The Nazis simply substituted bodies for automobiles.

We know now that the first primitive computers manufactured and sold by IBM helped organize the Jewish population for death. They were also responsible for tabulating everything that went on in the concentration and death camps. All of this was to separate as far as possible the human element in the destruction of Europe's Jews. By manufacturing and tabulating corpses, the Nazi encounter with the Jews they killed was limited. Or so they thought.

How much more so today, with weapons of mass destruction proliferating and with sophisticated, less-powerful weapons like unmanned drones that are guided and monitored far from the war zone itself. At least in the United States, most of us watch wars on television as we continue on with our lives. Is that part of the reason that we can continue on with our daily routine without encountering the Other who is suffering and dying?

So even with the uncertainty that attends our encounter with *Thou*, at least we have a face-to-face encounter with the depths of our humanity. Turning away from encounter, we retreat to what seems like safety. While seeking safety through objectification allows us to avoid encounter, the objectification does great damage to others whom we also objectify so as to avoid encounter.

The ultimate objectifying of the Other allows us to kill. To kill we have to turn the person's *Thou* into an *It*. Only then can we project methods and technology toward death. Today nations feel free to violate others in an abstraction that leads to the murder of hundreds, thousands, even millions. Living through the Nazi period, Buber knew this firsthand.

Violence is dependent on abstraction. When an Other is denied their integrity, it is because we have abstracted their identity from their person. Violence is only possible when we objectify the Other and ourselves to such an extent that we enter into the world of the object, *It*. Paradoxically what seems to be objective is the ultimate abstraction.

When we violate each other and nature, we turn away from relation. Though relation that is encounter may be difficult and frightening, our ability to stand within the unknowable also changes our ability to relate in our everyday lives. Our firsthand encounters make it more difficult to abstract our lives and the lives of others. Buber believed that as we become more sophisticated, we are more removed from the elements in our lives that are unpredictable and unknowable. We seek more and more control over nature and human beings. With increased technological power and less encounter, what was formerly impossible becomes permissible. Buber asked whether there is any limit to objectifying the world.

With violence we enter Buber's understanding of the *It* world that also exists in the language and ritual of ideology and religion. We are free to objectify the Other using ideology and religion. In doing so, we objectify *Thou* and turn *Thou* into an *It*. Buber saw this as the realm of unfreedom. He used the word "caprice" to signal a person who uses relational vocabulary while using the *It* world to advance a non-relational, ego-centered quest. For Buber, for those who employ caprice, what lies ahead is doom.[23]

As we have seen, Buber finds Jesus to be the master of the "unconditional relation." Buber contrasts Jesus with Napoleon to demonstrate that though the *I* in both exists, all depends on how the *I* lives in the world. Though his mission is fated, Jesus is free. In that freedom Jesus represents the possibility of community. Even in the glory of empire Napoleon is capricious and doomed. For Buber, Napoleon represents the "severed *I*," the *I* living exclusively in the *It* world, the *I* severed from *Thou*. When combined with material, economic, and military power, for Buber the severed *I* is the demonic.[24]

Though seemingly focused on the individual, Buber believes that true relation brings forth community. Here the *I* is more broadly connected in a communal relation. What is abstracted is unconnected with the *Thou* of being truly with others. When what is severed is empowered, this leads toward personal, economic, and political empire. Empire is domination over others. The empire can be small, a parent over a child, or large, community leader over a community. It can be national and even international. Buber experienced dictatorship in Nazi Germany and the Cold War. Dictatorship and empire is impossible without abstracting the people being dominated and ruled.

Empire promises freedom but it is the freedom to use and abuse. For Buber, however, empire provides only the illusion of freedom; true freedom is found in relation and community. In some ways, Buber sees empire and community as the two poles of encounter and life. The question for him is which one is being pursued. Empires promise an illusory community built on everything that defeats true community.

Empire often garners the support of the spirit to aid and abet its designs. This is the false spirit that Buber spoke of in his lecture in Prague. Community is a struggle within empire, and conversely even within community are the seeds of empire. The struggle between empire and community is a constant in history and like the prophets, the struggle often is lost. Yet the struggle itself upholds the very possibility of community.

As with *Thou*, Buber sees relation and community as a difficult struggle with ups and downs along the way. Like freedom, relation and community are also fated. Buber sees this struggle as representing the "direction of return that leads through sacrifice."[25]

Buber argues against the privatization of relation and encounter. In fact, Buber sees the division between public life and the interior of the person as a modern falsehood that we tend to accept at face value. In modern life this split between the public and the private yields little satisfaction in either realm. The split between the public and private is contrived, almost anti-human. If relation and encounter are essential to the human being, how can these be absent in our collective life? Buber's sense of community strikes a needed balance between the public and private, a balance that encourages growth and flourishing for both.

We should not mistake this sense of relation and community with happiness as our society defines it (but in many ways runs counter to it). There is a "lonesomeness" to life that, like all of Buber's concepts, can move in different directions. One direction is toward relation, sacrifice, and the prophetic. The other is toward ego gratification, self-aggrandizement, and power. Buber distinguishes between solitude and isolation. The person who chooses relation and freedom is connected and alone because the world conspires against the depth that such a person experiences.[26]

We feel this aloneness, especially if we espouse a hope that is different than the status quo around us. Often our arguments go nowhere with others and bouncing back to our ears, they even may seem hollow to us. Buber encourages those who feel the isolation of speaking the difficult truth that others do not want or cannot hear. When it becomes possible for a person to say what was defined as impossible, the world can seem to be conspiring against what is said—and the person himself.

For Buber, solitude is in a dynamic tension with solidarity and is at the very heart of the prophetic. Who experiences solitude more than the prophet whose calls for justice are often rejected by the rulers and sometimes even by the people? The prophet is also close to those who are suffering and therefore, for Buber, the prophet is at the very heart of history. When committed and engaged, those who experience solitude are in a more profound sense connected to others and history. They are also connected to the spirit, to *Thou*, to God.

All of us can experience closeness or, in Buber's terminology, enter into or be within closeness. For Buber, closeness comes through deed, risk, and openness—through a deep encounter in history.

Buber's mysterious approach to closeness contrasts with James Joyce's famous aphorism: "History is a nightmare from which I am trying to awake." History as a tragedy is real, but for Buber that is only a surface sensibility. Even in tragedy there are levels of possible meaning, which may have less to do with redemption than with grasping of part of our humanity.

No prayer or particular action can achieve closeness. For Buber it is through a lived relation within history that one finds his or her calling. Closeness is that calling and calling is the fruit of our freedom. It also becomes our fate. Yet like freedom and the prophetic, closeness cannot be summarized as success in the world or even a sense of personal achievement. The more probable feeling is one of failure. For Buber, there is a mystery in failure, which may be the key to redemption.

Isaiah's Arrow in the Quiver

Some years ago I stopped going to synagogue. On a particular day, perhaps the holiest day of the Jewish year, Yom Kippur, the Day of Atonement, I sometimes feel guilty that I am not there. Buber would not be there either.

As a child I recognized intuitively what Buber describes with regard to religion. For him, religion suffers from a category mistake by taking the original encounter with *Thou* and transforming this into an accomplished, once-and-for-all act. The religious person is enjoined to observe that encounter and reenact it from a distance.

Religion often turns the encounter and God into *It*. Religion speaks about *Thou* as an *It* and creates a theatric reenactment of a drama that originally was ongoing and unpredictable. Unlike religion's reenactment of the original encounters, true encounter is orienting and disorienting. True encounter subverts the known and unknown, including the known of religion. For Buber, religion is the subversive when known and tamed. It is a system of deflection. The unpredictable power of encounter becomes a religious calendar. *Thou* is banished to "once upon a time."

Sometimes, in spite of religion, that ongoing encounter becomes articulate again. Other times it lapses into silence. Sometimes that ongoing encounter is conditioned by our time and place in the world. At other times, encounter breaks through and becomes again the unconditioned. When this happens we are in a different realm of time and history.

Thou is that moment when the condition and unconditioned meet and where, in our own struggles and limitations, we become more than we were. Life is more abundant. We stand in an unsettling place of truth that is both weak and strong. For most of the encounter we are without words. Our anxiety and strength fuse together. When we return, we are different. We await another encounter.

What we witness in encounter is a gathering of *It* and *Thou* into a new configuration, akin to the ancient Israelites standing at Sinai. For Buber, such encounters are formative events from which our individual and communal lives are changed. "A great history-faith does not come into the world through interpretation of the extra-historical as historical, but by receiving an occurrence experienced as a 'wonder,' that is, as an event which cannot be grasped except as an act of God," Buber writes. "Something happens to us, the cause of which we cannot ascribe to this world; the event has taken place just now, we cannot understand it, we can only believe it."[27]

Once the formative event is recorded and caught up in religion, it is quickly perverted. The original primal encounter elicits a journey into the unknown. Once religion claims the formative event as its own, it becomes unrepeatable in history, though it is repeatable on a daily basis in liturgy and study. When claimed, prayed over, and studied, the formative event becomes owned and interpreted by those who "own" it. It then becomes known as "truth," which is used to draw boundaries of inclusion and exclusion. Over time the formative event as truth claim is used as a blunt instrument against others, meaning redemption for some and suffering for others.

Here I think of what the Cross means to Christians and what it means to Jews. For Christians the Cross is a sign of their faith, for Jews a sign of their oppression. Today, Christians hardly want the Cross to signify oppression and Jews are free from Christian oppression. Still, the Cross remains a symbol of a time when both religious communities were trapped by what was claimed and acted upon. Strangely and sadly, today Jewish symbols in Israel are often a sign of oppression to Palestinians. Even the Exodus story of the Promised Land is used against Palestinians in the land they love and call home.

The inversions are obvious and can shift again. Yet with Buber, I wonder if the formative event claimed forever and as one's own is the problem here. Projecting out a formative event into other decades or centuries is like sending an army into war. Is it any wonder that the symbols closest to Jews and Christians, the Star of David and the Cross, are often feared by others?

When tied to religion or an ideology, formative events become a tangle. When one's redemption causes the suffering of others, can it be truly redemptive? For Buber, once religion harnesses the power of the formative events like the Exodus or Jesus, events that promise liberation become sets of dogmas and creeds that divide the world into the chosen/saved and the damned. When this happens Buber believes that religion itself has to be called to account.

The original formative event is complex. Primal encounters themselves, like the liberation of the Israelites and the life of Jesus, are not without conflict, tragedy, and death. The problem arises when claims are placed upon this complexity and the complexity itself is simplified to divide us from them.

Once again Buber calls upon the prophetic. Here Buber distinguishes between the prophetic and the apocalyptic. The prophetic is worldly and calls for justice in the world; it represents an interruption of history within history. The apocalyptic is otherworldly and argues that a break in history will occur that brings us out of history. Buber identifies the prophetic with Jewishness and the apocalyptic with Christianity.

Though bold in its assertion, rather than breaking with history the prophetic often is hidden there. If the prophets suffer, as indeed they do in every age, they suffer because they pronounce judgment in angry and unsettling language to and in the world. In a worldly sense the prophets are doomed, yet they also experience a great sense of freedom. Though largely unsuccessful in the annals of history from an elite perspective, the failure of the prophets is skin deep. They create a path for future generations. They are the engines of a transformed world within history. In opposing unjust power, the prophet lives contrary to history.

Contrary to history means standing up for the essence of life—which the rulers and the people rarely want. It is easier to glide along the surface taking what we can get and leaving others to scavenge for what they need. Being with history as it is known is to succeed and to go with the flow. The disaster within what is known and approved remains hidden. When the prophet announces the doom ahead, it becomes apparent that everyone who pretends not to know actually does. If the prophet said what was truly unknown, why would the prophet be scolded, abused, and sometimes killed?

To move contrary to history also means to move contrary to the nature of human beings. The prophet says "no" to what the affluent and the powerful think is naturally theirs, to what they see as part of their destiny to rule over others. Interrupting the destiny of the powerful is rarely greeted with applause. Buber knows that penetrating to the heart of another sense of history is unpopular. It often means exile and sometimes death.

Buber asks the question of which side we are on in situations of injustice. Who is engaged in the *It* and who the *Thou*? Is there also a moment where judgment is suspended and we are there only as a witnesses?

Though we often think of the Ten Commandments as rules and regulations for personal and societal conduct, Buber understands the Ten Commandments as *Thou's* address to the person who has a choice in responding to them. One chooses either to listen to this address or not. For Buber there are no rewards or punishments attached to our decision. Translating these commandments into societal needs is what moves the Decalogue from *Thou* to *It*. The commandments contained in the Decalogue are so powerful that they subvert the world as we know it. Because of their power, religion immediately translates them into dogma and creed. In this form they are used by society and ultimately the state as rules and regulations. Then we are commanded to obey the Ten Commandments, and if we don't we are punished. Rather than encountering *Thou* in the Decalogue, we experience *Thou* as an *It*, as a force of control and domination. The power of the commanding voice of *Thou* becomes the *It* world objectified.[28]

Contra Buber, the Decalogue as presented in the Torah seems the very word of God to form society within a chosen and holy nation. There are penalties for violation of the Decalogue that form part of a larger and evolving covenant. According to scripture these penalties are invoked by God. In the Bible, a society that does not enforce these penalties is far from God. Thus, the claims of choseness and promise that are dependent on fulfilling the covenant are up for grabs. In the Torah, then, it seems that the Ten Commandments are not simply a personal address. Rather, they are an obligatory set of societal regulations that seek to bring the people into conformity with God's will. Still, Buber's understanding takes hold; his shocking reformation of the Ten Commandments forces us to think again.

Is this the way we have received the description of ancient Israel's encounter with *Thou*? For Buber all descriptions of the encounter are translated and placed into a framework that those who experienced it can understand. We also seek to place what is contrary to history and human nature into a more conforming and understandable framework, as religion does. For Buber, the case in point is Judaism.

Here, *Thou* is turned into the all-powerful and omnipotent God of history. When Buber discusses *Thou*, it mostly is a force within and outside of us that escapes definition. Those who encounter the Eternal *Thou* are overwhelmed by the sheer power of the encounter. In what follows, we as humans seek to describe these experiences. All descriptions of encounter are approximations and contextual to the times in which we live. This is true for God as well.

In biblical times the encounter is described within the framework the ancient Israelites knew. The encounter in our time will be described as we can describe it, in different ways. The point is to resist becoming trapped in any one description or any one encounter as *the* encounter. Buber believes as well that we should avoid becoming tied to any one account of God. Beyond God is the Eternal *Thou*. God as we describe God can only be an image, a shadow of our encounter. When God is invoked as a ruler and a regulator, the Eternal *Thou* behind the description is absent.

As we have seen, Buber claims that the soul of Judaism is pre-Sinai and he references Jacob as the heart of that soul. Jacob is the biblical figure that wrestled with God. Jacob proclaimed within that wrestling a truth that was, even in his time, hidden. What moves Buber most with regard to Jacob, however, is his lament for his lost son Joseph. Buber notes Joseph's arrival in the court of the Egyptian Pharaoh, the importance of his interpretation of dreams, and his brilliance in guiding Egypt through famine. However, Buber highlights the drama of Joseph's reconciliation with his brothers and father. He views the connection and reconnection of father and son as the *Thou* that transcends society and progress.

Here failure and tragedy take hold in Buber's mind. The pivotal point of the narrative of Israel is the prophetic that has within it a kernel of suffering and servanthood not obvious in the public sphere where the prophet lives. "And finally, this glorification of failure culminates in the long line of prophets whose existence is failure through and through," Buber writes of Isaiah's metaphor of the arrow in the quiver. "This existence in the shadow, in the quiver, is the final word of the leaders of the Biblical world: this enclosure in failure, in obscurity, even when one stands in the blaze of public life, in the presence of the whole national life."[29]

Buber leaves us with many questions. Are the public proclamations of the prophet more or less important than the personal suffering that these proclamations ultimately cause the prophet? Are the public proclamations conditional, an outer shell, and the personal call the essence, the soul? Is the outer proclamation that is heard everywhere at the same time an interior solitude that is unremitting and to some extent unforgiving? Buber's conclusion is difficult to fathom: "The truth is hidden in obscurity and yet does its work; though indeed in a way far different from that which is known and lauded as effective by world history."[30]

Buber's Intriguing Bible

What do we do with the truth hidden in the prophet's quiver? What do we do with the religions Buber scorns? And what do we do with Buber's need to topple the many images of God that obscure the eternal *Thou* that cannot be named or owned?

Over time Buber increasingly uses the name *God,* but this seems only a compromise so that his public speech can be understood. Buber continues to believe that most images of God need to be left behind. Why, then, is it that so many of these images of God seem to be necessary?

In privileging and also relativizing the towering figures of Moses in the Jewish tradition or Jesus in the Christian tradition, and by insisting that we are called to the same encounters in our own lives, what are we doing with the founders of our faith traditions? Do we go back behind them and contextualize them as Buber does? Is remembering their encounter as a guide for our own encounter enough, or are they *the* encounters that we need to venerate and observe?

Buber's evocation of the biblical figures is respectful. Still, for Buber the Bible is not *the* truth nor are there lessons to be drawn from it. Instead, the Bible is a record of primal encounters that are deep and formative. We are to read the Bible in this way, or better, we are called to encounter the Bible as if we know nothing about it in advance. Encountering the Bible sets the stage for our own encounter. For Buber, there is no scripture in the sense of a canonical text that binds us forever. Scripture is forever unfolding, with descriptions of encounters that are true for their time and context.

For some the attempt to displace received images of God or even the Bible as received truth is akin to heresy. For Buber, it is simply paring the images that have grown up around God. Buber is aware that for many people destroying the very images of God may make it more difficult to conceptualize the Eternal *Thou.* The challenge remains. Buber doesn't turn away from it.

Religions and religious authorities are often patronizing, claiming to know that mysteries behind the text are too difficult for the ordinary believer to grasp. Therefore they share only what the people can accept and make of it a "truth." For the most part, Buber operates without this filter. He seems to be unaware that different people might be on different levels and therefore certainty might be important to preach even if he knows it is more complicated. Refusing to topple the images or relativize a central figure like Moses may be essential to Judaism. In turn, Judaism may be essential as the vehicle through which Jews wrestle with their vocation. By saying that the essence of Jewishness is pre-Sinaitic, Buber collapses the normative conception of Judaism. In this he may be more than naïve, even a heretic.

Buber can justifiably be seen as a religious outlaw. Should we also see him as a religious anarchist? Buber thinks of Jewish law, the very structure of Rabbinic Judaism, as a way Jews are distanced from primal encounters. Yet Buber's critique of law is far from the traditional critique of Jewish legalism. In the Christian framework, Jesus has also undergone a transformation with regard to law. Buber calls upon Jews and Christians to break the law of their traditions for the sake of deep encounters in their own history.

Like other Jewish lawbreakers in history, Buber believes that he does so for the good of others and for the sake of his conscience, which refuses to be conformed to power. Buber's refusal to be conformed involved the state as well as religion. For Buber, religion provides the state with all the reasons to conform and anchors that conformity in eternity. At the same time, religion disciplines the prophetic in conformity to the needs of the state by covering over the very subversive content of the prophetic. By breaking the religious law, the prophet is freed once again to act within the larger world.

I wonder if it is possible that each one of us has a way of approaching God and that Buber's "mysterious approach to closeness" is just that—our own approach, hearing our own address, grasping our own destiny. While there may be *a* truth in the universe, it seems that each religious tradition provides space for differences in personality and approach. Buber denies the "truth" of any and all religions. Is truth found instead in the mysterious approach to closeness?

The particulars of *Thou* may be essential to the embrace of truth. *Thou* may be truth. Or the embrace of truth may come from an encounter a long time ago. If this is so, we can only approximate such an embrace in our own life. We do so by embracing the truth through those who embraced it originally, such as Moses or Jesus.

For Buber, however, our encounter is the very same as those who went before us, including those whom we place on a religious pedestal. Moses and Jesus have priority only because they are more ancient. In principle, at least, we can have the same encounter these biblical figures did. We also can describe our encounters in our own way.

The encounters recorded in the Bible and read by us must come alive in our lives. It is only by reading the Bible in search of our own way of encounter that the Bible comes alive. In this way the Bible is to be read as if it had never been read before. For Buber, the known in the Bible must be reconstructed and become unknown as if those who experienced the encounter didn't know what was going to happen beforehand. Buber believes we must encounter the Bible as we encounter the unknown and unknowable, deepest levels of our being.

If, as Buber points out, Jews embody the biblical message, or rather the primal message that is recorded in the Bible, the Jewish community I grew up in knew little about the details. Though I read stories from the Bible from a young age, I cannot remember one sustained discussion about the Bible at home, at Hebrew school, or among my peers in the neighborhood. So Buber's essays on the Bible were irrelevant and unavailable to me until I arrived in the Bible Belt in the American South and entered a culture still permeated by biblical themes and literature.

When I decided to come to this region, I knew that it would be important for my spiritual journey but had no sense that this would revolve around the Bible.

Then one day my oldest son, Aaron, came home and asked me to read the Bible with him. My first question to him was obvious: Why the Bible? He answered that everyone was referring to it. My second question was how much of the Bible he wanted to read. He answered: the Bible in its entirety. So I began reading the Bible out loud to Aaron that evening and continued everyday for several months until we had read the entire Bible. I thought I was doing it for Aaron but came to realize that I was reading the Bible for myself. As Buber would have it, I was encountering the Bible for the first time. Though not completely ignorant of its contents, I had been spared an early grounding in the Bible. This saved me from "knowing" it.

I also had spared myself from "knowing" more of the Bible so as to avoid modeling myself on any of its themes or characters. I had lived a full life without knowing these models, at least in their details. I was now free to see my life as having been shaped by the very details I had not known. In encountering the Bible at this point in my life, I found my story and my voice there. For the first time I realized that my individuality had been shaped by more than contemporary culture or even contemporary Judaism.[31]

As I harkened back to the Bible, the Bible moved toward me. I experienced what Buber called the "movable, circling midpoint" of the biblical narrative. For Buber, the moving midpoint of the Bible cannot be bound to any set time. Rather, it is the "moment when I, the reader, the hearer, the man, catch through the words of the Bible the voice which from the earliest beginnings has been speaking in the direction of the goal." Buber continues: "The Jewish Bible is the historical document of a world swinging between creation and redemption, which, in the course of its history, experiences revelation, a revelation which I experience *if I am there.*"[32]

Now when I read the Bible, I do have this sense of being there *and* here at the same time. It is as if the narrative I am reading is my narrative. Being modern, I also know that I am not *really* there and the Biblical narrative is not *really* here. Still I hear my destiny in the biblical narrative. Rather, I hear my destiny in the encounters I read because I have had my encounters, encounters I have described in my own language and time.

Some of the details of the biblical narrative fill me with horror. When Aaron and I read the story of the killing of three thousand Israelites after the Golden Calf incident, he interrupted my reading and referred to that God as a "dictator God." So too the entry into the land that is used by some Jews today to justify the ethnic cleansing of Palestinians. In conscience, I hope I would have said no to that cleansing. Wasn't there another way for the people Israel to have a land of their own?

I have a better sense of what I would have done then by saying "no" to the injustice Israel has committed against Palestinians in my lifetime. Having our encounters, saying what has been unsaid in our own lives, makes reading the Bible come alive. From outside the strictures of received tradition, I can better understand how the biblical figures lived.

Some want to cleanse the biblical narrative of its outrageous material. Others want to uphold a biblical literalism that has never been literal. Some who read the Bible through a Rabbinic framework interpret it in an almost fanciful way. I am now able to open myself to the biblical narrative as it is recorded while realizing that its application as a codified, dogmatic, or fanciful religiosity would end its power for encounter.

I believe that such readings of the Bible drown out my voice and become a substitute for my own encounter. When I read the Bible out loud to Aaron, Buber's biblical understandings came alive. Buber writes that "according to the Biblical insight historic destiny is the secret correlation inhering in the current moment. When we are aware of origin and goal there is no meaningless drift; we are carried along by a meaning we could never think up for ourselves, a meaning we are to live—not to formulate. And that living takes place in the awful and splendid moment of decision—your moment and mine no less than Alexander's and Caesar's [Abraham's and Moses'?] And yet your moment is not yours but rather the moment of your encounter."[33]

Just as we do not own the Bible, we do not own our encounter. It is ours and *not* ours. It *is* and never *was*. The moment is always possible, as it was then and as it can be. This is Buber's understanding of biblical revelation: "To endure revelation is to endure this moment full of possible decisions, to respond to and to be responsible for every moment." This responsibility is real, the source a mystery. As we have seen, it is here that Buber's faith is found: "Real faith means the ability to endure life in the face of this mystery: For to believe means to engage oneself."[34]

Buber's writings are as diverse as his religious sensibilities. His *I and Thou* period was followed by a necessary and transformative deepening of his Jewish commitment during the Nazi period. We cannot know whether this deepening would have come without the rise of Hitler and the Nazis. Nonetheless, it did arrive in the most terrible of times. After the defeat of Nazism, Buber chartered still other ground in the complex life of Palestine and Israel. Buber was a spiritual Zionist who believed in creating a Jewish homeland alongside a homeland for the Arabs of Palestine. Living together in a unified state, Jews and Arabs would share the land in peace and equality. This, too, seems remarkably relevant today.

Buber's first transformative movement was from an other-worldly mystical religiosity to a this-worldly spirituality that focused on encounter with others and the building of community. This occurred in the 1920s before the rise of

Nazism. His explanation for this shift is poignant and reflective, based on a particular experience that has implications far beyond its particularity. Buber calls it a "conversion."

After the Holocaust, Buber added conversation to conversion. As usual, he did so in a startling way. He was invited to address the annual book fair in Frankfurt, Germany, and to receive a literary prize. Surprising to many, since it was so soon after the Holocaust, Buber accepted the invitation and the prize from the same country that he was forced to leave under duress.

By his very presence and specifically in his address, Buber called for a genuine conversation as *the* possibility for reconciliation and peace after the Holocaust. Still more, Buber offered a way forward beyond Nazism and as well a way out of the cycle of violence and atrocity that Jews and others had suffered. Buber felt that if Jews and Germans could forge a new relationship after the Holocaust, the world could walk a path beyond injustice and war. Buber began his address with the Nazi era:

> About a decade ago a considerable number of German men . . . killed millions of my people and my fellow believers in a systematically prepared and executed procedure, the organized cruelty of which cannot be compared with any earlier historical event. I, who am one of those who remained alive, have only in a formal sense a common humanity with those who took part in this action in any capacity. They have so radically removed themselves from the human sphere, so transposed themselves into a sphere of monstrous inhumanity inaccessible to my power of conception, that not even hatred, much less an overcoming of hatred, could have arisen in me. And who am I that I should here presume to "forgive"?
>
> It is otherwise with the German people. From my youth on I have taken the real existence of peoples most seriously, but I have never, in the face of any historical moment, past or present, allowed the concrete multiplicity which exists in this moment within a people . . . to be obscured through the leveling concept of a totality which is constituted and which acts in one particular way and no other.
>
> When I think of the German people of the days of Auschwitz and Treblinka, I see, first of all, the great many who knew that the monstrous event was taking place and did not oppose it. But my heart, which tells me of the weakness of men, refuses to condemn my neighbor because he was not able to bring himself to become a martyr. Next there emerges before me the mass of those who remained ignorant of what was withheld from the German public, but also did not undertake to discover what reality lay behind the rumors which were circulating. When I think of these

men, I am seized by the thought of the anxiety—likewise well-known to me—of the human creature before a truth which he fears that he cannot stand. But finally there appears before me, from reliable reports, some who have become as familiar to me by sight, action, and voice as if they were friend—those who refused to carry out or to continue to carry out the orders and suffered death or put themselves to death, or those who learned what was taking place and opposed it and were put to death, or those who learned what was taking place and because they could do nothing to stop it killed themselves. I see these men very near before me in that especial intimacy which binds us at times to the dead and to them alone; and now reverence and love for these German men fills my heart.[35]

Buber's emphasis on conversion and conversation seems to contradict directly the tact that Rubenstein and Wiesel later took with reference to the Holocaust. Much earlier than either of them, Buber tried to defuse group think on one side or the other. Buber separated the perpetrators and the bystanders, judging the former and trying to understand the latter. Though he could not identify a human bond with the perpetrators, Buber does have a bond with those who did not have the courage to be martyrs. How much more then is honor due to those who refused to kill or even gave their lives to protect the innocent? With these Germans he had a "special intimacy" that "binds us at times to the dead and to them alone."

This special intimacy is like the conversion Buber underwent before the Holocaust. For Buber, the lesson was as it is with the Bible: we can only be present if we place ourselves and our attention to the person and the reality before us. By objectifying the Other and the situation, we remove and excuse ourselves from delving deeper into our hearts and souls. By staying on the surface we allow ourselves the luxury of abstraction. Dwelling in abstraction, we come closer to what we are condemning.

Surely if the tables were reversed we would want the Other to ascertain the questions we have and could not articulate. So too in situations of grave injustice and atrocity, even the Holocaust. If we were on the other side of history, wouldn't we want someone to sort out the difficulties involved and, without excusing the murderers, have empathy for those who could not rise to the level of martyrdom?

We must leave Buber here, at least for now. From the moment I encountered Buber, I wondered if there was any more provocative and haunting figure in twentieth-century spirituality. That rings true today.

Abraham Joshua Heschel
(1907–1972)

3

Encountering God *After*

Abraham Joshua Heschel

Abraham Joshua Heschel was born in 1907 in Warsaw as a descendent of important Hasidic dynasties. After receiving a Jewish education in Poland, he entered the University of Berlin and in 1934 received his doctorate for a study of the biblical prophets. In 1937 Heschel became Martin Buber's successor at the Judisches Lehrhaus in Frankfurt. The following year, while directing adult Jewish education in Germany, he and other Polish Jews were deported by the Nazis. After short stays in Warsaw and London, in 1940 he came to the United States, where he accepted a teaching position at the Hebrew Union College. In 1945 Heschel became Professor of Ethics and Mysticism at the Jewish Theological Seminary in New York. During his time at Jewish Theological Seminary, he published a series of works on diverse topics related to Jewish life. He also wrote and spoke on the contemporary moral and political issues of the Vietnam War and the civil rights movement. Heschel became highly respected among religious scholars of many faiths and played an active role in Jewish-Christian dialogue. He died in 1972.

Before leaving Europe, Heschel developed a close and sometimes contentious relationship with Martin Buber. In Frankfurt during the early years of Hitler and the Nazis, Buber helped open a house of study for German Jews, *Judische Lehrhaus*. This was a place where Jews suffering religious and political persecution could learn more about their heritage and gain strength from one another. Buber offered to bring Heschel to Frankfurt to teach, and the relatively unknown Heschel became a valuable addition to the teaching staff. He also became a personal tutor to Buber on a variety of topics.

In this time of great crisis, Buber and Heschel's relationship was close. However, this closeness was clouded by strains in their relationship that had surfaced some years earlier. Heschel, to Buber an unknown Hasid from Poland, had solicited Buber's advice on his religious explorations. Buber lacked enthusiasm for Heschel's work and Heschel felt that Buber ignored him. From that moment on there was a competition between them. Though their clashes were partly based on contrasting styles and egos, Samuel Dressner and Edward Kaplan, Heschel's biographers, see their early rupture as stemming from differences that came to characterize part of the post-Holocaust Jewish journey.

> Each man misread the other for good cause. For Buber, Heschel's implicit claim to "know" divine "emotions" from the God-side was perilous. For Heschel, the sacred origin of the mitzvoth justified their legal and ritual authority in Jewish religious life. Buber, for his part, refused to assume that human beings can experience God's "feeling," just as he did not consider the mitzvoth to be prescriptive of God's will. For each thinker, the hermeneutical conflict had immediate implications for Jewish continuity.
>
> At the time of the personal debate, it was well-known that Buber was not an observant Jew. Although Buber assumed the reality of the divine *Thou*, he subordinated the Law to human initiative, and in his early discussions with Franz Rosenzweig he insisted that the person should feel "called" by the Law in order to accept its obligations. Heschel was more militantly loyal to the divine Subject; he wanted to justify regular observance as a path of return to Judaism. Heschel gave priority to God. Even the human self (the *I* of *I-Thou*) was not, in itself, complete, but "something transcendent in disguise."[1]

The importance of observance is already there in the Buber-Heschel dialogue, but beneath and around it was another question: What is Judaism and what does it mean to be a Jew? As the Nazi period came upon Jews, there were more urgent survival matters at hand. Still, at the foundation of Jewishness, what could buttress the individual Jew in a time of crisis?

For a brief time in Germany, both men worked hand in hand. Later, the issue would arise again between them. By then they were separated by geography, Heschel living in New York City and Buber in Jerusalem. They still kept in touch by mail and saw each other occasionally, when Buber came to the United States or Heschel to Israel.

Though they seemed very different to each other, both Heschel and Buber were working on the same issues regarding Jewishness and Judaism in the modern world. They also approached the subject from more or less the same perspective, taking the ancient and mixing it with the modern. Both were among the first Jews who received doctorates in European universities. Both couched their ancient Jewish message in the most modern of garb.

This mixture of the ancient and modern is what is so disarming about both men. Their learning of the tradition was deep and thorough; separately and together they covered a wide range of Jewish learning. Still, it was the infusion of the modern that set them apart. During and after the Nazi period, Heschel and Buber became guides for Jews caught between the lure of modernity and its failure. Both thought that neither tradition nor modernity was sufficient for Jews in the post-Holocaust era.

Even in America, Heschel was shadowed by the Holocaust. Edward Kaplan describes the Holocaust horrors Heschel experienced:

> In April 1943, German soldiers began the liquidation of the Warsaw Ghetto. Heschel's mother and sister Gittle were among the seven hundred thousand Jews remaining in the district where he grew up. On 19 April . . . German troops entered the ghetto walls, where they were met by the heroic Jewish uprising. In early May the Germans assaulted the Jewish resistance command post; several of its leaders committed suicide to avoid capture. On 16 May the Nazi commander, General Jürgen Stroop, reported that "the Jewish section of Warsaw no longer exists.
>
> In Cincinnati, Heschel was on the verge of collapse. He couldn't sleep; he could hardly speak . . . he learned that his mother had died of a heart attack when German soldiers stormed their apartment. He responded to the news as would any traditional Jew, gathering a *minyan* (a quorum of ten men) together to hold a service in his dormitory room to honor her. Later he was informed that his surviving sister, Gittle Heszel, had been deported to Treblinka, where she was murdered.
>
> The following month Heschel attended a memorial service at the college to honor the dead of the Warsaw Ghetto. Raw with emotion, he was distressed by a song from the pulpit that he felt was not appropriate. It would have hurt the Jews of Warsaw to hear it, he said.[2]

The disconnection with the war in Europe and the suffering of Jews, including his own family, must have been incredibly difficult. This was compounded by being in a strange American culture and an even stranger American Jewish culture, which Heschel felt lacked the basic rudiments of Jewish learning and liturgy. Heschel was sleepless and speechless because his family with others of his community were being murdered and because he thought that no one understood his Jewish sensibility. Further, the world stood silent as European Jewry was being destroyed. Heschel doubted that the Judaism he experienced at Hebrew Union College was worthy of this great tradition. Was this the end of the Judaism he had known and inherited? If it were the end, what would this mean for Heschel, himself wandering in America without family or even a Jewish community he could respect?

Ultimately, Heschel decided that America was his new home and that he would become a force for remembering the Jewish world that had passed. He would also contribute to the Jewish world that was in the making here. In some ways, Heschel accomplished both, though certainly not without controversy. Soon Heschel's anger and hope were evident as he rose to prominence in America. He was feted by both Jews and Christians but also disparaged as a European interloper. The academic and religious leadership of the Jewish world was split, though in the end few disputed the courage and audacity that Heschel embodied.

In the early 1960s, Heschel became friends with Elie Wiesel. Wiesel recalls their early friendship in America in a way that evokes Heschel's diverse interests, commitments, and presence:

> I made friends with another Yiddish poet and thinker from Warsaw, Abraham Joshua Heschel, the great-grandson of the Rebbe of Apt, whose name he bore. Heschel was profoundly Jewish, a deep believer and a sincere pacifist who wrote lyric poems in Yiddish (one of which I recited at his funeral). He also produced a magnificent work on Rebbe Mendel of Kotz, and two volumes of Talmudic studies in Hebrew, as well as theological works in English. He was generous with his advice when I was writing on Hasidic masters.
>
> We spent hours together, sometimes strolling up and down Riverside Drive discussing God, prayers, Polish Hasidism compared to Hungarian Hasidism, Lithuanian Yiddish folklore, and Polish literature. He loved to reminisce about Frankfurt, where in the thirties he succeeded Martin Buber at the Institute of Jewish Studies. Heschel was a man motivated by humanism and civic virtue as well as Hasidic fervor. Nor did he conduct his quest for knowledge from an ivory tower. He was an active opponent of the war in Vietnam. One Sabbath afternoon he confided to me that Israeli friends had asked him—possibly on the initiative of American officials—to keep a lower profile in his struggle against Lyndon Johnson's policy in Southeast Asia. "What can I do?" Heschel asked. "How can I keep silent when week after week thousands of Vietnamese civilians are being killed by our bombs? How can I forget the Jewish concept of *ra'hmanut*, of pity, of charity? How can I proclaim my Jewishness if I remain insensitive to the pain and mourning of men, women, and children who have been deprived of sleep for years because of nighttime bombing?"
>
> Heschel was a major spokesman for Jewish ecumenism, a Jewish friend of all the oppressed. He was among the first to fight for Russian

Jews and—it should be noted—for American blacks. It was he who introduced me to Martin Luther King, Jr., whom he revered. In the civil rights
movement they called him Father Abraham, as a result of which certain
Orthodox circles kept their distance from him, which grieved him. "He's
too close to Christians," they said. Nonsense, I replied when I heard
such criticism. What is wrong with a Jew teaching Judaism to non-Jews
while defending the honor and tradition of his people? When he went to
see Pope Paul IV in Rome, it was to discuss the Catholic Church's anti-
Semitism. He believed that a Jew should not lock himself into a kind of
spiritual ghetto, forever separated from a society that envelops or opposes
him. It is not human, it is not Jewish, to ignore everything that is not Jewish. Scripture teaches us the value of human life—all human life, whether
Jewish or not.[3]

What Wiesel shows is the breadth of Heschel's commitments in America
and how he brought his Eastern European roots to his life here. Though deeply
European, Heschel did not act as a stranger in America. It seems that his European roots allowed him some distance to work through his own social and
political commitments without paralyzing him or being used as an excuse for
inaction. Still, Heschel maintained his distance from American life even as he
resolutely plunged into its rhythms. He quickly entered into the struggles that
were defining America as if he was a native-born citizen. Soon after landing
in America he developed his language skills to such a degree that some of the
most lyrical writing on religion was penned by this recent immigrant whose
primary languages were Yiddish, Hebrew, and German.

As Wiesel points out, Heschel joined movements that were controversial
within America—the civil rights movement—and one that was controversial
among some Jews as well—opposition to the Vietnam War. The civil rights
movement was an obvious place of commitment for Jews, since Jews wanted
a more open society for themselves and could see the plight of African Americans within the context of Jewish marginalization in history. In his opposition
to the Vietnam War, Heschel faced a similar struggle with Martin Luther King
Jr. Many in the civil rights movement cautioned King against opposition to
the Vietnam War because they thought it might divert attention from their
movement and would further the criticism of the movement as anti-American
and communist. Heschel was cautioned against opposition to the Vietnam
War because the state of Israel was increasingly reliant on American power to
guarantee its survival and American military and economic aid to buttress its
defense and economy.

On the scale of Jewish history, the state of Israel would have to take precedence over Vietnam. Why then risk the ire of the American government with

the opposition of one of the most high-profile Jews in America? Nevertheless, when King delivered his famous speech against the Vietnam War at Riverside Church in Manhattan in 1967, sitting on the dais was Heschel himself.

Caution about American foreign policy increasingly preoccupied American Jewish leadership, especially after the 1967 Arab-Israeli War. With the Holocaust and Israel becoming central to Jewish identity, the universal outreach that came with a strong sense of Jewish particularity lessened over time.

Heschel was the last major Jewish figure in America who was able to keep the universal and the particular in a positive and constructive tension. Being so public about his opposition to the Vietnam War was testament to Heschel's commitment that the strength of one's Judaism made possible a commitment to the world. Heschel believed that Judaism could have a positive presence in the world and be respected as such only if Jews refused to remain silent on the supreme ethical and justice issues of the day.

There was a profoundly personal dimension to Heschel's commitments to civil rights and his opposition to the Vietnam War. While most American Jews had never experienced significant discrimination or warfare, Heschel and his family had. Discrimination, dislocation, and civilian deaths were parts of Heschel's past that he carried with him daily. The feeling of helplessness he experienced in the face of the Nazis and the death of his family was ever present. He could not stand idly by as injustice and a senseless war claimed deaths by the thousands. Besides, many young Jews were for civil rights and opposed to the war. Heschel saw his own former youth in them. Perhaps together they could build a renewed sense of being Jewish in the world. In many ways, Heschel had given up on the Judaism he saw around him.

Bridging the Interfaith Divide

Heschel's interfaith work was important to him. Like Buber, Heschel sought to bridge the gap between Jews and Christians, though they were also at odds on important issues. Buber was suspicious of religion in general, and neither Judaism nor Christianity escaped that judgment. Buber's difficult relationship with normative Judaism and Jewish law made it easier for him to cross the boundary between Judaism and Christianity. As a religious outlaw, Buber could embrace Jesus without hesitation, holding him up as the role model for encounter without embracing Christianity. By embracing Jesus as his brother, Buber also distanced Jesus from Christianity. At the same time, Buber indicted the boundaries of Judaism as drawn by Rabbinic Judaism. Buber saw Jesus as distinctly Jewish in a way that neither Judaism nor Christianity could affirm.

Though thoroughly modern, Heschel was much more traditional than Buber. Though he might affirm Jesus as the apostle to the Gentiles and affirm Christianity as a path to God and the interrelationship of religions, Heschel had a distinctive view of Judaism and Jewish law. While Buber saw Jewish law primarily as block to encounter, Heschel saw it as a vehicle to encounter.

Like Buber, Heschel knew that Judaism continually had to be reinterpreted. Still, he affirmed the foundational elements of Judaism as given, essential, and commanded. If traditional Judaism was losing its hold on Jews, Heschel felt it was because Jewish religious leaders had lost the depth of the tradition. They were guilty of what Heschel called "pedestrian" religious thinking. The task ahead was less to jettison tradition than to penetrate to its depth. When the tradition was communicated in its depth, Heschel believed that Jews would embrace it even in a modernity chastened by the Holocaust.

When Heschel wrote of the interconnection of Judaism and Christianity, he viewed each religion as holding a part of the world in place. Thus they complemented each other, because no religion could do the job alone.

Heschel was a religious pluralist while Buber was a religious subversive. For Heschel, Christianity was a significant religion and should be affirmed as authentic by Jews. The same was true for Christianity vis-à-vis Judaism. Where the religions could and did cross was in their core values of justice, peace, and the inherent dignity of the person. In his inaugural lecture as the Harry Emerson Fosdick Visiting Professor at Union Theological Seminary in New York City in 1966, Heschel spoke of the challenge of interfaith dialogue in relation to his own past:

> I speak as a member of a congregation whose founder was Abraham, and the name of my rabbi is Moses.
>
> I speak as a person who was able to leave Warsaw, the city in which I was born, just six weeks before the disaster began. My destination was New York; it would have been Auschwitz or Treblinka. I am a brand plucked from the fire, in which my people were burned to death. I am the brand plucked from the fire of an altar of Satan on which millions of human beings were exterminated to evil's greater glory, and on which so much else was consumed: the divine image of so many human beings, many people's faith in the God of justice and compassion, and much of the secret and power of attachment to the Bible bred and cherished in the hearts of men for nearly two thousand years.[4]

Heschel continued:

> The religions of the world are no longer self-sufficient, no more independent, no more isolated than individuals or nations. Energies, experiences

and ideas that come to life outside the boundaries of a particular religion or all religions continue to challenge and to affect every religion.

> *No religion is an island.* We are all involved with one another. Spiritual betrayal on the part of one of us affects the faith of all of us. Views adopted in one community have an impact on other communities. . . . For all the profound differences in perspective and substance, Judaism is sooner or later affected by the intellectual, moral, and spiritual events within the Christian society, and vice, versa.[5]

Heschel then spoke about nihilism—the opponent to religions of all kinds. Only a joint effort among the world religions could stem the tide of a nihilism that threatened to drive religion underground. Therefore, Heschel asks whether religions should "refuse to be on talking terms with one another and hope for each other's failure? Or should we pray for each other's health and help one another in preserving one's respective legacy, in preserving a common legacy?"[6]

Imagine sitting at Union Theological Seminary, the very place of historic Christian progressive thought, and listening to Heschel speak of his own life and the role of religion in the world at the time when the world was at the crossroads of darkness and light. Religion had been chastened by its own history and by the modern world. Was there a future for Judaism and Christianity? Were there a future, what would it be, especially in light of the assault on our common humanity? Heschel laid out the possibility of religious collaboration and mutual solidarity in bold and revolutionary terms.

> What divides us? . . . We disagree in law and creed, in commitments which lie at the very heart of our religious existence. . . . What unites us? Our being accountable to God, our being objects of God's concern, precious in His eyes. Our conceptions of what ails us may be different; but the anxiety is the same . . . the embarrassment is the same, and so is the sign, the sorrow, and the necessity to obey. . . . Above all, while dogmas and forms of worship are divergent, God is the same.[7]

Heschel's interreligious stance was controversial. The controversy cut at least two ways. From the side of the Orthodox Jew, religions in dialogue, even while maintaining Judaism's separate beliefs, was dangerous. If Judaism were shared in dialogue with Christians, the appreciation might become mutual, with Christians becoming interested in parts of Judaism and Jews becoming interested in parts of Christianity. Though the first possibility made perfect sense for Christians—since by embracing their Jewishness they could enhance their Christianity—the opposite embrace might signal a loss of Judaism for Jews. If interfaith dialogue was built on reciprocity, how could Jews insist on a one-way street? Moreover, there was a fear that Jewish exposure to Christianity would encourage Jews to search out elements of Christian belief and life that might be attractive to them. What then would happen to Jews in the interfaith dialogue? Would they cease to be Jewish, or would they bring that attraction back to Judaism as a critique of the limits of contemporary Judaism?

Some Jews felt that Heschel's description of what Jews and Christians held in common gave over too much to Christianity. If Jews and Christians shared the same God, did both share the same fear and trembling before God? If the language and liturgy, dogma and creeds were different—and should remain as such—was it true that each religion believed or should believe that Jewish and Christian accountability before God was the same? If the conscience of Jews and Christians was the same, was the necessity to obey the same? This way of thinking might signal an ultimate equality between Judaism and Christianity. If there was an essential equality between the two faiths, it would be difficult to emphasize the differences. What should religious bodies do with another of Heschel's positions: "Religion is a means, not the end. It becomes idolatrous when regarded as an end in itself. Over and above all being stands the Creator and Lord of history. He who transcends all. To equate religion and God is idolatry."[8]

The second point of controversy revolved around what Heschel brought to the interfaith dialogue. Thoroughly Americanized Jews brought a shared Americanism to the dialogue table with American Christians. Sharing American culture was a secure meeting ground that could trump theological differences. A level of security was important to American Jews who wanted to avoid the foreigner designation that European Jews suffered from in relation to European Christian society. If America was different and would continue to be, then a common culture and citizenship would be the anchor.

With Heschel, the Eastern European dimension was reintroduced. To his last days, Heschel spoke with a European accent and his Judaism was far from what Christians—and most Jews—had experienced in America. Heschel was learned in Judaism in a way that few American Jews were or could be. He literally came from another part of the Jewish world.

Though he communicated openness, Heschel's Judaism was demanding. His combination of openness and commitment intrigued Christians. It was distinctive and captivating. At the same time, it was so different from the Judaism they encountered that it placed no demands upon them. Jews in the interfaith dialogue were faced with Christian attraction and a demand by Heschel that they be more Jewish than they were, or Jewish in a way they could not be. Thus, Jews in the interfaith dialogue were placed in a difficult situation.

Heschel was a Jewish weathervane and a lightning rod. He was born in the east of Europe, which in the broader arc of European and American Judaism and Jewish culture was seen as a hinterland. The Holocaust changed much of this perception of Eastern European Jewry. After the Holocaust, American Jews adopted a romanticized version of this life and culture. They also tried to distance themselves from it. American Jews wanted it both ways, singing Hasidic melodies from the old country as they lived a thoroughly modern life in America. Heschel embodied Eastern European Jewry while at the same time defying its stereotypes.

Heschel arrived in the United States as Eastern European Jewry was being annihilated. That destruction allowed American Jews to embrace the destroyed culture as its own without having to confront its reality. American Jews could also escape any judgment Eastern European Jewish culture might have upon how they as American Jews were appropriating that culture.

Heschel's presence provided an outside set of Jewish eyes regarding the Jewish future. As Wiesel points out, Heschel was a controversial figure on a variety of fronts, not the least of which was his sense that he came from an authentic Judaism that was now only limping along in America. Did Heschel believe that American Jews were really Jewish?

Few religious Jews with a public platform could speak with such direct connection to the Holocaust as could Heschel. Though Heschel demurred from using the Holocaust as part of his theology, he was not adverse to speaking to Christian audiences of his direct connection with the destruction of Europe's Jews at a time when the Holocaust was also beginning to redefine Christian life. Heschel spoke directly to Christians about what their faith might mean once it was joined to a positive appreciation of their Jewish heritage and the continuing importance of Jewish life in the contemporary world.

Directly across from Union Theological Seminary stands Jewish Theological Seminary, where Heschel spent his last years teaching. Few among the faculty there could speak from such experience and with such eloquence as did Heschel when he spoke of himself as a "brand plucked from a fire" whose destination could just as easily have been Auschwitz or Treblinka. The religious and experiential authority that Heschel naturally assumed could hardly be looked upon neutrally.

Like Buber, Heschel was a charismatic figure in Jewish life and assumed a significance for Christian renewal after the Holocaust. This assertion into Christian life was only the beginning of a journey that continues with twists and turns today. His force can still be felt.

As in the case of Wiesel and Buber, I was introduced to Heschel by Richard Rubenstein. Rubenstein had been a student of Heschel's both at Hebrew Union College and Jewish Theological Seminary.

Heschel was almost the direct opposite of Rubenstein and the other seminarians at Hebrew Union, a quintessentially American seminary of the Reform Jewish movement. With his Hasidic identity and leanings toward the modern

Orthodox movement, at Hebrew Union College Heschel entered into a Jewish world that surprised and often disappointed him. He was a flamboyantly distinct figure of old world Judaism at a seminary on the cutting edge of Jewish assimilation into American culture.

Edward Kaplan describes Heschel's life at the seminary. On the one hand, Heschel helped students understand Jewish spirituality through conversations and his own observance. On the other, few of the rabbinical students sympathized with his spirituality. Those who gathered around Heschel were referred to derisively as the "Kavanah Boys." *Kavanah* is the Hebrew word for "intention" and denotes the spiritual fervor associated with prayer and Hasidism, a type of prayer wholly out of place in the seminary at the time. In interviews with some of Heschel's former students, Kaplan was able to draw this portrait of Heschel's trials and tribulations:

> The other students were equally unimpressed by Heschel. Although Heschel inspired many students outside the classroom, his formal teaching almost destroyed his reputation—and his morale. Cultural differences were largely responsible for this hostility. The European Heschel was disconcerted by his American students' lack of respect. In European universities, students would rise when the professor entered the classroom. (In fact, members of Heschel's Hasidic community in Warsaw used to rise when he, the Hasidic prodigy, entered the room.) Teachers sat at a desk, and lectured from notes, often without looking up, while students silently noted the material being presented to them. American students, however, expected to interact with their teachers, and they expressed themselves freely.
>
> In addition, Heschel's teaching methods were old-fashioned. He did not present his lessons methodically but proceeded by means of digressions, a style more appropriate to a yeshiva than to an American college. He would begin by discussing a prayer, then move to its Talmudic background, then its Hasidic background, then its sources in mystical literature, and so on. He referred to so many works that were unfamiliar to them that most students were lost, able to grasp only bits of the lesson. When he tried to arouse them to an awareness of holiness, his ultimate aim in teaching, he could not get through to them. He would ask the class, "Gentleman, look at this prayer. What does it say to you?" but the students would only sit uncomfortably and smirk. "It's magnificent," he would say, attempting to convey its wonder, but to little effect.[9]

As Kaplan found it, though a minority of students admired Heschel, the majority did not know what to do with him. His style and sensibility was an "affront" to their rationalism and American ideals. They also saw Heschel as aloof, poorly organized, and hostile. Sometimes Heschel displayed his displeasure through sarcasm. For the student's part, they often teased Heschel about his understandings of God and his Yiddish accent. They also played pranks on Heschel in the common dormitory. As Kaplan reports, the pranks were childish. They were a form of humiliation for Heschel.[10]

There were some students who appreciated Heschel. For them, he conveyed his love of worship and through his counseling of those in need opened the student to a deeper spirituality than the seminary offered. With these students personal bonds developed.

Heschel and Rubenstein interacted on a number of occasions. Rubenstein recalls that when he asked for advice on pursuing the rabbinate, Heschel told him that he was better fit for an academic post. When Rubenstein inquired again, Heschel replied, "You can but the demands will be too much for you. You'll have to prepare a sermon every week, maybe two. You'll have to go to meetings, more meetings than you'll be able to stand. You'll start out convinced that you can achieve something, but you'll give up sooner or later. You'll hate yourself when you do. Don't do it. You've got something you don't want to lose." Heschel continued with a note of sadness. "When I think of what our people have accumulated over the centuries that nobody will ever know about it, it seems like a second Holocaust. Hitler destroyed our people. Now we let their spirit die. We train rabbis for sisterhoods and men's clubs, but nobody knows our people's literature. You have a lifetime of work ahead of you. You have the mind and depth to do it. You mustn't become a rabbi. You'll only waste your time."[11]

Rubenstein did become a rabbi, but Heschel was ultimately right. Some years after ordination Rubenstein left for the academic life that he survived only in exile. As for me, when I listened to Rubenstein relate his interaction with Heschel, it made perfect sense. I came to Jewish Studies in an official way midway through my teaching career and barely survived—also in exile.[12]

For Rubenstein, Heschel breathed Judaism as if it was his total environment. His learning was acquired as much as it was inherited and lived. So Heschel taught Judaism simply by being who he was. When I asked Rubenstein what it was like to encounter such a teacher, Rubenstein related that he knew he would never have Heschel's knowledge or grounding in Judaism. Yet encountering Heschel, he also felt that it was less knowledge per se that was important than it was to know enough to ask the questions each generation needed to ask. Sometimes teachers like Heschel knew everything and for a variety of reasons could not ask the next question that was needed. Rubenstein knew enough, in fact knew everything he needed to know, to ask the next question. As it turns out, this next question was the breaking point between himself and Heschel.

On the Jewish future, Rubenstein asked the question that Heschel could not ask, as in some ways Wiesel and Emil Fackenheim were similarly unable. Buber also asked questions that the others were unable to ask.

In the history of a people, questions asked—and responded to—are rarely buried forever. They remain in the tradition awaiting another day and another challenge. When the configuration of Jewish life changes yet again, the disputes between the giants of Jewish life become relevant once more. So the task before Jews of every generation is to know enough to ask the right questions for their time. Then a response needs to be fashioned, however provisional that may be. But "provisional" is life. It is the essence of fidelity in history.

Over the years differences developed between Heschel and Rubenstein, and in the end they became a chasm. Rubenstein was not a consensus builder; he saw the burning issue and struck while the iron was hot. So too with Wiesel, Buber, and Heschel. For each the fate of the Jewish people was at stake. Moreover, they felt themselves to have the proper response to the question they asked. When others refused the question or suggested a different response, open warfare was the result.

Was this because each saw the truth of their being as *the* way forward? The wide-ranging quality of thought and the sheer force that each exhibited is a marvel. Yet the downside to this was the warfare itself. Where there might have been a broader consideration, the declaration of war limited the options ahead. It also limited their vision of the Jewish future.

Of course, egos were involved, perhaps also the sense that only by removing others from the field of inquiry could one's voice be heard. One wonders if the civil war in Jewish life is specific to these generations or will be endlessly repeated until there is nothing left to fight over. Civil wars tend to end when the corpses are piled up so high that it is impossible to see over them. Surveying the Jewish future, this might be our fate, laying down our arms when it is already too late.

Even during my time as a student, I felt that these Jewish thinkers were fighting a rear-guard battle. They also were in mourning for a fight that was already lost. All the Jewish figures we have surveyed so far thought their questions and responses were more or less doomed, even when they placed them before the world with the authority of a commandment.

The divide between Heschel and Rubenstein had all of these elements and more. It also represented yet another twist in an increasingly tangled landscape of post-Holocaust Judaism. For the most part, Wiesel and Rubenstein agreed on the question of God after the Holocaust, though in the 1970 exchange they broke completely on where that would leave Jews and Judaism. Rubenstein's break with Heschel, however, was specifically on the question of God.

Rubenstein described these differences in *After Auschwitz* without mentioning Heschel by name:

> The Jewish community has experienced more monumental changes in the twentieth century than at any other time in its very long history. . . . Furthermore, the upheavals must be seen in the context of a world radically in flux. . . .
>
> In the face of so radical a change, some men romantically turn to an irretrievable past, yearning for a restoration of its virtues. . . . It is better to recognize the irretrievability of the past and to explore the potentialities inherent in the present, regardless of the radical hiatus with accepted traditions this may imply. . . . It would have been better had six million Jews not died, but they have. We cannot restore the religious world which preceded their demise nor can we ignore the fact that the catastrophe has had and will continue to have an extraordinary influence on Jewish life. Although Jewish history is replete with disaster, none has been so radical in its total import as the holocaust. Our images of God, man, and the moral order have been permanently impaired. No Jewish theology will possess even a remote degree of relevance to contemporary Jewish life if it ignores the question of God and the death camps. That is *the question* for Jewish theology in our times. Regrettably most attempts at formulating a Jewish theology since World War II seem to have been written as if the two decisive events of our time for Jews, the death camps and the birth of Israel, had not taken place.[13]

Rubenstein is quite clear that the credentials of extraordinary Jewish learning or having lived through the Holocaust were not enough to qualify or disqualify anyone from navigating the future of post-Holocaust Jewish life. Something new and destructive had become the center of Jewish reflection on the future. For Rubenstein, Rabbinic Judaism had collapsed. Evading this collapse was not enough. Moreover, the time bought by evasion was wasted. Indeed, it was only making the problem more systematic and deeply seated. Rubenstein set about to expose the evasion. But one person's evasion is another's deeply held foundation. Rubenstein did not expect a peaceful acquiescence to his assault. He did not receive one.

Rabbinic Judaism had been forged in the destruction of the Temple and Jerusalem, almost two thousand years ago. Now another event of destruction had occurred. For Rubenstein, Rabbinic Judaism had lost its credibility and its ability to respond to the future of post-Holocaust Jewry. Yet Jewish theologians like Heschel continued to sing its praises.

According to Rubenstein, only a misplaced nostalgia prevented Heschel and other religious figures from acknowledging that what had guided the

Jewish people for almost two thousand years had lost its plausibility. They could not admit it was over. When someone like Wiesel struck back, Rubenstein was amazed. Heschel struck the same note of alarm and dismissal. Rubenstein remained adamant.

For Rubenstein, the very ground of Rabbinic Judaism was in ruins along with European Jewry. Rubenstein saw these ruins as uninhabitable. They had been destroyed once and for all. There was no chance of return or rebuilding. Rubenstein doubted that an Eastern European Jew whose Jewish world had just been destroyed could have much to say to the future of Jews and Judaism in America.

Rubenstein explicitly denounced Heschel's understanding of Jewish life as a nostalgic view of the past. Though Heschel himself mourned the end of Eastern European Jewish life, and in many ways represented that end, he thought that somehow, even in a modified form, Rabbinic Judaism would survive.

Rubenstein believed that a *novum* had occurred in Jewish history that mitigated even the vast and deep liturgy of destruction that helped keep Jews and Judaism alive through the ages. Though this mourning allowed a certain depth, even hope in Jewish life, Rubenstein did not see it as part of the Jewish future. It was a mistake to assert that it could be a future, even as a form of nostalgia. The world remained a dangerous place to live. For Rubenstein, nostalgia was dangerous and could bring about yet another destruction. It was also counterproductive. The destruction of Europe's Jews was too massive for mourning. To engage in mourning and remembrance as a way of Jewish revival missed the very lessons Rubenstein felt the Holocaust had bequeathed to Jews. Now was the time to protect the Jews who were left. Invoking tradition and God was a luxury Jews could not afford.

Soon Wiesel would throw down the gauntlet and announce a Jewish future of remembrance for the Holocaust martyrs and Jewish empowerment in the state of Israel. Rubenstein said no to martyrdom and yes to Israel but for political reasons. Heschel agreed with Wiesel's mourning, though Heschel mourned more the passing of the spirit and liturgical sensibilities of East European Jewry, with less focus on the Holocaust than Wiesel. Heschel also charted a different path than Wiesel on God and Rabbinic Judaism.

Whereas Wiesel saw God in the past, Heschel saw God in the present. Rabbinic Judaism was past for Wiesel. For Heschel it lived on. In general, whereas Rubenstein and Wiesel saw an almost complete severing of the past and present Jewish life because of the Holocaust and broke ranks on the question of what continues on, Heschel saw continuity in Jewish life despite the destruction of European Jewry. Buber acknowledged parts of both sides and charted a course that hardly can be characterized as a middle way. He was and remains an outlier.

A Disturbing Nostalgia?

From Rubenstein's perspective, Heschel's theology could handle neither the Holocaust nor the state of Israel. Since Rabbinic Judaism had been formed after the destruction of the Temple, Rubenstein saw it as a religion built around political and military defeat. In their defeat the rabbis agreed to be a demilitarized Diaspora minority within majority empowered cultures largely hostile to Jews and Judaism. For Rubenstein, the combination of Jewish powerlessness and hostility to Jews was a powder keg waiting to explode. The result of Jewish powerlessness was a wandering and vulnerable community. For more than fifteen hundred years, Jews survived their plight by negotiating with their foes, bribing them, agreeing to further restrictions on the life of the community, flight, and even sacrificing some members of the community for the greater good of the community's survival.

In Europe, the hostile population was Christian. The long history of Christian anti-Semitism featured a series of violent assaults on the integrity and bodies of the Jewish people. Still, Christians limited the violence against Jews because Jews were the ultimate testimony to the rightness of Christianity and demonstration of God's punishment for the rejection of the messiah. Jews were Christianity's "eschatological reserve." When even the blinded Jews recognized the truth of Christianity, the last ages when Christ returned to earth would begin. The Nazis took the final step on this slippery slope of devaluing Jewish life. Their eschatology was the elimination of Jews altogether.

For Rubenstein, Jewish leadership relied on traditional responses to Christian anti-Semitism and failed to recognize that the Nazis had changed the rules of the game. With the Nazis and without power, Jews were as good as dead. Thus, the state of Israel was *the* response to the failure of Rabbinic Judaism and its system of religious and political thought to protect Jewish life. Rubenstein thought that Jews needed a political theology that encouraged Jewish empowerment. Rabbinic Judaism was hardly up to this because it discouraged political action on behalf of Jews as a community. Nor did Rabbinic Judaism know what to do with Jewish state power.

Jews could not effectively empower themselves if they had one foot in a Jewish state while the other stayed in a theological system that was born and developed when Jews were powerless. Jews needed a new synthesizer and engine for Jewish life, a clean break with its past. From Rubenstein's viewpoint, Heschel's haunting and beautiful spirituality hindered the transformation that was inevitable and necessary.

Even more disturbing for Rubenstein,the Nazi plan to annihilate the Jews of Europe become feasible only with a compliant Jewish leadership. This went back to the deal that the rabbis made with the Romans as Jerusalem fell.

Although Rubenstein never personally linked Heschel or others in this way, he did indict the rabbinic system and ethos that emanated from it.

The ghettoization of Jews that allowed them to be subsequently moved into the death camps was organized by the *Judenrat*, the Jewish Councils. Jewish leadership was operating within the established framework that for more than a thousand years had allowed assaults on individual Jews and Jewish communities throughout Europe. Jewish leadership traditionally waited out anti-Semitism, tried to buy off the mobs that were assaulting the community, or begged for institutional protection of the religious and political powers that be. With the Nazis, such bargaining was over. The endgame was total annihilation.

As Rubenstein pondered Heschel's spirituality, he thought of his magisterial works on Jewish philosophy and theology published in the first decade after the Holocaust, *Man Is Not Alone: A Philosophy of Religion*, published in 1951, and *God in Search of Man: A Philosophy of Judaism*, published in 1955. Heschel's popular work, *The Sabbath: Its Meaning for the Modern Age*, published in 1951, also fit Rubenstein's critique. Heschel's meditations on the Sabbath evoked the time and place of his upbringing. It was a world lost yet still living within him. It is strictly rabbinic, emphasizing a ritual that involves the mystery of creation and the world to come. The Sabbath is that world of creation and the end time of justice and peace here for a day in an unredeemed world. When Heschel asks what is so luminous about the Sabbath, his language is pre-modern: "What is so precious to captivate the hearts? It is because the seventh day is a mine where spirit's precious metal can be found with which to construct the palace in time, a dimension in which the human is at home with the divine; a dimension in which man aspires to approach the likeness of the divine." Rubenstein asks whether this and other of Heschel's understandings could be held in a post-Holocaust world and what they meant to a Jewish world that needed to look forward but might lapse into nostalgia for this lost world.[14]

Though Rubenstein felt that Heschel's rendering of the Sabbath was romanticized, he also acknowledged the power of his images. As with Wiesel, perhaps the very power of Heschel's personality struck Rubenstein as dangerous. For Rubenstein, Wiesel's and Heschel's powerful images and personalities made it more difficult for Jews to break away from forms of spirituality and religious thinking that had been and today were dangerous to the physical safety of Jews.

Though Heschel could not be blamed for recalling the world he came from and loved, Rubenstein felt that he had a broader obligation to the Jewish people. Private mourning could be respected. Mourning in public that could produce the opposite result had to be confronted.

For Heschel, the covenant remains in place—if only Jews will renew it. Furthermore, the question of God's responsibility for the Holocaust is misplaced.

The Holocaust comes from human hands and from humans turned away from God. Contra Rubenstein but in a similar fashion to Wiesel, Heschel speaks of the martyrs of the Holocaust. Yet unlike Wiesel, Heschel's covenant is the original one rather than the additional covenant harkening to a past time when God was with the Jewish people. Indeed, with Heschel's spirituality, God remains and is waiting for us to redeem the world.

Heschel believes the original vision of Judaism remains. Again, contra Rubenstein, Heschel calls for reclaiming ideals and refusing to adopt a military strategy of Jewish empowerment for its own sake. Didn't the Nazis make an idol out of empowerment? Instead, Heschel calls for a return to Jewish piety and a return to God. Heschel writes that "God will return to us when we are willing to let Him in—into our banks and factories, into our Congress and clubs, into our homes and theaters." For Heschel, "God is everywhere or nowhere, the father of all men or no man, concerned about everything or nothing."[15]

Rubenstein is very far away from this sensibility. Of course, the strain on Heschel was immense as he watched from afar as his family and community went up in flames. What world could Heschel evoke except his own?

Though written during the war years, Heschel's message changed little with time, and his language remained much the same. His litany of what went wrong to produce a world such as they were experiencing is haunting: "The conscience of the world was destroyed by those who were wont to blame others rather than themselves"; "Let us remember, we revered the instincts, but distrusted ideals. We labored to perfect engines and let our inner life go to wreck." Heschel accesses the primal rabbinic tradition he grew up with, which Jews grew distant from at their own peril. So too when he writes, "We ridiculed superstition until we lost our ability to believe. We have helped to extinguish the light our fathers had kindled. We have bartered holiness for convenience, loyalty for success, love for power, wisdom for diplomas, prayer for sermon, wisdom for information, tradition for fashion."[16]

This is Heschel at full throttle. In contrast, Rubenstein believes that we live in a "functionally Godless world" because there is no practical affect that comes from belief or non-belief in God. So how can Heschel believe that calling Jews or others back to God will mean anything in relation to the world?

For Rubenstein, it is almost blasphemous to think that the cause of World War II and the Holocaust is distance from God. It links the desire for worldly power with distance from God rather than the natural and ever present desire for power. Even if power over others comes from distance from God, Jews cannot afford to return to God when others do not, or assume that even a mutual return to God would ultimately protect Jews.

For Rubenstein, power is protection. In a functionally Godless world, Jews need to concentrate on power.

Even as Heschel places the blame for the Holocaust on human beings, he invokes the name of God with ease. Heschel's arguments with God are limited and redirected. The availability of God has not changed. If anything, God is even more present in calling Jews and others back to him. Heschel believes that the covenant at Sinai remains intact. This is not about nostalgia or idealizing a future after the Holocaust. It is about remembering and once again embracing the truth.

Heschel believes that Judaism with all its strictures and possibilities is the hope for the Jewish people. If Jews abandon Judaism as it has been known through the ages, where will Jews find their anchor? If Jews are called to be a holy people, where else could Jews find a rationale for being Jewish?

Power for its own sake made no sense to Heschel. There is always power, first and foremost, the power of God involved with humanity. Without the involvement of God and the engagement of human beings called to ethics and justice, what will keep any of us from pursuing power for power's sake? Jews especially know this since without this bond with God, why be Jewish and what does Jewish suffering mean? Why would Jews willingly undergo suffering and be willing to sacrifice for others if there were not an ethical core and calling from God?

Heschel also knew that there would always be a God that was worshipped, if not the true God of Israel then the God of power. A recurring theme is that of choice; we are always turning in one direction or another, and each has consequences. Rubenstein argued similarly, but they differed in how that direction could be appraised. For Heschel, turning toward the God of Israel represented an efficacious and worldly power. Just the opposite was true for Rubenstein. Without military power, we know the consequences. The consequences unfolded even as Heschel cried out to God and the world.

Though he lived through the Holocaust, Heschel never adopted the Holocaust—or the state of Israel—as central to Jewish belief or commitment. Though both become more important for Heschel over time, they remained as other events in Jewish history had been, framed within an overarching rabbinic sensibility. Such events had to be placed in a system that is beyond current events.

Heschel believed that historical events were important in calling Jews to a renewed commitment to the ancient Judaic framework. The Holocaust should be remembered within the Jewish calendar, which also includes other attempts to destroy the Jewish people. If those events did not change the face of Judaism and the covenant, it would be an act of hubris to see the present cataclysm as doing what other events did not. For Heschel, this did not minimize the horror of the Holocaust. Despite his own personal losses in the Holocaust, he continued to stress a religious framework in which the Holocaust would remain along with other events of Jewish suffering.

Wiesel went far beyond Heschel in emphasizing the Holocaust, but he did not consider it to be a result of Jewish detachment from God. Nor does Wiesel call for a return to God. For Buber, the Holocaust is a call back to our essential humanity, which includes encounter. Like any other event in history, the Holocaust does not block such an encounter but highlights our need to return to the primal source. This is far from Heschel's God, which for Buber it is too traditional and too causal. Yet like Heschel, Buber also believes in a destiny for the Jewish people that is primal and that cannot be displaced. Here Buber is closer to Heschel and Wiesel than Rubenstein. The difference is what each makes of the relation of the Holocaust and God.

God of the Prophets

Rubenstein broke with Heschel at the height of his popularity. This took courage. Rubenstein paid a price. It was also an opportunity for Rubenstein to make his mark on the Jewish future. After making this break, the post-Holocaust discussion quickly moved on. Rubenstein's future disputes were with Wiesel and Emil Fackenheim who, though respecting Heschel, had also broken with him.

Neither Wiesel nor Fackenheim announced their break with Heschel. By that time, Heschel was a towering figure in the Jewish imagination. It was best to critique Rubenstein without mentioning his name than to take on Heschel. It may be that neither Wiesel nor Fackenheim felt that they had broken with Heschel. Heschel was a power on his own. It was easier to concentrate on Rubenstein.

Like Heschel, Buber became increasingly marginal in the years ahead. In fact, though Fackenheim had been quite immersed in Buber's understandings of Judaism, in the aftermath of the 1967 war, Fackenheim broke with Buber in a similar manner that Rubenstein had broken with Heschel. Rubenstein also broke publicly with Buber. As with Heschel, Rubenstein accused Buber of being spiritually and politically naïve.

With Buber's death in 1965 and Heschel's in 1972, the passing of the torch to a new generation of Jewish thinkers became easier. In my short time with Heschel, it was clear to me that the torch had already passed. Though it was hardly clear then, Buber and Heschel's shadow hung over the next generation. Was the new generation of Jewish theologians—Rubenstein, Wiesel, and Fackenheim—up to the task ahead of them? Or would they fail in significant ways as they had accused the generation before them of having failed?

It was in the context of Rubenstein's disagreements with Heschel that I first encountered Heschel in person, just months before he died in 1972. Only years later did I come to understand that Rubenstein was addressing Heschel in the opening paragraphs of *After Auschwitz*. In turn, Heschel responded to Rubenstein without using his name: "The central issue is not man's decision to extend formal recognition to God, to furnish God with a certificate that He exists, but the realization of our importance in God's design; not to prove that God is alive, but to prove that man is not dead."[17]

Many years later I began to read Heschel. Partly this was for my enrichment and partly because I felt how he framed religion might be easier for my Christian students to understand. I thought Heschel would raise new questions within their Christian faith, broadening while also deepening it, which turns out to be the case. At first, I find that the students enter the realm of Jewish spirituality and end their essays with how Christian spirituality is different. Then I advise them to bracket their Christianity and interact with the readings as if they are Jewish. The students then explore Jewish spirituality on its own terms. Though we also read Buber, Heschel speaks to them at the deepest level, awakening within them the traditions they too cherish. They see continuity between Heschel's evocation of God and their own lives.

When I met Heschel he appeared old, though this could have been simply our age difference. He also appeared tired. He continued to travel and lecture despite health warnings from his doctor. I wondered if someone so well known had to travel so much and to such universities as mine. Speaking to students like me was complex and could be interesting from the older generation's perspective. Or they could consider it a waste of time. Was it worth it?

I remember little of Heschel's lecture. I do remember the reception held for him after the lecture. Heschel sat in a soft, cushioned chair. We students sat on the floor. Heschel answered our questions thoughtfully, sometimes gently, and other times with a sense of exasperation that we needed to read and know more.

One of the students asked Heschel about his understanding of the prophetic and about God. Heschel seemed caught off-guard. He responded that he had written extensively on the subject and that we might want to read what he had written. With an impish smile on his face, Heschel continued that after the student read the material, he would be able to ask more informed questions and receive more direct responses. I took Heschel's gentle admonition as a guide for the future. Even then though I wondered who would read Heschel in the future. Who would be able to respond to the questions his writing evoked?

In the early 1980s I was lecturing at the New School for Social Research in New York City. After the lecture, two women approached. It was Sylvia Heschel, Heschel's widow, and her lovely daughter, Susannah, already a firmament in the Jewish religious world.

I was taken aback at meeting Mrs. Heschel. We had a nice chat and she extended an invitation to come to her apartment for Shabbat. Several weeks later, I went there. She continued to live in the apartment that she shared with her late husband. In taking in the surroundings, I was encountering Heschel again. Later I found Susannah's reminiscences on the Sabbath, especially relating to her father:

> Walking with my father was not a matter of reaching a destination but of creating a private time for talk. He would stop every few feet and discuss a point, then go a little farther. He loved to take walks on the Sabbath afternoons, in Riverside Park, across from the apartment building. When I was a little girl, he was always delighted to play games to keep me amused . . . and when I grew tired from the walk, he would put me on his shoulders and carry me. . . .
>
> My father's book on the Sabbath, one of the most popular of his writings, evokes the spirit he created with my mother in our home, in which the Sabbath was both peacefully quiet and filled with celebration. The book beautifully describes the rabbinic, kabbalistic, and Hasidic understandings of the Sabbath experience; together, my parents brought the text to life.
>
> The Sabbath was the time my parents entertained. . . . Nearly all my parents friends were professors who had come to the United States from Europe, and they loved to tell stories about European Jewish life, or reminisce about professors and colleagues and rabbis they had known in Europe. There was some sadness that they were describing a world that no longer existed, but their stories had such vividness that they seem to keep that world alive.[18]

Susannah notes how her father died on the Sabbath. Planning to go to synagogue on Saturday morning, she discovered that her father died peacefully in his sleep. In the Jewish tradition, it is considered a blessing to die in one's sleep and even more so to die on the Sabbath. As Susannah writes, "Such a death is called a kiss from God."[19]

Encountering Susannah was a delight and how much more so in the context of her father's life and the very apartment where he had lived. Without knowing it, I had joined in a long tradition of Sabbath observances at the Heschel's.

Now that she was a scholar in her own right and carrying her father's name, it was both easier to succeed and more difficult to be accepted for her own contributions to Jewish life. In our conversations, I became aware of how so many Jewish figures her age claimed her father as a spiritual father and often saw her as the child she was when they knew her father years ago.

Susannah is a feminist, and this has caused problems with parts of her extended family that move in the Orthodox world. Since her father had feet in different parts of the Jewish and non-Jewish world, there were those who championed him. Some felt he had left his roots behind. Others thought he was too traditional. In some ways Susannah suffers the same trials and tribulations.

Having read Buber and now listening to Heschel and meeting his wife and daughter, I wondered about their understandings of God. They were so different than Rubenstein's and Wiesel's. Could either of them help me with the question of God?

Certainly Buber had a different sense of God after the Holocaust than Rubenstein, Wiesel, or Fackenheim had, and there were significant differences between Buber and Heschel. Buber also understood that darkness had settled over the question of God. "These last years in a great searching and questioning, seized ever anew by the shudder of the now, I have arrived no further than that I now distinguish a revelation through the hiding of the face, a speaking through silence," Buber wrote. "The eclipse of God can be seen with one's own eyes, it will be seen. He, however, who today knows nothing other than to say, 'See there, it grows lighter!' he leads into error."[20]

In the beginning I had difficulty with Heschel's understanding of God, and to some extent this remains so today. Unlike Buber, Heschel had a palpable sense of the traditional Jewish God who was with Jews in history and had a concern for Jews and humanity. Even more, Heschel believed that God is so involved with humanity that God suffers when humanity does. Heschel called this the "divine pathos."

By divine pathos, Heschel means a God that is active in human affairs. God is embedded in history. Heschel writes that though the divine pathos is "rooted in God's free will," it makes itself known in life itself. For Heschel, the category of divine pathos "leads to the basic affirmation that God is interested in human history, that every deed and event in the world concerns Him and arouses His reaction." He believed that the divine pathos represented a unity binding together the eternal and temporal, the rational and irrational, the metaphysical and the historical. This unity provided the foundational relation between God and humanity, the correlation of Creator and creation, and the dialogue between God and the people Israel.[21]

Heschel raised questions about other ways of looking at God, especially since his view was sometimes criticized as being anthropomorphic. "Is it more compatible with our conception of the grandeur of God to claim that He is emotionally blind to the misery of man rather than profoundly moved?" Heschel asks. "To conceive of God as not an onlooker but as a participant, to conceive of man not as an idea in the mind of God but as a concern—the category of divine pathos is an indispensable implication. To the Biblical mind the conception of God as cold, detached, and unemotional is totally alien." With Heschel, the divine pathos illustrates a connection between God and humanity, one that originates with God and continues to be involved with humanity. God views the world and its events and experiences and judges them. God's relation to the world is what Heschel calls God's "transcendental attention to man."[22]

As with Buber, though in a different way, Heschel believed that the prophets are the conduit for God's message: "According to the prophets of Israel, from Moses to Malachi, God is concerned with small matters," Heschel writes. "What the prophets tried to convey to man was not a conception of eternal harmony, of unchangeable rhythm of wisdom, but the perception of God's concern with concrete situations. Disclosing the pattern of history, in which the human is interwoven with the divine, they breathed a divine earnestness into the world of man." This led Heschel to see God in light of the prophets as a "spirit of concern for life. What is a thing to us is a concern to God; what is part of the physical world of being is also a part of a divine world of meaning. *To be* is to *stand for*, to *stand* for a divine concern."[23]

As for God's presence in history, Heschel writes:

God is present in His continuous expression . . . imminent in all beings in the way in which a person is imminent in a cry that he utters: He stands for what he says. He is concerned with what He says. All beings are replete with the divine word which only leaves our viciousness profane and overbears His silent, patient presence.

We usually forget where He is, forget that our own self-concern is a cupful drawn from the spirit of divine concern. There is, however, a way of keeping ourselves open to the presence of that spirit. There are moments in which we feel the challenge of a power that, not born of our will nor installed by it, robs us of independence by its judgment of the rectitude or depravity of our actions, by its gnawing at our heart when we offend against its injunctions. It is as if there were no privacy within ourselves, no possibility of either retreat or escape, no place in us in which to bury the remnant of our guilt feelings. There is a voice that reaches everywhere, knowing no mercy, digging in the burial places of charitable forgetfulness.

God is not all in all. He is in all beings but He is *not* all beings. He is within the darkness but He is not the darkness. His one concern permeates all beings: He is all there, but the absence of the divine is also there. His ends are concealed in the cold facts of nature.

The impenetrable fog in which the world is clad is God's disguise. To know God means to sense display in His disguise and to be aware of the disguise in His most magnificent display.

God is within the world, present and concealed in the essence of things. If not for His presence, there would be no essence; if not for His concealment, there would be no appearance.

If the universe were explainable as a robot, we could assume that God is separated from it and His relation to it would be like that of a watchmaker to a clock. But the ineffable cries out in all things.[24]

"The ineffable crying out" is quite a different sensibility than Buber's. Like Buber, Heschel looks to the Bible and finds encounters throughout. However, Heschel's understanding of encounter with God is much more concrete and traditional than Buber's. Instead of a mystery beyond words that is then translated into language and story, Heschel stays with the text and mines it. At the same time, Heschel's vision of the biblical God is quite different than the God of history whom Rubenstein rejects:

The Bible is primarily not man's vision of God but God's vision of man. The Bible is not man's theology but God's anthropology, dealing with man and what He asks of him rather than with the nature of God. God did not reveal to the prophets eternal mysteries but His knowledge and love of man. It was not the aspiration of Israel to know the Absolute but to ascertain what He asks of man; to commute with His will rather than with His essence.

In the depth of our trembling, all that we can utter is the awareness of our being known to God. Man cannot see God, but man can be seen by God. He is not the object of discovery but the subject of revelation.[25]

Heschel returns to the prophets, who posit meaning in the world. Rather than viewing history as a "superficial succession of causes and effects in the world; they saw it rather as a meaningful relation among events." The prophets see God as related to the world and that is why they have no interest in the question of what God is. Rather, they are interested in discerning God's activity in the world and, because of that activity, what is to be done. From Heschel's point of view, the world is unfinished, out of joint, and ready to be fulfilled. The project is between God and humanity together. The prophets are God's hands on earth. The prophets confirm that there is an intention in the universe that depends on free will and decision. Humankind, indeed the people of Israel, can either embrace that intention or turn away from it.[26]

The prophet's life is far from simple or easy, but for Heschel there is the consolation in that the prophet and God suffer together.

The *pathos* of God is upon him. It moves him. It breaks out of him like a storm in the soul, overwhelming his inner life, his thoughts, his feelings, wishes, and hopes. It takes possession of his heart and mind, giving him the courage to act against the world.

The words of the prophet are often like thunder; they sound as if he were in a state of hysteria. But what appears to us as wild emotionalism must have seemed like restraint to him who has to convey the emotion of the Almighty in the feeble language of man. His sympathy is an overflow of powerful emotion which comes in response to what he sensed in divinity.

Like a scream in the night is the prophet's word. The world is at ease and asleep, while the prophet is hit by a blast from heaven. No one seems to hear the distress in the world; no one seems to care when the poor are suppressed. But God is distressed, and the prophet has pity for God who cares for the distressed.

A single crime—to us it is slight, but to the prophet—a disaster. The prophet's scream which sounds hysterical to us is like a subdued sigh to him. Exaggeration to us is understatement to him.[27]

Can Heschel's words about the prophet be read *after* the Holocaust? Be understood as speaking directly to us? After the Holocaust can we honestly say that God is concerned with the individual Jew, with Jews as a people and other peoples who struggle and suffer? Can we speak about the prophets or experience the prophets in the way that Heschel conveys their sympathy and connection with God? If we were hit by a blast from heaven, would we keep quiet about our experience? If we named our calling, would we be seen as deluded?

Though Heschel and Wiesel are close in some areas, they understand the prophets quite differently. For Wiesel, if they had previously claimed God, that quickly and decisively left them when they witnessed the Holocaust. *Night* begins with the young Eliezer living within a Jewish world where Heschel's understandings made sense. The smoke of burning children ended that world for Wiesel. How then could Heschel hold onto it?

For Heschel, the prophets represent a deep embrace of God and humankind. Where that might lead on a practical level Heschel leaves others to map out. Certainly, commitments for justice are called for, the civil rights movement being a case in point. Still, the needed transformation of society seems too large for Heschel's prophetic. Or is this just a post-Holocaust pessimism that needs to be shaken up and turned around by Heschel's lost world?

If Heschel is nostalgic in his understanding of God, he is nostalgic in the boldest of ways. Heschel thinks that God is in search of us and that God needs us to complete God's work. God and humans are in a covenantal partnership. Part of that partnership is to complete the work on earth that God wants done. If God is concerned about humanity, God is unable to complete his task without us. Our act of completion is carried out through deeds. They reveal aspects of our life that are known to us before we act. Other aspects of our lives become known to us as we act. What is known and unknown to us is already known by God.

As with Heschel's theology in general, the obvious is complemented by that which is not. Acts are shadowed by evil and the possibility of doing good in the world. Heschel writes that "it is in *deeds* that man becomes aware of what his life really is, of his power to harm and to hurt, to wreck and to ruin; of his ability to derive joy and to bestow it upon others; to relieve and to increase his own and other people's tensions. It is in the employment of his will, not in reflection, that he meets his own self as it is; not as he should like it to be. In his deeds man exposes his immanent as well as his suppressed desires, spelling even that which he cannot apprehend. What he may not dare to think, he often utters in deeds. The heart is revealed in deeds. The deed is the test, the trial, and the risk." Referring to the Holocaust and no doubt to the atomic age that was inaugurated at the end of World War II, Heschel writes that it is "so easy to hurt, destroy, to insult, to kill. Giving birth to one child is a mystery; bringing death to millions is but a skill. It is not quite within the power of human will to generate life; it is quite within the power of the will to destroy life." In Heschel's view, what we do rather than what we say defines who we are as human beings.[28]

The other side of violence and destruction is justice and peace. For Heschel, God has a question for us and a task. The question is whether we will respond to God's address to us as individuals. Whether we respond or not will define who we are in the world and our relationship with God: Not things but deeds are the source of our sad perplexities," Heschel writes.

> Confronted with a world of things, man unloosens a tide of deeds. The fabulous fact of man's ability to act, *the wonder of doing*, is no less amazing than the marvel of being. Ontology inquires: what is *being*? What does it mean to be? The religious mind ponders: what is *doing*? What does it mean to do? What is the relation between the doer and the deed? Between doing and being? Is there a purpose to fulfill, a task to carry out?[29]

For Heschel, the Bible is important here: "In the midst of such anxiety we are confronted with the claim of the Bible. The world is not all danger, and man is not alone. God endowed man with freedom, and He will share in our use of freedom. The earth is the Lord's, and God is in search of man. He endowed man with power to conquer the earth, and His honor is upon this faith. We abused His power, we betrayed His trust. We cannot expect Him to say, Though thou betrayest me, yet I will trust in thee. Man is responsible for His deeds, and God is responsible for man's responsibility." Again what we do, we are. Choices are before us and the choices are ultimately religious choices. Our religiosity is defined more by what we do than what we say, even in prayer. For Heschel, the Biblical witness is clear.[30]

In specifically addressing Jews and Jewish history, Heschel is direct: "Jewish thought is disclosed in Jewish living." For Heschel, *mitzvot*, good deeds, are the key. By living as Jews "we attain our faith as Jews." For Heschel, a Jew does not have faith because of deeds, but faith can be attained only through "sacred deeds." Heschel continues, counseling that through right action we are already in the presence of God:

> A Jew is asked to take a *leap of action* rather than a *leap* of *thought*. He is asked to surpass his needs, to do more than he understands in order to understand more than he does. In carrying out the word of the Torah he is ushered into the presence of spiritual meaning. Through the ecstasy of deeds he learns to be certain of the hereness of God. Right living is a way to right thinking.
>
> The sense of the ineffable, the participation in Torah and Israel, the leap of action—they all lead to the same goal. Callousness to the mystery of existence, detachment from the Torah and Israel, cruelty and profanity of living alienate the Jew from God. Response to the wonder, participation in Torah and Israel, discipline in daily life bring us close to Him.[31]

As with Buber, Heschel understands doing to be more than activism. By creating a life responsible to humanity, the person is close to God. For Jews this has to do with carrying out the commandments God has given Jews. In turn, these commandments are a way of coming closer to each other and to God. For Heschel, doing is a way of going beyond our own needs to the needs of others and to God's need. God wants his creation to be just and peaceful. The earth cannot become such a place without our intentional action.

Jewish law, for Heschel, is the "discipline in daily life" that commands right doing. Right doing leads to right thinking. Right doing and thinking means attachment to God. Detachment leads in the opposite direction. If we are detached from right doing then we are detached from right thinking and from God. Heschel asks whether creation can be made right if we distance ourselves from God's way. Here Heschel departs from Wiesel and from Buber as much as from Rubenstein. Without a structure that commands us to surpass our individual needs, how can we be close to God and God's plan for the Jewish people and for humanity?

God is experienced internally for Heschel. This interior experience is an address by a reality that is not us and yet is intimately related to us. God's address is deeply personal and to the people as well. This address means that as individuals and as Jews we have a destiny. Even if we turn away, the address remains. God calls us at the deepest part of our individual and collective being to respond to God's presence in our lives.

We know that the "I" is more than we can grasp and know, a presence that is more than we are. So for Heschel, God is not so much the thundering God of history as the presence within that prompts us to ever deeper levels of spirituality and acts of justice.

Acts of spirituality and justice are our response to God's address. Heschel differentiates between the speculative mind that sees the world as an enigma and the religious mind that sees the world as a challenge. To the speculative mind the question of God is impersonal, while to the religious mind the question of God is personal. The first seeks an answer to the cause of being and the second to what is asked of us.[32]

On the one hand, Heschel's understanding of God is quite traditional—he invokes the biblical witness. He is comfortable with Rabbinic Judaism and Jewish law providing the essential structure of Jewish life. Yet he uses contemporary philosophy to deconstruct the self in a way that today would be seen as postmodern.

Heschel writes about a return to God as the beginning of recovering the human face so that we can do God's work on earth. He also thinks about the "I" that is not mine, the "mystery of our own presence": "I am endowed with a will, but the will is not mine; I am endowed with freedom, but it is a freedom imposed on the will. Life is something that visits my body, a transcendent loan; I have neither initiated nor conceived its worth and meaning. *The essence of what I am is not mine.* I am what is not mine. I am that I am not."[33]

Yet how can Heschel's God be so traditional and so modern at the same time? If the traditional God of Israel is obsolete, diminished, and distanced after the Holocaust, how can Heschel write so boldly about that God? But if the God of Israel as traditionally perceived is under attack, is it not equally bold to assert a God who is within us and calls us to a destiny that is uniquely our own? Even bolder is Heschel's proclamation that both the traditional understanding of God and the modern understanding of God are joined at the hip. For Heschel, there is no contradiction here. Indeed, there are questions and mysteries. Both tell us that humanity is not alone.

It follows for Heschel that God is in search of us, individually and collectively. Further, the traditional way of Jewish life provides the framework for God and the individual Jew that adds up to more than the sum of its parts. The covenant is unbroken and present now, if we only are present to it. Are these claims not subversive for post-Holocaust Jewish life?

That is one interpretation. Another is that Heschel's sense of God is too traditional and too modern to accept completely after the Holocaust. I cannot imagine Fackenheim's 614th commandment in Heschel's theology. Nor can I imagine a Commanding Voice of Auschwitz. Wiesel's additional covenant is too distant, Buber's unstructured encounter too ephemeral. Rubenstein's functionally Godless world is blasphemy leading humanity into nihilism.

Yet Heschel asks the question as to whether *after* is only important with reference to the Holocaust. Could *after* also apply now to post-Holocaust questions about theology and spirituality? To post-Holocaust political sensibilities? Could Heschel's traditional/postmodern sensibilities, as chastened as they might be, become part of a new religious configuration in the Jewish future?

Rendezvous with Destiny

It is difficult, if not impossible, for Jews today to see the state of Israel only as Rubenstein's site of Jewish empowerment or as Wiesel's dream response to the nightmare of the Holocaust. Indeed, the expulsion of Palestinians and the continuing expansion of Israel at the expense of Palestinians make Israel more and more problematic for Jews. Does this mean that Jews today come after the Holocaust *and* after Israel?

The hard lesson that Jews have learned in the post-Holocaust era is that simply placing "Jewish" before "state" does not modify the state's nature. As it turns out, Israel does everything every other nation-state does. It is difficult for Jews to admit this. Knowing the ways of the world, we shouldn't be surprised that a Jewish nation-state acts like other nation-states.

We return to the conception of most Jewish thinkers that Jews are somehow different. Here, Rubenstein is alone in questioning this understanding, even though Jews being isolated in the world is itself a Jewish distinctive. Wiesel argues movingly for Jewish distinctiveness. As we enter the second decade of the twenty-first century, Wiesel still argues that the state of Israel is different. His tribute to the Israeli soldiers in the 1967 war remains, though it has become somewhat muted over the years.

Wiesel has never indicated that Israel is a state like other states. In 2010 he published a full-page, paid statement on Jerusalem in major newspapers around the United States. The theme: Jerusalem is the eternal Jewish capital and is above and beyond politics. However, it is hard to think of a more politically contested city than Jerusalem.

Though mindful and often critical of contemporary Jewish life, Heschel holds to Jewish exceptionality. Whatever faults Jews have, it is because Jews have lost their connection with God. Jewish sin is found throughout history yet, comparatively speaking, Jews are innocent. Heschel rarely if ever speaks about the internal workings of a power structure within the Jewish community. Nor does he detail internal aspects of Israeli society. But then, none of the Jewish thinkers comment extensively on how Jews live together in Israel. They simply assume a just and ethical society in a Jewish state simply because Jews live there in the majority and govern themselves.

In some ways the contemporary Jewish debate has moved on from Rubenstein and Wiesel, but in other ways it remains the same. Still, a further question has emerged: Is Israel a true protection for Jews or a new danger zone? The discussion now is whether Jewish ethics can survive when Jews have power, or whether Jewish ethics was simply a set of principles that Jews lived out when they were powerless.

As much as the question of God was at stake in the Holocaust, the question of Jewish ethics is at stake in the state of Israel. In recent years the debate about God has lessened or moved to a debate about Jewish ethics in an empowered state of Israel. Perhaps this is the same debate under different guises.

Heschel linked God and ethics in a traditional and a postmodern way. If Heschel is correct, then the challenge of ethical behavior in a Jewish state may be even more protracted and deeper for Jews than the question of God after the Holocaust. If the argument is about more or less the same thing, God and ethics being linked, what kind of leap of action is necessary regarding the policies of the state of Israel in relation to the dispossession of Palestinians?

It may be that Heschel has little to say of importance on either the Holocaust or Israel as we view them today. If Heschel was unyielding on the question of God after the Holocaust, he also had a fairly conventional Jewish understanding of Israel. Though he was far from a militant who celebrated the Jewish use of power, at least publicly, he rarely showed a deep understanding of the violence used against Palestinians in the birth and subsequent history of the state of Israel.

In the 1950s and early 1960s, Heschel visited Israel on several occasions. Though he believed in the importance of a Jewish state, for the most part he concentrated his energies on infusing Israeli nationalism with an open and inclusive Jewish spirituality.

Along with most Jews, Heschel celebrated Israel's victory in the 1967 war. Just weeks after the end of the war, Heschel traveled to Israel and wrote what became a book length series of diary entries and essays. Heschel was caught up in Israel's victory, and his writing is reminiscent of his earlier evocations of the Sabbath of his childhood.

Yet the difference in context is striking. Heschel seems to miss that difference or believes that the ancient dream of the Jewish return to Jerusalem transcends it. Even the title of his collection—*Israel: An Echo of Eternity*—places the people of Israel and the state of Israel outside the framework of time. As Susannah Heschel comments, her father knew that Jews existed in both time and space. How else could Jews carry out their activities in the world? Yet this experiment in Jewish self-governance occurs within the context of a state. It exists in time and space. Israel is an exercise in Jewish memory and realpolitik. Heschel skirts the edges of both in a moving and poetic way:

> July 1967 . . . I have discovered a new land. Israel is not the same as before. There is great astonishment in the souls. It is as if the prophets had arisen from their graves. Their words ring in a new way. Jerusalem is everywhere, she hovers over the whole country. There is a new radiance, a new awe.

The great quality of a miracle is not in its being an unexpected, unbelievable event in which the presence of the holy bursts forth, but in its happening to human beings who are profoundly astonished at such an outburst.[34]

Heschel continues, echoing the tone of Wiesel's description of Israel's miraculous victory and the forces of Jewish history behind it. "I did not enter on my own the city of Jerusalem," Heschel writes. "Streams of endless craving, clinging, dreaming, flowing day and night, midnights, years, decades, centuries, millennia, streams of tears, pledging, waiting—from all over the world, from all corners of the earth—carried us of this generation to the Wall. My ancestors could only dream of you—to my people in Auschwitz you were more remote than the moon, and I can touch your stones! Am I worthy? How shall I ever repay for these moments?"[35]

For Heschel, Jerusalem represents an "inner force." He feels that force emanating from Jerusalem itself. "Is Jerusalem higher than the road I walk on? Does she hover in the air above me?" Heschel asks. "No, in Jerusalem past is present, and heaven is almost here. For an instant I am near to Hillel, who is close by. All of our history is within reach." Though that joyous exclamation is filled with lament of the Holocaust dead, Heschel resonates with a sense of expectation that has finally arrived.[36]

Almost alone among those who have written on the Holocaust from a theological perspective, Heschel is explicit about God's return in the 1967 war. Or rather, he is the one most explicit about God and the war. Perhaps since Heschel wrote little about God in the Holocaust, laying the responsibility for the destruction of European Jewry at the hands of human beings cut off from God and their consciences, it was easier for him to simply state God's active presence in Israel's war:

We have arrived at the beginning; the night often looked interminable. Amalek was Führer, and Haman prevailed. For centuries we would tear our garments whenever we came into sight of your ruins. In 1945 our souls were ruins, and our garments were tatters. There was nothing to tear. In Auschwitz and Dachau, in Bergen-Belsen and Treblinka, they prayed at the end of Atonement Day, "Next year in Jerusalem." The next day they were asphyxiated in gas chambers. Those of us who were not asphyxiated continued to cling to Thee. "Though they slay me, yet I will trust in Him" (Job 13:15). We come to you, Jerusalem, to build your ruins, to mend our souls and seek comfort for God and men.[37]

Heschel's rhetoric soars. He reads like a biblical text in modern times. Though Heschel is poetic in his description of Jerusalem, he was also, along with Buber and Hannah Arendt, the most analytical of the Jewish religious thinkers on the subject of Israel. As he waxed eloquently on what Jerusalem means to Jewish history, his conscience was also awakened to the plight of the Palestinian Arabs. At least he affirms their presence and some of their needs. Obviously Buber affirmed this presence long before Heschel and in his own way, but because Buber died in 1965, we do not know how he would have reacted to the 1967 war.

Though sometimes analytical, Heschel sees matters almost exclusively from the Jewish perspective, which is where most of the Jewish community was at the time. In some ways even after these many years, Heschel's view of Israeli and Arab history remains the normative view of the American Jewish community. Strange, though, that missing in Heschel's view on Israel is his sweeping and subversive insight that he applied to Jewish spiritual life.

Could Heschel, who accused religious thinkers of the sin of being pedestrian rather than deep and challenging, have succumbed to that same sin when analyzing the state of Israel? It is important to remember, however, that for some parts of the Jewish community his hopes for the Middle East were ahead of his time. Perhaps he was even further ahead but held his tongue so as not to scandalize the community or air Israel's dirty laundry to the outside world.

Susannah Heschel recalls that "contrary to the claims of some of his critics, my father's Zionist writings did not begin in 1967, nor was his commitment to Israel mitigated by his depiction of Judaism as a religion concerned with holiness in time." Moreover, in his earlier writings Heschel warned that neither statehood nor cultural nationalism could become a substitute for the religious teachings of Judaism. As she writes: "He presented these views in the United States and in Israel, often at Zionist conventions, where he warned that simply living in the state of Israel was no panacea for resolving issues of Jewish identity."[38]

It is worth spending time on Heschel's analysis, keeping in mind as well that his most prolific writing on Israel's situation in the world appears in the same book with his lyrical expressions of Jerusalem's overwhelming beauty and as the place of Jewish destiny. Heschel kept both the lyrical and analytical together in his own mind and theology, which would become more difficult if not impossible over the years. If Heschel had lived into the 1980s and beyond, I wonder if he would have lost the ability to hold these views together.

Heschel begins his chapter "Jews, Christians, and Arabs" by demarcating two different strands that shaped Jewish thinking through the ages. The first is the rational that is historical and realistic, stressing the concrete aspects of life with human values and the natural order of things. The second strand is the prophetic or apocalyptic, which from the point of view of the transcendent is concerned with supernatural events that seem miraculous and paradoxical.

According to Heschel, combining these ways of thinking leads to a messianic and prophetic sensibility within Judaism that allows the supernatural to be joined with the historical and political. Though there is an obvious tension between the two realms, he believes that this tension is productive. By maintaining the tension, Jews are able to operate on multiple levels of life and faith simultaneously, without one realm overwhelming the other. For Heschel, counterpoising the historical and political with the supernatural could overpower our reason or leave us with reason alone. As human beings and as Jews we need both the heavenly and earthly.

After Israel's victory in the 1967 war, there was much discussion about these issues. This included the possibility that Israel's victory and the retaking of Jerusalem signaled the arrival of Messianic times. Rubenstein was explicit that the 1967 war was no "royal road back to the God of History." Wiesel is evocative words on Israel's victory stopped short of naming God in the process. Fackenheim's 614th commandment came from voices emanating from the Holocaust rather than God. Since Heschel had never lost God, it was perhaps inevitable that Heschel would see God's hand in Israel's victory.

The early chapters of Heschel's book come very close to verifying that a new era had come into being. There is a messianic thrust in his writing. At the same time, however, Heschel cautions against this very thinking. At least he wants to hold the messianic in check. "A central concern in Jewish thinking is to overcome the tendency to see the world in one dimension, from one perspective, to reduce history exclusively to God's actions or to man's actions, either to grace or to man's initiative," Heschel writes. "The marvelous and the mundane, the sacred and the secular, are not mutually exclusive, nor are the natural and the supernatural, the temporal and the eternal, kept apart. The heart of the relationship of God and man is reciprocity, interdependence. The task is to humanize the sacred and to sanctify the secular." Heschel cautions further that the "spiritual without the political is blind, the political without the spiritual is deaf."[39]

Heschel then traces Christian and Muslim historical understandings of the meaning of a possible return of Jews to Jerusalem. This section is short and serves to set up his main argument, the irresponsible rejection of the state of Israel by Palestinian Arabs and Arab nations. Heschel begins with the complexities of Israel for Jews. For him there was a divine hand in the formation of Israel and its victory in the 1967 war, but this is complicated by what is involved in governing a state and conducting wars. Euphoria should not disguise the hard work that lies ahead: "The Lord of history has always placed us in predicaments, and this seems to be part of our destiny, never to relax in complacency, but to face difficult tasks, to live by the challenge. In this world there is no gem which is not in need of refinement, no wheat without chaff, no vineyard without weeds, no roses without thorns. Light and shadow are mingled. The joy and exaltation that comes from Israel reborn are mixed with pain and chagrin over the suffering and bitterness that are found in the Middle East today." As Jews celebrate there is much work ahead.[40]

Heschel cautions Jews against a premature sense of Israel's victory ushering in Messianic times, since history always presents new challenges. What seems like divine intervention and the unfolding of a divine plan needs probing thought. Heschel begins this probing by citing the need for Arabs, especially their leaders, to rethink their hostility to the Jewish state: "The return of the Jewish people to the land of Israel which was first welcomed by Arabs living in the land has, under the influence of reckless leaders, become a bone of bitter contention. At the beginning, many Arabs correctly realized that in the millions of square miles in the Middle East there was ample room for Jewish and Arab nationalism to grow in harmony in the process of achieving self-determination. The clash which subsequently occurred was due to the extremist character of Arab nationalism, a condition that continues to exist." Heschel's sense of Arab rejectionism is strong:

> The thing that separates us from the Arabs is the claim of two per cent of the area of the Middle East, while the values and interests that unite us comprise 90 per cent of our personal and social being. As a result, efforts to bring about a reconciliation between Jews and Arabs, to bring about good will and readiness to cooperate by asking Arab consent to a bi-national state in Palestine, have found no response on the part of Arab leaders. On the contrary, Jewish settlements were menaced with terror. And the intransience of Arab leaders did not abate.[41]

Heschel follows with a rendition of the historical conflict between Jews and Arabs in Palestine that remains normative in the Jewish world. He believed that the Jewish settlers in Palestine wanted coexistence with the Arabs of Palestine from the beginning but that Arab leaders rejected it for their own political reasons. As the 1948 war for Israel's independence proceeded and Arabs streamed out of Palestine, Heschel claims that the Palestinian Arab flight was inspired and encouraged by Arab leaders while Jewish leaders "did what they could to arrest this exodus." Then after the creation of the state of Israel, Arab armies invaded, seeking Israel's destruction. Heschel believes that the Palestinian Arab refugee crisis was created by the Arab governments "out of this design" and the Palestinian Arab refugees are a "victim of a barren policy" conceived by their own leaders. Heschel concludes that had there been no wars against Israel "there would not be a single Arab refugee today" and that once the refugee crisis was created Arab governments have "used the Arab refugee as a prime political weapon in the campaign against Israel." As well, "every proposal for the absorption and rehabilitation—and there have been many—has been killed so as to guarantee that the refugee problem should live on, endlessly, as a tool of propaganda and hatred."[42]

At no time in Heschel's writing is there a sense that Jewish settlers in Palestine might have been seen as a legitimate threat to Palestinian Arab leadership on a purely political level. Nor does he ponder how Arab nationalism in Palestine might have seemed as important to Palestinian Arabs as the creation of Israel was to Jews. Also, it seems that Heschel cannot envision ordinary Palestinian Arabs feeling threatened by increasing numbers of Jewish settlers.

In Heschel's view, Israel is part of a specific Jewish destiny. At the same time, he is unaware of any specific destiny Palestinians might have for themselves. It is as if Palestinian Arabs and indeed the Arab world simply exists, living better or worse, almost without a history they can access and champion. Jews have a destiny already foretold in ancient times. Palestinians can live anywhere in the Arab world.

Heschel recounts the numbers of Jews who left or were forced out of Arab countries in the tumult surrounding the founding of Israel. He estimates that the number of Jews were roughly the same as the number of Palestinian Arabs who departed from what became Israel. Calling this a "legitimate population exchange," Heschel cites what he considers to be the difference: "The major difference—and a very material one—is that . . . the Jews who came to Israel were totally and constructively absorbed into the country, the financial burden being borne mainly by the state of Israel and the Jewish people. In the case of the Arab refugees, however, a strict policy designed to keep them uprooted has been pursued, with the inevitable result that they have remained an object of international charity, the burden falling upon the United Nations and the international relief agencies. The plight of these refugees has been turned by Arab propaganda into a great international issue, while the outside world has hardly become aware of the mass exodus of Jews from Arab countries." Despite all of this, Heschel believes that the "Jewish people of Israel as well as Jews everywhere are most eager to contribute generously toward a just and charitable solution to this human tragedy."[43]

Heschel clearly is aware of the emerging criticism of Israel that will amplify in the years ahead. As an avid supporter of Israel, he is supportive of Israel's history and morality. Voicing this support, his main audiences are Jews in America and Christians in Europe and America. He also predicts that the road ahead will be rocky, though primarily because of what he considers to be Arab intransigence, again, mostly among the leaders of Arab nations. While for Heschel Israel is primarily a spiritual reality, the Arab world is defined by corrupt politics that keep their people enslaved.

Heschel echoes other Jewish commentators at the time with his belief that Arab leaders are keeping their people poor and backward. Further, he believes that Israel and the Jews within it are poised to help the Middle East emerge from backwardness and help usher them into modernity. Thus, Heschel writes of Israel reborn as a "blessing to the Arab world, to play a major role in their renaissance." As Heschel sees it, "The Jews of Israel are not an outpost of any foreign domination. Their ambition is to integrate themselves into the modern structure of reviving Asia. At the same time, they are anxious to make their contribution to the great bridge-building between modern Asia and the rest of the world. They claim what is the natural right of any people on the face of the earth—that as many of them as possible should live together in their own country, freely develop their civilization, make their contribution to the common stock of humanity, and be self-governing and independent."[44]

On account of their desire to contribute to the Middle East and their natural right to an independent existence in their land of birth, Heschel concludes that there is "no greater fallacy than to regard Israel as a 'colonial' phenomenon":

> No state in the world expresses the concept of nationhood more intensely than Israel. It is the only state which bears the same name, speaks the same tongue, upholds the same faith, inhabits the same land as it did 3,000 years ago. Recently a group of young Israelis near the Dead Sea came across some parchment scrolls written 1900 years ago. They are entirely intelligible to a young citizen of Israel today. Israel is not alien to the Middle East, but an organic part of its texture and memory. The long separation has had less effect on the region's history than the original birth and the modern renewal. Take Israel and all that has emanated from Israel out of Middle Eastern history—and you evacuate that history of its central experience. Arab political and intellectual leaders have never made a serious effort to understand, even in reluctant mood, the tenacity, depth, and authenticity of Israel as a national reality with deep roots in the Middle East.[45]

Here Heschel responds to a criticism within the Arab world and much of the third world. He also anticipates a criticism that spread to some in Europe and the United States as the twenty-first century dawned. From the creation of Israel and then with its expansion over the years, there have been questions about Israel's Western orientation and support and how this mirrored other colonial projects in history. Israel was founded at the time that the third world was throwing off its colonial past. Countries that had colonial outposts were reassessing their own history. For Heschel, Israel's Jewishness trumps that charge. Should he have expected Palestinian Arabs and other Arabs to accept his Jewish trump card?

With long roots in the Middle East and with the talents of the Jewish people, Heschel thought that the possibilities of a political and economic renaissance were at hand. Heschel is quite detailed about this renaissance: improvements in transportation by air and sea, agricultural and industrial development, advances in education and health, increasing water resources through desalination processes, the conquest of tropical diseases, and the sharing of knowledge and experience. Also, a peaceful and cooperative Middle East would attract tourists and pilgrims in an area rich in natural beauty and spiritual history.

Heschel concludes his chapter on this element of hope with a warning. If the Arab world does not reframe its hostility toward Israel, they will remain prisoners of their own making. Their "blind hatred" prison is self-defeating. Arabs themselves need to become aware that their "intransigence is responsible for the continuation of suffering and terror." Jews on the other hand must be vigilant. Though the tradition of Jewish-Arab cooperation is "ancient and rich," Israel will remain with or without Arab approval: "We have a right to demand, 'Love thy neighbor as thyself.' We have no right to demand, 'Love thy neighbor and kill thyself.' No moral teacher has ever asserted, 'If one stands with a knife threatening to kill you, bare your heart for him to murder you.' There is no moral justification for self-destruction."[46]

Again, Heschel asks the Jewish question about the state of Israel. Surely he is correct that no moral teacher teaches that love of neighbor means self-destruction. Yet Heschel does not apply this to Palestinian Arabs who have lost their homeland in the creation of Israel. He does not ask whether Jews, even after the Holocaust, can demand that the need for Jewish land take precedence over the Palestinian loss of land. Nowhere in Heschel's writings are Palestinians allowed to make their own demands.

Heschel ends his book by returning to the glory of Jerusalem and the revival of a Jewish nation in Israel. As a refugee from the Nazi period and having lost his immediate family in the Holocaust, Heschel reiterates what it felt like for him in the days leading up to the 1967 war. "*Terror* and *dread* fell upon Jews everywhere. *Will God permit our people to perish*? Will there be another Auschwitz, another Dachau, another Treblinka?" Heschel continues: "The darkness of Auschwitz is still upon us, its memory is a torment forever. In the midst of that thick darkness there is one gleam of light: the return of our people to Zion. Will He permit this gleam to be smothered?" Comparing the days before and during the war to the Day of Atonement when Jews wait for God to decide their fate, Heschel reverses this power of judgment and declares: "Some of us felt that these were days of judgment for the Holy One of Israel. Will He desert us? Will He hide His face again?" The pressure worked both ways, and perhaps out of defiance to God, if Israel should lose the war and be destroyed, Heschel and some of his friends maintained that they would commit suicide.[47]

There are lessons for Jews in relation to Israel's victory in and after the war. Heschel believes one of the lessons is that "Auschwitz is in our veins. It burns in our imagination. It trembles in our conscience. We, the generation that witnessed the holocaust, should stand by calmly while rulers proclaim their intention to bring about a new holocaust?" Another lesson is gratitude, which should be expressed to fellow Jews and to God. The God who hid himself during the Holocaust "went forth from His place of hiding." Just as there should be no apologies from Jews about their support for the state of Israel, neither should there be an apology from God: "Must God apologize for His audacity in performing wonders in 1967?"[48]

Heschel believes that amidst the celebration there has to be soul searching among Jews who previously have taken Israel for granted. Heschel asks what part Israel played in the daily life of the Jews outside the land before the 1967 war: "It was a footnote to one's existence enjoyed as a fringe benefit, a nice addendum, a side dish, a source of self-congratulation and pride. Israel was a place to visit, a place of pleasure and tourism, not a challenge, not a voice demanding meditation, not an urging for spiritual renewal, for moral re-examination. We have been occupied with many vitally important issues. We disregarded the challenge of Israel. We have failed to clarify its meaning, its value to our existence." Heschel continues as to what is necessary now that the importance of Israel has been clarified: "One of the great insights learned from the great crisis of May, 1967, is the deep personal involvement of every Jew in the existence of Israel. It is not a matter of philanthropy or general charity but of spiritual identification. It is such personal relationship to Israel upon which one's dignity as a Jew is articulated."[49]

This personal involvement and spiritual identification with Israel soon becomes central to Jewish identity. In some ways, Heschel is articulating what many Jews had begun to feel. Yet one wonders if Heschel has left behind the tension between the supernatural and the political/historical. Has he opted for the supernatural without the political/historical? Or has he defined the political/historical in such a way that the tension with the supernatural is already resolved?

The political/historical is in tension with the supernatural when it has a critical edge, when it asks hard questions. The messianic is tamed or at least doubted when the political/historical rendering of the past and present involves a variety of analytical angles. Sometimes this includes the underlying propositions of how we view history and the political. If everything in those realms leads up to the creation of the state of Israel and its victory in the 1967 war, then the backing of the supernatural seals the deal. Or has the political/historical already been predetermined by the supernatural?

In Heschel's writing there seems to be a lacuna in relation to critical thought. At the outset, it would seem necessary to listen to and take seriously what the Palestinian Arabs feel about the supernatural and the political/historical as they articulate this, believing that they feel, suffer, and hope as deeply as do Jews. This might have helped Heschel see the task before Jews and Israel differently.

Without doubt, the 1967 war was a moment of clarification about the importance of Israel. But important to whom? Obviously, Israel was always important to Jewish Israelis living there. Israelis have an existential relation to the land in which they live, and wars for their survival are dealt with like any other nation. Yet, Heschel's audience is primarily American Jews. He articulates the need for Jews to develop a similar existential connection with Israel, especially when Israel is under duress. The euphoria must engrave this existential connection into the heart of every Jew outside of Israel because Jews now realize that Jewish history after the Holocaust is intrinsically bound up with Israel. Yet Heschel's analysis, though heavily theological and politically and historically detailed, is decidedly one-sided. Not only is the story told primarily from the Jewish side, neglecting or speaking with prejudice against the Arab side, but the Jewish side of the question is selective and often narrow.

Heschel is strong on the Holocaust. However, he says little about Zionism or the historical debates within the Zionist movement. When he mentions bi-nationalism he does so without historical context; it is only to show that the Arabs did not want to live with Jews. Nowhere does Heschel write about the forces of state Zionism that overpowered the bi-nationalist movement within the Jewish political realm.

Heschel is also silent about non-Zionist and anti-Zionist movements within the Jewish world, and about those Jews who did see Israel as a colonial enterprise. In short, Heschel leaves out the forces within the Jewish world that might also help Jews understand the road ahead in a diverse and challenging way.

In the future, and after Heschel's death, a strong challenge came from within the Jewish world. During these years Israel developed settlements in the territories that Israel occupied after the 1967 war, thereby continually expanding its territory at the expense of Palestinians. Israel invaded and occupied parts of Lebanon in the 1980s and, a few years later, crushed the Palestinian uprising that sought to establish a Palestinian state alongside Israel. Where would Heschel have stood on these events?

What would Heschel have thought of Israel's re-invasion of Lebanon in 2006 and Gaza in 2008? Would he have held to the majority Jewish position, at least in public? If the policies that Israel followed bothered his conscience would he have spoken out, fulfilling his penchant for speaking his mind? Or would he have remained silent, knowing that speaking out might forever damage his reputation in the Jewish world?

It could be that voices such as Heschel's might have turned the tide in the Jewish world, forcing even the state of Israel to change course. Yet if he had spoken out and been rejected for it, his mourning over Jewish life would have deepened. For someone who had experienced the Holocaust on such an intimate level and survived, this might have been the final heartbreak. Heschel's death in 1972 may have saved him from another reckoning that was too painful even to contemplate.

Praying with My Feet

As we have seen, Buber was a bridge for Jews on the cusp of modernity. So was Heschel. The bridge to modernity was interrupted by the Nazis or, if we follow Rubenstein's analysis, the Nazis were thoroughly modern in how they pursued and carried out mass death. Jews, then, most intensively experienced the two sides of modernity, progress and mass death. On the one hand, Jews embraced secular modernity's promise to become free of a restrictive and discriminatory Christianity and thus full and equal citizens in the societies in which they lived. On the other, Jews suffered from the power of modernity to exclude, dislocate, and murder. Even with this divided record, after the Holocaust Jews re-embraced modernity.

With Buber's and Heschel's attempts to develop a modern form of Judaism, we are left to ask whether their project was as naïve as the initial Jews' embrace of all things modern. Though the Holocaust interrupted Jewish participation in modern life, Jews who survived the Holocaust once again embraced modernity. Jews have taken up their role as advance agents of the modern world and flourish within it. Clearly, there is no way back to the worlds from which Heschel and Buber came. Regardless, religious or other attempts to embrace the pre-modern are done from a modern vantage point. Even Orthodox Judaism, which pretends to be anti-modern, is a modern response to a secularizing world.

Heschel was emblematic of the tensions Jews experienced in modernity. With his traditional background, like Buber, he pursued advanced degrees in secular higher education. His post-Holocaust life was lived in New York City, the engine of modernity in the United States and the powerful engine of modernization worldwide.

Heschel's background and experience may have prepared him to help his fellow Jews think through the modern project, especially in the realm of spirituality. He was a curious mix of both traditional and modern. He knew that there was no turning back the clock of the modern world and that the question was what Jews would make of modernity for themselves and with others.

In some ways, the questions Heschel faced remain. Will modernity's assumptions about life, especially in splitting the traditional bonds of faith and community and its proclivity toward unbridled and unethical power, move forward without reckoning with those dislocated and oppressed by modernity? Or will Jews, in concert with others, embrace the promise of modernity critically, thus infusing modernity with a justice that brings its power to a moral and ethical accountability?

Heschel became known in America as a proponent of social justice and an advocate for the oppressed. He saw action for justice as the Jewish vocation within modern society. He supported and marched with Martin Luther King Jr. and protested against the war in Vietnam through his participation in interfaith conferences and organizations opposed to the war.

Heschel's theological understandings supported such actions. Instead of a post-Holocaust retreat into Jewish particularity over against others or a Jewish particularity that trumped the universal thrust of Jewishness and Judaism, Heschel argued for a Jewish particularity with universal implications. He recognized that modernity could be called to account only through the mobilization of Jewish particularity in concert with the particularity of other communities. To some extent, he foresaw and experienced the coming exile of Jews and others of conscience from their own religious communities. I wonder if he also knew that his attempt to infuse Jewish tradition into a modern setting was failing and destined to fail in the future.

In his lifetime, the Jewish community and others were embracing the modern project as the new and most powerful religion of all. In that embrace, the critical element so important to keeping modern life honest went missing. Heschel was strongly against this uncritical embrace. He could be scathing in his critique in large public events of Jewish organizations. In 1965 Heschel spoke forthrightly to a general assembly of the Council of Jewish Federations and Welfare Funds:

> Our institutions maintain too many beauty parlors. Our people need a language and we offer them cosmetics. Our people need style, learning, conviction, exaltation, and we are concerned about not being admitted to certain country clubs.
>
> To paraphrase the words of the prophet Isaiah: What to me is the multitude of your organizations? says the Lord. I have had enough of your vicarious loyalty. Bring no more vain offerings; generosity without wisdom is an evasion, an alibi for conscience.
>
> We are ingenuous in fund-raising, which is good; we are shipwrecked in raising our children, which is tragic. We give of our wealth to many good causes; we lose our substance in abandoning our children

to fetishism. I wish we could give priority to teaching and inspiring our children to live as Jews.

We may claim to be a success, but in the eyes of Jewish history, we may be regarded as a failure.[50]

Heschel's biting rhetoric is beyond the polite criticism that is sometimes encouraged by the organizers of formal events. He doesn't disguise his disdain for American Jewish leadership or American Jewish life itself. "Our community is in spiritual distress, and some of our organizations are too concerned with digits. Our disease is loss of character and commitment, and the cure of our plight cannot be derived from charts and diagrams." Heschel then circles back to how the affluence of the Jewish community is embedded in the American dream of affluence: "Judaism is *spiritual effrontery*. The tragedy is that there is disease and starvation all over the world, and we are building more luxurious hotels in Las Vegas. Social dynamics is no substitute for moral responsibility. The most urgent task is to destroy the myth that accumulation of wealth and the achievement of comfort are the chief vocations of man."[51]

Whatever else can be said about Heschel's soaring, almost-messianic rhetoric, here Heschel is in his prophetic mode. To speak to organized Jewry in this way could be received only as a wholesale rebuke to the American Jewish way of life. Yet Heschel seems unaware that his criticism of the failure of American Judaism might be connected with the soon-to-be embrace of Israel by the same Jews he saw as failing in America. Could the embrace of Israel be yet another form of vicarious loyalty?

As Heschel excoriated the Jewish community for its failures he, along with some other Jews, was becoming deeply involved in the civil rights movement. This was the context for his 1963 telegram to President Kennedy:

I LOOK FROWARD TO PRIVILEGE OF BEING PRESENT AT MEETING TOMORROW AT 4 P.M. LIKLIHOOD EXISTS THAT NEGRO PROBLEM WILL BE LIKE THE WEATHER. EVERYBODY TALKS ABOUT IT BUT NOBODY DOES ANYTHING ABOUT IT. PLEASE DEMAND OF RELIGIOUS LEADERS PERSONAL INVOLVMENT NOT JUST SOLEMN DECLARATION. WE FORFEIT THE RIGHT TO WORSHIP GOD AS LONG AS WE CONTINUE TO HUMILIATE THE RIGHT OF NEGROES. CHURCHES SYNAGOGUES HAVE FAILED. THEY MUST REPENT. ASK OF RELIGIOUS LEADERS TO CALL FOR NATIONAL REPENTANCE AND PERSONAL SACRIFICE. LET RELIGIOUS LEADERS DONATE ONE MONTH'S SALARY TOWARD FUND FOR NEGRO HOUSING AND EDUCATION. I PROPOSE THAT YOU MR. PRESIDENT DECLARE STATE OF EMERGENCY. A

MARSHALL PLAN FOR AID TO NEGROES IS BECOMING A NECES-
SITY. THE HOUR CALLS FOR HIGH MORAL GRANDEUR AND
SPIRITUAL AUDACITY.[52]

Heschel had just met King at the National Conference on Religion and
Race sponsored by the National Conference of Christians and Jews. In his initial keynote, Heschel denounced racism and the morality that allowed it. A key
sentence of Heschel's written speech, "Racial or religious bigotry must be recognized for what it is: atheism," was changed as he orally delivered his speech
to "Racial or religious bigotry must be recognized for what it is: Satanism, a
blasphemy." In the heated atmosphere, Heschel thought that injustice was less
a product of disbelief than it was product of perverted belief. Heschel then recognized the "Negro problem" as "God's gift to America" and as a "magnificent
spiritual opportunity" to test the integrity of the nation." Heschel wondered
whether the nation would rise to the occasion.[53]

Heschel and King became good friends and colleagues. They shared a
similar understanding of the Bible, and their life experiences of discrimination
and the struggle against injustice infused both of their lives. Both had come
from respected and important religious families. The conference was a success and was featured in *Time* magazine, which praised Heschel as "one of the
most illustrious Jewish theologians" and as a "mordant critic of religious ineffectiveness of U.S. race questions." *Time* characterized his conference address
as "prophet-like." [54]

Heschel went on the offensive, speaking at different venues around the
country on behalf of civil rights. Soon he was marching with King and others
from Selma to Montgomery. Heschel was in the front of the march, as King
himself suggested. There were fears for everyone's safety, including Heschel's.
Along with racial bigotry, those who opposed the march also expressed a bitter anti-Semitism. Hostile police were everywhere and the FBI, having tracked
King for years, was also tracking Heschel. Heschel was emboldened. In a private
memorandum to King after the march, Heschel wrote about "having walked
with Hasidic rabbis on various occasions. I felt a sense of the Holy in what I
was doing. . . . Even without words our March was worship. I felt my legs were
praying."[55]

In 1968 Heschel was honored at the Rabbinical Assembly of the Conservative movement on the occasion of his sixtieth birthday. The honor cited Heschel's
social activism and his contribution to Jewish scholarship. As part of honoring
Heschel, Martin Luther King Jr. was invited to be the keynote speaker at the event.
The rabbis honored King by singing "We Shall Overcome" in Hebrew. After the
song, Heschel introduced King and praised him as a modern prophet: "Where in
America do we hear a voice like the voice of the prophets of Israel? Martin Luther

King is a sign that God has not forsaken the United States of America. God has sent him to us. His presence is the hope of America." King returned the compliment, also referring to Heschel as a prophet and thanking the rabbis for translating the civil rights anthem into the language of the biblical prophets.

Two weeks after King and Heschel saluted each other, King was assassinated in Memphis. Heschel was asked to participate in King's funerals and went to King's house with other national leaders to pay his respects. He attended a morning service at King's Ebenezer Baptist Church and a memorial service at Morehouse College. At the invitation of Coretta Scott King, Heschel selected a passage from the Hebrew Bible he felt described King most profoundly. As a final tribute to King, Heschel read a passage from 2 Isaiah (53:3-5).

> He was despised and rejected by men;
> A man of sorrows, and acquainted with grief;
> And as one from whom men hid their faces
> He was despised, and we esteemed him not.[56]

Heschel's last television interview before his death again featured social justice as foremost in his mind and as the center of Jewish spirituality. When the interviewer asked Heschel why he made Vietnam a religious issue, Heschel responded: "Of course it's a religious issue, for what does God demand of us primarily? Justice and compassion. What does He condemn above all? Murder, killing innocent people. How can I pray when I have on my conscience the awareness that I am co-responsible for the death of innocent people in Vietnam? In a free society, some are guilty, all are responsible.[57]

As the follow-up question, Heschel was asked to comment on a recent trial in Harrisburg, Pennsylvania, where a Catholic priest, Father Daniel Berrigan, along with other priests and nuns were on trial for various protests against the Vietnam War. One after another perspective jurors said they thought it was wrong for clergymen to be involved with politics and that their vocation was to cater to spiritual needs. Heschel responded:

> That's a very good statement. In fact, it's such a good statement that if the prophets were alive, they would already be sent to jail by these jurors. Because the prophets mixed into social-political issues. And, frankly, I would say that God seems to be a non-religious person, because if you read the words of God in the Bible, he always mixes in politics and in social issues.
>
> My Lord, you, God, should worry about spirituality and not about politics and injustice. Do you hear me? Pardon me.
>
> This is precisely what I said before. The prophets are forgotten. No one reads the prophets. They have not touched the mind of America. And

this is why such statements come out. What is the greatest concern in the Bible? Injustice to one's fellow man, bloodshed. What is the greatest dream of the prophets and of the Bible? Peace.

The only men in antiquity—no philosopher anywhere in the world, in India or China, was capable of dreaming even that there would be a time when war would be abolished and there would be peace. This is the message of the prophets.[58]

Here was Heschel's sense of moral grandeur and spiritual audacity in the realm of politics. In Heschel, the Jewish prophetic was a call to conscience. The prophetic was alive and speaking to the modern world. Heschel thought that modernity in its own grandeur and audacity lacked a foundational base for the moral and the spiritual. Only by infusing the ancient into the modern through the Bible and the prophets could modernity be held to account.

For Heschel, modernity was lost in its own theoretical constructs. It had no moral compass. No matter their failures, Judaism and Christianity retained a moral and ethical base. The problem was translation, how the ancient could be brought into the modern without losing its ability to speak truth to power. Though Rubenstein accused Heschel of a religious and cultural nostalgia and felt that Heschel's backward leaning toward an intact religiosity could no longer live after the Holocaust, Heschel was actually forward looking in his religious outlook.

Other Jewish thinkers wanted to bring the ancient into the modern by conforming the modern to the ancient, but Heschel rejected this approach. He understood that the only way the ancient could survive in the modern world was through a justifiable and relevant critique of modern forms of discrimination and modernity's use of unjust power.

Heschel did not call for a return to ancient religiosity. Rather, he attempted to address the deepest calling of humanity to a life of meaning beyond the material. With all its scientific advancement and technological power, Heschel felt that modernity was silent about meaning. This silence created the danger that amidst the tremendous power of modernity, the human heart and hope would be lost. Heschel feared the possibility that without faith as a foundation the world would be seen as absurd. If the world is absurd, why struggle against our own material interests and for others? Why suffer for a cause greater than our self when it would be easier to cause suffering for others?

Heschel believed that this human heart and hope could not be sustained without God as modernity proposed. As we have seen, Heschel proposed deeds infused with the spirituality of justice. The bedrock of deeds was the judgment of God. Without God, modernity had only itself as judge. "The moral imperative was not disclosed for the first time through Abraham or Sinai," Heschel wrote. "The criminality of murder was known to men before; even the institution to rest on the seventh day was, according to tradition, familiar to Jews when still in Egypt. Nor was the idea of divine justice unknown. What was new was the idea that justice is an obligation to God, *His* way not only His demand; that injustice is not only something God scorns when done by others, but that which is the very opposite of God; that the rights of men are not only legally protected interests of society, but the sacred interests of God.[59]

Heschel experienced a massive heart attack in 1969. Despite this, his last years were full of activity. Though he was feted in certain circles, Edward Kaplan feels that Heschel's stance in the Jewish community was eroding. Perhaps Heschel's sense of being in an uphill struggle was playing out. Kaplan describes Heschel's last years this way:

Although prized by activists as a model of piety and biblical dissent and praised in mass circulation magazines like *Time* and *Newsweek*, Heschel endured personal isolation. Some of his Jewish critics believed that he gave himself so fully to interfaith work, the civil rights movement, and the Vietnam protest because they brought him acceptance and admiration from Christians. But vanity had little to do with his engulfing commitments. For the sake of truth and compassion he jeopardized his health, compromised his writing and teaching, and undermined his prestige within the Jewish community, which was turning toward the ideological right. He paid an exorbitant price for maintaining his witness on these several fronts—his untimely death.[60]

Hannah Arendt
(1906–1975)

4

Encountering Jewish Politics

Hannah Arendt

Hannah Arendt was born in 1906 in Hanover, Germany, the only child of secular Jews. In 1922 she began her studies in Classics and Christian theology at the University of Berlin and in 1924 entered Marburg University, where she studied philosophy with Martin Heidegger. She then moved to Heidelberg, where she studied with Karl Jaspers. She wrote her dissertation on St. Auguine's concept of love. With the rise of the Nazis in 1933, Arendt fled to Paris. Following her detention as an "enemy alien," she immigrated to America where, in 1951, she published her now classic The Origins of Totalitarianism. *After a series of positions at American universities, she spent her last years teaching at the New School for Social Research in New York City. In 1961 Arendt traveled to Jerusalem to cover the trial of Adolph Eichmann for the* New Yorker. *Her controversial reporting was later published as* Eichmann in Jerusalem: A Report on the Banality of Evil. *In subsequent years, she also published a number of influential books, among them* On Revolution, Men in Dark Times *and* The Life of the Mind. *Arendt died in 1975.*

When I first probed Hannah Arendt's work, I was trying to find a way beyond the ominous direction in which the state of Israel seemed deeply invested, and was finding little in the contemporary Jewish discussion that was helpful. Reading her, I began to see that there was a history of Jewish dissent within Zionism. Indeed, from the beginning there were Jews who wanted a Jewish homeland in Palestine alongside the Palestinian Arabs. This is also when I discovered

Martin Buber's different take on Zionism. Heschel briefly alluded to this desire for accommodation with the Palestinian Arabs before Israel was created but then dismissed it as a Jewish dream the Palestinian Arabs rejected.

After reading Buber and Arendt, I found Abraham Joshua Heschel's brief rejection of homeland Zionism misplaced. In reading Buber and Arendt, I found a different historical account, and some possibilities for the Jewish future.

Obviously, Jews and Palestinians are not going to return to pre-state days. It is doubtful that Palestine is going to be resurrected as a bi-national state where Jews and Arabs live in harmony. Yet the present state of affairs is impossible to maintain. Year after year there is settlement after settlement, uprising after uprising, war after war. There seems no end to the cycle of violence and atrocity between Jews and Palestinians.

When Heschel spoke of a "beauty parlor" kind of Judaism or the claim of American Jews being a success—though in the "eyes of Jewish history regarded as a failure"—I couldn't help but fast forward to the decades that followed. Heschel gave his address in 1965, the year when I became a Bar Mitzvah. Everything he said was part of my own experience as a young Jew. Yet now, the generation that was being educated during the time he spoke is being confronted with the same judgment.

What would Heschel say now about how we are educating Jewish youth? What kind of example are we setting? Where have we put everything on the line and where have we been silent? Would Heschel today speak of Israel as American Jewry's new "beauty parlor"? Or would he say that Jews have substituted a Settler Judaism for a Judaism that should be a spiritual effrontery?

Like Heschel, Hannah Arendt was an affront to many Jews. Despite her secularity, or maybe because of it, there are references to and echoes of Arendt throughout Richard Rubenstein's reflections on the Holocaust. Despite her refusal to address the religious elements of the Holocaust, and even warning against it, Arendt shadowed the discussion of the Holocaust from its inception. Could her atheological understanding of the mass murder of Europe's Jews help all of us with the question of God—*after*?

In 2008 I held a conference to celebrate the centenary of Arendt's birth. The conference was electric, with Jewish scholars discussing Arendt's contributions to philosophy and related disciplines. Like Buber and Heschel, Arendt was unrestricted by academic disciplines. She wrote on whatever she felt important, often crossing disciplines to do so.

As with Buber and Heschel, Arendt's academic pedigree was European and, like them, she suddenly found herself a refugee in a foreign cultural and linguistic environment. It is remarkable how easily all three adapted to their new environment and language.

Remembering that Rubenstein had addressed a similar centenary conference in honor of Martin Buber in 1978, I invited him to address the Arendt conference. As usual, his lecture was probing. It brought back memories of his lecture at the Buber centenary conference thirty years earlier.

Buber and Arendt opposed a Jewish state because they knew where nation-states led. What witness could the Jewish homeland have to Jews around the world and the broader global community if every resource to build the homeland was used to maintain a nation-state? Again with Arendt, Buber thought that the creation of a Jewish state in the Middle East would be seen—correctly—as, among other things, a colonial venture. Buber's Jewish spirituality could not thrive in such a colonial context. The Jews of Europe suffered from an internal European colonialism for more than a thousand years.

Rubenstein found flaws in Buber's commentary on the trial of Adolph Eichmann. Eichmann was the Nazi bureaucrat whose primary task was to organize the destruction of European Jewry. At the end of the war, Eichmann evaded capture and escaped to Argentina. In 1960 Eichmann was kidnapped by Israeli operatives and placed on trial in Israel for facilitating millions of Jewish deaths during the Holocaust.

The trial gained international attention. It was a compelling drama of a Nazi being tried in a court of law. That the court trying a Nazi war criminal was in the state of Israel highlighted the drama, as was the fact that Eichmann had been kidnapped by Israeli agents. This was the most high profile trial of a Nazi since the Nuremburg Trials. Eichmann was being tried for his role in the final solution of the Jewish "question" in Europe. Few trials captured international attention in the pre-Internet age. The Eichmann trial was one that did.

Rubenstein found Buber's opinion that Eichmann had committed crimes against humanity, rather than against the Jewish people, to be superficial. He criticized Buber's assertion that an international rather than an Israeli court should have been the forum for Eichmann's trial. Rubenstein was also troubled by Buber's stance against the execution of Eichmann. He did agree with Buber that a far worse punishment for Eichmann would be forcing him to live the rest of his life within Israel, after his own failure to eliminate Jews from the earth.

Buber was strong on the issue of state-sponsored execution in a Jewish state. This became such a public issue that when Eichmann's death sentence was announced, Buber called and requested a meeting with Israel's first prime minister, David Ben-Gurion. Buber reiterated his opposition to capital punishment and proposed that Eichmann be forced to work the land on a kibbutz in Israel. In this way, Eichmann would experience concretely his failure in annihilating the Jewish people. Buber considered executing Eichmann to be "too facile and commonplace a way out of this unique dilemma." Buber was also worried about

making Eichmann a martyr for German youth who had enough trouble dealing with the history they inherited and were working toward a humanism that
would decry the Nazi past. Buber believed that no punishment fit Eichmann's
crime. As he remarked after Eichmann's execution, "for such crimes there are
no penalties." He continued saying that the "death sentence has not diminished
crime. . . . Killing awakens killing."[1]

Rubenstein disagreed with Buber for reasons related to political power and
the state. Buber did not believe that the victims of the Holocaust should be
the judges of those who perpetrated it. Could they really be objective and fair-
minded? Rubenstein countered that the Eichmann trial provided the first time
in two thousand years where those who committed crimes against Jews could
be tried in a state where Jews held power.

Rubenstein also disagreed with Buber's opposition to the death penalty in
general. As difficult a decision as it is to sentence a person to death, the state
holds that right as part of its monopoly of power and its mandate to protect
its citizens. If Jews have a state, Rubenstein thought that the same rights and
obligations had to exist there. If a Jewish state could not try and punish those
who committed crimes against its own community, even unto death, then how
could having their own state change the vulnerable Jewish condition to one of
strength? In his lecture honoring Buber, Rubenstein stated it this way:

> The state was founded largely because of the terrible lessons to be drawn
> from the experience of Eichmann's victims, but it itself was no victim. On
> the contrary, the purpose of the state was to offer hope that the succes-
> sor community would no longer be the gathering place of future defense-
> less victims. This meant that the state of Israel not only had the right but
> was compelled to acquire and, at times, to employ instruments of coercion
> against both internal and external adversaries. Regrettably, human nature
> is such that this may at times involve war and capital punishment. To assert,
> as did Buber, that the state has no right to take human life is to betray a
> fundamental ignorance of the nature of political sovereignty as well as the
> imperatives confronting a sovereign state. A state founded on law has no
> right *capriciously* to take human life, but to ask that the state uncondition-
> ally forego that right is tantamount to asking for its ultimate dissolution."[2]

Here, the difference between Rubenstein and Buber was in full flower.
Though by this time Buber had accepted that there was a state of Israel, he
continued to try to minimize its state-like quality and maximize what was left
of its homeland sensibility. What for Rubenstein necessitated and characterized
a Jewish state for Buber undermined the very qualities he sought in the Jewish
return to the land. While Rubenstein demanded the ordinary aspects of the

state so that Jews could enjoy its protection, Buber saw the Jewish state as a mistake that might lead to doom.

Judging Eichmann

Along with the 1967 Arab-Israeli war, the Eichmann trial paved the way for the development of Holocaust consciousness. In reflecting on the development of Holocaust Theology in the 1980s, and researching some of the reporting on the Eichmann trail, I found a curious coincidence. Through Rubenstein, I knew that Hannah Arendt had attended and reported on the Eichmann trial. Her reporting, originally published in the *New Yorker* magazine and later as a book, instantly became and remains one of the most controversial commentaries on the Holocaust.

What I did not know was that the then-unknown Elie Wiesel was also at the trial. To support his travel and stay during the trial, Wiesel wrote reports for the *Jewish Daily Forward, Commentary,* and *l'Arche.* He listened for hours to survivors' intense depositions and recalled his own memories and those of other survivors. The trial was traumatic for everyone involved, as people in the audience broke down in tears or seemed dazed. In his autobiography, Wiesel records his impression of Eichmann:

> I could not take my eyes off the defendant, who sat in a glass cage impassively taking notes. He seemed utterly unmoved by the recitation of the crimes against humanity and the Jewish people of which he was accused. He looked like an ordinary man. I was told he ate heartily and slept normally. Considering the crushing pressures, he seemed to bear up well. Neither the prosecutors nor the judges were able to break him.
>
> I thought I remembered him. I knew that he had been in Sighet to supervise the deportation, and I wondered whether he was the man I had seen at the station, visibly saddened because there were no more convoys to send of this town now emptied of its Jews.[3]

In reading what both Wiesel and Arendt were reporting on the trial, I found an immense contrast between their writing. To begin with, Wiesel's poetic and evocative style read like a liturgy of judgment and horror. Arendt's style was analytical and with a biting understatement that seemed sarcastic or indifferent.

Already at the trial, no love was lost between Wiesel and Arendt. In many ways, the relationship between the two anticipated Wiesel's later relationship with Rubenstein. In his memoirs, Wiesel records his impressions of Arendt:

Hannah Arendt was surrounded by her coterie. Many Israeli journalists avoided her, finding her arrogant and condescending. She knew everything before and better than everyone else. I met her only later, at her home, where we discussed her theories of the "banality of evil," which some survivors found simplistic and offensive and which I was invited to refute in print. She greeted me amiably, telling me she had read and liked my work. Was she being sincere or merely courteous? I found her disconcerting and chillingly aloof. How could one delve into the tragedy and still retain that hardness in one's eyes? The question I asked her was simple: "I was there and I don't know. How can you possibly know when you were elsewhere?" Her reply: "You're a novelist; you cling to questions. I deal with human and political sciences. I have no right not to find answers."[4]

One either took to Arendt or resented her. In reading through the various biographies of her life, Wiesel's description of her is often confirmed and often disputed. Everyone who met her knew that she was single-minded. Others who were also single-minded had difficulties with her. Wiesel's impression of Arendt was complicated by the intensity of the personal tragedy that befell him and his family. Yet as a refugee from Nazi Germany, life had not been easy for her either.

The gulf between Wiesel and Arendt was represented by their different understandings of Jewishness and the way they saw the future of Jewish life. Even in this early period, tempers between them flared. Emotions were raw. Throughout his life, Wiesel had trouble with anyone who claimed to know what the Holocaust was about and to be able to define it, which for him ultimately led to the Holocaust being explained and compared to other events. When Arendt referred to Wiesel as a novelist and herself as a human and political scientist, unknowingly she had thrown down the gauntlet. She appeared to be saying that it was she rather than a victim like Wiesel who would arbitrate the history of the Holocaust.

The Eichmann trial was dramatic. It was the first time in almost two thousand years that a criminal charged with crimes against the Jewish people was tried by Jews in a Jewish state. The difference between Wiesel's and Arendt's reporting on the trial was equally dramatic. The emphasis on *banality* in Arendt's writing became as famous and infamous as the content. Wiesel's reporting was virtually unknown at the time and, even to this day, there is little or no reference in the scholarly literature to his presence there.[5]

In his reporting, Wiesel is indignant that there was even a trial for Eichmann, whom Wiesel portrays as a monster. That Israel would provide a lawyer for Eichmann is, for Wiesel, an insult to the dead and survivors of the Holocaust. He imagines that the dead of the Holocaust and the survivors are in the courtroom. They are there to judge Eichmann as only they can. All of the victims of anti-Semitism throughout history are present in the courtroom as well.

For Wiesel and the gathered witnesses, Eichmann deserves only a swift and sure judgment. For such a monster, there should be no attempt to understand, analyze, or provide him with the safeguards of an impartial legal system. As a survivor, Wiesel witnessed the crimes against the Jewish people. As a reporter, he experienced the trial as a prolongation of the Holocaust agony.[6]

Like Wiesel, Arendt was a refugee from Europe, but unlike Wiesel, her imprisonment during the Nazi era was short and her physical suffering limited. Wiesel spent his youthful years in Auschwitz while Arendt escaped to France and then to the United States. As well, Wiesel became a reporter and then a writer of memoirs and fiction. Arendt was trained and functioned as an intellectual.

Arendt's commentary on the trial is the opposite of Wiesel's. Rather than emotional, her commentary is analytical, or as Wiesel and others would say, detached. The guilt of Eichmann is clear to Arendt, yet she questions what in fact he is guilty of and how that relates to the twentieth century and the future of humanity. She also probes the historic responsibility of the Jewish community in Palestine and Jewish leadership in Europe during the Nazi era. Had they done enough for the Jewish community during the Holocaust? Rubenstein's later work is heavily indebted to Arendt on these controversial matters.

Arendt is critical of all parties involved in the Holocaust and the trial. However, she seemed to have little idea of how emotional the subject of Eichmann was for Jews. From Arendt's perspective, she was reporting on a trial that dealt with a history and politics through which she had lived. She did not approach her reporting from the standpoint of being a victim, nor did she cater to the emotions of the victims. Though Arendt heard and sympathized with the victims who testified, she also was certain that emotion obscured the understanding of the Nazis and Eichmann himself. True to her academic training and interests, Arendt wanted to understand what had happened and why. Her concentration on analysis made it difficult for her to hear or report on the more primal aspects of the trial and how they played out in the larger Jewish world.

As Wiesel's strong opinion of Arendt stresses, her focus was divided. History, sociology, and philosophy were as important in her judgments as was her concern for the feelings of traumatized Jews. Arendt resisted the idea that the crimes the Nazis had committed should be seen primarily as against the Jewish people. Theirs were crimes against humanity, even though disproportionately against Jews.

Whereas Wiesel found Eichmann to be a monster, Arendt found him to be shallow, without passion or ideology. In Arendt's view, Eichmann did not murder Jews because of his hatred of them. She even questioned his commitment to Nazi ideology. Instead, Arendt found him to be a functionary, a bureaucratic climber who hoped to advance in the reigning ideological system of his time. She felt that seeing Eichmann as a monster missed the point. It was too simplistic to think that only anti-Semitism drove the Nazis, or that their hate of Jews was the sole reason for the death camps. For Arendt, it was a peculiar combination of ancient prejudice and a thoroughly modern system of totalitarian thought and politics that doomed the Jews of Europe. Added to this was the position of Jews in Europe who were either apolitical, adopted the wrong kind of politics, or were unable to create a politics that addressed their situation. This combination rendered Jews as easy targets in a world that defined Jews as outsiders and as superfluous to the coming Nazi world order.

Wiesel saw Eichmann and the Nazis as committing crimes of passion. Arendt saw Eichmann and the Nazis as committing crimes of logic. For Wiesel, Eichmann was a monster, for Arendt, a bureaucrat. However, Arendt upped the ante by suggesting that the extensive Nazi crimes of logic could not have taken place without the complicity of Jewish leadership. Without a compliant and failed political Jewish leadership, Arendt concluded that the Holocaust, at least in the extent that it occurred, would not have taken place.

The idea of Jewish complicity was another extremely complicated and controversial understanding that characterizes Arendt's analysis and, again, from which Rubenstein later draws. According to Arendt, the *Judenrat* (Jewish Councils) helped organize the ghettoized Jewish communities of Eastern Europe and therefore unintentionally contributed to the organizational apparatus that led Jews to their death. This was a controversial and provocative understanding. It was very far from Wiesel's sense that even a trial was too good for a Jew-hater and Jew-murderer.

Could it be, as Arendt thought, that Jews were caught up in a nightmare that ensnared them, as it had others, and could happen again to non-Jews? Such an analysis could be argued and disputed. Yet more was at stake. Many Jews felt that the Nazis targeted Jews solely because of anti-Semitism and that for this reason the Holocaust was unique. If Eichmann was not a monster, a Jew-hater of unparalleled proportions, then the issue shifted to the terror of totalitarianism, a near universal phenomenon. If the Holocaust was discussed in this way, where did this leave Jews and Jewish history? Could anti-Semitism be subsumed under totalitarianism?

Beyond their personal disagreements, Wiesel's and Arendt's differing interpretations on Eichmann anticipated later divisions in the Jewish community over the meaning of the Holocaust for the Jewish future. By the time of Arendt's death, Wiesel's views had won the day. Rubenstein carried Arendt's views as a minority position. If the Nazis were monsters, Jew-hatred would always exist in the world. If the Nazis' modern totalitarian system of domination was and could be applied to other target populations in the future, then anti-Semitism could no longer be highlighted. In sum, the question revolved around whether the Holocaust was about Jews only or about humanity in general.

Regardless of these differences with Wiesel, Arendt sided with Wiesel and Rubenstein on the subject of Eichmann's execution. Eichmann had supported and actively carried out mass murder. Arendt believed that Eichmann must be executed:

> Let us assume, for the sake of argument, that it was nothing more than misfortune that made you a willing instrument in the organization of mass murder: there still remains the fact that you have carried out, and therefore actively supported, a policy of mass murder. And just as you supported and carried out a policy of not wanting to share the earth with the Jewish people and the people of a number of other nations as though you and your superiors had any right to determine who should and who should not inhabit the world—we find that no one, that is, no member of the human race, can be expected to want to share the earth with you. This is the reason, and the only reason, you must hang.[7]

Although in the early 1960s Arendt's reporting was much better known than Wiesel's, the Jewish community ultimately vilified Arendt and followed Wiesel. From the time her first reports on the Eichmann trial appeared, her Jewishness and her love for the Jewish people were questioned. She was demeaned to be a lover of German culture and the Nazis. Like Rubenstein, she was labeled a self-hating Jew.

A milestone in this vilification came from the noted German scholar, Gershom Scholem. A German Jew by birth and a leading scholar on Jewish mysticism, Scholem left Germany for Palestine in the 1920s. Scholem was part of an important German Jewish circle of intellectuals, writers, and artists that included Walter Benjamin.

Scholem begins his letter of response to Arendt by noting the difficulties and complexities inherent in writing about the catastrophe of European Jewry. Yet it seems to him that at each decisive juncture of Arendt's analysis, the weakness of the Jewish people is emphasized. In his mind, her analysis loses objectivity and instead acquires "overtones of malice." In fact, he finds so much malice in Arendt's writing that he is left with a sensation of bitterness toward and shame for Arendt herself. Scholem considers why he should have such feelings:

> In the Jewish tradition there is a concept, hard to define and yet concrete enough, which we know as *Ahabath Israel*, "Love of the Jewish people." In you dear Hannah, as in so many intellectuals who came from the German

left, I find little trace of this. A discussion such as is attempted in your book would seem to me to require . . . the most old-fashioned, the most circumspect, the most exacting treatment possible—precisely because of the feelings aroused by this matter, this matter of the destruction of one-third of our people—and I regard you wholly as a daughter of our people, and in no other way. Thus I have little sympathy for the tone—well expressed by the English word "flippancy"—which you employ so often in the course of your book.[8]

Arendt's response to Scholem is striking:

I found it puzzling that you should write "I regard you wholly as a daughter of our people, and in no other way." The truth is that I have never pretended to be anything else or to be in any way other than I am. . . . I know, of course, that there is a "Jewish problem" even on this level, but it has never been my problem—not even in my childhood. I have always regarded my Jewishness as one of the indisputable factual data of my life, and I have never had the wish to change or disclaim facts of this kind. . . . To be sure, such an attitude is pre-political, but in exceptional circumstances—such as the circumstances of Jewish politics—it is bound to have also political consequences though, as it were, in a negative way. The attitude makes certain types of behavior impossible—indeed precisely those which you chose to read into my consideration.[9]

Much earlier in relation to the question of Palestine, Arendt predicted what she experienced directly in the controversy surrounding her interpretation of Eichmann. The issue would revolve around Jewish unity rather than thought, and a demonstrable commitment to a people rather than rootedness in a people as a platform for free inquiry. In relation to the internal disputes over Palestine and the Jewish settlements that were there prior to the creation of the state of Israel, Arendt wrote of this demand for unanimity:

It would be frivolous to deny the intimate connection between this mood on the part of Jews everywhere and the recent European catastrophe, with the subsequent fantastic injustice and callousness toward the surviving remnant that were so ruthlessly transformed into displaced persons. The result has been an amazing and rapid change in what we call national character. After two thousand years of "Galut mentality," the Jewish people have suddenly ceased to believe in survival as an ultimate good in itself and have gone over in a few years to the opposite extreme. Now Jews believe in fighting at any price and feel that "going down" is a sensible method of politics.

Unanimity of opinion is a very ominous phenomenon, and one characteristic of our modern mass age. It destroys social and personal life, which is based on the fact that we are different by nature and by conviction. To hold different opinions and to be aware that other people think differently on the same issue shields us from a god-like certainty which stops all discussion and reduces social relationships to those of an ant heap. A unanimous public opinion tends to eliminate bodily those who differ, for mass unanimity does not stop at certain well-defined objects, but spreads like an infection into every related issue.[10]

Arendt's Jewishness was judged with regard to both the Holocaust and the state of Israel. In her lifetime, both events would be spoken of in a unified voice, or a unity would be established by defining dissent as being out of bounds, as un-Jewish or even anti-Jewish. But in the 1940s, long before the Eichmann trial and the 1967 Arab-Israeli war, Arendt was already fearful of what the quest for one point of view would mean for individual Jews and the Jewish people.

Arendt asked how individuals and the community could survive and think, even discern the best way to move forward, if thought were censored and motives suspected at every turn. If every dissenting thought could be thought only under the threat of being labeled disloyal, what kind of thought would emerge? Censorship could move in different directions but the least likely was through mature thought and action. Instead, a general bullying would be substituted for critical thought. This attitude would hardly be helpful in creating a thoughtful and discerning Jewish future.

Arendt also thought that the "infection" of unanimity would spread like a disease. If certain issues were considered off-limits, all issues would be tainted. A general thoughtlessness would pervade Jewish life, and this in a tradition that prized itself on critical thought. Soon, censored thought would become an empty and symbolic device, used by the Jewish community to further dampen thought. At some point, what could not be thought would also become unspeakable. Jews would become their own worst enemies.

The Jewish community followed Wiesel's path rather than Arendt's, with ramifications far beyond the Eichmann trial itself. The particular emphasis in the Eichmann trial on crimes committed against the Jewish people resonated in Jewish support for an exclusive Jewish state of Israel. Arendt's bi-nationalism, which she developed before the Eichmann trial, represented her attempt to create a structure where Jews and Arabs could live together in Palestine. Yet an integrative structure for Jews and Arabs in Palestine could make sense only if the universality of Eichmann's crime were recognized. If in the Holocaust only the particularity of crimes against Jews were emphasized, then a more universal settlement of Israel/Palestine could hardly be envisioned. How could Jews live without a state of their own, if anti-Semitism were eternally defining of the Jewish experience?

Arendt did not believe that anti-Semitism was defining or eternal. Rather, she thought of anti-Semitism in a broader array of issues that sometimes came to the fore and other times remained latent. She also felt that Jews had some responsibility in anti-Semitism, primarily by how Jews responded to such sentiments in their cultural and political environment. In short, Arendt criticized the scapegoat theory of anti-Semitism and the doctrine of eternal anti-Semitism. Richard Bernstein, a commentator on Arendt's Jewish thought, describes her position:

> Both types of theory turn away from confronting how modern Jewish history has been entwined with modern European history; they divert us from understanding the specific historical ways in which the Jewish people responded to the concrete situations in which they found themselves. They turn us away from honestly confronting the question of the Jews "share of responsibility."
>
> Arendt is raising the explosive issue of the responsibility (or more accurately, co-responsibility) of the Jewish people for what happened to them. We must be careful not to misinterpret what she is claiming. For the issue is not one of blame, guilt, or even moral responsibility. It is, rather a question of political responsibility: of how Jews have (and have not) responded to the concrete political situations in which they have found themselves.[11]

Arendt was hardly denying the existence of anti-Semitism. The question was how to struggle against anti-Semitism with others who also were struggling for an open and just society. What Arendt wanted was the development of a Jewish politics where Jews would fight for their rights as Jews in a broader polity.

Though a distinct Jewish politics developed in her day, Arendt thought it to be too dependent on the scapegoat and eternal theories of anti-Semitism. In a sense, Jews were practicing a Jewish politics that others had practiced against them. Or at least, Jews were employing the theoretical constructs of others as levers for their own political response. It was as if the Jewish community needed the existence of anti-Semitism to make sense of itself. Arendt thought that these understandings of anti-Semitism almost always missed the real challenges confronting the Jewish people. They were straw concepts rather than real life political challenges.

The rejection of these theories, and her desire for a different kind of Jewish politics, guided Arendt's critique of the general Jewish reaction to Eichmann and what became the normative support for a Jewish state. She felt that both these understandings locked Jews into an embrace of a form of Jewish particularity that was apolitical and defensive. Such an apolitical sense did not explain the challenges facing the Jewish community in the post-Holocaust era. Nor would it help develop the politics that might be needed in the Jewish future. That future could not be determined in advance.

In spite of Rubenstein's devotion to Arendt's work, he came to an opposite conclusion regarding the need for a Jewish state, siding instead with Wiesel, Fackenheim, and Heschel. Arendt thought that anti-Semitism was contextual rather than eternal; it could be struggled against by an intelligent and considered Jewish politics in concert with a broad coalition sharing mutual interests. Rubenstein was pessimistic about this possibility. Though he borrowed freely from Arendt, his sense that modernity was an iron cage forced him to be pessimistic about the limits of moral and ethical action. For Rubenstein, the fate of the Jews was to be singled out.

Already at the Eichmann trial, Arendt's more analytical understanding of Jewish politics was under assault. By the 1967 war, her arguments about the need for Jews in Palestine to coexist with Arabs in a structure that bound their mutual interests in a just and peaceful society were shut down. Over time, the increasing demand for the Jewish character of the state of Israel skewed the politics of Jews in Israel and America in a more tribal, emotional, and religious direction.

Although Rubenstein rarely commented on Arendt's bi-nationalism, he did take up Arendt's analysis of the Holocaust as a thoroughly modern exercise in total domination that would have been impossible without the bureaucracy, social organization, and advanced technology of modern society. These elements of modern society had an ambivalent effect on the world. On the one hand, they were the engines of progress. On the other, they were used to isolate, dislocate, and destroy millions of people. Fewer people were needed to labor and contribute to society, which rendered large segments of the world's population increasingly superfluous. The lesson of the twentieth century was that superfluous populations are relegated to a ghettoized life or eliminated altogether. Progress thus carried within itself the shadow side of mass death.

Rubenstein also appropriated Arendt's idea that it was only the political that guaranteed the rights of the person. Without the political protection of the state, human beings were rendered vulnerable to state power and to whatever force might harm them. This was yet another lesson of the Holocaust that applied to others in the future.

In her book *The Origins of Totalitarianism,* published soon after the Holocaust, Arendt referred to this situation as the "tragedy of our time" where "only the emergence of crimes unknown in quality and proportion and not foreseen by the Ten Commandments made us realize what the mob had known since the beginning of the century; that not only this or that form of government has become antiquated or that certain values and traditions need to be recon-sidered, but that the whole of nearly three thousand years of Western civiliza-tion, as we have known it as a comparatively uninterrupted stream of tradition, has broken down; the whole structure of Western culture with all its implied beliefs, traditions, standards of judgment, has come toppling down over our heads." For Arendt the implications of this were devastating and needed to be reconsidered for the future: "Whether we like or not, we have long ceased to live in a world in which the faith in the Judeo-Christian myth of creation is secure enough to constitute a basis and source of authority for actual laws, and we certainly no longer believe, as the great men of the French Revolution did, in a universal cosmos of which man was a part and whose natural laws he had to imitate and conform to."[12]

Rubenstein's writing on the "functionally Godless world" of modernity is found already in Arendt. Obviously, God and the religions that championed God had failed to protect Jews and others in the twentieth century. But Ruben-stein added, again from Arendt, that the terror of our time was found precisely in the fact that the Enlightenment sensibility there to protect us where God could not had also broken down.

Arendt believed, as does Rubenstein, that only a politics of citizenship and inclusion can provide the protection individuals and communities need in modern mass society. When that protection is lost, Jews and other minorities are threatened with statelessness. Becoming stateless, the populations are then further defined as "superfluous." In the twentieth century, the fate of the state-less is sealed with impoverishment, ghettoization, and death. The twenty-first century seems to be following the same path.[13]

For Arendt, Wiesel's view of the Holocaust and Israel was too religious. Instead, we needed a secular understanding of both. This means that we have to think philosophically and politically without reference to the transcendent. By thinking too religiously, Arendt believed we missed the primary lesson of the twentieth century, that secular and political sensibilities should limit our com-munal and religious loyalties and provide the protection necessary to insure human freedom and survival. For Arendt, the movement toward totality, even with the best of intentions, truncates the more natural plurality of life and attempts to foreclose elements of initiative, surprise, and rebirth that character-izes the human journey.

Not surprisingly, Arendt thought about the search for totality as encom-passing the political and the intellectual. The only way politics could be worthy of its own vocation is to be free and diverse. She considered the engine of poli-tics to be thought and action. Positing events or attitudes as somehow transcen-dental or eternal gave them a God-like mystique. That mystique acts back upon politics and thought, depriving them of their critical edge.

If politics and thought make sense only if they conform to a reality posited as transcendent, how can the flow of information and discernment continue? Transcendental positing of earthly matters is an ideological blinder placed on earthly reality in a way that confuses and interrupts the human. That is why Arendt believed that totalitarianism was fundamentally interested in remaking the human into a thing. This could happen in nation-states as well as in much smaller communities, especially communities that made claims on identity by referring to realities outside of history, that claim eternal verities.

Arendt's secularity was more than an abdication or defiance of religion or faith. Secularity is itself a way of engaging the world on its own, for the sake of the world. Though other levels of meaning come into play, Arendt believed they should be restricted to their own sphere. To mix the religious and the secular is to confuse belief with thinking.

Arendt believed that plurality is necessary for public speech and action that seeks human flourishing. This can help interrupt injustice and provide space for alternative and more human paths. Where totality reigns, the rights of the person are necessarily interrupted. The quest for totality places humanity itself in doubt. It is only a short step from there to declare portions of the population superfluous. Being so defined, everything can be permitted in the name of that totality.

Thus, thought needs to be intentional and have a place in the world that involves others. Especially in the modern world, where social systems move toward totality and ever more people are deemed to be superfluous, Arendt believed it was crucial to protect humans from forces that might seek to define them as superfluous and then eliminate them. She could not escape those questions nor place them beyond the reach of the human capacity to act in the world.

The Hidden Tradition

In April 1944 Arendt published her essay, "The Jews as Pariah: A Hidden Tradition." She defined the hidden tradition as a dissenting one that had been pioneered in Europe by that part of the Jewish community that was fully integrated neither into Jewish nor European culture. This involvement and distance allowed for critical thought to develop and mature. What was beneficial from either culture could be borrowed. What was not could be jettisoned.

As the hidden tradition evolved, a boundary position emerged where critical inquiry was possible. Being in between, each culture had less power over the individual thinker. Being on the margins of both cultures, individual thinkers were not dependent on either for legitimation. Critical thought was necessary for the same reason. Authorities of both cultures wanted to censor the critical thought that emanated from thinkers who were independent. Importantly, those on the margins of cultures constantly had to define where they were. This also spurred exploration. Being in between, the pull and push of cultures sometimes made life precarious, yet in the end much more productive and exciting.

According to Arendt, the hidden tradition began with the Enlightenment and Jewish emancipation in Europe. This allowed greater participation of Jews in society, even though they remained outsiders in the social and political realms. This outsider status gave rise to two types of Jews: the "conscious pariahs," who transcended the boundaries of nationality to weave the strands of their Jewish background into the general texture of European life, and the "parvenus," who tried to achieve status by raising themselves above their fellow Jews into the respectable world of Christians. Arendt wrote about those like herself who chose to place themselves as conscious pariahs.

Arendt endured a dual difficulty that all conscious pariahs shared: she was marginal to European society and to the Jewish community as well. Ron Feldman, an editor of her Jewish writings, notes that conscious pariahs were "neither parochially Jewish, like their Eastern European cousins, nor were they part of the wealthy Jewish upper class of bankers and merchants that controlled Jewish-gentile relations." They constituted a hidden tradition because there were few links among those who affirmed this pariah status, such as Heinrich Heine, Sholom Aleichem, Franz Kafka, and Walter Benjamin, nor between them and the rest of the Jewish community. Conscious pariahs were loners and experienced this acutely. Nonetheless, they also formed a community and ultimately a tradition. Standing exclusively neither inside nor outside their Jewish or European heritage, conscious pariahs used both as platforms from which to gain insight into the other.[14]

This understanding of the hidden tradition allowed Arendt an extraordinary independence and clarity of thought, in short, a freedom to think about the crucial issues facing the Jewish people in Palestine in the 1940s and later in the Eichmann trial in the early 1960s. As we saw in the Eichmann trial, Arendt was free of some of the constraints that other Jewish reporters had internalized. Though Arendt's independent thinking hurt her popularity, it also allowed her to articulate her insights in a way that would have been impossible for a Jew beholden to the Jewish community for support and affirmation. She wrote earlier about the Jewish homeland in Palestine with a similar independence. It was the collapsing of that hidden tradition that Arendt both feared and experienced in her own life. Perhaps it was her articulation and participation in the hidden tradition, as well as the collapse of that tradition during her lifetime, that makes her thought even more relevant now then it was in her lifetime.

As we have seen, Arendt's understanding of Palestine revolved around support for a Jewish homeland and a political framework in which Jews and Arabs could interact from positions of equality. Here was another example of Arendt's participation in the hidden tradition as applied to a deep and important political issue. The hidden tradition involved creativity in the arts and literature and in critical thought and politics. It was this very worldliness of the hidden tradition that attracted her. She became one of this tradition's most ardent and perhaps last writers on public affairs.

On the question of Palestine and the Jewish settlement, Arendt was prolific and timely. Her proposal of a Jewish homeland in Palestine was consistent with her overall view of the reconstruction of the post-World War II world. It was a time of decision and Arendt wanted Jews to play their part. From her perspective, Palestine could become a model of how to overcome the problems that led to totalitarianism in Germany, the problems of mass society and the deterioration of the nation-state.

According to Arendt's biographer, Elizabeth Young-Bruehl, Arendt saw the kibbutzim, the socialist farming communes of the pre-state Jewish community in Palestine, as promoting "a new form of ownership, a new type of farmer, a new way of family life and child education, and new approaches to the troublesome conflicts between city and country, between rural and industrial labor." As well, the possibility of Arab-Jewish cooperation in Palestine foreshadowed Arendt's answer to the problem underlying racism and the possibility of a new concept of humanity. Since Arendt saw the problem underlying imperialism as one of "organizing a constantly shrinking world in which we are bound to share with peoples whose histories and traditions are outside the Western world," she also saw Jewish-Arab cooperation as another contribution that the Jewish homeland could make in the post-World War II world. In Palestine, she hoped to see the elements of her political theory realized: new social forms, local political councils, a federation, and international cooperation.

Arendt hoped that the victims of totalitarianism could offer a vision of institutions and government beyond totalitarianism. Her hopes for the Jewish community in Palestine conformed to her understandings of the post-war world that would develop, choosing either empires or federations. Arendt's conviction was that the Jewish people would survive only if they chose the model of federation. She also saw this empire/federation choice on a global scale and felt that the future of the world hinged on that choice. The Jewish victims of totalitarianism could create a politics with a non-Western people and show the global community the way forward.[15]

In 1948, just months after the state of Israel was declared, Arendt wrote an important essay about her hopes for the future. Its title was hopeful though shadowed by despair: "To Save the Jewish Homeland: There Is Still Time." The essay was filled with a sense of doom and alternately with a detailed constructive plan. She viewed the two great contributions of the Jewish settlement in

Palestine, the kibbutz movement and Hebrew University, as well as the great precedent of cooperation between a European and a colonized people, as being in danger of collapse. The advantage of the Jewish people not having an imperialist past was also threatened. Thus, their ability to act as a vanguard in international relations on a "small but valid scale" was being lost. Arendt felt that even if Jews won the war and affirmed their claim to statehood, the unique possibilities and achievement of Zionism in Palestine would be destroyed:

> The land that would come into being would be something quite other than the dream of world Jewry, Zionist and non-Zionist alike. The victorious Jews would be surrounded by an entirely hostile Arab population, secluded inside ever-threatened borders, absorbed with hysterical self-defense to a degree that would submerge all other interests and activities. The growth of a Jewish culture would cease to be the concern of the whole people; social experiments would have to be discarded as impractical luxuries; political thought would center around military strategy; economic development would be determined exclusively by the needs of war. And all of this would be the fate of a nation that—no matter how many immigrants it could still absorb and how far it extended its boundaries (the whole of Palestine and Transjordan is the insane Revisionist demand)— would still remain a very small people greatly outnumbered by hostile neighbors.[16]

The ends of a failed endeavor were clear to Arendt. In the near future, Israel as a Jewish state would degenerate into a warrior state and the political initiative would devolve into Jewish, terrorist hands. The Jewish state could only be erected at the price of a Jewish homeland. Unwilling to concede defeat, Arendt closed her essay with a plan to overcome the future that she thought was inevitable if the present course continued:

1. The real goal of the Jews in Palestine is the building up of a Jewish homeland. This goal must never be sacrificed to the pseudo-sovereignty of a Jewish state.

2. The independence of Palestine can be achieved only on a solid basis of Arab-Jewish cooperation. As long as the Jewish and Arab leaders both claim that there is "no bridge" between Jews and Arabs (as Moshe Shertok has just put it), the territory cannot be left to the political wisdom of its own inhabitants.

3. Elimination of all terrorists groups (and not agreements with them) and swift punishment of all terrorist deeds (and not merely protest against them) will be the only valid proof that the Jewish people in Palestine has

recovered its sense of political reality and that Zionist leadership is again responsible enough to be trusted with the destinies of the Yishuv.

4. Immigration to Palestine, limited in numbers and time, is the only "irreducible minimum" in Jewish politics.

5. Local self-government and mixed Jewish-Arab municipal and rural councils, on a small scale and as numerous as possible, are the only realistic political measures that can eventually lead to the political emancipation of Palestine. It is still not too late.[17]

Arendt was able to see these questions in the Eichmann trial and in the formation of a Jewish state because of her connection with, yet independence from, European and Jewish cultures. She witnessed the difficulties of living and thinking in a marginalized status, but this allowed her to draw on the riches of both European and Jewish cultures while remaining free from the confines of either. Arendt was able to participate in a dialogue between cultures that had often been bloody, a dialogue that she believed, even after the Holocaust, could help lay the foundations for a world beyond death and destruction. Her intuitions as well as her intellectual vision included the need for dialogue partners.

Seen through Arendt, the hidden tradition comes into view. It is found in a willingness to stay in the tension between cultures and to maintain a critical distance from both while being engaged in communal, national, and international affairs. Arendt represented grounding in the humanist and religious traditions that did not seek to subvert one nor place them in a false unity. She was not fully invested in any one culture per se and thus was free to borrow what was needed to think critically. She was also able to criticize or simply leave behind parts of any culture that censored or held her thought hostage.

The tension of secular and religious in the hidden tradition perhaps is best exemplified by the Jewish German critic and philosopher Walter Benjamin. Benjamin was a friend of Arendt's. After his suicide during World War II, as he tried to avoid arrest while attempting to cross from France into Spain, Arendt championed his work and brought him to the attention of the post-war world.

Whereas Arendt's writing on history is completely and intentionally secular, Benjamin's meditation on history crosses back and forth from observation and theology to mysticism and Marxism. While Arendt wrote scholarly volumes, Benjamin mostly wrote essays, one titled, "Thesis on the Philosophy of History." Here, shortly before his death in 1940, Benjamin saw the forces of material history shaped and challenged by a theological voice that too often was employed by the powerful to legitimate injustice. However, when theology was hidden it could be subversive of that very same power. Though kept out of sight, theological insight speaks for the dead and the dying in a world where power rules with injustice and murder. This insight is weak yet messianic. Its power subverts those who use politics and theology to murder. Benjamin sees a continual need to prevent this theology from becoming a tool of the ruling classes.

Benjamin views the task of every generation to wrest theology and the tradition that uses it from a "conformism that is about to overpower it." Here, the historian is important, by speaking for the dead. The hidden quality of Benjamin's theological insights is found in a meditation on a painting by Paul Klee, the Swiss painter:

> A Klee painting named *Angelus Novus* shows an angel looking as though he is about to move away from something he is fixedly contemplating. His eyes are staring, his mouth is open, his wings are spread. This is how one pictures the angel of history. His face is turned toward the past. Where we perceive a chain of events, he sees one single catastrophe which keeps piling wreckage upon wreckage and hurls it in front of his feet. The angel would like to stay, awaken the dead, and make whole what has been smashed. But a storm is blowing in from Paradise; it has got caught in his wings with such violence that the angel can no longer close them. The storm irresistibly propels him into the future to which his back is turned, while the pile of debris before him grows skyward. This storm is what we call progress.[18]

Benjamin concludes by commenting on "messianic time":

> The soothsayers who found out from time what it had in store certainly did not experience time as either homogeneous or empty. Anyone who keeps this in mind will perhaps get an idea how past times were experienced in remembrance—namely in just the same way. We know that the Jews were prohibited from investigating the future. The Torah and the prayers instruct them in remembrance, however. This stripped the future of its magic, to which all succumb who turn to soothsayers for enlightenment. This does not imply, however, that for the Jews the future turned into homogeneous, empty time. For every second of time was the strait gate through which the Messiah might enter.[19]

Benjamin's insight is that our experience forbids us to conceive history in fundamentally theological or atheological terms. Often, "progress" is a disaster, and when it comes the victims are defenseless. Yet what seems to be victory can be turned into the victor's very own disaster. When the victor struts on his stage, the overturning of that victory has already begun. Messianic time is right around the corner.

Clearly this is also a thesis on the "progress" of Nazism and its dissolution, which Benjamin did not live to see. Nonetheless, he felt the Nazi defeat to be inevitable. Was the survivor of Nazism also destined to become a new oppressor?

According to Benjamin, the wise person pays attention to history without giving everything over to it. There is a human and transcendent element in history that can be broken but not destroyed. When empowered, theology is part of the ideological sweep that spells disaster, yet when wrested away from conformism, it is necessary and sustaining. "The tradition of the oppressed teaches us that the 'state of emergency' in which we live is not the exception but the rule," Benjamin writes. "We must attain to a conception of history that is in keeping with this insight. Then we shall clearly realize that it is our task to bring about a real state of emergency, and this will improve our position in the struggle against Fascism." He believes that this and other struggles will be "nourished by the image of enslaved ancestors rather than of liberated grandchildren."[20]

In Benjamin, Arendt sees a man of letters who barely made it economically, who was between cultures and misunderstood by almost everyone, and had difficulty even understanding himself. For Arendt that was a badge of honor: "Unlike the class of the intellectuals, who offer their services to the state as experts, specialists, and officials, or to society for diversion and instruction, the *hommes de letteres* always strove to keep aloof from both the state and society. Their material existence was based on income without work, and their intellectual attitude rested upon the resolute refusal to be integrated politically or socially." Arendt identifies Benjamin as the last of this tradition, a tradition that combined the rebellious with the revolutionary. Again referring to the tradition to which Benjamin belonged, Arendt writes of their Jewishness: "What was decisive was that these men did not wish to 'return' either to the ranks of the Jewish people or to Judaism, and could not desire to do so—not because they believed in 'progress' and an automatic disappearance of anti-Semitism or because they were too 'assimilated' and too alienated from their Jewish heritage, but because all traditions and cultures and all 'belonging' had become equally questionable to them."[21]

Knowing, loving, and being part of this hidden tradition, Arendt also knew it to be fated. As the bottom fell out of the Western tradition, there was no place for the hidden tradition. In 1944 she laments its passing:

> So long as the Jews of Western Europe were pariahs only in a social sense, they could find salvation, to a large extent, by becoming parvenus. Insecure as their position may have been, they could nevertheless achieve a *modus vivendi* by combining what Ahad Haam described as "inner slavery" with "outward freedom." Moreover, those who deemed the price

too high could still remain pariahs, calmly enjoying the freedom and untouchability of outcasts. Excluded from the world of political realities, they could still retreat into their quiet corners there to preserve the illusion of liberty and unchallenged humanity. The life of the pariah, though shorn of political significance, was by no means senseless.

But today . . . the bottom has dropped out of the old ideology. The pariah Jews and the parvenu Jew are in the same boat, rowing desperately in an angry sea. Both are branded with the same mark; both alike are outlaws. Today the truth has come home: there is no protection in heaven or earth against bare murder, and a man can be driven at any moment from the streets and broad places once open to all. At long last, it has become clear that the "senseless freedom" of the individual merely paves the way for the senseless suffering of his entire people.

The old escape mechanisms have broken down, and a man can no longer come to terms with a world in which the Jews cannot be a human being either as a parvenu using his elbows or as a pariah voluntarily spurning his gifts. Both the realism of the one and the idealism of the other are today utopian.

There is, however, a third course—the one that Kafka suggests, in which a man may forgo all claims to individual freedom and inviolability and modestly content himself with trying to lead a simple decent life. But . . . this is impossible within the framework of contemporary society. . . . The man of goodwill is driven today out of isolation. Like the Jew-stranger at the castle. He gets lost—or dies from exhaustion. For only within the framework of a people can a man live as a man among men, without exhausting himself. And only when a people lives and functions in consort with other peoples can it contribute to the establishment upon earth of a commonly conditioned and commonly controlled humanity.[22]

On the one hand, Arendt champions the hidden tradition as a tradition of dissent and freedom. On the other hand, she believes that of necessity it was apolitical and thus no longer viable.

Here, Arendt stresses the particularity of Jewish peoplehood and the need for all Jews to recognize their identity. This goes against Wiesel's and Scholem's critique of her Jewishness. What they resented, and what she emphasizes, is the need for relentless honesty among Jews, an honesty that some would characterize as indecency. For Arendt, the new sense of Jewish peoplehood must dispense with the illusion of some Jews, the conscious pariahs, that they are free of Jewishness and the illusion of other Jews, the parvenus, that the Jews are only those who are fully or properly Jewish. In short, the divisions among Jews collapsed as the war was being collectively waged against them. In that collapse, however, a new vision of Jewish identity and the relations of Jews and non-Jews had to emerge. The division of Jew and Christian spelled disaster for both groups. Now both have to take responsibility separately and together for envisioning a new world.

Arendt comments that "refugees driven from country to country represent the vanguard of their peoples—if they keep their identity." This refers to a political identity. Jews will be treated as such, wherever they go. Yet it also means belonging to a tradition with multiple levels that are being compressed by history. Whereas communities of Jews previously could wall themselves off from other Jews, today that is no longer possible. All Jews are in the same boat, initially placed there by others and now having to recognize this fact as Jews, with all the consequences that result when squeezed together. Everything uncomfortable comes to the fore, and though defined as one people, Jews now realize how separated they really are: "Those few refugees who insist upon telling the truth, even to the point of 'indecency,' get in exchange for their unpopularity one priceless advantage: history is no longer a closed book to them and politics is no longer the privilege of the gentiles. They know that the outlawing of the Jewish people in Europe has been followed closely by the outlawing of most European nations. Refugees driven from country to country represent the vanguard of their peoples—if they keep their identity."[23]

Refugees are thrown out. They are also thrown together. Being thrown out/together also creates new possibilities for life. In the first place, it collapses the previous distinctions of class, education, and status and highlights the limitations of each grouping as well as their strengths. The idea that these distinctions will be recreated in the new environment is a natural hope of regaining what has been lost. For Arendt, though, it is part illusion that such a recreation will occur, since part of the reason Jews are refugees is the failure of the old world configurations.

Reading Arendt many years later, more to the point is that some European categories of Jewish life were recreated in America and many were not. Those who became the vanguard were mostly refugees like Arendt herself, but the Jewish community itself split again into a variety of classes with varying status and the divergent politics. Though Arendt lived into the 1970s and saw the Jewish community evolve, she died before the almost complete abandonment of what she had hoped would be done with this new freedom.

Jews are no longer refugees. Instead Jews are deeply entrenched at elite levels of American society. What today would force Jews to reconsider their new found Jewish identity? If refugees were the vanguard of the Jewish people, what kind of Jews can form that vanguard today? Remembering that Arendt saw a solidarity among refugees of other peoples as well, what can we expect from other communities in America, most of which have lost their refugees status and like Jews have sought and been assimilated into the American mainstream?

In the post-Holocaust world, even Arendt believed that the hidden tradition had lost its grounding and become distant. In a Jewish community where power and privilege is assumed, along with the neo-conservative politics such power and privilege allows and perhaps demands, where can Jews go and with whom can they affiliate for a critical assessment and projection of a different Jewish future?

Certainly it is more than a Jewish future that Jews must be thinking through and acting to create. Arendt believed that Jews as a people needed to act with other groups and peoples. That was the abiding lesson of the collapse. What had been separate could no longer remain separate.

Arendt saw the integration of Jews and non-Jews as good if the identity of each kept evolving separately as well. This joint evolution was the new freedom Arendt saw, but this would come to fruition only with critical thought. Although the hidden tradition as it had been known was over, a new aspect of it would have to evolve. This could be among Jews or between at least some Jews and non-Jews. Once Jews and non-Jews declared their independence, the hidden tradition could take many forms.

Arendt's point about the possibility of structuring a life together of Jews and Arabs in Palestine is important here. If the Western tradition had come toppling down, so that Jews and others from the West had to create a new ethic of life and politics, this was the case for other traditions and peoples as well.

The Holocaust and its aftermath exaggerated the pace of this collapse in the West, making it so dramatic and awful that it could not be bypassed. Yet other non-Western traditions for their own reasons—including colonialism, war, and modernity—were also experiencing collapse. After World War II and the Holocaust, the flood of refugees from Europe seemed unending. Yet that flood has only intensified in the decades since, primarily from other parts of the globe. Diaspora populations from Africa, Latin America, and Asia now help define the world, including within America and Europe. Sadly, Jews have also created a Palestinian refugee population in the creation and expansion of Israel.

Does this mean that the evolving hidden tradition will be partly defined by refugees from all over the world, if they keep their identity? The immigrants from these lands are in between their own geographic culture and the new cultures in which they live and interact. Since Jews pioneered the hidden tradition and since most Jews have assimilated to American culture with power, affluence, and status, does that mean that Jews can only watch as this hidden tradition changes hands? Or do dissident Jews still have access to the hidden tradition?

It may be that Jews have a special relationship to the hidden tradition that will continue to the extent that Jews are in contact with and struggle with the new refugees. This of course means that there is something about Jews and Jewish history that drives them toward the hidden tradition. Is there more to being Jewish than context and politics? Is Jewishness more than a constituent part of being born a Jew? This may be the question Wiesel and Scholem were asking Arendt, though they could only communicate it with derision. Perhaps they were unable to pose the question more positively because they could not answer their own question.

Jewish Identity(s)

If the whole of Western civilization has come crashing down, and if after the Holocaust Jews are completely invested in the West, in what situation do Jews find themselves today? Since the Holocaust, the center of Jewish population and energy has shifted to America and to Israel. If in many ways Western civilization came toppling down on the heads of European Jews in a murderous fury, and if Jews reside in and identify with the West after the Holocaust, how are Jews to negotiate their presence in the very civilization that built gas chambers for them?

Even in her understandings of a Jewish homeland in Palestine, Arendt's frame was Western, as was Buber's. Both wrote of the benefits that would accrue to the Arabs because of the Western sensibilities that Jews brought to the region. Although they decried the more obvious colonial aspects of Jewish settlement in Palestine, linking colonialism with the formation of the Jewish state of Israel, which they opposed, they were unable to disentangle themselves from the Western assumptions of technological progress, agricultural and industrial advances, democratic forms of governing, and support for human rights.

Heschel's angle was also decidedly Western. Indeed, as a colonial sensibility it was more Western than Jewish to argue that Jews needed a homeland and that Palestinian Arabs could forfeit their homeland and live anywhere else in the Arab world. At the same time, Heschel thought little about Palestinian or Arab history or destiny. What may have been their sense of history and destiny was characterized by Heschel as misguided nationalism and cynical politics that held the Arab people hostage. To be sure, Heschel does not speak of Jewish history and destiny as nationalism. Rather, he saw the creation of Israel and its victory in the 1967 war as part of the return of the people Israel to its patrimony. Though different politically, Arendt was closer to Heschel's Western sensibility that she would want to admit.

At least in the contact that Arendt and Buber proposed between Jews and Arabs, a mutual meeting place could surface where they could work out their differences in culture and religion. In proposing a Jewish homeland alongside and in solidarity with a Palestinian homeland, with joint municipal councils and other institutional mechanisms for living together, the hope was that over time, a give-and-take relationship could emerge.

This was Arendt's model for the meeting of different cultures where prejudices and differences could be faced directly, negotiated, and worked through. Undoubtedly, aspects of Jewish Western particularity and Arab Eastern particularity would remain, even as a broader Jewish-Arab culture emerged. The fear of the state Zionists in this area was clear: too much interaction between Jews and Arabs would inevitably bring about a broader Jewish-Arab particularity, which in turn would jeopardize the Jewish character of the Jewish population. This meant that many Western Jews had difficulty recognizing a Jewishness that was not Western. But there had been Jews living in Palestine who were Eastern in their Jewishness and hundreds of thousands of Arab Jews living in the surrounding Arab countries. Soon many of these Arab Jews came to Israel to live. Buber, Arendt, and Heschel rarely mentioned these non-Western Jews.

Even with this Western bias, Arendt's analysis was global in scope. Unfortunately, Arendt's prediction that those on the margins of society are likely to be declared superfluous and condemned was not only true for her time. It became the defining theme of the late twentieth century. It is poised to become definitive for the twenty-first century as well. The number of people seen as superfluous continues to increase. So too do the measures to deal with them.

Gil Eliot, a British thinker, has named those who die in diverse circumstances and geographical locations caught up in ideologies and wars in the twentieth century, or who were murdered because they were seen to be superfluous, as "the nation of the dead." It is also true that billions of people around the globe have been moved from poverty to destitution in our time. Though they remain alive, they are essentially dead in life. Are they the nation of the living dead? What kind of politics can address the nation of the dead and the living dead?

The nations of the dead and the living dead are outside normal political configurations of power and status. Does this mean that those with a politics of power and status have to develop a politics of inclusion and justice so as to keep the nations of the dead and the living dead from increasing in size? Since Arendt's time, programs to address the plight of superfluous people have increased greatly, but so too has the problem. The quest for a new international economic and political order has yet to be fulfilled. Meanwhile, for many in the nations of the dead and the living dead it is already too late.

While Arendt sees the ineffectiveness of the Judeo-Christian tradition to block out the evil workings of the powerful, as a theologian Rubenstein also explores the culpability of theology and God. Even so, the social and moral reconstruction that Arendt envisions in *Origins* and pursues in her later work is absent from Rubenstein's analysis and from Elie Wiesel's writings for that matter. It is absent for the most part from reflections on the Holocaust. Arendt reflects on the end of Western civilization as we knew it and what is needed for the future:

> In historical terms this would mean not the end of history, but its first consciously planned beginning, together with the bitter realization that nothing has been promised to us, no Messianic Age, no classless society, no paradise after death. . . . No longer separated by space and nature and, consequently, by spiritually insurmountable walls of history and culture, mankind will either find a way to live in and rule together an overcrowded earth or it will perish—an event which will leave the sublime indifference of nature untouched.
>
> The most immediate political consequence of this new historical situation, where mankind actually begins to occupy the position formerly assigned to nature or history, is that some of the factual responsibility shared by the members of every national community for all the deeds and misdeeds committed in their name has now expanded to the sphere of international life. The peoples of the world have a vague foreboding of this new burden and try to escape from it into a kind of nationalism that is all the more violent because it is constantly frustrated. They know that they will be "punished" for sins committed at the other end of the globe, and that they have not yet had the opportunity to learn that they may also benefit from every step in the right direction that is taken elsewhere.[24]

Arendt believes we have entered unexplored human territory. The choice before us is to explore that territory or die. Neither God nor any ancient or modern code of conduct we have inherited will do what needs to be done. In contrast to Arendt, Rubenstein seems stuck in the absence of God and solidarity. With him, as with Max Weber, modernity is an "iron cage." With Arendt, Rubenstein believes that we cannot go back behind modernity to a less powerful and destructive world. Unlike Arendt, however, Rubenstein has difficulty envisioning a more inclusive and pacific one.

For Rubenstein, what makes for the material progress that some experience in modernity is also what makes for the increasing desperation of the majority of the world's population. Programs to advance those on the losing side of modernity fail, and the urge to power among the affluent extends their advantage at the expense of those on the margins. The political experiments as in the Soviet Union and Nazi Germany that sought to diminish or eliminate altogether the plurality of the world ended in societies of total domination and massive destruction. There are few, if any, models to guide us into the future.

Perhaps part of this despair comes with the passage of time. At the end of World War II there was a tremendous optimism about the future. Looking back, the paradoxical nature of this optimism is obvious. How could a world that had just experienced devastation look upon the future with optimism? It might be that the devastation itself demanded a new beginning. Optimism may have acted like adrenaline that flows in the body during moments of danger. After the initial adrenaline surge was over, after the rebuilding of post-war Europe was accomplished, the questions became more complex. Still, even before the adrenaline flow abated, the world was involved in what became a protracted Cold War. Initiatives were frozen. Critical thought was discouraged and punished. The freedom to create and reconstruct the world was held in check.

It might also be that the choices for Arendt were so obvious that she could only afford envisioning the world being reconstructed along new lines. The Cold War interrupted much of that optimism since the world's two superpowers, the United States and the Soviet Union, were almost immediately locked in a nuclear confrontation. Since hopes for a new beginning were stillborn, many thinkers lost the ability to project a world order beyond what was known. Regardless, in the destruction that Arendt experienced, there is a sense of uplift, as if the concerted energies of humanity are up to the task ahead.

Arendt's optimism is contagious. Was she also, inadvertently, naïve and utopian? Like the other Jewish thinkers I am exploring, and despite the criticism launched against them, it may be the naïve and utopian aspects of their life and thought that are the most available to us today. Sometimes hope is tucked away in critical and seemingly pessimistic thought. Critical thought is a form of hope, if in facing the truth of our situation we can find a way forward.

When I read Arendt's argument for the sharing of Palestine, I wonder if her belief that Jews and Arabs could live together in peace and harmony was a case of naiveté and utopian thought. Or was the seemingly realistic idea of her critics, that Jews could only survive and flourish if separated in a state of their own, actually a form of pessimism? Was it naïve and utopian for Arendt to believe that anti-Semitism was not eternal and could effectively be fought against by Jews in concert with non-Jews? Or was it realistic to assume that anti-Semitism was eternal, and in every age just waiting to rear its ugly head again?

Once again, I encounter Arendt's ideas on the coexistence and mutual solidarity of Jews and Arabs more than six decades after she wrote them. Though the path she laid out was discarded as it was written, it is difficult to fathom anyone on either side of the Jewish and Arab divide reporting honestly that the passing decades have been anything other than disastrous.

With regard to anti-Semitism, relations between Jews and Christians have never been better. To describe the United States as anti-Semitic, or to see anti-Semitism lurking around any and every corner, is to assert that anti-Semitism is an eternal threat against which Jews need to mold and maintain their Jewish identity. Today, some Jewish commentators speak and write about the "new" anti-Semitism, usually defined as those who support Palestinian human rights and criticize Israeli policies toward them. Whereas traditional anti-Semitism was essentially religious and emanated from Christianity, the new anti-Semitism is supposedly sponsored by peoples and institutions of the Third World or by institutions that also support anti-colonial and anti-imperialist movements. To call these understandings overreach is to belabor the obvious.

In Arendt's language, the Jewish community has substituted a transcendent concept of Jew-hatred, now morphed into Israel-hatred, for a political analysis of why Palestinians, Arabs in general, and others, including some Jews, might support Palestinian human rights and be critical of Israeli policies. Traditional anti-Semites had Jews on their mind, seeing Jewish conspiracies everywhere. Today there are politically based criticisms of certain behavior sponsored or acted upon by Jews. Here, Arendt is important, reminding us that we cannot remain stuck since there continues to be too much at stake.

Hope is missing in Rubenstein and in much of post-Holocaust Jewish life. With an "iron cage" mentality, the cycle of power can only continue on its foreordained path. Yet even though Arendt was a refugee from Europe and analyzed the horror of the Nazi period, her work seeks to break through this iron cage mentality. In doing so she posed possibilities of reconstructing values so violated in the Holocaust. Rubenstein was not so inclined. Perhaps Arendt could not afford the break that Rubenstein saw as definitive. As a European refugee rather than a native born American analyzing the effects of the Holocaust, Arendt *had* to construct a world for herself in another place.

Was Arendt more like Wiesel in her affirmation of a future for Jews and humanity? Though Arendt and Wiesel kept each other at arm's length, each being suspicious that the other was entering their own iron cage mentality, the truth lies somewhere in the middle. For Wiesel, a defined Jewish particularity was the way out for Jews, or at least the only way to be faithful to Jewishness and Jewish history. With the Holocaust as the guide, the question of meaningless suffering could be rescued, and thus the people who had suffered could be likewise rescued from oblivion. If Arendt were interested in rescuing anyone, it was humanity, Jews among them, but she was certain that a rescue had to be built rather than felt. It would involve concerted work rather than appeals to history. Without that appeal to history, history was open. For Arendt, the iron cage was not defining. It was also less important for her to know the kind of future the world was heading toward. Defining that in advance could interrupt disruptive thought. In Arendt's world, thought needs to be confronted by thought and action by action. How else could the possibility of a future remain open?

In her essays on life as a refugee, Arendt is hoping against the tide of her life and that of other Jewish refugees. This is one of the few places where she despairs, over what the refugees have been dealt in their new lot in life. The desperation is palpable, the tone sarcastic.

Arendt points out that, in the first place, she and others do not like being called refugees. "We ourselves call each other 'new comers' or 'immigrants,'" she writes. "Our newspapers are papers for 'Americans of German language'; and as far as I know, there is not and never was any club founded by Hitler-persecuted people whose name indicated that its members were refugees." The old meaning of the term refugee that applied to someone who had committed certain acts or held certain opinions did not hold. Arendt and the other Jewish refugees had to flee simply because they were Jewish. Moreover, out of pride the refugees wanted to deny that they were foreign and in need. They preferred the term "immigrants" or "newcomers." As she writes, this somehow made them feel better, at least on the outside.

As for the optimism the refugees exuded and that some found admirable, in Arendt's view it was only skin deep. They wanted to keep the more horrible aspects of their journey hidden to others, and for themselves, the trauma was too deep: "The story of our life has finally become known. We lost our home, which means the familiarity of daily life. We lost our occupation, which means the confidence that we are of some use to the world. We lost our language, which means the naturalness of reactions, the simplicity of gestures, the unaffected expression of feelings. We left our relatives in the Polish ghettos and our best friends have been killed in concentration camps, and that means the rupture of our private lives."[25]

"We were told to forget; and we forgot quicker than anybody could ever imagine. In a friendly way we were reminded that the new country would become a new home; and after four weeks in France or six weeks in America, we pretended to be Frenchmen or Americans. The more optimistic among us would even add that their whole former life had been passed in a kind of unconscious exile and only their new country now taught them what a home really looks like." The refugees began to think all of this was true, including the possibility that they spoke English perfectly and that they had already forgotten their mother tongues.

Forgetting was hope. It also was impossible. Was hope impossible as well? Arendt cuts to the point when she analyzes the greeting the refugees received and the responses they gave: "In order to forget more efficiently we rather avoid any allusion to concentration or internment camps we experienced in nearly all European countries—it might be interpreted as pessimism or lack of confidence in the new homeland. Besides, how often have we been told that nobody likes to listen to all that; hell is no longer a religious belief or a fantasy, but something as real as houses and stones and trees. Apparently nobody wants to know that contemporary history has created a new kind of human beings—the kind that are put in concentration camps by their foes and internment camps by their friends." Arendt then turns to the issue of suicide:

> No, there is something wrong with our optimism. There are those odd optimists among us who, having made a lot of optimistic speeches, go home and turn on the gas or make use of a skyscraper in quite an unexpected way. They seem to prove that our proclaimed cheerfulness is based on a dangerous readiness for death. Brought up in the conviction that life is the highest good and death the greatest dismay, we became witnesses and victims of worse terrors than death—without having been able to discover a higher ideal than life. Thus, although death lost its horror for us, we became neither willing nor able to risk our lives for a cause. Instead of fighting—or thinking about how to become able to fight back—refugees have got used to wishing death to friends or relatives; if somebody dies, we cheerfully imagine all the trouble he has been saved. Finally many of us ending by wishing that we, too, could be saved some trouble, and act accordingly.[26]

Perhaps Arendt's experience of the dark side of life as a refugee was part of the reason for her concentration on forgiveness. Without leaving the past, how could she and her fellow refugees escape being mired in a dynamic of past and future that rendered them homeless in both? How could they embrace the world in all its contradictions and build a future for themselves and others? With their own particular experience, how could Jewish refugees bond with refugees of other peoples to create a world without refugees? Then again, if Western civilization had come toppling down over our heads, perhaps all of us are refugees in some ways, traveling without our "home" into a foreign land.

When I first encountered the role forgiveness plays in Arendt's work I was surprised. How could forgiveness, a term I associated with Christians and, from my perspective, often in such a hypocritical way, be part of Arendt's vocabulary?

Two of my encounters prepared me to understand Arendt's sense of forgiveness. In the first, in the mid-1980s, I had been invited to teach in a Development Studies program by an Irish religious order.

During my second day of teaching, a Catholic nun in the program asked softly but with an intensity that bordered on violence: "You hate Hitler in your heart, don't you? You can't forgive Hitler!" Already knowing the charge made by Christians that Christians were forgiving whereas Jews were not, I was stunned by the force of her comment. I experienced her words as an accusation against me, Jews, and Jewish history. As she hurled her accusation, I had to think of my relation to Hitler. I had never hated Hitler. Perhaps that was bringing him too close to me. As she spoke, I felt a void within me. I couldn't hate Hitler because

I could not relate to him. Therefore, I didn't think that the category of forgiveness applied. Yet it did raise the question of what forgiveness was and wasn't. I had never thought that the way Christians spoke about forgiveness made sense anyway. Could it make sense with Hitler?

As these thoughts raced through my mind, another Christian, a priest from Uganda, rose to my defense. He stared straight at the Sister and told her that if Muslims came to his village to steal and rape the Christian women he would take out his gun and blow their brains out. Two sides of the contemporary Christian narrative, from the developed and developing world, were playing themselves out in front of me.

I stood there stunned, still feeling her accusation. The violence of both statements was too much for me. I was speechless. With the violence of her accusation and his threatened action, I couldn't go on. There had to be another way to move forward. Violation upon violation seemed endless. I was violated by her accusation. I couldn't accept the priest's defense of me either.

My second encounter was through a book, *Revolutionary Forgiveness,* authored by a group of American Christians who travelled to Nicaragua during the years of the Nicaraguan revolution, which American-supported armed forces were fighting against. The American Christians came in support of the revolution and to stand as a witness against the American government's support for its foes. They wondered how the people could be so kind and forgiving toward them. A Nicaraguan spoke up, saying that their opposition to the policies of the American government meant that because they were taking action for justice, Nicaraguans could forgive them. The forgiveness was revolutionary because justice was at its core.[27]

Taking this as my cue, I began to think of revolutionary forgiveness being applied to Jerusalem, where Jews and Palestinians, two peoples after their own divided and violent history, could gather and begin a new history of equality and justice. This would mean a confession by Israel about the wrongs it has done the Palestinian people and a willingness to pursue justice in the future. Over time, as justice became a reality, the possibility of forgiveness might open up.

With Jews and Palestinians living together and mutually invested in each other's future as part of their own, history and historical memory would take another shape. It would allow both Jews and Palestinians to embrace a different future. Old grievances would remain at first, over time dissipating and one day even disappearing.

Though revolutionary forgiveness would impact Israeli and Palestinian relationships most immediately, it would inevitably spread to other historical issues. The process of revolutionary forgiveness could impact Jewish-Christian relations, even the ways Jews relate to the Holocaust. The investment that Jews have in dividing Jews and Palestinians and maintaining a focus on the Holocaust would be examined thoroughly and critically. What would Jewish identity look like if Jews and Palestinians lived together in equality, peace, and justice? What would Jewish identity be if the wounds of the Holocaust were healed rather than maintained?

Surely there is very little forgiveness in Jewish life. Arendt has never been forgiven for her writings on the Jewish homeland or her reporting on Eichmann. Is the difficulty in forgiving Arendt because of a Jewish insistence on keeping divisions and wounds open because Jews fear a healing? Healing means a future beyond what Jews have known in the past. Arendt was a messenger of a future that many Jews continue to reject.

As I encounter Arendt, the cost of rejecting healing has become more and more obvious. Where have our wounds brought us? Can our new found power be used for healing instead of further violence? Has our violation of the Palestinians, ostensibly to secure the Jewish place in the world, secured our place in the world? Or has it brought a further wounding to Jewish being in the world?

Since Arendt is a secular and Jewish thinker, I thought forgiveness would be foreign to her. Moreover, her understanding of forgiveness is only peripherally, if at all, connected to the question of God. Arendt rarely wrote about God, and when she did it was only to mention the role religion traditionally played in ethics. Her closing thoughts in *Origins* emphasized the end of the era where God and the traditions that purported to represent God played any role at all in shaping society. Rights were not guaranteed by God nor could we rely on nationalism or any ideology to do so. For Arendt, it was only on an international and regional level that the right to life and security could be achieved. Arendt thus became one of the first proponents of human rights in a global setting. Her final paragraphs of *Origins* set her vision:

> Only a consciously planned beginning of history, only a consciously devised new polity, will eventually be able to reintegrate those who in ever increasing numbers are being expelled from humanity and severed from the human condition. The recognition of the crime against humanity will, by itself, achieve neither liberty nor justice, for these are the concern of the daily strife of all citizens; it can only secure the participation of all men in the strife. The concept of human rights can again be meaningful only if they are redefined as a right to the human condition itself, which depends upon belonging to some human community, the right never to be dependent upon some inborn human dignity which *ipso facto*, aside from its guarantee by fellow-men, not only does not exist but is the last and possibly most arrogant myth we have invented in our long history. The Rights

of Man can be implemented only if they become the pre-political foundation of a new polity, the pre-legal basis of a new legal structure, the, so to speak, pre-historical fundament from which the history of mankind will derive its essential meaning in much the same way Western civilization did from its own fundamental origin myths.[28]

Arendt's main theme is a social and philosophical reconstruction of a world when the memory of the death camps is recent and the Cold War is already in full bloom. The rights of men and women can flourish and be protected only if they are respected as constituent of human beings without any reference to any theological or ideological structure above them. In essence, while there can be arguments about how the social, economic, and political realms should be constructed, the arguments about what constitutes a human being and the rights of human beings to freedom and dignity must come to an end.

The ideologies of the past decades, especially Fascism and Communism, were arguments over what a human was in essence and how human beings could be changed to fit the preconceptions both ideologies had of the human. That is why Arendt argues for the pre-political, pre-legal, and pre-historical recognition of human rights, to prevent attempts by political and ideological forces to change humanity beyond recognition.

Perhaps surprisingly, Arendt mentions Jesus of Nazareth as the "discoverer of forgiveness in the realm of human affairs." Yet this is couched in non-religious language. Arendt cautions that too many contributions from religious thinkers and actors have been lost to contemporary public discourse because of their religious nature or have been used in ways that end up denying fundamental human rights and freedom. The conceptual contribution of forgiveness has to be stripped of its specific religious nature in order to be available to a broader public and freed from aspects of religion that may be coercive or invasive. Then forgiveness can assist in the reconstruction of the public realm after the catastrophic Nazi era.[29]

For Arendt, there are two sides to forgiveness: forgiveness itself and promise. Promise is essential for action in the world so we have a sense that the present and future are continuous. Even under the best of intentions, promise is often compromised and even betrayed. Forgiveness is needed so that a promise broken can once again be trusted as a possible future. Forgiveness allows the individual and the community to begin again after the promise falls short.

Forgiveness and promise are initially religious sensibilities. Therefore, in Arendt's understanding they are private and wordless. She strictly separates the private and public realm. In private, we can be who we are and believe what we want. In public, we move beyond the private and live with others, transcending ourselves to share a common life. According to Arendt, in public life forgiveness and promise become founding blocks of a secure and stable public life. In this sense, they are worldly.

In the public realm, respect rather than love prevails. Respect is a friendship without intimate closeness, a "regard for the person from the distance which the space of the world puts between us . . . independent of qualities which we may admire or of achievements which we may highly esteem." Love, often associated with Christian forgiveness, is different. When transported into the public realm, love becomes dangerous.[30]

"Love, by its very nature, is unworldly," Arendt writes, "and it is for this reason rather than its rarity, that it is not only apolitical but anti-political, perhaps the most powerful of all anti-political human forces." If forgiveness is public because of the distance it allows people in the public realm, promise is also public because it creates the possibility of meaning and stability in a world where neither is self-evident. The unpredictability of human affairs and the unreliability of human beings necessitate a "promise" into which "certain islands of predictability are thrown and into which certain guideposts of reliability are erected." For Arendt, forgiveness and promise come together because without either the dynamic of finitude and the search for meaning and coherence collapse. Though both forgiveness and promise are never assured, she believes that both are necessary if individuals and communities are to avoid becoming lost in violation or in uncertainty.[31]

Arendt believed that to create order, people and institutions had to transcend their natural tendency toward inwardness and selfishness. This is an ongoing process of trial and error because action in the world is unpredictable. Only through willingness to risk—which involves promise—can a future be envisioned. But only with a willingness to forgive can risk, stymied by error, be taken again.

Arendt ponders whether we can live without promise, without a hope that is certain or at least attainable. Since promise is often compromised or we arrive at the end of the promise with the outlook being different than we expected, it is improbable that we can live without forgiving others and ourselves. Shortcomings introduce the prospect of instability in life. They also represent possibilities beyond our initial imaginings.

Acting on promise involves risk. Risk is part of life; it is also unnerving. Therefore, in order take a further step into the unknown, we need assurance that forgiving and being forgiven are possible. Arendt envisions life as a series of trials and errors that keep reaching across the unknown and into the future. We need assurance that a future is possible, even when we or others fail. Our assurance is that, regardless of success or failure, we will remain in the cycle of public life. Even if we fail, we have to trust that we won't be banished from society.

Arendt views failure and trespassing as everyday occurrences. Both are directly related to the risk of establishing new relations within a broader web of relations, which is how Arendt refers to the constantly evolving public realm. Therefore, she believes that failure or trespassing "needs forgiving, dismissing, in order to make it possible for life to go on by constantly releasing men from what they have done unknowingly."[32]

In the broader web of relations, the role of punishment is important. Acting in dynamic concert with forgiveness and promise, punishment is an action taken within the public realm. Such punishment reminds the person and the community of the frailty of the human enterprise and the ability of the person, once the punishment has been carried out, to reenter the process that sustains life. In Arendt's understanding, punishment is a way of maintaining the possibility for the future interaction of the individual within the broader web of relations. It also makes it possible for the community to entertain promise again, even for the once guilty individual.

If everyone who fails and trespasses is exiled, too many people are lost to the community. Over time, the community will lose trust in itself. Moreover, if those who fail and trespass are exiled, those who remain will hesitate to risk in their thought and action. If those who fail and trespass are not reincorporated, the enterprise of building and rebuilding the world is seriously compromised. If punishment points to failure and trespass is wrong, when corrected both point in the direction of recovery and continued life.

For Arendt, human activity represents the possibility of new beginnings. All acts are beginnings that interact with other acts in unpredictable ways. This interaction represents new beginnings. Adi Ophir, an Israeli philosopher, explains the dynamic of Arendt's understandings:

> The one who forgets cannot forgive, but the one who forgives (or is forgiven) is free to forget; forgiveness unties. Similarly, he who fulfills promises is free to let his memory loose and untie the knot that promise creates. Before forgiveness, or before the fulfillment of a promise, forgetfulness acts like a virus in the network: it prevents the untying of old entanglement and loosens ties necessary for successful coordination and cooperation among actors. After forgiveness has been granted or a promise fulfilled, it is memory that becomes the virus: it infects the network with unnecessary ties that block new beginnings; it distorts identities; and it increases the burden that the past and the others who represent it exert on unforgetful actors.[33]

Arendt sees life as both being bound and unbound in a dynamic process where the very binding and unbinding is a web that moves into the future. We are responsible for our beginnings, which recur and must be allowed to fail and trespass so that new beginnings are possible. Where our actions lead is unknown, which is why a constant monitoring must occur without judgment falling too heavily on those whose participation is essential.

Fixed identities are problematic, if not impossible, in Arendt's analysis. If all continually is beginning, and with interactions being unpredictable as to where they might lead, how can origins and a destiny of any particular identity be affirmed? Arendt sees the world constantly deconstructing and reconstructing itself. Identity changes simply because of the way the world operates. Therefore, projecting any kind of identity—say Jewish, Christian, or Islamic—remains unreliable. Such projections can interact in the public realm only if their definitions of identity are not imposed upon the public realm.

Arendt is aware of how important communal identity is for many in the world. It is highlighted especially in times of duress. Nonetheless, she believes that identity formations are highly political and must be seen as such. Rather than hardened, identities move with and against the times, depending on what is necessary at the time. Identity is contextual. No identity is carved in stone.

Arendt is doubtful about the prospect of any particular Jewish identity. Clearly, Jewish identity evolves and takes on different formations at different times. Elements of Jewish identity have developed at different times in Jewish history and, as well, certain aspects of Jewish identity come and go in Jewish memory. Aspects of Jewish identity that have been carried over time might become irrelevant in certain contexts, when new ways of being Jewish come into being. Jewish identity, like politics, is in flux with ever changing configurations.

On the matter of anti-Semitism, Arendt feels that understanding such occurrences in history as foundational to Jewish identity is bound to become outdated and magnified in a negative way. The very concept of anti-Semitism as a viable construct independent of the changing world is, for Arendt, like a virus that blocks new beginnings. The same is the case when Jews adopt an outmoded nationalism as the age of nation-states recedes. Though the nation-state is a newly formed possibility for Jews, Arendt believes that it represents an old entanglement that distorts the Jewish politics necessary in the post-Holocaust world.

When I encounter Arendt's sense of identity entanglements, I think of the Jewish investment in identity formations for specifically political reasons and how much more authority we seem to have when Jewish public principles are anchored in historical destiny or transcendent truth. Still, it is true that many Jews hold principles they believe to be so anchored. After all, life is not just lived in public, and the search for the meaning of human existence often is all consuming.

In my own lifetime, I have seen the anchors of, for example, Christian or Islamic life emphasized to such a degree that the distinction between public and private is so diminished that it hardly exists. This is also true for Jewish life.

The Holocaust happened to Jews. Does that mean suffering and murder affected Jews alone? The Holocaust of Jews in Europe is memorialized by the United States government, and that historical event became a cornerstone of Jewish identity in such a way that the Holocaust functions to force a particular identity upon a broader non-Jewish community. Does the Holocaust as central to Jewish identity, and exclusive of others, also force a particular identity upon Jews themselves?

When the Holocaust becomes defining for both Jews and non-Jews alike, "Jewish" becomes boxed in for both communities. When circumstances change, as they have, the present identity formation that is already past becomes a present that is fixed as eternal. Any deviation from affirming Holocaust identity formation is punished. A conversation about Holocaust identity becomes impossible, most especially when such a discussion needs to occur.

Perhaps this is why Arendt's commentaries on a Jewish homeland and the Eichmann trial were so contentious. Arendt and her opponents foresaw the time when the interpretive framework of the Holocaust and Israel would determine the contours of Jewish identity. Those who held different views of Jewish identity would therefore square off in verbal fights that know few, if any, bounds.

For Arendt, the stress on a Jewish particularity that necessitates Eichmann as a criminal against the Jewish people and Israel as a Jewish state requires a fixed sense of what it means to be Jewish. Having established this fixed sense of Jewish identity, it is too dangerous to allow any unpredictable thought or action. Of course, in Arendt's system of thought the future is unpredictable anyway, no matter how identity is policed and disciplined. The unpredictable is in the order of things. Ironically, the Jewish establishment's fight against Arendt has, unpredictably from their point of view, increased her importance and her popularity in the decades since her death.

When I encounter Arendt's thought, I am amazed at how disciplined, punished, and exiled she was. I also think how her thought continues to resonate through the contested lines of Jewish identity. Her voice was prophetic, denouncing injustice and promoting justice while also predicting what would happen if the present course of the Jewish community went unchallenged. Trying to discipline Arendt was therefore like trying to discipline the prophetic voice. From the establishment's perspective, Arendt's exile demonstrated to Jewish dissenters how costly their dissent can be. But through her Jewish dissenters also learn how rigorous and critical thinking takes on a life of its own. It continues to live and become more valuable over time.

Arendt became the test case for the policing of Jewish dissent. In the short run, the policing was successful. After the Eichmann case, Arendt stopped writing about Jewish affairs. On the Jewish scene, Arendt more or less dropped out of sight. Nonetheless, the victors continued to refer to Arendt as the poster girl of what would happen to those who ventured over the line. It is amazing how her Jewish prophetic voice survived and how often Jewish dissidents point to Arendt in a positive way. She remains a heroine to many Jews, perhaps even more so than when she was alive.

Behind the scenes, those who argued with Arendt over what it means to be Jewish were also anxious about Jewish identity after the Holocaust. If Jewish identity is not fixed but fluid, if the outcome of contested identities is unpredictable, could that mean that somewhere down the line an increasing number of Jews will cease identifying as Jews?

We return to Rubenstein's exchange with Wiesel. Ostensibly, their exchange was over whether the Holocaust dead were victims or martyrs. At a deeper level, however, they were discussing the contours and possibility of Jewish identity after the Holocaust. Where Wiesel parted company with Rubenstein, he also parted company with Arendt. Wiesel could not imagine Rubenstein's vision of the void of Jewish life after the Holocaust and, though Arendt had no defined end point of Jewish life as Rubenstein seemed to have, Wiesel had difficulty finding any content to Arendt's Jewishness. At least Rubenstein argued a specific content, the God of history who failed, which Wiesel could counter if not answer in the affirmative. Arendt had no conception of the God of history and therefore was without a specific content to which Wiesel could respond.

Arendt's response to Scholem was hardly enough to inspire confidence in Scholem or Wiesel that she was a Jew, that she recognized herself as such, or that she could be a force for the continuation of Jewish identity. The new beginnings Arendt posited were too frightening for many Jews, even though the Jews who criticized her were themselves contributing to a new beginning. Jewish identity was changing, as it always has. The argument was about the direction in which it would change. Arendt saw Wiesel's direction as being as dangerous as he saw hers.

Arendt's view of forgiveness, promise, and new beginnings coincides with her view of the structural elements of human action and the public realm in which it occurs. Ophir describes Arendt's vision in this way: "Plurality, new beginnings, open-endedness, uncertainty, the weaving and unweaving of flexible, loosely structured networks of interrelations embodied in the spaces of mutual visibility, in which identities are never fixed, and no pre-established teleology resides." Clearly, there is little room here for primal origins or eschatology.[34]

Does that mean Jewishness is only contextual, here and there, and perhaps one day will cease to exist? On Arendt's sense of Jewishness as she embodied it, her niece, Edna Brocke, says it best:

> Like a great many Jews, she was conscious of being a Jew without being Jewish in a religious sense. This was apparent on the one hand in her very close relationship to her small family in Israel, and on the other in her circle of friends in New York, which consisted for the most part of Jewish emigrants. This deeply rooted Jewish awareness conditioned her political and historical observations of the reality of her times, as well. She herself described this sensation in a letter to Karl Jaspers: 'As far as the Jews are concerned: You are historically correct in everything you say. Nonetheless it is a fact that many Jews are like me entirely independent from Judaism in a religious sense and at the same time Jews. Perhaps this will bring about the end of this people, there's nothing to be done about it. What one can do is only to strive for political conditions that will not make their survival impossible.'[35]

Many people, including her Gentile friends in New York as well as many of her readers in Europe, were never able to understand this central aspect of Arendt's identity. "I was sitting together with a couple of American friends a few days ago—a history professor, two famous journalists and a woman novelist; all non-Jews with many Jewish friends. They were drawing up an imaginary list of people who could be relied upon in the struggle for civil liberties; suddenly one of them said: Isn't it funny, only Hannah of all those Jews is with us."[36]

Arendt's plurality and the ever-evolving network of life are vital to her post-Holocaust sensibility. Her sense that reconstruction is part of our destiny, since act we must, complements her belief that the future is open because of the unpredictability of the interaction of these acts.

For Arendt, the collapse of the Western tradition has an unpredictable series of outcomes. Therefore, even the end is a beginning that is not determined in advance. Even the errors committed in the reconstruction are part and parcel of the way forward. So how then can we affirm an iron cage from which there is no escape?

With humanity, so too with Jews. Because there is a collective sensibility, for Jews to exaggerate the differences with others is a mistake. Collective identities are constructed in history, therefore they can be reconstructed. The construction of identity is above all political and therefore changes with politics. Even within a collective identity there is plurality, or rather, in Arendt's view, plurality is more evident in the collective. Does that mean that an assertion of Jewish identity is fanciful, aspiring to a totality that is only fiction and ultimately destructive? In the end, Arendt's vision is a new form of universal solidarity.

Bracketing Jewishness

Since Arendt's birth in 1896, the world has changed considerably, as has the Jewish community. Jews have moved upward and out of an impoverished, selectively protected, and often communally abused European reality. The cost, however, has been enormous.

The most immediate cost is obvious with the Holocaust. A less obvious cost comes within the empowerment of worldwide Jewry after the Holocaust. There is reason to denote a "before" of Jewish life, when Jewish life was modest and sometimes completely disempowered, and an "after" of Jewish life, where Jews are upwardly mobile and actively empowered.

Still, such a linear sequence of "before and after" is deceptive. Because of the complexities of Jewish history, Jews live in a time where the before and after commingle. Positions shift in light of historic and contemporary events, or at least how Jews perceive the meaning of events. Jews do not think primarily in linear terms now and perhaps never have. Of all the characteristics of the Jewish journey, this may be the most distinctive. This is why Arendt's words on universality, politics, and forgiveness are so relevant today.

Initially, it might seem contradictory that during World War II Arendt argued for the formation of a Jewish army to fight the Nazis alongside the Allied powers. Yet for Arendt, this represented a conscious political act to assert the Jewish dignity that was under assault. It also reflected her desire for Jews to think and to be thought of as worldly.

Arendt proposed that the Jewish army emanate from the Jewish community in Palestine but include Jewish volunteers from around the world. She thought that a Jewish army would usher in a new understanding of Jewish politics, where the political would be characterized by a sense of the interdependence of the peoples of the world. A Jewish army would have the added benefit of Jews refusing to be seen as a community of victims in need of protection.[37]

Arendt wrote of the need for a Jewish army in 1941, as the assault on the Jews of Europe was about to reach its apex. Like other Jewish intellectuals, she felt the dignity of Jews could be asserted only through political action in consort with others who were seeking similar goals. Her essay is short and to the point; it is a call to action. "The Jewish Army" ends with a question: "The Beginning of a Jewish Politics?"

> Today Jews seems obsessed with their own insignificance. In part they hope this will enable them to leave the political stage once again; in part they are honestly in despair at belonging to a powerless and apparently completely depoliticized group. We too are not immune to the disease which has affected the European nations: despair, the cynicism that comes from disappointment and feeling of helplessness.

The storm of indignation that the formation of the Jewish army of volunteers from all over the world will cause in our own ranks and will make it clear to honest doubters that we too are only human; that we do engage in political action, even if it usually has to be laboriously pieced together from obscure petitions organized by notables and charities, and even if this kind of politics has proved particularly adept at alienating the people from politics. However, we are by no means the only ones to have been led to the brink of the abyss by a plutocratic regime. As Clemenceau put it, war is too serious a matter to leave to the generals. Now, the existence of a nation is definitely too serious a matter to leave to wealthy men.

The formation of a Jewish army will not be decided upon in secret talks with statesmen, nor by means of petitions from influential Jews. We shall never get the army unless the Jewish nation demands it and unless hundreds of thousands are prepared to arm themselves to fight for their freedom and for the nation's right to life. Only the nation itself, young and old, rich and poor, men and women, can turn public opinion, which today is against us, in our favour; *only the nation itself is strong enough for a real alliance.*[38]

Arendt's call for a Jewish army was not a call for the militarization of the Jewish psyche or of Jewish communal life. Rather, she saw this as a contextual political response to a situation of powerlessness and oppression. Though she included in her essay the need for Jews to defend the Jewish community in Palestine, Arendt's proposal for a Jewish army was not seen by her as a precursor to a Jewish state in Palestine. Indeed, as a bi-nationalist, Arendt warned that promotion of a Jewish state exhibited a similar understanding of politics that led to Jewish powerlessness.

Though at the time some felt that the state of Israel, with guarded borders and a significant military, was the natural extension of Arendt's call for a Jewish army, she felt the opposite. Arendt thought that drawing borders of a nation-state in Israel would lead to a future bedeviled by an angry Arab Palestinian population and a disgruntled Arab world in general. Israel would also be stalked by the injustices committed by Jews in their desire to create a Jewish state. Because of this, a state of Israel might become an iron cage whose unpredictable future would spell ruin for Jews there and beyond. As a Jewish state, Arendt saw Israel's future as an armed garrison that would perpetually be in danger. This was the opposite of the interdependent empowerment Arendt envisioned.

For Arendt, the Jewish community was at a crossroads. Emotions were running high on all sides. Those who wanted a Jewish state were framing the question in an all-or-nothing scenario. They were pushing their case to the extreme. Arendt asked what this might mean for the Jewish future:

The moment has now come to get everything or nothing, victory or death; Arab and Jewish claims are irreconcilable and only a military decision can settle the issue; the Arabs—all Arabs—are our enemies and we accept the fact; only outmoded liberals believe in compromises, only philistines believe in justice, and only *schlemiels* prefer truth and negotiation to propaganda and machine guns; Jewish experience in the last decades—or over the last centuries, or over the last two thousand years—has finally awakened us and taught us to look out for ourselves; this alone is reality, everything else is stupid sentimentality; everyone is against us . . . in the final analysis we can count on nobody except ourselves; in sum—we are ready to go down fighting, and we will consider anybody who stands in our way a traitor and anything done to hinder us as a stab in the back.[39]

Her predictions as to where such understandings would lead also resonate:

Palestine and the building of a Jewish homeland constitute the great hope and the great pride of Jews all over the world. What would happen to Jews, individually and collectively, if this hope and pride were to be extinguished in another catastrophe is almost beyond imagining. But it is certain that this would become the central fact of Jewish history and it is possible that it might become the beginning of the self-dissolution of the Jewish people. There is no Jew in the world whose whole outlook on life and the world would not be radically changed by such a tragedy. . . .

The loss of the kibbutzim, the ruin of the new type of man they have produced, the destruction of their institutions and the oblivion that would swallow the fruit of their experiences—this would be one of the severest blows to the hopes of all those, Jewish and non-Jewish, who have not and never will make their peace with present-day society and its standards.[40]

Arendt feared that a Jewish state would feed off the scapegoat and eternal anti-Semitism she felt to be false. Now a Jewish state and its needs would be added to it, thus boxing Jews into a reality that would inevitably be hostile. The Jewish state would need anti-Semitism and a hostile neighborhood in order to keep it going. This would provide a continuing rationale for a life of separation in an area of the world that has historically been diverse. Instead of celebrating and affirming plurality as a politics, the only type of politics that Arendt thought would protect and enhance Jewish life, Jews were choosing the opposite.

If Jews in Europe had been isolated to their detriment, did they think that as a small minority in the Middle East they could survive their isolation simply because they were armed to the teeth? At the same time, the notions of anti-Semitism and the military needed for a Jewish state would dominate and over time eradicate the contributions that a Jewish population in Palestine could make to Jews, the Middle East, and the world. For Arendt, choosing a sense of Jewish particularity that revolved around anti-Semitism and statehood was anti-political. It was a folly with devastating consequences—to Arabs and to Jews.

What did Arendt think was possible with a Jewish population who lived side by side with the Arabs in Palestine? Her dream was a new form of cooperation between peoples, the growth of a Jewish culture in the land, and social experiments of small communities that were beginning anew. All of this would be consumed with the military necessities of the new found state of Israel.

Arendt also saw a fracturing and militarization of world Jewry, who would have to respond to the needs of Israel. However, since Jews in America and in Israel would be traveling in two different directions, propaganda would have to be used to persuade Jews in America to bend their politics to the needs of Israel. Instead of attending to their needs in America, Jews would increasingly be focused elsewhere. In the end, world Jewry would be left living two political illusions melded into one. Arendt's hope of the new era would be dashed.

To a large extent, Arendt predicted what is Israel today. The initial hopes for a Jewish homeland have largely evaporated. Even among the most ardent supporters of Israel, the days of soaring rhetoric about the need and possibilities inhering in a Jewish state are absent. The rhetoric of Wiesel or Heschel just after the 1967 war is impossible to imagine today. Both Wiesel and Heschel saw Israel as a rendezvous with destiny. Today, the question is what kind of rendezvous Israel is and where that destiny leads.

Though Heschel counseled a direct involvement of Jews in Israel as a sign of authentic Jewish identity, what would he think if he were alive today? Many of the few American Jews who settled in the Jewish state after the 1967 war left Israel years ago. Today there is a continuing exile of Jews from Israel, including Jews who were born and raised in Israel. Some estimate that almost a million Israelis permanently reside outside of Israel, some twenty percent of Israel's Jewish population. Universities, think tanks, and businesses in the United Kingdom and America are experiencing an ingathering of Israelis. The exit of other Israelis to countries around the world is already redefining the Jewish Diaspora.

Arendt did not foresee this exodus from Israel. Yet many of her predictions, already partially fulfilled in her lifetime, serve as a cautionary note. As we have seen, especially after the publication of *Eichmann in Jerusalem*, Arendt was systematically vilified and verbally expelled from the Jewish community.

When I first began to read the literature addressed to Arendt during the Eichmann controversy, I was horrified. The invective used against her was extreme. Even Wiesel's reflections on meeting Arendt at her home are so negatively skewed as to make one pause. Though I was somewhat prepared for this literature, having already read invectives directed toward Rubenstein, her vilification still startled me.

Arendt's death in 1975 spared her future disquiet on the Israel front. Like Abraham Joshua Heschel who died before her, Arendt was spared the Israeli bombing of Beirut and Israel's repression of the Palestinian uprising in the late 1980s and early 1990s. She was also spared the continuing expropriation of Palestinian land in Jerusalem and the West Bank, as well as the building of settlements that are for all practical purposes mid-size cities. Arendt also was spared Israel's use of helicopter gunships and guided missiles against the Palestinian uprising in 2000 and Israel's practice of "politicide," depopulating the political ranks of Palestinian leadership so that the very possibility of Palestinian national aspirations would disappear.[40]

Arendt foresaw that the abandonment of her sense of the political in Jewish life would lead to disaster. That is why she argued for the creation of the Jewish army. Her call for a Jewish army was not first and foremost a call for a revival of the military tradition in Jewish life, but she did view it as a necessary first step in a new politics that could defend Jews and then, more importantly, reintegrate Jews as a force for good in the world. Though largely unstated by Arendt, but crucial for us now, is the other side of the Jewish abandonment of the political. It is difficult to see how the Palestinian Arabs and other Middle Eastern countries can practice a politics of compromise and integration when Israel and the Jewish community does not.

Hannah Arendt is important today not as a way of proffering a solution to the Israeli-Palestinian conflict, or even as a substitute for commentary on the political complexities of the decades since Arendt called for a Jewish army and Israel as a Jewish state emerged. I lament the almost total absence of reflection today regarding the plight of Arendt within the Jewish world of her time and the silencing of her significant and critical contribution to Jewish history because of her stand on Eichmann and the creation of the state of Israel. This deprives Jews and the Jewish community of the significant wisdom needed to move forward, as it were to seize the moment, just as others whose voices we desperately need have been and are now being exiled from the Jewish world.

The vilification of Arendt and her loss to the Jewish community as a Jewish thinker and her disappearance as a political thinker in the world of Jewish politics is more than cautionary. It is instructive because her predictions about the future of Jewish politics and debate have come to pass. In many ways, the attempt to address the Jewish community from within a Judaic framework, a tactic adopted by Wiesel and Heschel, has failed to develop a real Jewish politics. It seems, at least for the time being, that it is the Judaic framework itself that contributes to the impasse.

In a strange twist of fate, the very accusation hurled at Arendt by Scholem and others in the wake of the Eichmann trial—that she did not think or write in Jewish ways and that she lacked a love for herself and the Jewish people—might be an asset in assessing the Jewish condition in the twenty-first century.

Arendt's responses to Scholem's accusations are instructive. By responding that she had always accepted herself and defended her rights as a Jew, at the same time working to defend the Jewish community against injustice, but could not love a condition that she took for granted, Arendt may have been ahead of her time. She stated that she was Jewish. That was that. Arendt was completely Jewish in background, upbringing, experience, and political organizing. A good portion of her writing was devoted to analyzing the Jewish historic and contemporary condition. Yet Arendt, at least to some extent, bracketed her Jewishness, even as she embodied it.

Arendt found no reason to glory in or deny what was constitutive of her being. Furthermore, to pledge loyalty to a people in the way she was asked to diminished her ability to think through the questions that faced Jews individually and collectively. From our vantage point today, it is hard to argue with Arendt about her ability to think "Jewishly" by deflecting questions about her Jewishness.

Arendt felt she was being asked to give up her right and obligation to think, a pattern that she analyzed in the Soviet and Nazi quest for totality. She also felt her Jewish loyalty flowed from her critical engagement with the Jewish community and the world. For here to have a loyalty above that was to enter into group-think. Group-think isn't good for anyone, least of all Jews.

By remaining independent of community demands, by staying distant from Jewish institutional life except in the activities of refugee work, Arendt was able to see realities that those arguing from a specifically Jewish point of view could not. This was her major point in relation to Israel. By abandoning an independent position on the margins and by investing everything in group loyalty, the ability of Jews to think through a politics of engagement, compromise, and interdependence—the very possibility of a mature Jewish politics—was lost.

What did Hannah Arendt think about the Jewish question that is relevant for the Jewish future? Will the twenty-first century be different than the twentieth century for Jews, and how? What can be said now about Rubenstein's comments at Buber's centenary regarding Buber's politics and his naiveté? Even though Rubenstein adapted much of Arendt's framework on other issues, she was much closer to Buber than to Rubenstein. Isn't Israel a garrison state much like the one Arendt predicted? Do the differing commentaries offered by Arendt and Wiesel at the Eichmann trial have any relevance today, and should we come back to their relevance for the issues before us now?

It may be time for yet another attempt by Jews to redefine the political. I wonder if this redefinition will come through the embrace of Jewishness or by bracketing it. It might be possible to do both at the same time, but it is doubtful that Rubenstein or Heschel will be the guides we need for the future. It may be that a response to Arendt is also a response to Heschel and Rubenstein, as different generations face the Jewish condition *after* the Holocaust but now also *after* Israel.

Not surprisingly, Arendt's work seems to be at the intersection of the twentieth and twenty-first centuries, complicating an assessment of her work in general. Though her writing on the situation of Jews that led to the Holocaust is now historical, and her pleas on Palestine seem naïve to many, the search for a Jewish politics may be more important now than in her lifetime. Certainly Arendt's views need renewed consideration in an era of unparalleled Jewish empowerment and in this post–September 11 era when the discussion of anti-Semitism is assuming a new prominence. With new democratic movements surfacing in the Arab world, the time may soon be ripe for a further reassessment.

In a 1997 conference on Hannah Arendt in Jerusalem, Amnon Raz-Krakotzkin of Ben-Gurion University revisited Arendt's critiques of Zionism for its importance in contemporary Israel. For Raz-Krakotzkin, though the bi-national option is no longer viable in the way it was in the 1940s, its significance lies in the path toward reconciliation with the Palestinians in the present as well as an alternative sensibility that could remind Jews of the original purpose for a renewed Jewish presence in the Holy Land. Asserting that the question now is not only how to prevent a further expulsion of the Palestinians but how to ensure Palestinian national and civil rights, Raz-Krakotzkin feels that this can be achieved in the framework of a two-state or one-state solution. Regardless, the concept of bi-nationalism is essential for the process of reconciliation:

> In both solutions, national definition would depend on the recognition of the other, including the rights of the Palestinian refugees and awareness of the Jewish question. In both cases, it is necessary to establish procedures that will ensure the equal distribution of resources such as land and water. Any other solution preserves the present status of the Palestinians as an inferior group, as well as the process of apartheid. The principle of bi-nationalism is therefore the starting point for imagining and developing

different political alternatives. It is not necessarily a fixed solution, but at least a direction that fosters resistance to the present situation.[41]

At the same time, Raz-Krakotzkin sees Arendt's understanding of the Eichmann trial as instructive because of the tendency of Israeli society and the Jewish establishment in America to accuse those who criticize Israeli policies of blaming the victim.

> "Blaming the victim" was a charge directed against Arendt herself on a different occasion, when she claimed Jews as pariahs should feel responsible for what society had done to them. Her analysis of the Eichmann trial was misinterpreted as an accusation of the Jews. But in that case, Arendt demanded that the Jews should take responsibility for their own deeds and develop a political approach stemming from the experience of the victims and the analysis of their victimization. But blaming the victim continued to be the foundation of Zionist historical perception.[42]

Blaming the victims, in this case the Palestinians, is akin to blaming Jews for their own situation during the Nazi era. The political, at least as far as Arendt understood it, is more complex. At the same conference in Jerusalem, Richard Bernstein pointed to Arendt's sense of the political as a key to her complex understanding of Zionism, as well as her understanding about action and politics:

> Politics in the normative sense, that is, politics as it ought to be practiced and, according to Arendt, as it has been practiced at those rare moments when the revolutionary spirit has burst forth, presupposes genuine plurality. Politics involves active agonistic debate, discussion, and deliberation. Politics involves a contest of a plurality of perspectives that are publically displayed and tested in public places. These are the public spaces in which freedom becomes a tangible reality. Politics dies when unanimity takes over—a unanimity that is intolerant of dissent.[43]

Arendt's understanding of the hidden tradition allowed her an extraordinary independence and clarity of thought, in short, a freedom to think about the crucial issues facing the Jewish people in Palestine in the 1940s and later in the Eichmann trial in the early 1960s. This ability allowed her to avoid groupthink on the issues of Holocaust and empowerment.

Arendt was a Jewish thinker who lived and wrote within the context of Jewish suffering and the consequent grappling with empowerment. Her thought was distinctly European, even though she lived her last decades in America. Though she was part of the seismic shift in Jewish population and cultural milieu during the middle years of the twentieth century from the Jewish heartland of Europe to America and Israel, Arendt experienced both as an outsider.

Arendt came from the Jewish historic tradition of dissent in Europe and also embodied the evolving tradition of dissent so important to the Jewish future. In her formative years, she lived between the Jewish and European community, belonging to both while not being fully within either. In her later years, she was part of both the American and Palestine (later, Israeli) discussions, without being at home in either. Arendt lived between a vanished Europe, an America that intrigued her but was foreign in language and culture, and a Jewish community in Palestine/Israel that could embody either a new, more mature phase in Jewish politics or become a tragedy of unparalleled proportions.

Since the European culture that Arendt represented no longer exists, she became, like Buber and Heschel, an emissary from the vanquished past. Yet it is also true that the refugee status she brought to America, and her being born before Israel was created, is also past. Jews are not refugees in America. Even the children of those European Jews who fled Nazi Germany are now at home in America.

Arendt's last, albeit brief comments on Israel were amid the emotional turbulence of the period before and after the 1967 Arab-Israeli war. If Arendt was before and after the end of European Jewry, she was also within the refugee/ survivor period of the Holocaust and before the empowered state of Israel. In a significant way, Arendt was one of the last voices before the Holocaust and Israel became central to Jewish identity.

Since Jews are empowered in America and Israel, is there any need for the continuation of the hidden tradition that features critical thought and dissent? If the continuation of that tradition is needed, what form will it take?

The situation remains urgent, as it was in Arendt's time. The Holocaust looms larger in the Jewish psyche as time marches on. Israel also looms larger, even as the founding spirit of Israel wanes. The Middle East is fraught with dangers that accelerate with each war. Though the devastation has been great, the one ingredient that has been missing is a catastrophe of unimaginable proportions. That catastrophe might be right around the corner.

The ability of Israel to burn others is well documented. Israel's 2006 invasion of Lebanon simply confirmed its earlier military prowess. During this invasion, the ability of Israel to be burned also came into sharp relief. Lebanon was burning. So was Israel. The sight of Israel burning is a sign of a possible future. Yet this future would not be the Holocaust, the past event where Jews had no army or state. It would be within the context of empowerment and failed politics. The debate over whether the former or present condition were more tragic would be academic in the worst sense of the term.

If Arendt speaks to us boldly in any arena today, it is her force of thought and her desire to forge ahead, especially in times of great crisis. She was always thinking—without ideology or flags. My encounter with Arendt shows this to be a sign of maturity and strength. But where on the Jewish landscape today is such a thinker?

Without thought, we are banished to the thoughtless and worse, we are consigned to a world without new beginnings, stuck as it were in a conundrum without points of entry and exit. Jewishness can be that place of being stuck. But it can also be a place of freedom, the way out, to begin again.

Beginning again, do we fear the loss of our Jewishness and our place in the world? Do we fear betraying our past suffering and the Jewish state that came into being to address that suffering? Betrayal comes in many forms, and today the fear of betrayal itself is a Pandora's Box where everyone is out to harm Jews, including many dissenting Jews who demand another way, another way of being Jewish in the world.

There is always a way out. That way out is carrying our past and present with us, content to be who we are and ready for the next question before us. Today, that next question is one of Jewish identity in relation to others, the nation-state, and the continual struggle over our direction as individuals and as a people—toward the isolation of empire or toward the solidarity of community.

Arendt reminds us that neither direction is preordained. Nor do we reach either and remain there for long. Wherever we are there is movement, the movement of life and new beginnings. Now is the time, as she argued in 1948. There is still time, but for how much longer?

There were many sides to Arendt. For every person who found her cold and aloof, perhaps arrogant and disconnected from Jews and Judaism, there were others who found her tough, loving, and always engaged. At her funeral, Jerome Kohn, Arendt's research student, spoke of Arendt as a teacher: "She was one of the great teachers of our times. Her knowledge was vast and she gave it gracefully." Arendt's publisher, William Jovanovich, spoke of Arendt as a public figure: "She was passionate in the way believers in justice can become and that believers in mercy must remain. . . . She followed wherever serious inquiry would take her, and if she made enemies it was never out of fear. As for me, I loved her fiercely." Elizabeth Young-Bruehl writes of her funeral and life:

> In the crowded room, among the three hundred mourners, there were many who felt fiercely about Hannah Arendt; though they were seldom without memories of anger or hurt or bewilderment, they felt as Jonas said, that "the world has become colder without your warmth." She was, for those who loved her, part of the "world," not just of the circles of family

and friends and colleagues in which they had known her. They were aware that there were many strangers at the funeral, Arendt readers, even a contingent of them in denim overalls wearing Farm Workers buttons. These were from the "world." It was not—and still is not—easy for those who loved her to locate their Hannah Arendt in the multifaceted light of Hannah Arendt's public *fama* or in the many layers of privacy which she had kept around what some of her friends would have called *Innigkeit,* some her *vivid avis animi,* and some her soulfulness. The night before her funeral, friends and family had debated fiercely whether Jewish prayers should be said for her—as she had debated whether they should be said for her non-Jewish husband! The conclusion of the debate was a compromise: Arendt's Israeli niece read a psalm in Hebrew and then it was read in English by the Klenborts' son, Daniel."[44]

Emmanuel Levinas
(1906–1995)

5

Encountering the
Jewish Prophetic

Emmanuel Levinas

Emmanuel Levinas was born in 1906 in Kaunas, Lithuania, into a traditional Jewish family. At Strasbourg University in France, he majored in philosophy, and in 1928 he moved to the University of Freiburg to study with the great philosopher Edmund Husserl. He wrote his doctoral thesis on The Theory of Intuition in Husserl's Phenomenology. *Levinas became a naturalized French citizen in 1930 and professor of philosophy and director of the Ecole Normale Orientale of the Alliance Israelite Universelle in Paris. Mobilized to fight in the French army in 1939, he was captured and spent the war in a prisoner-of-war camp. After the war Levinas returned to Paris, taught in a Jewish teacher-training college, and in 1951 completed his state doctoral study,* Totality and Infinity, *regarded today as a classic text in philosophy. He subsequently held philosophy chairs at Poitiers, Nanterre, and the Sorbonne. Steeped in the Talmudic tradition of textual analysis, Levinas published many essays of biblical exegesis and essays on Judaism, notably* A Difficult Freedom *(1963). He died in 1995.*

The philosopher Emmanuel Levinas was one of the few European Jewish intellectuals who continued living in Europe after the Holocaust. Similar to but also substantively different from Martin Buber, Levinas explored Judaism and the prophetic with great acumen. A primary concern for both was the Jewish vocation in the world, which was the lens through which they considered Judaism, the Holocaust, and the state of Israel. While Buber and Hannah Arendt wrote extensively on the emerging state of Israel, arguing for certain political structures of the community and against others, for the most part Levinas commented on the larger sweep of Jewish history.

Levinas wrote poignantly about the Jewish journey, offering fresh perspectives about the Jewish past and future. Like our other Jewish thinkers, Levinas was strong in his views and ambivalent about the Jewish future. Levinas knew Jews needed power but was haunted by where that power might take Jews in the future.

Levinas brings together the different sides of issues that Buber, Arendt, and Abraham Joshua Heschel argued singularly. Like them, his intellect and ability are wide ranging. Arguing for the renewal of Jewish life and thought on the very continent where millions of Jews were murdered lent a certain gravitas to Levinas's voice. Perhaps he thought that it was in the land where the Holocaust had occurred that Jewish life and history could take another turn and be healed.

Through the lens of the European future, the destruction of European Jewry has had a profoundly negative effect on European intellectual and spiritual life. The cultural and spiritual ground from which these Jewish thinkers emerged has been destroyed and can never return. Though often Jewish life before the Holocaust is romanticized, our Jewish thinkers testify to the diversity and energy of pre-Holocaust European Jewish life. Though the relative absence of Jews in Europe today has a profound effect on Europe's post-Holocaust life, the destruction of European Jewish culture has had a devastating effect on post-Holocaust Jewish life.

Because Elie Wiesel is still alive and Buber, Heschel, Arendt, and Levinas live on through the study of their ideas and spirituality, the effect of the Holocaust on Jewish intellectual and spiritual life may be experienced for the first time in the coming decades. The Holocaust cannot be tucked away as a historical event. The reverberations of the Holocaust continue. The less obvious effects, like the loss of certain kinds of Jewish intellectual and spiritual foundations, may only be recognized in the coming years.

Buber, Heschel, and Arendt were pioneering Jewish influences on the study of religion and philosophy during the 1960s and 1970s. Levinas assumed that role in the 1980s and beyond. In the twenty-first century, there has been much attention paid to him in universities around the world. Journals and books are filled with discussions of Levinas's philosophy and ethics, so much so that his name has become a signifier of a certain kind of ethical argumentation. Still, the intellectual arena where he is discussed is very different than the ground from which he came. That ground no longer exists.

This peculiar disjunction reorients the discussion of Levinas and others. Did their displacement or that of the community itself also reorient the thinkers themselves? On the one hand, Levinas continued to be rooted in Europe after the Holocaust, and was, obviously, the same person. On the other hand, his own experiences interrupted his intellectual life, and the community from which he came ceased to exist. Everything around him changed. Levinas's audience became significantly different.

Levinas's popularity in intellectual academic circles today often leaves behind the difficult questions of tradition and commitment. Loosened from the European Jewish tradition and often from the Jewish tradition itself, Levinas's thought floats freely and is used to illumine different issues. Too often his pathos is left behind. Yet as with our other thinkers, it is Levinas's Jewishness that anchors him. In some ways this also happened to Buber and Arendt. From my perspective, the universal appeal of their thought takes on depth only when it comes out of their particularity.

Hannah Arendt is rarely analyzed today as a Jewish thinker. How can she be stripped of her Jewish angle of vision and still be understood? Can Jewish thinkers be taken only as universal, without the particularity of those who use them also being stripped away?

University-oriented, academic analysts pick and choose aspects of great thinkers to teach and write about. Yet only Levinas of our Jewish thinkers had academic life as his primary vocation in their early years. The others commented on the issues of their time as intellectuals and religious figures who then also taught in universities and seminaries. Their route to the classroom was indirect and rarely their main focus. Until my generation, Jewish intellectuals were much larger than the university. Instead of being readers of the great thinkers, they themselves have become read.

Imagine Elie Wiesel filling out application forms for academic employment. What discipline would he fit into? Imagine Richard Rubenstein being judged for promotion to full professor. Should the discussion about promotion emphasize his decision that in the Holocaust God was absent and therefore could no longer affirm the Jewish covenant?

It is hardly surprising that Levinas's Jewishness is rarely highlighted. Where his thought leads on the Jewish prophetic and the state of Israel are rarely analyzed. Thus, the deepest and most problematic aspects of Levinas are discarded or not even known. My sense is that the unknown and discarded Levinas tells us much about the Jewish future. The underside of his thought helps illuminate those aspects that usually are emphasized. As we shall see, the difficult question is whether this underside invalidates being able to call on his insights for the future.

While areas of Rubenstein's thought are harsh and ill-considered, he is up front about pushing the envelope against liberal thought. He had to cross the boundaries of liberal thought in order to think clearly. Without an adversary to engage, Rubenstein could be polite. Only a thinker who forced Rubenstein back on his heels was worthy of his attention. Levinas is different. Though there is a trajectory in his thought, it is sometimes interrupted by other considerations needing to be thought through.

As a thinker, Levinas is compassionate and inclusive, as well as Judeo and Euro-centric. The latter two aspects undergird his compassion and inclusiveness but sometimes undermine both. Levinas seems unaware of how his own dialectic of affirmation and negation are affected by his Jewish and European roots.

With regard to Jewish particularity, Levinas shares the same fate as did Buber and Arendt on questions that were of great importance to them. When analyzed and used by others, our Jewish thinkers exist in a netherworld, with their Jewishness stripped away in favor of an elusive universalism. Jews also have trouble dealing with the particularity of these thinkers. By eliminating the Jewish world that gave birth to much of Jewish thought, the Holocaust also deprived Jews of their own foundations. This makes for a disconnect within Jewish life between Jews living today in America and Israel and Jewish thinkers who came from a very different world.

It is important to analyze aspects of Levinas's Jewish writings for the questions he asks about the future of Jewishness, Judaism, and the state of Israel. Some aspects of his thought are incredibly instructive and haunting in their depth. Other aspects are troubling. Both are crucial here in yielding insight into the Jewish future.

I was introduced to Levinas by one of my students who had a spiritual search of his own. He had been born into a Catholic family and only later discovered that part of his family was Jewish. He was drawn to that part of himself he felt to be Jewish. Though he remains Catholic, the search for his Jewish roots has become increasingly important to him.

Having encountered a number of Christian students with a Jewish background, I have been surprised to find how many broken threads of Jewishness there are in our world today. Recovering their Jewishness is like a bridge that suddenly appears on the horizon. I invite them to walk over and see what is on the other side of the bridge, opening up another world that is also deeply theirs.

Increasingly, the Jews I encounter are fenced in by their Jewishness—or the version of Jewishness they carry. I have encountered this in myself as well. The Jewishness I carry forth in the world is both my own and shared. I also know that I, and we, need to subvert our known and knowable Jewishness if we are going to move out of the Jewish present into the Jewish future. Levinas has his own Jewishness that confronts our own. In turn, aspects of his Jewishness need to be confronted.

Experiencing this newfound Jewishness with students is remarkable. There is a personal layer of inheritance. There is also a communal layer that the person discovers. My student suddenly discovered another part of himself, a sense of Jewishness that is more than constructed.

In our post-Holocaust world, Jewishness may extend even further to those who have had no familial contact with the Jewish world. This may be the reason that Jewish thinkers resonate so deeply in the non-Jewish world. More than a decade after Levinas's death, he continues to generate an international discourse about violence, justice, and the Other. The reason for this influence could simply be the power of his thought. Yet the power of thought might also flow from his Jewishness or, as in Arendt's sense, because he lived between Jewish and European culture.

Though they rarely refer to each other, clearly Levinas finds his place in Arendt's hidden tradition of Jewish dissent. Or perhaps Levinas occupies a particular branch of this evolving tradition, because he was more overtly religious in his language and style. It might that the hidden tradition of Jewish dissent today is more religious, though a kind of religiosity that is distinct from normative Jewish religiosity and the more prominent Jewish secularity.

Over the years, the teacher/student inversion has become more common in my life. In my mind as a student, Rubenstein was already formed. I could not imagine him needing students to broaden his outlook. It is only when the student becomes a teacher that he recognizes that he, too, is evolving and that the students he teaches are part of that evolution. Rubenstein had set me on a journey, but even then I knew his understandings could not sustain me. His path was not my own. The Jewish intellectuals he introduced me to have been crucial for my journey. Yet there were other parts of me I knew I had to explore. I needed other guides. The journey of the Jewish world during my adult years has raised urgent new moral and ethical questions relating to Jewish empowerment in America and the state of Israel. The journey continues.

Levinas was the last of our great Jewish thinkers with whom I became acquainted, and he became one of my mentors. Mentors help us discover aspects of ourselves that lie beneath the surface, but in the end we are responsible for our own journey. Like all Jews of the contemporary period, Levinas's depth was riddled with contradictions. Could I escape the same plight?

The Passion of Passions

The first Levinas essay I read was "A Religion for Adults," which was originally a lecture he gave in 1957 to monks at the Abbey at Tioumliline in Morocco. It was a Christian institution in a nation where the majority of the population is Muslim. At that time, interfaith conferences were rare, but the need for such was heightened in the aftermath of World War II. There was the hope that a world beyond war could be created and sustained. Coming after two world wars in close succession, that hope was shadowed by desperation. For many it was doubtful that the world could sustain the destruction of another world war.

One of the issues at this conference was whether religions, which have often been part of the world's divisions, could help create a more peaceful world. To do so, they would have to sort out what divided them and what they held in common.

A theme in the post-war interfaith dialogue was how each religion's particularity could be retained while also celebrating what the religions held in common. This could be a way forward. Whether retaining a religion's particularity was possible while joining in a more universal interfaith embrace was controversial in the post-war era. It continues to be so in our post–September 11 era.

Solidarity among religions and their adherents is a delicate balancing act, especially among the followers of the monotheistic religions of Judaism, Christianity, and Islam. Political ideologies have led to destruction, and religions have also played a role in division and war. The challenge remains when these same culpable religions become catalysts in creating a new world order based on mutual recognition and love.

In Levinas's essay there is something strikingly original, as if he was addressing the world on these issues for the first time. Certainly, his conceptual framework for Judaism and the world religions would have been experienced as provocative at that time. Especially unusual, however, is how Levinas carves out the special place of Judaism in this new economy of religious solidarity.

Levinas begins with a belief in God as the commonality that Jews, Christians, and Muslims share. He sees this commonality as a civilizing force for each community and for the wider world. It is the shared belief that there is a reason for humanity beyond itself, anchored in God, that allows each religion to inculcate in its followers a humanism above political ideologies and the shifting sands of nationalism. Though the monotheistic religions often lose their way, Levinas believes that the future of civilized humanity is dependent on rediscovering each religion's particular mission.

"We all in fact maintain that human autonomy rests on a supreme heteronomy and that the force which produces such marvelous effects, the force which institutes force, the civilizing force, is called God," Levinas writes. What is needed now is the rediscovery of this common belief that allows a special language of a humanism that comes from and with God. Especially after the years when that language was "confronted by the proud affirmation of energies at free play, and drowned out by the overflowing of purely natural forces," the special language of religion has also become a "common life." For Levinas, this common life was rediscovered spontaneously, as if the crisis of catastrophe forced each religion back unto itself and toward other religions. A choice was presented to each religion and to religion in general: either speak fully and together and engage the world from your depths or remain on the sideline and be swept away by history.[1]

As he affirms a common God and civilization, Levinas immediately shifts to the uniqueness of the Jewish landscape of faith and the suffering Jews have just undergone in the Holocaust. He addresses his Christian audience in language with which they are familiar. Instead of using the word "Holocaust," a term still in its infancy, he takes a more direct and provocative route, characterizing the recent suffering of Europe's Jews as the *Passion*. In using this term of utmost religious significance, Levinas highlights his belief that something more than suffering happened to the Jews of Europe.

Levinas's move is bold. It transgresses specifically Christian boundaries. Why use a term so central to Christian faith when it was Christian anti-Semitism that laid the groundwork for the destruction of European Jewry? For a Christian audience, Levinas adopts a symbol for what happened to the Jews that defines the essence of the Christian faith. Thus Levinas throws into question just what redemptive suffering is or indeed if suffering is redemptive as Christians claim. By defining Jewish suffering in Christian terminology, Levinas also crosses a Jewish boundary that before and after the Holocaust has been seen as sacrosanct.

Levinas opens up the dilemma of what becomes of Christianity and Judaism once the boundary of violence and atrocity is crossed. Though he uses the terminology without explanation, it seems that Levinas is pushing back on both Jewish and Christian presumptions about their own religions, at least as they are presented in the world. Judaism and Christianity are already on the sidelines of history. They need to be shaken up at the core. Only then can their presence become more relevant.

Even today, Levinas's use of the Passion imagery is striking. It forces us to rethink both the Christian and the Jewish side of the meaning of suffering. It might even compel us to rethink the Holocaust imagery that has now assumed an orthodox sensibility among Jews and Christians today.

Levinas believes that when pushed to the wall of human endurance, Jews reclaimed their vocation in the world. The Passion that Europe's Jews experienced thus has meaning for the Jewish future. While Christianity's task is to awaken and revaluate its very being in the world, so too Jews are presented with the challenge of what Israel's vocation is in the world:

I should like to remind you of what the years 1933–1945 were like for the Jews of Europe. Among the millions of human beings who encountered misery and death, the Jews alone experienced a total dereliction. They experienced a condition inferior to that of things, an experience of total passivity, an experience of the Passion. Chapter 53 of Isaiah was drained of all meaning for them. Their suffering, common to them as to all victims of war, received its unique meaning from racial persecution, which is absolute since its paralysis . . . refuses any conversion, forbids any self-abandonment, any apostasy in the etymological sense of the term; and consequently touches the very innocence of the being, recalled to its ultimate identity. Once again, Israel found itself at the heart of the religious history of the world, shattering the perspective within which the constituted religions had enclosed themselves and re-establishing, in the most refined consciences, the link—which until then had incomprehensibly been hidden—between present-day Israel and the Israel of the Bible.[2]

For Levinas, the people Israel have their own particular path in the world. Many of the Christian and Muslim faith had come to believe that Judaism helped give birth to them but that the original impetus of Judaism carried by Jews had either disappeared or become enfolded in their religions. However Judaism was imagined by Christianity and Islam, Jews as individuals and as a community remained visible. Since the living significance of their religion had been usurped, living Jews were seen as archaic and were often derided. Being invisible and blatantly visible led to the mix of theology and ideology that defined the contemporary Jewish Passion.

For Christians and Muslim, Jews as contemporary carriers of a specific vocation were no longer important to the world. They had become obsolete. Oddly, more than a few Jews also felt that Judaism was obsolete and that the reasons for maintaining a Jewish life had vanished. Levinas sees both visions as strange and troubling.

For Levinas, the slaughter of Europe's Jews subverts this sensibility. The mass killing of Europe's Jews forces reconsideration on all sides. Because Jews were totally innocent in their suffering and because there was no way out for Jews, even through conversion, the stakes of their murder were heightened. Therefore, Jews had to reconsider their own being in the world. Levinas believes that Jews re-embraced their unique destiny and reclaimed the continuity between the people Israel in the Bible and Jews today. This was a leap for Jews who had given up their Judaism and sought assimilation in the cultures that surrounded them. Since the connection between the Israel in the Bible and Jews today could not be thought through as an intellectual exercise, how could the connection make sense? It was the experience of the Passion that explained the connection Jews encountered within themselves and as a community.

Levinas's Passion inversion also raises the question of whose suffering counts in the modern world and whether Christians who claim the Passion as their guiding belief can make that claim without keeping the unique destiny of the Jewish people in the forefront. Or in Levinas's view, has the claim of the Passion switched hands, reverting to the original carriers of Israel's destiny?

Although Levinas makes the reference without probing it further, it is hard to believe that his audience of monks missed the point. Today we are more accustomed to borrowing and even inverting religious imagery. Still, at a time when interfaith dialogue stressed the integrity of each faith tradition and their fundamental separation, Levinas's appropriation of the Passion for the Jews of Europe raised hackles.

Marc Chagall's paintings of Jewish suffering do include the imagery of the Crucified Christ wrapped in a *Tallus*, a Jewish religious shawl, in a way similar to how Levinas inverted Christian imagery. Still, Chagall was an artist, and the eye of the beholder decided what these images meant. As a survivor of the Holocaust and a philosopher, Levinas is much more direct. He proceeds without asking permission. Yet he is speaking to monks and other Christians who have committed their lives to the proposition that there was only one Passion, that of Jesus Christ. This scandal of particularity could hardly contain Levinas's broadening, especially because according to him it now included millions of Jews whose ancestors had been accused of the crime of deicide. Levinas's lecture preceded by some years the Second Vatican Council, when Jews were absolved of the murder of Jesus. Still, Levinas's appropriation of the Passion moves in a much more radical direction than the Council intended.

By appropriating the Passion for the Jews of Europe, Levinas implicitly criticized Christian history, minimizing Christianity as a religion and perhaps even undermining its very foundation. That Levinas could speak thusly and be applauded meant that indeed a new era of Christian history was beginning. It meant that Christians could listen to Jews as equals and also allow Jews as critics within the Christian framework. Levinas demanded something more than mutual assent, however. He was calling for a new Christianity. He did all of this without laying a groundwork or explaining what he had done and why.

How does Levinas accomplish this reversal? Though Levinas would hardly deny the Christian roots of anti-Semitism, he spends no time there. Instead, he pointedly refers to the "racial persecution" of Jews that even prevented their conversion and ostensibly their safety as converts to Christianity. Thus, he bypasses Christianity as an enabler of the Holocaust.

By emphasizing racial persecution, Levinas also shifts the ground from underneath most Jewish writers on the Holocaust. Levinas avoids a binary, more static division between Judaism and Christianity, as if by playing off Judaism and Christianity, Judaism as an independent religion is reestablished. Levinas is free to discuss Christianity in a somewhat different light. He does so as he continues his discussion of the Passion of European Jewry. Here Levinas also refers to Islam:

> At the moment of this experience, whose religious range has forever left its mark on the world, Catholics, whether secular, priests, or monks, saved Jewish children and adults both in France and outside France, and on this very soil Jews menaced by racial laws heard the voice of a Muslim prince place them under his royal sovereignty.
>
> I am reminded of a visit I once made, as part of a religious ceremony, to the church of Saint Augustine in Paris. It was at the beginning of the war, and my ears were still burning from the "new morality" phraseology that for six years had been circulating in the press and in books. There, in a little corner in the church, I found myself beside a picture representing Hannah bringing Samuel to the Temple. I can still recall the feeling of momentarily returning to something human, to the very possibility of speaking and being heard, which seized me at that moment. The emotion I experienced can be compared only with what I felt throughout the long months of fraternal detention spent in Fronstalag in Brittany with the North African prisoners; or with my feelings in a Stalag in Germany when, over the grave of a Jewish comrade whom the Nazis had wanted to bury like a dog, a Catholic priest, Father Chesnet, recited prayers which were, in the absolute sense of the term, Semitic.[3]

The fraternal sensibility, the note of the human he hears in Christianity in a time of inhumanity, and then after World War II in the discussion of the new morality, strikes Levinas to the core. He seems to describe this Christian witness during the Passion as calling him and Israel back to its destiny, as much as did the racial persecution.

Racial persecution reduced Jews to the level of animals. The compassion of a Catholic priest brought the Jewish victim back into the human community. Though Jewish prayers over the dead were preferred, the priest's Catholic prayers, tied as they were to the monotheistic tradition, were sufficient. Rather than being offended by this prayer over the death of a Jew, Levinas was himself brought back to life. He was reminded of the land of the living where Jews and others have meaning even when their deaths are intended to go unnoticed.

Levinas preempts the argument over whether the Holocaust dead were victims or martyrs by acknowledging that even a Catholic prayer is recognition of the worth of Jewish life. Prior to this, and for years after, Christianity had become absent in the Holocaust discussion, except as a negative, anti-Semitic force. For Rubenstein, Judaism and Christianity are rival religions and thus Jews should expect little from Christians when the chips are down. If Jews want to be free of persecution and demand that Christians relinquish their claims to be the New Israel, then Jews have to relinquish their claim to be God's chosen ones. In Wiesel, it is when the rabbis refuse to abandon their people that Christianity is addressed. In his town of Sighet, a group of priests offered the rabbis refuge in a nearby monastery, but Wiesel assumes they only wanted an alibi in case the military situation was reversed, so that they could say they saved Jews.

Rubenstein also takes on Christianity when he references a museum photograph of a Christmas celebration in the Westerbork concentration camp in the Netherlands. Rubenstein writes that those "responsible for the death of over one hundred and ten thousand Dutch Jews took time out of their grisly labors to celebrate the birth of their Jewish God in the very place where they were sealing the doom of every single Jew they could find." He also makes the claim that "former pastors were active leaders in the work of death."[4]

Levinas chooses a different path. As a means of interfaith solidarity, the three monotheistic faiths remind each other of their own particular way of speaking and being heard. It is striking that in this early period after the Holocaust and years before the Second Vatican Council affirmed the closeness of Judaism and Catholicism, Levinas outlines how that appeared in his life and, by extension, what it might mean for Jews and Catholics after the Holocaust.

To a large extent, this element is missing in post-Holocaust interfaith dialogue today, at least with the heartfelt sensibility of Levinas. Any closeness is trumped by the accusations of Christian complicity in the Holocaust because of historical Christian anti-Semitism. Though aware of this history, Levinas chooses instead to emphasize how without the possibility of a Jewish burial, a Catholic priest at least affirmed the humanity of the Jew who the Nazis wanted to "bury like a dog."

Levinas believes that Judaism, Christianity, and Islam are united because like the Nazis the modern world assumes that the ancientness of the monotheistic religions disqualifies them from speaking in the world or from being heard. For Levinas it is this very ancientness that makes them so needed. Their language is from a different time. Therefore it can shock the world out of its complacency, interrupt what is considered to be the norm, and offer a way forward.

When the Nazis were treating that Jew like an animal, denying him even a decent burial, what would affirm his humanity? The very assault against the human vision in the Holocaust and the lack of post-war systems of thought to address this made the ancient religions more relevant. Yet to do so, certain assumptions among Christians and Muslim must be confronted, such as that they had subsumed the Jewish role in the world. Though Christianity especially needed to provide space for Jews to reconsider their own place in the world, Jews have their own responsibility in this matter. Levinas places before

Christians, Muslims, and Jews the same question, "How can we hear the voice of Israel?"

Levinas's main concern is what the Jewish voice in the world is meant to be and how Jews can once again embody that. This may be the reason for his curious reference to Isaiah 53. That verse may have made perfect sense when addressing the monks and other Christians at the conference, seeing it is still used by Christians to signal the coming of Jesus Christ as the Messiah. Yet Levinas inverts the Passion imagery and applies it to the Jews of the Holocaust. In his reading the victims of the Holocaust replace Jesus and are now considered the Suffering Servant(s). Isaiah 53 also is important in Jewish life outside of the Christian interpretation. In Jewish life, Isaiah speaks of the people Israel as the Suffering Servant, chosen and derided, with a resurrected life to come. Thus, despite Christian interpretation, the Jewish reading or scripture remains valid.

Could Levinas be thinking that the suffering of Europe's Jews as somehow redemptive—even by Jews—must also be discarded? It is also possible that he is taking the possibility of Israel's suffering out of the theological and eschatological mix. The Passion of the Jews during the Holocaust could be a counter to the original Isaiah. At least for Levinas, Isaiah 53 can no longer be read in the same way by Christians or by Jews—*after*.

The question remains whether eschatology can be set aside in Judaism or Christianity while these religions remain as they have been throughout history. In naming the suffering of Europe's Jews as the Passion, Levinas transforms the Christian understanding of Jesus as Christ. Linking that suffering to racial rather than religious persecution also interrupts the Jewish sense of martyrdom. The choice for Europe's Jews was not one of faith or betrayal. Levinas also de-links, at least for the time being, the death of Jews to Christianity.

Levinas raises the question of what Judaism and Christianity are as religions. Do Jews and Christians have a destiny that is intended and prescribed, and if so, will it be fulfilled at the end of time? Is it the same for both religions? For either is there a transformative event that leads to redemption? If the Holocaust is now that transformative event, it is difficult to see anything redemptive coming from unmerited suffering that is not linked to religious choice. At the same time, perhaps paradoxically, such unmerited and unredemptive suffering calls the people Israel back to their own destiny.

Levinas does not specify what a destiny for the people Israel can be after the Passion, except to live out an adult faith. It appears that this has little to do with transcendence. At the same time, it is hard to see how Levinas's view of an adult life of religiosity can be found within Christian life.

Levinas's naming of the Holocaust dead has different levels. Referring to the Holocaust as the Passion means that the Holocaust dead experienced martyrdom and that their very innocence is the essence of that martyrdom.

Levinas believes the Holocaust ends vicarious suffering as redemptive. So without individual or collective suffering being redemptive, how can the Passion Jews have undergone be the conduit for Jewish renewal? Levinas simply asserts this connection as being real. It is Israel's innocence and persecution that made this special vocation reappear, this after it had gone underground in Christianity and Islam and even among many Jews. The recovery of Israel's ultimate identity has to do with the very innocence that was persecuted: "Once again, Israel found itself at the heart of the religious history of the world, shattering the perspective within which the constituted religions had enclosed themselves and re-establishing, in the most refined consciences, the link—which until then had incomprehensibly been hidden—between present-day Israel and the Israel of the Bible."

In their Passion, then, Jews experience the stripping away of the accumulated layers of Jewish history. Also stripped away were the intermingled layers of non-Jewish history that had found their way into Jewish life. In the Holocaust, both the psyche and religion of Jews were cut to the bone. Naked and suffering, life could not resume as it had been.

The martyrdom of the Jews of Europe forced this question to the fore. Instead of giving birth to other religions, Jews and Judaism were back at the beginning with their original vocation. Christianity and Islam were again distant and foreign entities. Indeed, as it is the very innocence of the people Israel that recalls Jews to their own vocation and their ultimate identity, it is for Jews to rediscover exactly what that destiny is—by themselves.

For Levinas, there is a method to the madness of history. Horrible events like the Holocaust have a meaning, perhaps even a purpose, that may or may not be intended. Other than Jews, what other people who undergo suffering—as do all victims of war—could make such a claim or have such an impact on themselves and the world?

At stake in the Holocaust was the possibility that the voice of the people Israel might be lost to the world. Other religions saw Israel as only a precursor to their own faiths. Israel also was unsure of itself. Was there any reason for an independent Jewish voice in the religiously saturated and yet increasingly secularizing West?

Levinas argues the opposite. The Holocaust reclaims Jewish particularity among the world religions and among Jews themselves. The question is what Jews have to contribute in the world today and with what voice they will speak.

Though for Christians the voice of redemption has been relativized or stilled by the Holocaust, Levinas believes the opposite is the case for Jews. Recovering the Jewish voice in the world is of utmost importance, and in many ways is Levinas's life project. Yet that recovered voice is chastened by the Holocaust itself. It is carried by a people in mourning. Thus, it seems that Israel's vocation has to be different than it was in the Bible. At least it has to be shorn of its accumulated metaphoric visions.

Levinas first argues the particularity of the Jewish path as its main contribution to the broader world. Judaism ceases to be for the world when it loses its own way. Nor can Christianity travel its specific path without recognizing Jewish particularity. Without Jews recognizing as well their specific and continuing contribution to the possibility of faith, Christianity is diminished.

Though Levinas affirms the need for Jewish-Christian solidarity, such solidarity is cultural rather than overtly theological. A Jewish-Christian culture is essential for both religions, with Christianity providing the space for Judaism and Judaism contributing the foundational principles. Both are important for structuring a civilization that speaks and hears justice.

On the specifics of how Judaism and Christianity interact, Levinas is guarded. "Lest the union between men of goodwill which I desire to see be brought about only in a vague and abstract mode, I wish to insist here precisely on the *particular* routes open to Jewish monotheism," Levinas writes. "Their particularity does not compromise but rather promotes universalism. For that reason, this monotheism must be sought in the Bible that is bathed by the sources in which, while being both common to both Jewish and Christian traditions retains its specifically Jewish physiognomy." Levinas is silent on how the particularity of the Christian tradition might also benefit Jews but direct on the independence of Jewish life and spirituality: "The paths that lead to God in this Judaism do not cross the same landscapes as the Christian path."[5]

Levinas's reference here is to Rabbinic Judaism, the Judaism that Rubenstein abandons because of its religious and political inadequacy after the Holocaust. Buber also refuses Rabbinic Judaism because he believed that, like all religions, Judaism tried to mediate the unmediated relation with *Thou*. Heschel is closer to Levinas in asserting the continuing validity of Rabbinic Judaism, yet Levinas's rhetoric is much starker. In the end, Levinas's Jewishness is bifurcated as Rabbinic Judaism and the prophetic are divided in his thought and perhaps in his life. Instead of burying the prophetic, Levinas highlights it.

Levinas's writing on the prophetic is clear and concise, unlike his rabbinic meditations, which are often wandering and abstract. In general, it is difficult to see how the rabbinic and the prophetic can be held simultaneously without resolving their contradictions. However, Levinas articulates both aspects of Jewishness without fearing that they cannot be held together. The only other Jewish thinker who attempted this bridge was Heschel, whose rabbinic and prophetic proclivities were much more traditional and grounded in an understanding of Jewish destiny that was, for the most part, uninterrupted by the Holocaust.

Paradoxically, what is lyrical and evocative in Levinas is the very starkness of his imagery. With Heschel, the Bible soars and his articulation of the biblical message carries the reader away with its beauty. Reading Levinas is like burrowing deeper and deeper until so little remains that the reader looks for relief. Levinas's writing travels the paradoxical road of despair infused with destiny.

In front of the audience of monks, Levinas is mostly silent on the prophets. Or perhaps he invokes the prophetic by emphasizing the Judaism that developed after the Hebrew Bible and the New Testament. In this Christian setting, and in a Muslim majority society, simply announcing a living Judaism was prophetic. Further, the use of the Passion for Europe's Jews is so unexpected and confrontational that it could be considered a prophetic act in and of itself.

For Levinas, Christians need to affirm Judasim, since Christians have traditionally affirmed the prophets of the Hebrew Bible as the precursors to Jesus. By affirming Judaism as it has developed since Jesus, Christians also have to affirm the particularity of the Jewish search and restrain any form of Christian triumphalism. From the beginning of his lecture, Christianity and Islam are back on their heels, among the world religions, with Judaism standing at the center with an independent voice that is startling to them. Those who have undergone the Passion of the Holocaust are independent of Christianity. The claim of the people Israel is ongoing. "If you had been shocked or amazed by that," Levinas continues. "You would have been shocked or amazed that we remain Jews before you."[6]

Two years earlier in an essay "Loving the Torah More Than God," Levinas meditated on the meaning of the Holocaust for faith:

> [T]he Passion of Passions . . . continue to resound and reverberate down the centuries. . . . What can this suffering of the innocents mean? Is it not proof of a world without God, where only man measures Good and Evil? The simplest and most common answer would be atheism. . . . But with what lesser demon or strange magician have you therefore filled your heaven, you who claim that it is empty? And why, under an empty sky, do you continue to hope for a good and sensible world?[7]

Here the Passion of the Jews has become the "Passion of Passions," thus upping Levinas's own theological inversion of Jewish and Christian theology. The Holocaust recalls Jews to their original vocation and Christians to understand the continuing special role of Jews as well. But what do Jews have to say to each other and to the world about God? Clearly Israel cannot affirm a God who "dished out prizes, inflicted punishment, or pardoned sins."

Levinas encounters the traditional sense of God in both the Jewish and Christian traditions but sees Christianity as more dependent on this childlike understanding than is Judaism. It is hard to imagine a religious system more foreign to Levinas than the Christian one where God becomes human and is crucified for humanity's sins, through which the world is redeemed.

Levinas asks about the need for God if most of the images of God held by believers are childlike. Does this invalidate any possibility of God? Perhaps the sanest option would be to let go of God. People, societies, and ideologies always posit Gods who promise prizes, punishment, and pardon. If the Jewish and Christian understanding of God changes, there will be other Gods to replace them. Or have Jews and Christians already been worshipping these other Gods? Levinas seems to be pointing to this when he writes of the "lesser demon or strange magician" that "filled your heaven, you who claim that it is empty?" Still, the further question is asked of the believer who no longer affirms a childlike God: "And why, under an empty sky, do you continue to hope for a good and sensible world?" Can the world be sensible, is there hope, can the world ever be just, if there is no God?

Without God able to lift us out of history or rescue humanity from suffering and death, there seems little reason to affirm God. If affirmation is simply a fairy tale, then we face a Godless world. Few events could be more compelling and less childlike than the Holocaust.

Levinas responds by again emphasizing the difference between the adult's and the child's God: "The path that leads to the one God must be walked in part without God," Levinas writes. "True monotheism is duty bound to answer the legitimate demands of atheism. The adult's God is revealed precisely through the void of the child's heaven. This is the moment when God retires from the world and hides His face." Here, Levinas works through the child's conception of God to reach another side of God. To do so, however, he must respond to the legitimate demands of atheism, a response that is hardly theoretical. The only way for the believer's response to make sense is by abandoning and walking without the known God:

> The God who hides His face is not, I believe, a theological abstraction or a poetic image. It is the moment in which the just individual can find no help. No institution will protect him. The consolation of divine presence to be found in infantile religious feeling is equally denied him, and the individual can prevail only though his conscience, which necessarily involves suffering. This is the specifically Jewish sense of suffering that at no stage assumes the value of, a mystical atonement for the sins of the world. The condition of the victims of a disordered world—that is to say, in a world where good does not triumph—is that of suffering. This condition reveals a God who renounces all aids to manifestation, and appeals to the full maturity of the responsible man.[8]

For Levinas, abandoning God comes about because human beings have been abandoned by God. In recognizing this real state of affairs, we are thrown back upon ourselves. This means we have to suffer, though now without recourse to salvation or a "mystical atonement."

Jews have this ability within their tradition because they have experienced suffering as part of their destiny, without being conscious of being saved. Levinas does not see this as a new condition directly related to the Holocaust. It is the human condition and specifically the Jewish condition, perhaps because of the Jewish emphasis on chosenness. Nonetheless, the Passion of Passions drives home this lack of rescue.

Levinas understands Judaism's peculiar route to God to be through atheism, a path to be walked without expecting to be delivered into a "child's heaven." This is a direct critique of the Christian vision of being saved from the harsh reality of the world, which Levinas believes also represents a form of violence. If the otherworldly can annul human responsibility, then it can be used as an excuse to violate others in its name. For Levinas, any spirituality proposing that we can be lifted out of our human predicament is false. Such beliefs are mobilized to demonstrate its truth. The violence from above is mirrored with violence here on earth.

For Levinas, the cycle of belief in and demonstration of an otherworldly faith is one way of understanding the violence of Christian history in relation to Jews. Jews have resisted the Christian interventionist and incarnational God and consequently have suffered at the hands of Christians. Though Levinas does not directly discuss Christian anti-Semitism as the cause of the Holocaust, it is difficult to avoid this conclusion when reading Levinas. In his vision, the adult believer knows there is no redemption and often no appeal. Those who have suffered the Passion of Passions know the reality of the unredeemed world. Those who assert redemption often do so at the expense of Jews who know different.

This may also be why it is difficult for Levinas to bring together rabbinic and prophetic understandings of Judaism. The prophetic believes in an interventionist God, as found in the Hebrew Bible, where violence is sometimes committed in the name of God who acts in history. The biblical God also sanctions rewards and punishments. Rabbinic Judaism is less appealing in these areas, yet Levinas refuses to jettison the prophetic as essential to Judaism and the world. But can the prophetic survive the end of the child's God?

Ethics as the Optic of the Divine

Levinas begins his commentaries on Judaism and the prophetic before Rubenstein and Wiesel enter the public scene. Buber was there already. In his speech to the monks, Levinas affirms Buber's comments on Christians regarding the Hebrew Bible as their Old Testament: "Thus it is that the voice of Israel is at best heard in the world only as the voice of the precursor, as the voice of the Old Testament which—to use a phrase from Buber—the rest of Jews have no reason to consider either a testament or old, or something to be situated in the perspective of the new." At the same time, Levinas parts company with Buber's transcendent sense of the Eternal *Thou* and the concept of *Thou* itself. The particular routes open to Jewish monotheism limit transcendence, even in encounter. At no point is being transported into another time frame positive.[9]

Where Buber envisions closeness, Levinas needs distance—the distance from the Other that allows ethical relations. Insofar as Buber attempts to overcome or enter deeply into Otherness, Levinas believes this violates the ethical. The sacred enveloping and transporting us is, for Levinas, a form of violence.[10]

Some years after writing *I and Thou*, Buber had the transformative experience of moving out of a transcendental mysticism toward what he called the "hallowing of the everyday." Even there, for Levinas, the Other is to remain as Other, without being entered into or absorbed. Rather, the autonomy and distance of the Other is the essential challenge to our own individuality that cannot be absorbed or detached.

For Levinas's taste, Buber remains far too enthusiastic in his description of spirituality. Levinas warns against any encounter that is less than a command, coming from the distant Other who is also, paradoxically, our neighbor. The neighbor as Other stands alone and can only be absorbed and assimilated through a violence that violates the Other's essential nature. For Levinas, Buber plays too fast and loose with the otherness of both the person and of God.

Wiesel's additional covenant and his almost mystical sense of the Holocaust and the state of Israel also fall into Levinas's critique of the "sacred" that envelopes and transports. Wiesel's sense that God's presence is past makes the appeal to the sacred less imposing in the present, but the Holocaust still is present and abiding. Wiesel's identification of the Holocaust with the sacred transports us to a different world that allows him and other Jews to make significant claims about ultimate reality, even if that reality is without God. For Levinas, the Holocaust cannot rescue us.

The state of Israel becomes part of this rescue, which perhaps is why Wiesel rarely comments on the particulars of Israeli policies toward Palestinians or its internal social and political life. As well, Levinas occasionally refers to those years of Nazi terror in order to reframe the questions of Jewish destiny. But Levinas views the Holocaust as an event wherein Israel is called back to its destiny rather than an event we can access through devotion. Still, by naming the murder of six million Jews as the Passion of Passions, Levinas does court that danger of mystifying the Jewish journey. As we shall see, Levinas's discussion of the state of Israel also runs that danger of opting for the sacred. Just as he seems to be moving there, however, he reverses course.

The sense that the people Israel have a destiny already seems to assert the sacred, even if the God ordaining that destiny is chastened. How can such a destiny claim to be made without acknowledging an interruption in history from outside, and how can such a claim be held up without being transported into the sacred?

Rubenstein refuses the transcendent God of history, yet Rubenstein drops the vital sense of Levinas's thought that affirms the movement of Jews and Judaism through atheism. Rubenstein breaks the tension that Levinas maintains between a destiny and the sacred. Like Wiesel, Rubenstein opts for a solution to the question of God. Levinas refuses a solution while also changing the perspective from which God can be named and asserted.

The suffering that Levinas envisions is partly found in the Jewish relation to a God who does not save. In the end, without comfort in his challenge of God, Rubenstein abandons this relation to God. In Levinas's framework, Rubenstein abandons the challenge of coming to a more mature adult conception of the tensions that living and suffering entail.

Levinas's stark geography of faith is less an argument with God, as in Wiesel, and more an engagement that cedes little ground to parts of the Jewish tradition with a more robust sense of God's presence and activity in history. Levinas is insistent on the responsibility of human beings and of the specific nature of the Jewish path. At the same time, his tone is one of insistence rather than anger.

Among the Jewish thinkers here, Levinas expresses the least anger with God and, except for Heschel, is the most insistent on God's presence. Though a philosopher by profession, his conception of God is deeply theological and has a transcendental aspect that highlights the human struggle with suffering. The importance of Jewish fidelity in history is thus underlined.

Levinas emphasizes that the willingness to suffer and persevere is essential to the Jewish journey. For Rubenstein, the power to forestall future suffering becomes the ultimate goal in his vision of post-Holocaust Jewry. Levinas is ambivalent about this quest for power. If Jews take on the violence of the world, won't they also need to affirm a sacred reality that saves? Whether that sacred is God or the Holocaust or the state of Israel matters little to Levinas. All eventually lead to idolatry, which Levinas equates with the embrace of a childlike and violent sacred reality.

Already in the 1950s, Levinas saw the danger of Jews and Judaism elevating the Holocaust and the state of Israel to the category of the sacred. Levinas wondered whether Jews who had walked the path of atheism because of their suffering could remain in that difficult tension of affirmation and negation. If the tension was resolved, Levinas believed that Jews would ultimately embrace the Holocaust and Israel as a sacred form of transcendence.

For Levinas, the voice of the people of Israel reclaimed after the Holocaust must avoid false transcendence. Then the Jewish voice would regain its resonance and authenticity. Additionally, embracing the Holocaust and Israel as sacred would remove both events from Jewish participation and analysis. This would release Jewish conscience from the challenges intrinsic in living a conscious and conscientious life.

If there is no transcendence that transports us outside of the reality available to us as human beings, and if positing such would be a form of violence, how is atheism related to an adult faith? For Levinas monotheism "de-charms" the world, which means to rid the world of false Gods, especially the Gods of nature and ideology. It also means that the Gods of religion are suspect as well. Any God who mainly comforts or takes away human responsibility must be opposed or banished.

Judaism contests the very "notion that religions apparently evolved out of enthusiasm and the Sacred" and resists "any offensive return of these forms of human elevation." Judaism denounces them as the essence of idolatry. For Levinas, this is why Judaism concentrates on applying intelligence first to biblical revelation, and then "the rigorous affirmation of human independence, of its intelligent presence to an intelligible reality, the destruction of the numinous concept of the Sacred." This entails the risk of atheism. "That the risk must be run," Levinas writes. "Only through it can man be raised to the spiritual notion of the Transcendent."[11]

Paradoxically, it is here that Levinas recovers the transcendent. Judaism does teach a "real" transcendence that involves a direct and immediate relation with God. This is crucial to a tension between a God who is there yet often absent and the responsible human beings who through intelligence and suffering make their way through life. Self-consciousness and conscience are as important here as is the Other, the neighbor, whom we face and who places demands on us.

For Levinas, the Other as a person is an independent being who challenges our self-perception and being in the world. This is what Levinas means when he says: "My neighbor's face has an alterity which is not allergic, but opens up the beyond." The Other keeps us alert and monitors our behavior. Our responsibility toward the Other increases, whereby we retain and even deepen our humanity.

In the otherness of the Other the paths of atheism and the transcendent cross. The otherness of the Other is the challenge that refuses our own desire for closure in life or in relation to God. What we do here is essential. "The Justice rendered to the Other, my neighbor, gives me an unsurpassable proximity to God," Levinas writes. "It is as intimate as the prayer and the liturgy which, without justice, are nothing."[12]

The practice of justice and ethics in relation to the Other are the opening to God. Though in much theology grasping and affirming truth are central, Levinas views actions as central. If actions are ethical with regard to the Other, then we can speak about God. The ethical relation unites self-consciousness with the consciousness of God. Rather than being a corollary of God, "ethics is an optic, such that everything I know of God and everything I can hear of His word and reasonably say to Him must find an ethical expression." That ethical expression is a commandment that we experience in the face of the Other, whereby we understand immediately that to "know God is to know what is to be done."[13]

If knowing and doing are in relation to the Other, then turning away from the ethical obligation is turning away from God. Levinas believes that Judaism developed a science interconnected to this ethical obligation. This is because Judaism provides the "austere discipline" that refuses false transcendence in practice and, grounded in daily ritual and commandments, maintains attentiveness to the needs of the Other for justice. Thus, Levinas can say that "the way that leads to God therefore leads *ipso facto*—and not in addition—to man; and the way that leads to man draws us back to ritual discipline and self-education." And: "The ritual law of Judaism constitutes the austere discipline that strives to achieve that justice.... Only this law can recognize the face of the Other which has managed to impose an austere role on its true nature. At no moment does the law acquire the value of a sacrament."[14]

In spite of his aversion to the transcendent, Levinas's language has an almost mystical force. Yet his distance from Buber's and Heschel's use of language remains. Levinas thinks that Buber's *Thou* transports us beyond the law and thus out of Judaism's ritual science, but for Levinas the daily ritual and commandments are there regardless of where we are spiritually. While maintaining the traditional structure of Judaism, Heschel also delves deeply into the meaning of the law as Jews carry it out. Levinas sees meaning here without delving further into any kind of symbolic or ritual enhancement. The law's rigor is stark and unremitting. Jewish law, the opposite of what is attractive to many in religion, continually calls us back out of the sacred. Rather than the sacred relieving us of our duties and suffering, Jewish law does just the opposite, reminding us of the daily obligations that root us in unredeemed reality.

Though Levinas does not think that the law is a yoke as Christians often assume it to be, it does require effort and indeed courage to be faithful to it in daily life. This dovetails with Levinas's sense of a practiced daily justice, as found in the Bible. "The fact that the relationship with the Divine crosses the relationship with men and coincides with social justice is therefore what epitomizes the entire spirit of the Jewish Bible," Levinas writes. "Moses and the prophets preoccupied themselves not with the immortality of the soul but with the poor, the widow, the orphan, and the stranger. The relationship with man in which contact with the divine is established is not a kind of spiritual friendship but the sort that is manifested, tested and accomplished in a just economy and for which each man is responsible."[15]

Our relationship with God is a test rather than the spiritual friendship that Christianity and some forms of mystical Judaism seem to offer. In spiritual friendship our eyes are turned toward God rather than the face of the Other. Levinas asks what a spiritual friendship with God could possibly mean in light of a just economy "where each man is responsible." Can a person be responsible to God without being always and everywhere responsible to the Other right next to him? Though we might speculate that a person can be responsible to the Other and also be in a spiritual friendship with God, Levinas is dubious. For him, the special route of Judaism precludes this. Levinas believes that the responsibility of persons with regard to others is such that even God cannot annul it.[16]

If Jews are violated and naturally seek to resist that violence, does that mean Jews can use violence in turn? If Jews counter violence with violence, where does that violence stop? What is too much counter-violence, and who makes this judgment? If human responsibility cannot be annulled even by God, does this mean God has no say at all on the matter of violence being used in self-defense?

While Levinas is not a pacifist, he worries over the prospect of Jews taking on the violence of the modern world. He worries about this over time and in a manner different from our other Jewish thinkers. Few Jewish thinkers address the role of violence in contemporary Jewish life, and when they do, it is reluctantly and only in relation to the Palestinian cause. For most Jewish thinkers and most Jews, the state of Israel is innocent; only the Other commits violence. However, Levinas is less naïve. Already in his 1952 essay "Ethics and Spirit," he devotes a section to this issue, under the title "You shall not kill":

> The face, for its part, is inviolable; those eyes, which are absolutely without protection, the most naked part of the human body, nonetheless offer an absolute resistance in which the temptation to murder is inscribed; the temptation to absolute negation. The other is the only being that one can be tempted to kill. This temptation to murder constitutes the very vision of the face. To see the face is already to hear "You shall not kill," and hear "You shall not kill" is to hear "Social Justice." And everything I can hear coming from God or going to God, who is invisible, must have come to me via the one, unique voice. "You shall not kill" is therefore not just a simple rule of conduct; it appears as the principle of discourse itself and of spiritual life.[17]

For Levinas, the face of the Other is the conduit for God, the only one available to us and the only one needed. In the face of the Other we hear the voice of God, which is Social Justice, a demand that we resent and want to end. Hence our temptation to murder the Other is our desire to be released from this demand. However, since the demand is really a command, our temptation to murder the Other is our temptation to silence the voice that comes from God.

It might be that murdering the Other is our best effort to murder God. However, encountering the Other, we already hear God's command. Consequently, there is no way to silence the voice of God. Being always invisible and visible at the same time makes the Jewish God omnipresent in our responsibility.

When heard in the face of the naked, vulnerable Other, "Thou shall not kill" grounds the voice of God in a responsibility that cannot be annulled except by annulling the Other. Yet by annulling the Other through murder, the Other's importance is highlighted by the aloneness the murderer experiences. This is what Levinas means when he calls violence a sovereignty that is also a solitude.

Power over the Other is an example of what happens when the face of the Other is foreclosed and the voice of God refused. What results is an aloneness that offers no respite from the Other. Even the Other's absence is another form of presence. Then the temptation to murder increases because, once involved in murder, each Other whom the murderer encounters presents the same command. With every murder the murderer's solitude increases.

For Levinas there are two sides to this solitude. The first is the aloneness that the difficult path through atheism presents. Belief in God will not transport us beyond ourselves or annul our responsibility. The second is the aloneness we feel when the face of the Other commands us to move beyond self-gratification and contentment. Perhaps the commandment "Thou shall not kill" is a corollary to "Thou shall not commit suicide," since the aloneness of the spiritual path might lead one to despair.

Throughout, Levinas places an enormous burden on the person. To begin with, the person must walk the path of God without God. Then the person hears the voice of God as a command through the Other, to practice justice. All of this is without the consolation of being saved or being rescued by God, even in a time of need. Further, a spiritual relationship with God is denied. This is so demanding that it is little wonder most religions prefer instead to transport the human into the sacred.

The difficulty of life for Levinas is establishing a society based on social justice without which we cannot approach God. The God we come before remains encased in the human face that we desperately want to transcend, perhaps because we want to transcend and therefore become God. The ethical relation also establishes society, which Levinas considers to be a miracle. Rather than spiritual friendship with God, society is the miracle of moving out of oneself while leaving the otherness of the Other intact. If for Levinas, violence is the attempt to violate the Other and thus release us from the Other's command to do justice, society is the framework for a life together that respects the commanding presence of the Other.

In society the Other is sovereign and our solidarity is found in respecting the Other's sovereignty, as ours is respected as well. Here, Levinas seeks a distance that allows respect and independence rather than intimacy and friendship. He is thinking of the "miracle" of human beings living with one another through restraint and self-transcendence.

Like Jewish law, society requires a daily routine and attention to detail that does not promise salvation or rescue. Levinas is making a connection between adult religion and adult society. Though Levinas does not state it directly, he seems to see a connection between certain understandings of Christianity and Fascism, Islam and Fascism, and even perhaps Judaism and Fascism. Levinas experienced Fascism as a political movement. If we can murder only "when one has not looked the Other in the face" and if the "commerce with beings which begins with 'You shall not kill' does not conform to the scheme of our normal relations with the world," then all ideologies, even formative events that become like ideologies such as the Holocaust and the state of Israel, must continually be reexamined for their propensity toward violence and totality.

On the one hand, we live in a world of violence and counter-violence. On the other, we have positions that over time become hardened and self-referenced. To keep them in place, they must also become religious in Levinas's negative sense, transporting us outside of ourselves. Following Levinas's logic, we turn away from the Other or define the Other in our terms, absorbing and assimilating them to our cause. But if, as Levinas counsels, the face of the Other forces us to depart and does not allow us to return to "self-contentment, self-enjoyment, or self-knowledge," and if the face of the Other also establishes society, doesn't that imply that Jews also have to recognize other collectives, such as the Palestinians, as our own interlocutor?

Expiating Blasphemy in Advance

After Auschwitz, the Jewish covenant may indeed be broken. Efforts to mend it may be doomed to fail. God language itself may be blasphemous in the face of burning children of the Holocaust. Yet the Jewish covenant is further tainted by a violence and atrocity Jews now perpetrate against Palestinians.

Levinas is cautious here. Sometimes his thought is convoluted. It is difficult enough to analyze past events. Even more challenging is to reflect philosophically and religiously on historical events that are still unfolding. This is especially true when millions of lives are at stake and when a nation-state such as Israel is acting on a domestic, regional, and international stage. Can Israeli society be established and maintained by instituting Levinas's understanding of the face of the Other? Does "You shall not kill" translate into a plan of action when confronted with powers internal to and outside of Jewish society? This is another way of asking how Levinas's ethics applies to the memory of the Holocaust and Israel as it lives and breathes.

If there is violence at the very heart of the covenant, it is hard to imagine that the prophetic can escape unscathed. For some Jews who criticize the policies of Israel, violence has become the marker of what it means to be Jewish in the world. Is this the preface to an exile from which there is no way back to a Jewishness that embodies ethics and justice?

It is difficult for Levinas to envision a broken covenant. Since for him God is not a rescuer, the matter of God's absence in the Holocaust is of little importance. Still, as a European Jew who survived the Nazis and then, living in the continent where the Holocast had occurred, witnessing the birth of the state of Israel, Levinas saw this struggle close-up. He was not indifferent.

As we have seen, Levinas wrote movingly of the Holocaust as the Passion of Passions and wrote of the hope and danger of the state of Israel. However, he hoped that the state of Israel would use violence minimally, only enough to survive. Otherwise, Israel might become like other nations, absorbing and assimilating the Other, until the distinctions between nations faded. If that were to happen, Jews could hardly avoid becoming like other peoples and Judaism like other religions.

On some issues, Arendt and Levinas are quite close. They both see certain uses of power and violence as an infection that moves beyond the particular act into the communal understanding of reality. Abuse of power and indiscriminate use of violence are for both like an infection that spreads everywhere.

Levinas explored the danger that Israel might take on the violence of the world as its *raison d'être*, becoming like the other nations and forgetting its own mission. Not coming to a resolution on this, he rarely if ever addressed the concrete policies of Jewish and Israeli power. In the end, he was diffident about the state of Israel and the need for Jews to take on the violence of the world. He knew only too well that the state of Israel could not take on the violence of the world without Jews and Judaism also taking on that same violence. What if Levinas had paid more attention to details of the history of the state of Israel? Its very creation, with the ethnic cleansing of the Palestinians at its origins, certainly challenged Levinas's understanding of "Thou shall not kill" and perhaps its logical extension, "Thou shall not displace."

Yet the death and displacement of Palestinians, at least initially, was bound up with the death and displacement of European Jews. The timing was so close that the imposition of Jews on Palestinians might be justified, at least from a

Jewish point of view, by the exigencies of history. Could it be justified within Levinas's thought? How many details of the formation of any state can survive Levinas's rigorous philosophical and theological investigation?

Regardless, Levinas's questions about Israel penetrate to the very core of what it means to be Jewish. As early as his 1952 essay "Ethics and Spirit," Levinas laid the groundwork for his exploration of Jewish identity after the Holocaust by raising the matter of the Jewish struggle against idolatry in the nineteenth century and the lost language of Jewishness, a complexity still relevant today. He begins with a lament about what he refers to as the "poor nineteenth century." During that time, religious Judaism sought to accommodate itself to the surrounding non-Jewish culture, an accommodation that threatened to eviscerate the roots of the Jewish prophetic for future generations. Although this became obvious only after Holocaust, by then the toll had been taken:

> Separated more and more from the rabbinical tradition and its exegesis, the morality offered in Western temples no longer contained a message to justify the messenger. It more and more resembled the generous but general formulae of the European moral conscience. The European moral conscience did exist! It flourished in that happy period in which centuries of Christian and philosophical civilization had not yet revealed, in the Hitlerian adventure, the fragility of their works. Philosophical morality never seemed more conformist, or Israel's mission closer to its term.
>
> And certainly the antiquity of the message, the existence of a Moses or an Isaiah in an age when Greece still wallowed in barbarism, sets the imagination racing. But historical worth cannot compensate for existing pointlessly. In the realm of the spirit, there are no automatic allowances to be claimed. Only a brilliant present can invoke its past merits without demeaning itself—or, if need be, can invent itself on the basis of them.[18]

Here, Levinas counterpoises the ancient voice of Judaism with its contemporary vision. In one sense, Jews were drawn to a foreign sensibility in the hope that they would be able to normalize their condition. For Jews, the freedom to enjoy the life of the average citizen was no small matter. Yet the hope of a European moral conscience was exposed as fragile and vanishing by Hitler and the Nazis.

In a time of their greatest need for solace and guidance, Jews were left bereft. Further, because of the desire of Jews to assimilate, Levinas believes that the ancient Jewish prophetic was rendered homeless. By the time the Jewish community called upon the ancient greatness of Judaism, it was only a shadow of itself. Judaism had strayed from its essential roots. It was on the verge of being lost.

Though Levinas thinks that ancient religions, including Judaism, constantly have to renew themselves to be present in the world, when assimilation goes too far there is the danger that the power of renewal will be lost. This is why Levinas believes it was the Holocaust that recalled Jews to their destiny. Being challenged to the very core forced a reappraisal of Judaism. It was almost too late.

When the essential reason for Judaism's existence is lost or abandoned, Jews no longer justify the message they have been given. Before the Holocaust, according to Levinas, some Jews refused this assimilation and continued the ancient tradition. To do so, however, they had to further distance themselves from the Jewish community and what was distinctively Jewish. In short, such Jews had to leave the Jewish community in order to be faithful as Jews.

If Jews and Judaism were accommodating to the surrounding culture, what could ground this refusal to assimilate? Levinas believes that the Jews who left Judaism were carriers of the underground prophetic, without articulating it as Jewish. Unknown to themselves or other Jews, these rebellious Jews were actually preparing the way for the survival of Jewishness and Judaism.

To live out their Jewishness, rebellious Jews became more deeply involved with a world and a language that was foreign to them. While these Jews continued on the trajectory of what Levinas believes to be the essence of Jewishness, identifiable and upstanding members of the Jewish community had departed from it.

Jews traveling the "right path" became involved in revolutionary movements addressing non-Jewish societal concerns. Some of these movements engaged in violence that they saw as just in righting the wrongs of the world. They plunged headlong into a revolutionary world that sometimes transgressed even its own stated values. In doing so, Levinas believes that they violated their own unarticulated Jewish values and lost their moorings in the world. Nonetheless, their witness was not lost on the world or the Jewish future. Levinas refers to these rebellious Jews positively as "denigrators of tradition" and as "atheists and rebels."

> But did Jews at least continue to bring peoples a prophetic morality through the examples of their lives? The virtues which, in the darkest periods of the Middle Ages, provoked the admiration of Christians of good faith, were shattered like the walls of the ghetto. Others replaced them but the Jews, in discovering certain freedoms, also took on much of the violence of the modern world. They joyfully espoused every form of nationalism, but equally burdened themselves with their quarrels and passions. Israel has not become worse than the surrounding world, whatever the anti-Semites say, but it has ceased to be better. The worst thing is that this was precisely one of its ambitions.
>
> Perhaps, from that age on, the Jewish presence manifested itself more in the Israelites participation in liberal and social movements—in the

struggle for civil rights and true social justice—than in the sermons to be heard in liberated synagogues. All these denigrators of tradition, all these atheists and rebels, unwittingly joined the divine tradition of intransigent justice which expiates blasphemy in advance. With these rebels, Judaism, which had scarcely been absorbed into the surrounding world, already opposed it on one level. But in this manifestation, it found itself deprived of its own language. Having nothing but will, it turned to a borrowed system of thought to understand itself.[19]

Levinas recognizes that the Jewish spirit is on the move here, alternating between escaping the singled-out Jewish condition and affirming it. Part of the Jewish ambition is to join the world, becoming no worse but also no better than other nations. This is Levinas's analysis of the Jewish struggle for emancipation and citizenship before and during the twentieth century.

In pursuing this prophetic vision, the vanguard of the Jewish people threw off the shackles of the ghetto and the ghettoized mentality of Jewish leadership. Some Jews also refused to accumulate privileges among the elite and joined movements for revolutionary change. Because of the fears of the Jewish establishment and restrictions placed upon Jews by society, these Jews were atheists and rebels of necessity. They wanted and needed to be free of Judaism and the Jewish community in order to struggle for universal justice in the wider society. In doing so they participated in what Levinas calls the "divine tradition of intransigent justice."

If his analysis were not provocative enough, Levinas also asserts that this very atheistic and rebellious attitude "expiates blasphemy in advance." Blasphemy cannot be present if a Jew is responding to the face of the Other in need. For Levinas, the departure of many Jews from an assimilating Jewish community was a positive sign. To leave the Jewish community, they had to become atheists because the Jewish religious authorities were brandishing the assimilationist God as the true God of Israel. As atheists and rebels, these Jews did more than rebel; they distanced themselves from the community and denigrated its traditions. Thus, their rebellion was experienced by the community as an assault, an assault that in Levinas's view was necessary. They were the modern day prophets who addressed the Jewish community and experienced more or less the same fate as the ancient prophets. Their task was similar: "With these rebels, Judaism, which had scarcely been absorbed into the surrounding world, already opposed it on one level."

In other words, for Levinas these atheists and rebels joined the "divine tradition," a tradition with origins in the Hebrew prophets and which through "intransigent justice" has proximity to God. This is an inflexible, obdurate, obstinate, intractable, and unbending will for justice that makes blasphemy impossible in advance. Their pursuit of justice eliminated the very possibility of calling their relation to God in question. Because the Jewish community was conforming to the world, this atheism was necessary. Exercising conscience, these rebels walked at least part of their path without God.

The problem was that they replaced the language of Jewishness with borrowed non-Jewish languages (from Europe and later America) that were foreign to Jews and Judaism and which therefore could not form the basis for *Jewish* dissent in the future. Levinas believes that ultimately only a "Jewish" language can undergird the Jewish mission to the world. He fears that Jews who rebel against their language will be lost to the Jewish world.

Is that true of such Jews today? Are Jews who flee the Jewish community on account of justice joining once again that "divine tradition" that "expiates blasphemy in advance?" The difference is that instead of moving out into the world and railing against the Jewish world that gave them birth, they are also engaged in a Jewish civil war. The assimilation of the Jewish community now is twofold—to the world and within the Jewish world.

Following and updating Levinas, there are Jews today who believe that the state of Israel has taken on the violence of the modern world and advanced it. Therefore, contemporary "Jewish" language revolves around the Holocaust and Israel. Insofar as the memory of the Holocaust has become a servant of Israel's power in particular, for these Jews it functions as a perpetrator of violence as well.

In our present context, what "language" can Jews use to "expiate blasphemy in advance?" What does it mean to be a Jewish rebel and atheist today and in what language is this rebellion and atheism spoken? As with previous periods of borrowed language, do these atheists and rebels "unwittingly" join the "divine tradition of intransigent justice?"

For Levinas, the divine tradition of intransigent justice is the prophetic that is foundational to Jewish life. Yet the prophetic and its language are always contextual. When Levinas limits prophetic speech to the language of Hebrew, a language that has rarely been used in public discourse in Jewish history, or to contemporary normative Jewish discourse and culture, does he stifle the creativity of the Jewish prophetic tradition? In the modern period at least, it has been the ability of Jews to counterpoise different "languages" that are part and parcel of Jewish insurgent thought.

Language for Levinas denotes a general discourse of Jewish concepts in an identifiably Jewish conceptual universe, thus it is not limited to Hebrew. The difficulty here is that with the rebirth of Hebrew as a spoken language in Israel, the Hebrew language itself may be part of the same assimilationist patterns.

Hebrew has become the national language of Israel and therefore is involved in all matters of the state, from planning water sewage systems in Tel

Aviv to building the Wall around Palestinians in the West Bank. Can the divine tradition of intransigent justice be carried out in Hebrew or must Hebrew now be counted among the languages from which atheists and rebels must flee in order to expiate blasphemy in advance? It may be that Hebrew, ostensibly the Jewish language par excellence, is so tainted with injustice and atrocity that it needs to be abandoned in order for Jews to be faithful today.

All of these questions are tied up with the "return" of Jewish life to Israel. The question is what this return means in practice. Since many Israelis are leaving Israel because they feel the injustice of Israeli policies toward Palestinians is too great, is this similar to why nineteenth-century Jews left the Jewish community, as a way of exercising their conscience as Jews? Do those Israelis who leave Israel for reasons of conscience expiate blasphemy in advance?

Even in Levinas's understanding, the language outside of normative Jewish discourse has been essential. The use of other languages by Jews has helped turn those languages upside down and inside out. A combination of Jewish and non-Jewish languages has historically fueled Jewish atheists and rebels, such as Sigmund Freud, Franz Kafka, Walter Benjamin, and Albert Einstein.

With the revival of Hebrew and Jewish renewal, the irony is that more and more Jews find both the Jewish language and the renewed celebration of Jewish life suffocating. Levinas seemed unaware of the conundrum that faces Jews who exercise conscience in the way he affirmed. He did not contemplate the possibility that there might be an expiration date on renewed Jewish commitment within an empowered Jewish world.

There may be an instability within Jewishness that rarely allows stasis. Just when Jewishness seems to be reestablished another break is inevitable. Perhaps the prophetic is cyclical. Jews leave the confines of Jewish life, then return, only to leave again. What may be different today is that the long-hoped-for return to Israel has occurred, while the disappointment in that return has engendered another exile. On the face of it, this might mean an exile without return to Israel or to the Jewish community anywhere else. This could be the final exile in Jewish history, the expiration date par excellence.

If the Jewish community in Israel and around the world is intent on following the assimilation to power and injustice that Jews who expiate blasphemy in advance reject, there may be no Jewish harbor left anywhere. Jewish atheists and rebels might then rest comfortably in the New Diaspora, made up of exiles from all peoples, religions, and lands. However, their children might not identify as Jews.

In this New Diaspora, what Jewish language is available? Are there Jewish atheists and rebels actually living Jewishness without claiming its name? Levinas doesn't ask whether Jewish language and living are inherently confined to those who identify as Jews, or whether identifiable Jews may lose their

Jewishness because their assimilation has an expiration date after which they are Jewish in name only. In a strange twist of fate, it may be that the normative Jewish community is no longer Jewish and those who never have or no longer claim Jewishness now carry the divine tradition of intransigent justice. They may be carrying that tradition against a normative Jewishness that itself will never return to its Jewish roots.

Still, Levinas's questions remain. If the "borrowed system of thought" comes in cultures and religious/ideological systems of nations outside of the people Israel, can Jews find a home there and be truly themselves? How will Jewishness be passed on to future generations if Jews will either never feel at home in the borrowed systems of thought or will be fully assimilated? Levinas poses a challenge:

> One cannot, in fact, be a Jew instinctively; one cannot be a Jew without knowing it. One must desire good with all one's heart and, at the same time, not simply desire it on the naïve impulse of the heart. Both to maintain and to break the impulse is perhaps what constitutes the Jewish ritual. Passion mistrusts its pathos, and becomes and re-becomes consciousness! Belonging to Judaism presupposes a ritual and a science. Justice is impossible to the ignorant man. Judaism is an extreme consciousness.[20]

Does this mean that the only way to be Jewish is through Jewish ritual? Is the science that Jews have known the only science that can be known as Jewish? If justice is impossible to one who is ignorant, what happens when we discover that well-educated Jews are quite capable of carrying out injustice and characterizing it as Jewish?

Levinas knows that Judaism can also become a cover for assimilation to injustice and power. Levinas argues an essence to Judaism—the prophetic—that abides even when Jews stray. This is akin to stating that though Christianity has assimilated itself to power for almost its entire history, the essence of Christianity is its initial marginalization and refusal to cooperate with unjust power. When do we simply conclude that so much of Christian history has been involved with colonial and imperial domination that its essence now includes these aspects of its history? The time is coming when we may need to ask the same question to Jewish history. The question Jews face is whether or not this assimilation to power and injustice has already permanently marked the Jewish world.

Asceticism and the Prophetic

In the long sweep of history even the origins of cultures contain elements of what went before. It is difficult to speak of borrowed languages as if any language is original or indigenous. Few linguists or anthropologists believe that languages, cultures, or symbol systems are pure, which also applies to religion. There is no pure and original Judaism.

Monotheism develops gradually in the Hebrew Bible, through struggle, prophetic denunciation, and sometimes violence. Jews have always been boundary crossers even when it relates to God. If Jews had been respecters of boundaries, there would be little need for the multitude of regulations that draw severe distinctions between the clean and unclean, between the worship of the one true God and the false Gods.

In Levinas's evocation of a Jewish "language," he seems to mistake continuity in Jewish life for an ever-changing pattern of Jewishness that is as discontinuous as it is continuous. Most often, Judaism and Jewishness are in flux, made up of borrowings, with perhaps a series of crystallized foci.

While Levinas cites those atheists and rebels of the nineteenth century, he has difficulty delineating what exactly sparked their opposition. What part of their Jewishness allowed or demanded that they leave behind the Jewish community? We cannot be sure what in their Jewish background prompted this rebellion. Nor do we know what elements are necessary to recover a certain Jewish language, and which ones will solidify that rebirth. Again, it may be an inherent instability at the heart of Jewish life that is the catalyst within certain contexts that come and go.

Is the prophetic itself this instability? In Levinas, the prophetic is relatively undefined in its details, though its outlines are clear in the Hebrew Bible. It may be that at certain times the prophetic simply comes to the surface, as if it can be contained for only so long. Though it can be modified and dismissed for extended periods of time, the prophetic resists categorization and banishment.

Levinas is mostly silent on the question of the character of God. Perhaps he sees speculation about God's nature as akin to a childlike enthusiasm rather than an adult concern. In the Bible, God, like the prophetic, lacks stability. The God of Israel's actions are often unpredictable, sometimes following a certain identifiable logic, at other times seeming to defy the logic that even God has laid out.

On occasion, biblical characters like Abraham and Moses alter God's perceptions and judgments. The incongruity of a lowly human being affecting God occurs more than once in the Bible. Abraham appeals to God's sense of justice while Moses appeals to God's ego. For Abraham, a just and all-powerful God could not condemn an entire city wholesale when there are righteous people within the city walls. For Moses, God could not abandon his chosen people in the desert because of their violations and thereby become the laughing stock of the world.

If anything, it seems that in the post-Holocaust era the attempt to recover a specific Jewish language has led to an uncritical embrace of the Holocaust and

Israel. Certainly that has led Jews further away from the extreme consciousness Levinas sees at the heart of Judaism. Post-Holocaust Jewish life may be another attempt to discipline the instability in Jewish history.

How can Jews live in constant instability? Can they afford the unstable prophetic in a time when Jews have lost one-third of their people and have founded a fragile and endangered Jewish state? Nonetheless, there are Jews who ask if it is time to seek another borrowed language to recover the critical consciousness that the Holocaust and Israel now occlude.

The idea of borrowed languages, cultures, and religions takes us further into identity formation. The challenge to Levinas is whether there is such a thing as a singular identity or even an identity that is differentiated from other identities. If historically we can seldom, if ever, speak of Judaism as univocal and separate, can we speak of Jewishness as distinctive? If we can still speak of Jewishness as distinctive, what it is that distinguishes Judaism from Christianity and Islam? The same challenge applies to Christianity, Islam, Buddhism, and Hinduism. As with Judaism, the identity claims of these religions are less meaningful when they claim their identity to be continuous and unitary.

Human beings have a need to demarcate origins and present-day orientations in the world. It is difficult to argue for meaning in the world if we have no place to stand that is unique. A sense of being set apart is an argument about meaning in the world. Jewish thinkers such as Levinas participate in this argument with a certainty that belies historical mixing and evolution. This is what makes Jewish thought so strong and attractive. It also is the Jewish Achilles heel, especially when Jewish identity formation is mobilized for power over others.

The toxic mixture of identity and power is true of any identity formation. Identity formation is important for survival when a community is under assault. It can be internally meaningful but lethal when mobilized against others. Assertions of a distinctive identity, especially when linked to a transcendent being or destiny, are often marshaled to commit violence against the identity and physical being of others. When identity is organized and militarized, dissidents have little choice except to flee to borrowed languages to speak and be heard.

Probing the origins and evolution of different religions and identities undermines the very idea of the prophetic as static. The prophets see all established religions as blasphemous and all received identities as covers for injustice. For the prophet, the very idea of religion is blasphemy.

Wherever the prophet stands, the prophet does so in relation to other attempts at prophetic witnessing. Even the prophetic has to be continually turned upside down and around. Otherwise, the prophetic might assimilate to what is expected of the prophetic.

Modernity sees itself as the alternative to a misguided identification with the sacred and with a given community. After involvement in the cycle of violence and atrocity over the course of the last centuries, it is difficult to see modernity being boastful about this achievement. Modernity has a worldview, eschatology, rituals and high priests, with sacred texts and demands for uncritical loyalty. Like all religions, modernity disguises its complicity and disciplines the prophetic.

Modernity promised a progress that would eliminate economic want, provide health and well being for all, and end superstition and war. Why, then, are so many in the world destitute? Modernity promised peace without end. Why, then, was the twentieth century so bloody a century with no end in sight? The prophetic shines a different light on whatever seeks to cloak its failings with garments of innocence. Modernity can be seen as the most powerful religion of our time. Traditional religions often try to soften some of the harsher aspects of modernity while functioning as modernity's enablers. I wonder what borrowed language will challenge modernity's claims.

Levinas views Judaism for the most part as independent of time and place. It is a touchstone to which Jews are periodically called back, even in dialogue with other religions and modernity. The Holocaust functions this way, in calling Jews back to their original destiny. Atheists and rebels flow in and out of Jewish history.

What then accounts for the power of the prophetic and its persistence over time? Here Levinas abandons the language of the rabbis and of Rabbinic Judaism itself. He opts instead for the origins of the people Israel.

If the prophetic appears in every age and culture in borrowed languages, can we speak of its essence? Levinas writes hauntingly on the nature and force of the Jewish prophetic:

> Judaism, disdaining this false eternity, has always wished to be a simultaneous engagement and disengagement. The most deeply committed person, one who can never be silent, the prophet, is also the most separate being, and the person least capable of becoming an institution. Only the false prophet has an official function. The *midrash* likes to recount how Samuel refused every invitation he received in the course of his travels throughout Israel. He carried his own tent and utensils with him. And the Bible pushes this idea of independence, even in the economic sense, to the point of imagining the prophet Eli being fed by the crows.
>
> But this essential content, which history cannot touch, cannot be learned or summarized like a credo. Nor is it restricted to the negative and formal statement of a categorical imperative. . . . It is acquired through a way of living that is a ritual and heartfelt generosity. . . . It is an asceticism, like the training of the fighter.[21]

This passage is from Levinas's essay "Judaism and the Present," which was published in the wake of the European and American youth movements that culminated in 1968. It was also written shortly after the 1967 Israeli-Arab war, though he does not mention the war in the essay. Though the conquering of Jerusalem, the West Bank and Gaza would lay further roadblocks for his vision of Jews rejecting the violence of the modern world, Levinas's focus is elsewhere. Most Jews, including Levinas, had little idea of what lay ahead.

Levinas was relieved that Israel won the war. Few then realized that within Israel's victory lay the making of its ethical undoing. Only later did it become clear that Israel's victory in the 1967 war sealed the fate of the Jewish prophetic—at least for a while. Arguments about the prophetic as being fomented by self-hating Jews and anti-Semites grew as Israel tightened its hold on the territories it conquered in the war. Theologians like Rabbi Irving Greenberg cautioned against the possibility of the prophetic undermining Israeli security, as that might lead to another Holocaust. Substantive criticism of Israel became the excommunicable sin of the post-Holocaust era.

Unbeknownst to Levinas and the Jewish community in general, an explosion of the prophetic was about to take place. The first stirrings of this occurred during the 1982 Israeli invasion of Lebanon and later came to fruition during the 1987 and 2000 Palestinian uprisings. Levinas did not understand the coming explosion during its first stirrings and did not live long enough to see its final flowering. Whether he would have embraced the prophetic in its later stages is unknown. What we do know is that Levinas fought its first stirrings, unable to see clearly where Israel was leading Jews and the Jewish community.

As the prophetic exploded, Jews borrowed yet another language to strike at an assimilationist community. The language that Levinas thought to be a homecoming for Jewish rebels and atheists was rejected. Similar to modernity's co-optation of the synagogues during the nineteenth century, the Holocaust and Israel had co-opted the synagogue in the latter part of the twentieth and early part of the the twenty-first century. Jewish critical consciousness had once again been assimilated to trends in society and to power.

As Jews engaged the prophetic, their exile became profound. This ever deepening exile poses the question as to whether any "Jewish" language will survive among those in exile. Most Jews today who speak a Jewish language are happily embedded in the Holocaust/Israel paradigm. Is this the conformism that Levinas wrote of when he praised those earlier atheists and rebels?

Levinas contributed both to the conformism of Judaism and to the rebirth of the Jewish prophetic. He played both sides of the issue, reserving judgment where judgment should be rendered and, at the same time, sketching out the contours of the future of the Jewish prophetic.

Levinas's understanding of the prophet is profound. He cites the "essential content" of the prophet as a core that "history cannot touch." Like Buber, Levinas does not think linear history or the political and economic systems of any period can define or judge the prophet. Levinas's code word for modernity, *Kantianism*, cannot wish away or replace the prophetic. Nor does the "particular privilege or racial miracle" of Jewish chosenness explain it. The prophet shadows the present context and the claims of Judaism as a presence that at times judges both.

For Levinas, humanity is constantly being offered "false" eternities, which the prophetic disdains. Judaism outlived the past and will outlive the present. It can participate fully wherever it is, while also remaining outside.

Clearly Levinas is writing here of a Judaism informed by the prophetic, rather than by Rabbinic Judaism. While the rabbinic aspect often, clear as it is, disciplines the enthusiasm of the prophet, Levinas skews the rabbinic toward the prophetic. Nowhere in rabbinic Jewish literature is the prophet and the prophetic evoked with such depth and force.

Levinas's prophetic Judaism is shorn of religious violence. It refuses sacred and military violence. It embraces the Other with the commandment "Thou shall not kill." Hence, Levinas sees the prophet as without official functions, without and against empire.

As in ancient times the prophet stands outside and against the religious hierarchy, independent of the social, political, and economic forces of his day. "Only the false prophet has an official function. The *midrash* likes to recount how Samuel refused every invitation he received in the course of his travels throughout Israel. He carried his own tent and utensils with him. And the Bible pushes this idea of independence, even in the economic sense, to the point of imagining the prophet Eli being fed by the crows."

Translated for our time, this means that the modern prophet functions outside the synagogue and Jewish institutional life and, insofar as possible, outside the economics and politics of modern life as well. For Levinas, the prophet is so deep in exile by refusing to compromise with injustice that she voluntarily carries her tent and utensils with her.

Levinas's writing on the prophets is his most eloquent and penetrating. The language he uses seems to exist independent of Levinas himself. He traverses the Jewish landscape with fascinating results. When he arrives at his place, Levinas is in a Jewish zone of his own making. With the prophetic, he is at home.

For Levinas, the prophetic cannot be learned or summarized in a credo; it can only be lived in a life characterized by a "heartfelt generosity." This is linked with asceticism. Instead of transcending history, the prophet burrows so deeply within history that he finds himself alone. This is difficult but necessary. If the prophet surrounds himself with the trappings of Judaism and the world, he would be called back to a conformism and an assimilation that belie his vocation. It is only by stripping away all attachments that the prophet can be who she is called to be.

The prophet also walks the difficult path of atheism, with a special consciousness linked to the face of the Other as the only way to God. Fixed on the face of the Other, the prophet cannot look away. This is part of the prophet's asceticism. When the prophet looks in the face of the Other, that face is always in need.

God does not rescue the Other, nor can the prophet. A further stripping away happens in this encounter because both the prophet and the Other have no appeal. Both are without divine or earthly protection. The prophet is not with God, nor is he in a mutual dependency with God, as in Heschel. In Levinas, as in Buber, the prophet is doomed, but that doom does not pave the way for redemption. Levinas believes that the prophet has an adult conception of being alone and without protection. Suffering is in the mix. Levinas does not chart a future for the prophet that brings social justice or redemption. The prophet is without destination.

This is the ground from which the prophetic practice Levinas calls extreme consciousness is born. Once born, such consciousness continues with and without God. For Levinas, the prophet is the crystallization of Jewishness and thus speaks the language of Jews and Judaism by his very being in the world. The prophet's appearance seems enough to provide hope for Jews and humanity.

For Levinas, the true prophet and the prophetic itself is only truly at home within Jewish history. Therefore, Jews are the carrier of the prophetic in the world. That peculiar configuration and power of the prophetic is found only among some Jews who bring the destiny of the people Israel to the fore.

So the prophetic is the lens through which Levinas sees the ultimate contribution of Jewishness to the larger world. The prophetic is a decidedly Jewish gift, perhaps the greatest gift in world history.

Few associate Judaism with asceticism, but Levinas provides us with a clue as to his definition, again within the realm of the prophetic. "Judaism is a non-coincidence with its time, within coincidence," Levinas writes. "In the radical sense of the term it is an *anachronism*, the simultaneous presence of a youth that is attentive to reality and impatient to change it, and an old age that has seen it all and is returning to the source of things." For Levinas, Judaism and monotheism in general "constitute the concrete fulfillment, beyond all mythology, of the primordial anachronism of the human."[22]

In this view, the prophet is attentive to the present as he brings forth a world from outside of the present. The prophet appears in a particular context with a vision that was born somewhere else and, though unannounced and unrecognizable by most, is the most subversive force in the world. Moreover, even as it is brought to bear on the present, the prophetic will outlast the present. Thus the "anachronism" is unexpectedly and vividly relevant, providing the prophet levers of insight and judgment, fully in the present and at the same time not here. The prophet refuses to be assimilated to the present.

How, then, does such a prophetic appeal work? How is it heard? What girds the prophet for the usual way prophets are received? One thinks of the prophet Ezekiel being called by God and then enjoined to eat the scroll that internalizes the prophetic call. God already foretells Ezekiel's doom, since the people of Israel will not listen.

Does God send the prophets and if so, once sent, do they have any further appeal to God? Here Levinas is silent, perhaps out of respect for the mysteries he is reluctant to utter or out of fear of the passions he might ignite. Nonetheless, Camus's question of whether it is possible to be a saint without God rings true here. For Levinas, the question is whether it is possible to have prophets with a God who is only accessible through the face of the Other, a God who does not call or protect the prophets.

Wiesel's additional covenant is one of mourning with Jews gathering in memory of God's presence. One can understand a liturgical memory as a vision for the future though it is absent in the present. Levinas's prophet, however, carries the memory of an ancient calling as a calling in the immediate present. Though Levinas's God is not officially past, we are unable to call on God in the present. Perhaps the prophet for Levinas is the Passion reappearing in the world, a sign of the just person who is completely aware and suffers for it. Perhaps Isaiah 53 retains a meaning for Levinas after all.

We return to the asceticism of the fighter. In Levinas's vision, the Jewish prophet, like Samuel, refuses invitations; Eli is fed by crows. This independence symbolizes the prophetic unwillingness to join the present as if it was the eschatological fulfillment of time and hope.

The prophet also refuses to assimilate to any one identity, as if it was chosen by God for all time. This leaves the prophet with little if anything to fall back upon when the going gets tough.

Levinas's imagery of Jews taking on the violence of the world is damning. Feasting at the table of injustice, the people Israel becomes one with idolatry. The prophet arises in opposition to the injustice of feasting while others are hungry. Instead of transcendence or redemption, the prophet calls the people Israel back to their true identity. That identity harkens back to Levinas's vision: "To see a face is already to hear 'You shall not kill,' is to hear 'Social Justice.' And everything I can hear coming from God or going to God. Who is invisible, must have come to me via the one, unique voice."

The prophet disturbs all the religious and secular credos and refocuses our attention on the face of the Other. Still, in Levinas, we rarely have a sense that the people are listening or being called. The prophet is so alone that the people Israel, the prophet's audience, are either assumed or relegated to the background.

Levinas's asceticism is the refusal to feast at the table of injustice, thus refusing idolatry. In thus refusing, the prophet denigrates what is proffered as tradition and rejects the accommodationist and assimilationist language in which that tradition is wrapped. By refusing to feast at the table of injustice and use the religious language of his day, the prophet expiates blasphemy in advance. By declining to bow to the God offered at that table of injustice, the prophet embodies God, even if God remains invisible and unnamed.

Levinas's Ambivalence

Some Jews believe that the very violence of the world has infected Judaism and Jewishness today. Though Levinas saw this as a coming possibility, he never embraced it as fact. Today, much of contemporary Judaism is learned through a catechism of empire. This is to project beyond Levinas, who died in 1995. But by then, Israel had been created through the ethnic cleansing of more than 700,000 Palestinians, permanent settlements had been build on parts of what remained as Palestine, for almost thirty years Israeli soldiers had occupied parts of Jerusalem, the West Bank, and Gaza, a brutal invasion of Lebanon had occurred, and nonviolent uprisings by Palestinians to establish their own state had been crushed by Israel. Levinas lived during the decades when the groundwork for Israeli expansion and the shrinking of Palestine was in full bloom. Why was he unable to connect the dots as to what Israel and Jewishness were becoming?

When I first encountered Levinas, I felt that despite the limitations of his thought his words on the prophetic opened up new horizons for the Jewish future. I still do. Through his words on the prophets, I heard the language of my life. However, I now also see his limitations more fully.

I had already been deeply involved in the issues of Israel and Palestine for many years. As with other Jewish dissenters, my expression of dissent had landed me in exile. My integrity was questioned and my job opportunities and speaking engagements limited. On my travels, private investigators stalked me. My Jewishness was questioned. One day after delivering a lecture, a young Jewish Studies professor opined that the language I used with regard to the state of Israel wasn't "Jewish." Then she left the lecture room in a huff. I wondered whether her expertise was in Levinas.

I also wondered whether, despite Levinas's ambivalence about the trajectory of Jewish life, he had created a context for analyzing Jewish life that held his own sense of the prophetic hostage. Despite his deep evocation of the prophetic, I wonder if he himself was afraid of the prophetic in Jewish life. Levinas may well have been afraid of the prophet within himself.

From the beginning, Levinas is ambivalent about the emergence of a Jewish state. As a European Jew, the Holocaust is uppermost in his mind. Moreover, he lived the rest of his life on the soil where Jews suffered mass death. Perhaps the priority for Levinas is that Jews are a nation with a mission before and beyond the state. Levinas believes that the special language for Jews is found in canonical and interpretative texts rather than in territory.

For Levinas, Jews read and interpret the texts of the Torah and the Talmud as the founding and unfolding of the special destiny of Jews and Judaism. It is from interpreting and living out these texts that Jews are able to contribute to the world. Nation-states come and go. Moreover, they use violence to survive. From Levinas's perspective, Jews have a special vocation to refuse the violence of the nations around them. After the Holocaust, Levinas asked what it would mean for Jews to take on the violence of the world. Once they did, Levinas asked how much violence Jews could adopt without ceasing to be Jewish.

Levinas knew that the state of Israel had taken on some of the violence of the world, which he believed necessary because Jews and Judaism had been assaulted in the world. It was also inevitable because all states need violence to survive.

Perhaps this was the essence of Levinas's ambivalence. On the one hand, Jews around the world were influenced by the state of Israel. On the other, who among the nations could or should lecture Jews about the violence of the state of Israel?

The people Israel must survive in the world to accomplish their mission. The danger to Jewish existence is what made the state of Israel necessary in the first place. Then again, the critics, Jews included, also lived in states with a history of violence. Looming in the background is the larger question of whether any collective, or individual for that matter, can survive in the world without violating others, including the Other who is our neighbor.

Shortly after the 1967 war, Levinas wrote a short essay, "Space Is Not One-Dimensional." In this essay, Levinas justified the creation of Israel as a state. In haunting language, Levinas explained the rise of the state of Israel from the ashes of the Holocaust:

> The Nazi persecution and, following the exterminations, the extraordinary fulfillment of the Zionist dream, are religious events outside any revelation, church, clergy, miracle, dogma, or belief. It was as such that these events, too heavily for their frame, entered the consciousness. . . . The Passion in which it was "finished" and this daring task or recommencement—despite the conflicting signs affecting them—have been experienced as signs of being chosen or damned—that is to say, of the same exceptional destiny. . . .

After twenty centuries of apparent anachronism, diasporic Judaism once more became, for the Christians themselves, the locus of the Divine Comedy. The creation of the state of Israel was produced at this level. It came alive once more in 1948, scorning all sociological, political, or historical improbability. The Zionist dream, which had evolved from the most implausible nostalgia, going back to the very courses of Creation and echoing the highest expectation, took shape at the cost of labour and sacrifices inspired by the glory invisible to the eyes of those who had not been haunted by the Dream and who have never been able to make it out, in contrast to their own tumbledown dwellings, anything more than a miserable arid land in the East, half-swamp and half-desert pretending to be milk and honey.

It is not because the Holy Land takes the form of a state that it brings the Reign of the Messiah any closer, but because the men who inhabit it try to resist the temptations of politics; because this state, proclaimed in the aftermath of Auschwitz, embraces the teaching of the prophets; because it produces abnegation and self-sacrifice. And certainly, this identity, geographically localizable through all Sacred History and nearly all Western history, holds great power over failings and wills. But it lends this power to all of the messianic institutions of Israel, all those who tear us out of our conformism and material comforts, dispersions and alienation, and reawakens in us a demand for the Absolute.

The resurrection of the state of Israel, its dangerous and pure life, can no longer be separated from its doubly religious origins: a Holy Land resuscitated by the state, in spite of the profane forms it assumes. To "go up" into Israel for a French Jew is certainly not to change nationality, it is to respond to a vocation. Others make espousals of faith, enter religious orders, go on a mission or join a revolutionary party. Through the appeal of the Holy Land, Jews hear new truths in their ancient books and enter into a religious destiny that cannot be summed up in dogmatics, but in history which its own limits cannot define.[23]

Clearly there is a different tone when Levinas describes the sacred here than in his earlier essays. Like most Jews, he is caught up and transported into an almost messianic-intoxicated enthusiasm in the aftermath of the 1967 war. Zionism is described as a "Dream," close to the "Sacred" that Levinas scorns. It becomes "Sacred History."

It is clear that Jews are involved in a sacred history, and Levinas describes the state of Israel in almost sacred terms. He asserts that the state of Israel can be analyzed to some extent as can other states. But unlike other states, Israel is also off limits to analysis.

Levinas struggles to retain aspects of his anti-messianic thrust. He affirms that the state of Israel has a profane shape, but what lay behind it is "the Holy Land," with its messianic implications. Moreover, he describes the prophetic aspects of Israel as a call for Jews to abnegation and self-sacrifice, even as he perceives the state of Israel as beyond nationality. Therefore, a French Jew who leaves to live in Israel embraces his vocation rather than changes nationality. There is something more about Israel than its state formation. That something more is found in its link with the ancient biblical promise.

Can any state, including the Jewish state, embrace the words and actions of the prophets? Levinas refers to the "Resurrection" of the state of Israel. If indeed Jews have experienced the "Resurrection" after their "Passion," then Levinas has made a further raid into Christian imagery. It is doubtful that Levinas could "borrow" anything more from Christianity and leave Christianity intact.

Levinas may simply be reappropriating beliefs that had been expropriated from Judaism by Christianity. Was he also reinstating the meaning of Isaiah 53 that he felt had been drained of its meaning by the Holocaust? If so, we would have to ask if this reappropriation of Jewish beliefs changed his own understanding of Judaism, extreme consciousness, and the refusal of the sacred as a form of violence. At least in the euphoric days of Israel's victory, Levinas seems to enter another sphere of religiosity, one that the bulk of his thought unceremoniously rejects.

Levinas always believed that there was a separate Jewish history with its own reference points. Still, the change here is important. Caught up in the moment, Levinas refers to the "Resurrection" of the state of Israel as a calling out of conformism to reawaken our thirst for the "Absolute." Should we expect any nation-state to call us back to the "Absolute?"

Levinas makes a distinction between the "Holy Land," "Sacred History," and the state of Israel. In most of his other writing, he argues against such distinctions as deceptive and as havens for idolatry. For Levinas, going up into the Holy Land or state of Israel is a response to a vocation or calling from God.

Levinas finds the appeal of the Holy Land to be the hearing of "new truths in their ancient books" and entering into a "religious destiny that cannot be summed up in dogmatics, but in history which its own limits cannot define." Like the call of the prophets, the state of Israel cannot be summarized in religious, nor for that matter political or sociological, categories. Nor can history as it is studied and written in universities and nations hold Israel's feet to the fire. Just as Jews have suffered the Passion of Passions that could not be defined in advance nor explained in accepted categories, the state of Israel, as part of the "Resurrection" of the people Israel, also defies categorization. For Levinas, Israel is a *novum* in Jewish and world history and therefore must be treated differently.

Before the 1967 war, Levinas was profoundly ambivalent about the trajectory of states, including the Jewish state. In "Means of Identification," published in 1957, Levinas expressed it this way:

> The act, word, and thought of a Jew have the formidable privilege of being able to destroy and restore whole worlds. Far from being a serene, self-presence, therefore, Jewish identity is rather the patience, fatigue, and numbness of a responsibility—a stiff neck that supports the universe.
>
> This primordial experience is expressed in a more tolerable way by Zionism, even if it gets turned into politics and nationalism in the process. For many Israelis, their identity card is the full extent of their Jewish identity as it is, perhaps, for all those potential Israelis in the Diaspora. But here Jewish identity runs the risk of becoming confused with nationalism, and from that point on, a loss of Jewish identity is probably the price to be paid in order to have it renewed.[24]

In 1969 Levinas addresses the question again:

> This struggle with the Angel is therefore strange and ambiguous. Isn't the adversary a double? Isn't this wrestling a twisting back on oneself, one that may be either a struggle or an embrace? Even in its most impressive struggle that Israel undertakes for the sake of its personality, even in the building of the state of Israel, even in the prestige it holds for souls everywhere, this sublime ambiguity remains: is one trying to preserve oneself within the modern world, or to drown one's eternity in it? For what is at stake is Israel's eternity, without which there can be no Israel. The combat is a very real one.[25]

Was this combat already lost when Israel became a state in 1948? As we have seen in the 1950s, Levinas was already writing about Israel taking on the violence of the world, though then he seldom specified whether he was writing about the people Israel, the state of Israel, or a combination of both. The context was the loss of Jewish particularity in the nineteenth and twentieth century and the desire of Jews to adopt the European "language" of morality and ethics. This is where Levinas wrote of Jews "joyfully" espousing forms of nationalism and burdening themselves with the quarrels and passions of the nationalisms that were not specifically Jewish. The result was that the people Israel, while not becoming worse than the surrounding world, ceased to be better. Levinas lamented that the "worst thing is that this was precisely one of its ambitions."[26]

Levinas does not write about the quarrels and passions that arose within the Jewish world about a Jewish nationalism embodied in the state of Israel, as Hannah Arendt did in 1948. Arendt predicted that in many ways the Jewish quarrels would be the same quarrels and passions that attend any nationalism.

Perhaps unlike Arendt, Levinas was too caught up in the Jewish trajectory of the state of Israel in Jewish history and its appearance in the post-Holocaust world to think through what might become of a Jewishness that had defense of a Jewish state as its preoccupation.

For thousands of years and especially in the nineteenth century, Jews had to guard against their adoption of other non-Jewish languages, lest "Jewish" be lost to Jews or Jews be lost to Jewish history. Though Levinas was for the most part ambivalent about the state of Israel and its relation to the violence of the world, he underestimated the energy and space it would take up in Jewish life in the ensuing years. Nor could he anticipate how much the Jewish world and language would conform to the external world to keep the Jewish state secure and flourishing.

It is difficult to find references in Levinas to America's role in Israel's flourishing, Israel's arms industry, or Israel's later arming of dictatorial regimes in Central America, apartheid South Africa, and elsewhere. Whatever the connection between the Holy Land and the state of Israel, the state is kept afloat by other interested parties and through its involvements in the affairs that are more than marginal to its existence.

Indeed, the state of Israel might have other significations than ordinary history. Nevertheless, at some point the practicalities of forming and running a state take on a life of their own. In general, Levinas is suspicious of the practical intrusions of nation-state life since this can only be conformed to violence in one way or another. Especially after the 1967 war, Levinas failed to understand that each day the actual life of the state of Israel worked against his own projection that the state is part of the resurrection of the Jewish people.

Levinas does warn that "Jewish identity runs the risk of becoming confused with nationalism, and from that point on, a loss of Jewish identity is probably the price to be paid in order to have it renewed." But once again, he seems to have underestimated the price to be paid. He was shortsighted about the increasing difficulties to come.

What if the renewal that he anticipated had ended with Jews being unable to find their way back to the Jewish substance that Levinas saw making the state of Israel distinctive from ordinary nationalism? What if the renewal were fraught with a violence that increased steadily during the last decades of his life, and even more since then? When does renewal itself become a wrong turn, taking such a toll that the way back to Jewish identity is precluded?

Identification with a state tends to conform to power, as Levinas well knew. The exact opposite is what he identifies as the essence of the Jewish spirit and vocation in the world. The biblical prophets Levinas invokes encountered this problem in their lives and called down the wrath of God on Israel's idolatry in its national life. Like many other Jews, Levinas saw in the state of Israel an ancient connection, though he and others emphasized only selective aspects of that connection. The judgment of God upon Israel's idolatry, as carried to the people through the prophets, is mostly absent in Levinas.

Still, the issue of the Jewish vocation in the world and how the state of Israel affects that is complex and ambivalent for Levinas. On the one hand, he warns Jews and the state of Israel of what is befalling them. On the other, he also demands that the world back off from its criticism. Having violated Jews for so long, the world has no moral lessons to communicate.

It is also disturbing that the Other, often characterized as the neighbor and of fundamental importance in Levinas's philosophy, is restricted. This is true especially when it comes to Israel's neighbors in the Middle East, as well as other peoples in the developing world. The Other, as the commanding voice that the self is responsible to and for, is primarily Jewish. Western non-Jews, mostly Christian, are also included. But the neighbor is rarely *Afro-Asiatic*, Levinas's encompassing term for the rest of the world, including Arabs and Palestinians.

For Levinas, the "Third World" is teeming with the uncivilized masses that he sometimes refers to as "hordes." In Levinas's vision they are waiting to invade the civilized West, which must be protected against them. It is ironic that Levinas views the West as civilized and the East as uncivilized, noting that it was the West that carried out the Holocaust.

On occasion Levinas vacillates, catches himself, and sometimes affirms Islam as part of the civilized world. In general, however, Levinas is Eurocentric and identifies Jews within that framework. Rarely in Levinas's work are Jews seen within the context of global humanity, except as separated and set apart. Nor does he acknowledge a Judaism that is indigenous to the Arab world.[27]

In his essay "Jewish Thought Today," published in 1961, Levinas expresses his understandings of non-Western people directly, especially as it relates to the newfound, post-Holocaust solidarity of Jews and Christians in the West:

> Surely the rise of the countless masses of Asiatic and underdeveloped peoples threatens this new-found authenticity? On to the world stage comes peoples and civilizations who no longer refer to our Sacred History, for whom Abraham, Isaac, and Jacob no longer means anything. As at the beginning of the Exodus, a new king arises who does not know Joseph.
>
> . . . [U]nder the greedy eyes of those countless hordes who wish to hope and live, we, the Jews and Christians, are pushed to the margins of history, and soon no one will bother any more to differentiate between a Catholic and a Protestant or a Jew and a Christian, sects that devour one another because they cannot agree on the interpretation of a few obscure books. They are a religious collectivity that has lost all political cohesion in a universe that is henceforth built around different structures.[28]

Even if the state of Israel is set apart and exists geographically in the Middle East, Levinas understands its existence and natural connections within the context of Europe. Though the negative reason for the state of Israel's existence is Europe, Levinas believes that Europe is its protection from the surrounding "hordes." Israel then is a demand on the European conscience because of its history of anti-Semitism and now a bond of solidarity as a civilizational barrier against the uncivilized masses of the East.

Though it inhabits the land of the Bible, for Levinas, Israel is located in an uncomfortable and disturbing neighborhood. Its only protection from this barbarism is Europe and its status as a European-oriented state. Lurking in the background is the people Israel's fight with the pagan world, now begun again in the Middle East. Salvation comes from Europe, ironically, the same place that damned the Jews during Levinas's lifetime.

Even in Levinas' early writing, Israel's Jewish population contained Jews from Arab and North African countries. Their percentage of the Israeli Jewish population grew considerably during his lifetime. Then and now, there are Palestinian Israelis among the citizens of the state of Israel. Both the Jewish and Palestinian non-Western populations of the state of Israel are rarely mentioned in Levinas, nor are the original Palestinian inhabitants of the land who were cleansed from Palestine in the creation of the state of Israel.

Though Levinas counsels against utopianism on all levels, the state of Israel comes close to being utopian for him:

> Zionism and the creation of the state of Israel means for Jewish thought a return to oneself in every sense of the term, and the end of the alienation that lasted a thousand years.
>
> The people of the book are forced to become a people of the earth. But the religious essence of Israel and its thought is ill-concealed behind the denial of God. The state of Israel has become the place where man is sacrificed, where he is uprooted from his recent past for the sake of an ancient and prophetic past, where he seeks his authenticity.
>
> While the spiritual personality of Israel was for centuries excused for its lack of participation in the history of the world on the grounds that it was a persecuted minority—not everyone has the chance to have pure hands because he is persecuted!—the state of Israel is the first opportunity to move into history by bringing about a just world. It is therefore a search for the absolute and for purity. The sacrifices and works which the realization of this justice invites men to make give body once more to the spirit that animated the prophets and the Talmud. The socialist dreams of Israel's builders do not become entangled in world circumstances. . . . The collectivist society of the kibbutz attempts socialism in one village! "The four

cubits of the Law" in which God took refuge, according to the Doctors of the Talmud, become the four hectares of the collective farm. We must not lose sight of the universal meaning that this work assumes in the eyes of the Israelis themselves, who believe that they are working for humanity.

Jewish universalism has always revealed itself in particularism. But for the first time in history, Israeli Judaism gauges its task only by its own teachings, which in some ways has been freed from an obsession with the Western Christian world, towards which it moves fraternally but without any feelings of inferiority or timidity.[29]

In 1982, Levinas's sense of Israel's participation in history was challenged most directly. During the Israeli invasion of Lebanon and Israel's bombing of Beruit, Lebanese Christian soldiers under the watchful eyes of Israel's army and with its permission were allowed into the Palestinian refugee camps of Sabra and Shatilla. A massacre of several hundred Palestinians ensued, followed by an international outcry and an upheaval within Israel itself. Israel was in crisis and Jews everywhere had diverse opinions on what to say and do in light of Israel's complicity in the massacre. When Levinas agreed to a radio interview in Paris, he knew it was bound to be difficult, as indicated in these selections from the interview:

> I have always thought of Jewish consciousness as an attentiveness which is kept alert by centuries of inhumanity and pays particular attention to what occasionally is human in man: the feeling that you personally are implicated each time that somewhere—especially when it's somewhere close to you—humanity is guilty. Close to you—as if one could anticipate that!

> Innocence is not the zero degree of conscience, but merely an exalted state of responsibility, which is perhaps the final nodal point of the Jewish conscience, among all those symbolized by the knots of our *tzitzit*: the more innocent we are, the more we are responsible.

> Evoking the Holocaust to say that God is with us in all circumstances is as odious as the words "Gott mit uns" written on the belts of the executioners.

> The Zionist idea, as I now see it, all mysticism or false immediate messianism aside, is nevertheless a political idea which has an ethical justification. It has an ethical justification insofar as a political solution imposes itself as a way of putting an end to the arbitrariness which marked the Jewish condition, and to all the spilt blood which for centuries has flowed

with impunity across the world. This solution can be summed up as the existence, in conditions which are not purely abstract, that is, not just anywhere, of a political entity with a Jewish majority. For me this is the essence of Zionism. It signifies a state in its fullest sense of the term, a state with an army and arms, an army which can have a deterrent and if necessary a defensive significance. Its necessity is ethical—indeed, it's an old ethical idea which commands us precisely to defend our neighbours. My people and my kin are still my neighbours. When you defend the Jewish people, you defend your neighbor; and every Jew in particular defends his neighbor when he defends Israel. However, there is an ethical limit to this ethically necessary political existence. But what is that limit? Perhaps what is happening today in Israel marks the place where ethics and politics will come into confrontation and where the limit will be sought.[30]

The conclusive statement Levinas makes is in response to the question as to whether the Other isn't also and especially the Palestinian. Levinas responds: "My definition of the Other is completely different. The Other is the neighbour, who is not necessarily kin, but who can be. And in that sense, if you're for the Other, you're for the neighbour. But if your neighbor attacks another neighbor or treats him unjustly, what can you do? Then alterity takes on another character, in alterity we can find an enemy, or at least then we are faced with the problem of knowing who is right and who is wrong, who is just and who is unjust. There are people who are wrong."[31]

Epilogue

Encountering the Jewish Future

Though my encounter with our great Jewish thinkers began many years ago, this book took shape as I was reconnecting in Korea with my student Father Mun and subsequently was developed for a lecture I was invited to give at the Rothko Chapel in Houston.

In the advertisement for my Rothko Chapel lecture, I noticed that, without discussing the matter with me, a response by "Three Rabbis from Houston" had been scheduled. This surprised and annoyed me. I felt that a double standard was being applied to me and to other Jews who held similar understandings about the Jewish future. The rabbis presumably were the authentic representatives of the "real" Jewish community in ways that I was not. At least that is how they presented themselves. Obviously, the administration at the Rothko Chapel had been pressured to agree to this. In the early years, no doubt, this had happened to Richard Rubenstein and Elie Wiesel as well. Had it also happened to Hannah Arendt? After protesting this double standard with the organizers, I decided to deliver my lecture as I had agreed. I am glad that I did.

The Rothko Chapel evokes a spirituality and commitment that flows from the murals of Mark Rothko. Since going there previously to see Rothko's murals, I delved deeper into his life and art. In preparing for my lecture I reviewed James Breslin's beautiful and engaging biography of Rothko. I noticed that Rothko signed the contract to produce his murals for the chapel in 1965, the year when I became a Bar Mitzvah. By that time Rothko had become affluent and famous. Yet he was also on the verge of giving up on the art world because he hated the commercialism that had invaded it. He also didn't want his paintings to be seen primarily as decorative objects in homes or museums. Art had to mean more than what the market could bear. Rothko longed to return to the connection between art and the sacred. As the one who approached Rothko to paint murals wrote: "What is wonderful about Mark is that he aspires, and is still capable of believing that his work can have some purpose—spiritual if you like—that is not sullied by the world."[1]

When you are in the Rothko Chapel, surrounded by his murals, you feel like you have entered sacred ground. Is it therefore outside the world? Or is sacred ground part of the world that is set aside for us to think again about the world we live in?

I think of Martin Buber and Abraham Joshua Heschel. The sacred is in the world. Sometimes the sacred survives the world or reenters the world we have barely survived. Sometimes the sacred surrounds those who have not survived the world but is carried by those who survive. I think here of the Holocaust as well as so many others traumatic experiences of displacement and destruction. Is there beauty after violence and atrocity? I also think of Emmanuel Levinas's invocation of the sacred as a place of violence. So many innocent people suffer around the world, victims of what others "know" is their redemption.

Rothko's murals were created in the world and survive in it. He did not. Several years after the murals were finished, he committed suicide. When you view these murals, all of various forms of gray, is it any wonder that Rothko created so much beauty and also committed suicide?

There is also light in the darkness of Rothko's murals, if we can see it. Light and darkness have to do with our ability and inability to see the light that is there. In darkness, we search for light. Sometimes it is found by us, other times by others. Light exists. It waits to be gathered. Then we can see again.

As with Rothko's art, there is much light to be found in the Jewish thinkers we have considered. There is also much darkness. We can see either, or both. The light we gather can be carried forth into the Jewish future.

We might experience the sacred surrounded by murals or in encountering Jewish thought. Most often, however, we experience the sacred in contested places in the world. That was the case for Rothko and for our Jewish thinkers. We might also experience the wrath of Levinas's sacred, as it comes from outside and from within the community that formed us. Projecting violence outside and within the Jewish community is part of the Jewish present. What we will do to quell that violence is critical to the Jewish future.

Rothko's art is without images. He believed that images of the human or even of nature represent something else. Representational images limit our vision while color invites us somewhere within and outside of ourselves. When

I view a Rothko painting, I experience a world that is unrestricted and undisciplined by the powers of the market, the family, or political and religious authority. I breathe free and enter the place of unknowing. I sometimes feel that this is the most religious place of all, an encounter that Buber envisioned.

Rothko was Jewish and raised Orthodox. He rebelled against both as an adult. But as his biographer points out, he explored and helped define a modern transcendence free of any particular religion or philosophy. When I think of Rothko, it is clear that he embodied the indigenous Jewish prophetic in the modern world. As most Jewish prophetic figures, he lived outside of the synagogue from which he was estranged. The Rothko Chapel had a Christian inspiration, though neither Judaism nor Christianity is mentioned there. This silence about tradition may be part of the Jewish and Christian future.

Throughout history most Jews who carry the prophetic have been outside the synagogue. They have found their home, as Jeremiah did, in exile. In different ways, our Jewish thinkers carried the prophetic, often against the wishes of the Jewish community and sometimes against the wishes of those outside it. From exile the prophets bring Jews and the world a message that is heard even when censored and repressed. It is heard precisely because it stands at the root of what it means to be Jewish—and human.

I am grateful for those who bring the prophetic, the greatest Jewish gift to the world, even under extraordinarily difficult circumstances. The prophet is one who encounters history and God on behalf of the broken, the widow, the orphan, the poor, and the stranger and draws us to them. Paradoxically, this drawing to those on the margins is also a movement inward to our deepest self. Through the Other we find our own otherness. In that movement outward and inward, if just for a moment, we experience Isaiah's ultimate vision of a reconciled humanity.

It is amazing that Jews continue to carry the prophetic. This persistence allows us to encounter, embrace, and live the prophetic today. The prophetic is about real people who have been cast aside the walls of society or imprisoned within them. Jews well know this experience of being walled in. Today, Jews also wall in others, the Palestinians.

Jews know what it is to live on both sides of what I have come to think of as the empire divide. Throughout Jewish history, Jews have stood on both sides of empire. Empire can be outside of us, as in powers that want to do us harm. The empires of others can be used by Jews to solidify our place in the world. We can also have our own empires, projecting power over others outside or within our own community.

Some Jews believe that only empire will save us, others that empire will destroy us. Those who embrace empire rail against the prophets. The prophets rail against empire. Jews birth prophets. Jews fight against them. We have seen this back and forth in our great Jewish thinkers. Many of them have taken their stand—on both sides of the empire divide.

The empire divide is outside and within Jews. It is also part of the Jewish future. Being on both sides of the empire divide elicits a struggle. This struggle bequeaths violence against Jews. It also bequeaths internal Jewish civil wars. These struggles are part and parcel of Jewish destiny. There doesn't seem a way out.

Rothko spoke about the meaning of his non-representational art: "I do not believe that there was ever a question of being abstract or representational. It is really a matter of ending this silence and solitude, of breathing and stretching one's arms again." Perhaps this is the inspiration for my encounters with Jewish thought and my hope for the Jewish future. I hope that we confront our silence and solitude and begin breathing and stretching our arms again.[2]

When Rothko began painting the murals for the chapel, he confronted the question of "how much a flat, blank, opaque, and humanity-obliterating black could he let in before the painting became unendurable." In some ways, this is the perennial challenge throughout Jewish history—what to emphasize, what to downplay, when to speak, when to be silent, when to dwell in the moment, when to look to the past. Sometimes dwelling in the moment or looking to the past invokes a future. Other times, such dwelling obscures the future.[3]

Although the ancient prophets were bleak at times, they also represented a difficult hope. The prophets were always told that it was the wrong moment to speak the truth. For those in power, there never is a right time to speak the truth. The prophets have their own time frame. Perhaps this is why Levinas thought of them as dwelling alone, bringing their own bedding, being fed by the crows.

Someone Has Deceived You, My Dear Friend

If all our efforts result in a circular pattern of life and death, with no distinction in how we live and with no destination, would either humanity or God matter? In Jewish life, there is intention, purpose, and destiny. This is laid out by the prophets, whether as God's spokespersons or as independent agents. It is also part of the covenant, whether it is broken, past, or renewed.

The Jewish present is replete with Levinas's atheists and rebels—who expiate blasphemy in advance. In the Jewish future I wonder whether these atheists and rebels of different stripes will come together or split farther apart. Even if they come together, they are unlikely to be embraced by the broader Jewish community. More likely, they will be driven deeper into exile.

Ezekiel is one called by God to deliver the prophetic word to the people Israel, which God already knows will be rejected by the people. Ezekiel must have been wondering why God or he should bother with the entire enterprise. Reading Ezekiel is like attending a one-act play written by God for God's edification. Since life is going to become incredibly difficult for Ezekiel, he might be excused for wanting to turn down such a role, but he accepts his mission. Asking him to "eat the scroll" is God's way of asking Ezekiel to internalize the message he will deliver to the people Israel. Internalizing the suffering, Ezekiel eats the scroll that, unexpectedly, tastes sweet, just like honey.

None of our Jewish thinkers has felt that sweetness for long stretches of their lives. Perhaps it is internalizing God's message that is sweet rather than the treatment the prophet experiences. Doing justice is sweet no matter the consequences. In the Jewish future, I wonder if the Jewish prophets without God will find what they internalize sweet. I also wonder what text they will eat and in what language the text will be written.

If history is our guide, the Jewish future will feature a new type of conscious pariah. Hannah Arendt's "in between" is difficult to imagine in advance. Can this be mapped out in advance or does it simply emerge when the hidden tradition of dissent begins to flow again? The "in between" situation may now be global, with a combination of self-critical secular and self-critical religious thinkers. Such an in between could mean a new and revolutionary solidarity with all peoples of conscience, as well as charting a new path of what secular and religious means. Jews cannot escape this redefinition nor should we. The only question is whether Jews will be in the forefront of this movement, as we have often been, or whether Jews will defend against it, handing over the core of our destiny to others.

Just days after the rabbis from Houston responded to my lecture in the Rothko Chapel, the linguist and political commentator Noam Chomsky traveled to the Middle East to speak at a Birzeit University in the Israeli-occupied Palestinian, West Bank city of Ramallah, where I also had lectured on a number of occasions. When he tried to enter the West Bank from Jordan, he was denied entry by Israeli authorities. The eighty-one year old Chomsky, consistently voted the leading intellectual in the world, was denied entry by Israeli authorities.[4]

Although Chomsky is Jewish, he rarely speaks about his Jewish background. As an American citizen, he is a consistent and vocal critic of American foreign policy. As a Jew, he was an early advocate of a bi-national Zionism, much along the lines of Hannah Arendt and Martin Buber. Now he is an advocate of a two-state solution. Most see Chomsky as a purebred American political radical, in some ways a throwback to the 1960s when he first became known in his opposition to the Vietnam War. Yet in many ways the Jewish Chomsky, with his first name Avram, should be seen as the latest incarnation of Hannah Arendt's conscious pariah. In an interview some years ago, Chomsky was asked about his background:

I was born in Philadelphia, in 1928. . . . My father was . . . a Hebrew scholar, . . . and my mother was a Hebrew teacher. . . . [B]y the time I was eight or nine, on Friday evenings my father and I would read Hebrew literature together. My parents were immigrants, and they happened to end up in Philadelphia, but my mother was from New York and my father from Baltimore. The Baltimore family was ultra-orthodox. In fact, my father told me that they had become more orthodox when they got here than they even were in the shtetl (town) in the Ukraine where they came from. In general, there was a tendency among some sectors of immigrants to intensify the cultural tradition, probably as a way of identifying themselves in a strange environment. . . .

The other part of the family, my mother's, was mainly Jewish working class—very radical. The Jewish element had disappeared. This is 1930s, so they were part of the ferment of radical activism that was going on in the thirties in all sorts of ways. . . . One that actually did influence me a great deal was an uncle. . . . He had grown up in a poor area of New York. In fact, he himself never went past fourth grade. . . . He had a newsstand . . . [that] became an intellectual center for émigrés from Europe, lots of Germans and other émigrés were coming. He wasn't a very educated person, formally . . . but maybe the most educated person I've ever met. Self-educated. . . . The newsstand itself was a very lively, intellectual center—professors of this and that arguing all night.[5]

The Jewish Chomsky. Avram. American—but not only.

Jews are hardly alone in encountering a challenging future. There is an entire community of exiles from all religions and geographic areas of the world. Though exiles think they are going home and returning to their native traditions and geographical locations, exiles never return home. Or their return home is so fraught that they exist in exile at home. This is the lesson for many exiles, including Jewish exiles. The Jewish community is not now nor will it ever be home again for exilic Jews. The same is true of Israeli Jews of Conscience who leave Israel. They will never go home again. Israeli Jews of Conscience may be the new stream of Jewish conscious pariahs. I think here of Oren Ben-Dor, Ilan Pappe, and Ronit Lentin, all decidedly secular Jews, all living outside of the Israel they were born within, who in their writing and actions on behalf of Palestinians expiate blasphemy in advance.

After the Holocaust, Jews needed to regroup, attend to identity needs, and seek empowerment. That very empowerment led to another, unexpected, crisis. After the return to the Jewish homeland in the state of Israel, another exile was precipitated by the violation of Jewish ethics. Now dissident Israeli Jews exist in exile, as do other Jewish exiles in the Diaspora. This is the base from which exilic Jews will live for the foreseeable future.

A few years before I reconnected with Father Mun in Korea, I stood with my son Aaron at Israel's Wall surrounding Palestinians, at the part that separates the Palestinian city of Ramallah from Jerusalem. The checkpoint we went through with the Palestinians represents the inhumanity of this most modern way of regulating human movement. Here, Jews regulate the movement of others. With Aaron, I viewed the Palestinian and the Jewish future that had already arrived.

When I encountered Rothko's murals in the chapel bearing his name, I thought of the first time Aaron and I saw the Wall that surrounds the Palestinian city of Bethlehem. Together we gazed at the huge welcome sign provided by the Israeli tourist authority. In English, Hebrew, and Arabic it welcomes tourists: "Peace Be with You!"

Only two of our Jewish thinkers, Elie Wiesel and Richard Rubenstein, were alive when the Wall surrounding the Palestinians in Jerusalem and the West Bank began in 2002. Neither has commented on it in any depth. Just days before I lectured at the Rothko Chapel, Wiesel published an "Open Letter to President Obama on Jerusalem," which again avoided the questions of Israeli policy toward the Palestinians:

> Jerusalem once again is at the center of political debates and international storms. New and old tensions surface at a disturbing pace.
>
> For me, the Jew that I am, Jerusalem is above politics. It is mentioned more than six hundred times in Scripture—and not a single time in the Koran. Its presence in Jewish history is overwhelming. There is no more moving prayer in Jewish history than the one expressing our yearning to return to Jerusalem. To many theologians, it IS Jewish history, to many poets, a source of inspiration. It belongs to the Jewish people and is much more than a city, it is what binds one Jew to another in a way that remains hard to explain. When a Jew visits Jerusalem for the first time, it is not the first time; it is a homecoming. The first song I heard was my mother's lullaby about and for Jerusalem. Its sadness and its joy are part of our collective memory.
>
> Today, for the first time in history, Jews, Christians, and Muslims all may freely worship at their shrines. And, contrary to certain media reports, Jews, Christians, and Muslims ARE allowed to build their homes anywhere in the city. The anguish over Jerusalem is not about real estate but about memory.
>
> Jerusalem must remain the world's Jewish spiritual capital, not a symbol of anguish and bitterness, but a symbol of trust and hope. As the

Hasidic master Rebbe Nahman of Bratslav said, "Everything in this world has a heart; the heart itself has its own heart."

Jerusalem is the heart of our heart, the soul of our soul.[6]

The response from dissident Jewish Israelis was prompt. In an open letter published in the Israeli newspaper *Haaretz*, Yosse Sarid, a well-known Israeli politician, wrote, "Someone has deceived you, my dear friend. Not only may an Arab not build 'anywhere,' but he may thank his god if he is not evicted from his home and thrown out onto the street with his family and property. Perhaps you have heard about Arab residents in Sheikh Jarrah, having lived there since 1948, who are again being uprooted and made refugees because certain Jews are chafing from Jerusalem's space constraints." Sarid continued: "Those same jealous Jews insist on inserting themselves like so many bones in the throats of Arab neighborhoods, purifying and Judaizing them with the help of rich American benefactors, several of whom you may know personally. Behind the scenes our prime minister and Jerusalem's mayor are pulling the strings of this puppet show while in public deflecting responsibility for this lawlessness and greed. That is the real reason for the 'new and old tensions surfacing at a disturbing pace' of which you warn in your letter." Then Sarid poses a final challenge: "'Jerusalem is above politics' you write. It is unfortunate that a man of your standing must confuse fundamental issues and confound the reader. Is it not politics that deals with mankind's weightiest issues, with matters of war and peace, life and death? And is life itself not holier than historical rights, than national and personal memory—holier even than Jerusalem? The living always take precedence over the dead, as must the present and future over the past."[7]

In *The New York Review of Books*, a group of one hundred prominent Israelis wrote their own response:

Dear Mr. Wiesel:

We write to you from Jerusalem to convey our frustration, even outrage, at your recently published letter on Jerusalem. We are Jewish Jerusalemites—residents by choice of a battered city, a city used and abused, ransacked time and again first by foreign conquerors and now by its own politicians. We cannot recognize our city in the sentimental abstraction you call by its name.

Our Jerusalem is concrete, its hills covered with limestone houses and pine trees; its streets lined with synagogues, mosques, and churches. Your Jerusalem is an ideal, an object of prayers and a bearer of the collective memory of a people whose members actually bear many individual memories. Our Jerusalem is populated with people, young and old, women and men, who wish their city to be a symbol of dignity—not of hubris, inequality, and discrimination. You speak of the celestial Jerusalem; we live in the earthly one.

For more than a generation now the earthly city we call home has been crumbling under the weight of its own idealization. Your letter troubles us, not simply because it is replete with factual errors and false representations, but because it upholds an attachment to some otherworldly city that purports to supersede the interests of those who live in the this-worldly one. For every Jew, you say, a visit to Jerusalem is a homecoming, yet it is our commitment that makes your homecoming possible. We prefer the hardship of realizing citizenship in this city to the convenience of merely yearning for it.

Indeed, your claim that Jerusalem is above politics is doubly outrageous. First, because contemporary Jerusalem was created by a political decision and politics alone keeps it formally unified. The tortuous municipal boundaries of today's Jerusalem were drawn by Israeli generals and politicians shortly after the 1967 war. Feigning to unify an ancient city, they created an unwieldy behemoth, encircling dozens of Palestinian villages that were never part of Jerusalem. Stretching from the outskirts of Ramallah in the north to the edge of Bethlehem in the south, the Jerusalem that the Israeli government foolishly concocted is larger than Paris. Its historical core, the nexus of memories and religious significance often called the "Holy Basin," makes up a mere one percent of its area. Now the government calls this artificial fabrication "Jerusalem" in order to obviate any approaching chance for peace.

Second, your attempt to keep Jerusalem above politics means divesting us of a future. For being above politics is being devoid of the power to shape the reality of one's life. As true Jerusalemites, we cannot stand by and watch our beloved city, parts of which are utterly neglected, being used as a springboard for crafty politicians and sentimental populists who claim that Jerusalem is above politics and negotiation. All the while, they frantically "Judaize" East Jerusalem in order to transform its geopolitics beyond recognition.

We, who live in Jerusalem, can no longer be sacrificed for the fantasies of those who love our city from afar. The Jerusalem of this world must be shared by the people of the two nations residing in it. Only a shared city will live up to the prophet's vision: "Zion shall be redeemed with justice." As we chant weekly in our vigils in Sheikh Jarrah: "Nothing can be holy in an occupied city!"[8]

"Nothing can be holy in an occupied city." That refrain echoes throughout Jewish history; we memorialize it annually. Now there are Jews who hear that echo in our empowerment. Perhaps we, too, have been deceived in the Golden Age of Constantinian Judaism.

We have little patience with those who say they were unaware of what was happening to Jews in the past. Rightly so. Shall we expect others to have patience with our denial?

Aaron Crossing the Empire Divide

What is Aaron to do with this discussion and my younger son, Isaiah, as well? When they enter the terminals that separate Jerusalem and Ramallah and see the welcome signs on the wall that surround Bethlehem and the heated "word signs" in the back and forth of Jews on Jerusalem, who will interpret them so they can understand fidelity in the Jewish future? Since the broader Jewish community seems oblivious, it may be that Jews need exiles from around the world to help in this interpretation.

Aaron and I looked on in amazement when we witnessed what Elie Wiesel had not seen—or was silent about when he wrote about Jerusalem. I had been traveling among Palestinians for decades. During his first visit to Israel several years earlier, Aaron joined with an Israeli group, Israeli Committee against Housing Demolitions (ICAHD), that rebuilt Palestinian homes that had been destroyed by Israel.

As he worked with fellow Jews and internationals, Aaron was asked to issue the first declaration on behalf of the group:

> In the village of Anata, revolution is in the air. We are resisting the Occupation in a nonviolent way, rebuilding a home. We, as an international group, are sending a powerful message to our respective communities: a message of peaceful coexistence. The presence of Israelis, Palestinians, and others, working side by side to provide housing for a family who has lost their home to the Occupation allows me to see the future of Israel-Palestine as I have never seen it before. If both Israelis and Palestinians can stand side-by-side and demand human rights and justice for both Israelis and Palestinians, there is hope for peace, forgiveness, and reconciliation.

If the Holocaust is a *novum* in Jewish history, there are other firsts in Jewish history occurring today: a Jewish father and son going through a checkpoint terminal with Palestinians under occupation, standing together at a wall surrounding Bethlehem "welcoming" tourists, visiting Palestinian territories occupied and patrolled by Jews; a young Jew reaching out to Palestinians, working with Jews, Palestinians, and others to rebuild what has been destroyed and then declaring this *the* reconciling revolution in Jewish life after the Holocaust and after Israel.

Aaron's statement is bold. Could it be that, albeit unknowingly, our Jewish thinkers led me and my son, along with other Jews of Conscience, to this very difficult place of solidarity with a people Jews have displaced? Joining together with Aaron at the place of Jewish empowerment after the Holocaust, I glimpsed the prophetic voice in Martin Buber and Hannah Arendt's vision of a homeland as opposed to state Zionism. I also felt Abraham Joshua Heschel's approach in his writing on the prophets, a voice that wavered after the 1967 war. I heard the hard edge of Emmanuel Levinas turning his back on the Jewish Other when, in the wake of the massacre at Sabra and Shatila, he declared that Palestinians were not the Other, the neighbor, that placed demands on Jews.

Aaron's vision was no doubt colored by the enthusiasm of youth. Reading that statement as it was issued left me with a different impression. In and around Aaron's words, I recognized immediately the prophetic voice that echoes throughout Jewish history. It was then that I realized that the Jewish prophetic voice will never die.

Aaron crossed the boundary that some of our Jewish thinkers approached and that others were unable even to see. In crossing that boundary, the question is whether Aaron left Jewish life or approached the center of it. In rebuilding a Palestinian home in the face of Israeli power, Aaron had either ceased to be Jewish or had embraced the prophetic as practiced in our time. Taking another perspective, perhaps in the oppression of another people Jewish life was leaving Aaron, a leave-taking he resisted. Recent studies have found that many young Jews want little or nothing to do with Jewish life, at least the Jewish life as presented by the mainstream Jewish community. Considering the state of denial, should this surprise us?

Some years ago I attended a Society of Jewish Ethics conference where a scholar lectured on a book he had written on the Jewish tradition of human rights. Predictably, he did not address the Palestinian question. When I raised the issue, I told the story of Aaron's work rebuilding a Palestinian home and how he felt that, by repairing the relationship of Jews and Palestinians, he was fulfilling part of his covenantal obligation as a Jew. The lecturer deflected the question and the session came to a halt.

After the session, a rabbi sympathetic with my comment offered a better way for Aaron to think about the issue. In Jewish tradition, he said, the covenant is only for Jews, so a covenantal obligation can only be between Jews. However, within that covenant, there is also room for concern for others. Though a secondary obligation, it nonetheless could be seen as flowing from the covenant itself. I thanked the rabbi but told him that it seemed to Aaron that justice for Palestinians is included within the covenantal obligation. Palestinians are not secondary, they are essential. The Jewish covenant has expanded.

After the Holocaust, much has been written about the Jewish covenant. As we have seen, some view the covenant as irretrievably broken or existing in the past tense only. Others think it remains as it was in essence, though our relationship to it has changed. Still others think that the way forward is for Jews to take even more covenantal responsibility. Whatever we can say about God after the Holocaust, Jews have to rely on themselves.

Having heard these ideas in conversation around the dinner table since he was a child, Aaron simply acted. He carried the covenant with him across the boundary that separated Jews from a different kind of destiny. With an intuitive and compassionate intelligence, he acted to heal the breach between Jews and God by reaching out to the Other whom Jews are now oppressing. Aaron was posting another commandment: "Thou Shall Not Demean, Dislocate, or Destroy the Palestinian People." In a positive formulation: "Thou Shall Embrace the Palestinians Whom You Have Displaced."

From the perspective of history, it is understandable when Jews link with empire for the sake of security and status. But those Jews who cross the boundaries of Jewish life for the sake of the Other cross them for the sake of Jews and Jewish history as well.

Aaron and I saw the Jewish future where Empire Jews build checkpoints and walls and where Compassionate Jews criticize Israeli policies toward Palestinians and rebuild Palestinian homes. This is the same divide I encountered in our Jewish thinkers. On one side, post-Holocaust Jews are hunkered down. They benefit from, endorse, enable, and project power over others, all the while holding to their innocence. Since the policies of Israel toward Palestinians in Jerusalem are widely known, perhaps this is why Wiesel writes of Jerusalem as if it is a dream. While this sense of innocence may have been excusable in the early years after the Holocaust, it is impossible to hold and be considered a Jewish spokesperson in the second decade of the twenty-first century. Or so one would think.

Wiesel and many other Jews remain in a timeframe that has long passed by. Aaron's generation of Jews cannot live in that time warp and be faithful as Jews. Encountering Palestinians in Palestine changes everything for Jews, including the perception of Jewish innocence. None of our Jewish thinkers encountered Palestinians in this way. Their perception of Jewishness was univocal and virtually "untainted" by such exposure. It is easier to declare Others outside of our concern if we shield ourselves from their presence. Perhaps it would have been important for them to witness Palestinian life as it is lived under occupation. Then they would have been forced to make the most difficult of decisions, whether to continue on as before or bring the disturbing message to our people. We might think of this as the Ezekiel Decision. But then, it seems Ezekiel had no choice.

After the Holocaust—without a definitive sense of God's presence—the choices we make are on us. In our suffering we rightfully complained about God's absence and silence. Who will complain about our absence and silence?

Though Hannah Arendt and Martin Buber crossed some Jewish boundaries, they did so with a typical Western sensibility. One benefit of a Jewish homeland was that Jews would bring parts of Western technology and democracy to the "backward" Arab Middle East. Even as they crossed boundaries, they kept others intact. Emmanuel Levinas is the most blatant here, with his fear of "Third World" peoples and his call to protect the Judeo-Christian civilization from them.

As we have seen, one of the problems with our Jewish thinkers is that, no matter how far reaching their thought, it remained Judeo-centric and Western. There were and are colonial and imperials aspects of Jewish identity that are unmentioned. Perhaps they could not even identify them. A problem contemporary Jewish identity deflects is that, like other religious identities in the West, we have colonial and imperial aspects at our core. If this is the case, no wonder Jewish thought is unable to embrace fully the Palestinian people. Increasingly this extends to other peoples in our globalized world. As Jews, we are more and more isolated in the world.

For a long time, the East and Arabs in particular have been seen through the Western gaze. Though Jews were often victims of that same gaze, while being defined as outsiders to the Christian enlightened West, we also internalized Western values and at first chance identified ourselves as Western. In doing so, we linked with the European and American sense of an empowered exceptionality. Thus we see Israel, despite its geographic location, as also being Western. With Jews being empowered in the West, and the state of Israel claiming to be part of the West, how could Palestinian Arabs be seen as anything but Third World outsiders with perfidious motives toward Jews and the Jewish state?

On the other side, Jews with compassion and justice cross boundaries toward others, projecting a prophetic power that includes others. They seek an interconnected empowerment. All religious traditions and communities have similar struggles and divisions, including the Palestinians. All need to struggle together to overcome these obstacles.

In the fourth century, the previously marginal sect of Christianity that had been linked with Judaism came into favor with the Roman emperor Constantine. Soon it became the empire's religion, Constantinian Christianity. Becoming the state religion gave it privileges and power.

Constantinianism as a religion-state power configuration continues to be present today among some Christians and Muslims. After the Holocaust and with the birth of Israel, Jews have entered a Constantinian phase. The Jewish community orients itself to power and influence and in turn identifies with empire in America and Israel. This is Constantinian Judaism. There are also Compassionate Jews, Jews of Conscience, who oppose Constantinian Judaism and commit themselves to the prophetic call of seeking community, justice, and reconciliation with the oppressed Other. Such Jews link with Christians, Muslims, and all others of conscience.

An important and vexing question is whether it is possible even for Jews of Conscience to avoid these colonial and imperial aspects of Jewish identity. In the post-Holocaust Jewish world, with Israel in power, it is doubtful that dissident Jews can escape the predicament of Jewish life. Since all Jews share in the same historical moment, it is important for Jews of all perspectives to recognize these colonial and imperial elements rather than pretend they can transcend them. This would be a step toward facing where we as Jews have travelled and what is needed to change direction.

If Constantinian types of different religions and communities belong together, so too do people of conscience. If Jews embrace communities of conscience, then they become part of them. Though Jews previously were leaders among people of conscience, in many areas we are now followers. This, too, is part of the Jewish future that has arrived.

It is difficult for Jews to admit the colonial and imperial elements in Jewish identity. Recognizing that Jews are as much followers as leaders is even more challenging. Whether Jews have been as exceptional as we believe we are, the additional factor of worldly empowerment makes it even more important for us to take stock. Asserting exceptionality without power is one thing. Asserting exceptionality with power is another.

Does this mean that the Judeo-centric bias of Jews must now be reevaluated or perhaps given up? Claiming innocence and a special place among communities now has to be reassessed in light of our place in the world. On the one hand, the dilemma facing Jews is whether Jewishness, with its special claims, can survive such a reevaluation. On the other, the question is whether Jewishness can be asserted without a sense of specialness. Whether Jews can adopt empire as our special calling, name it as such, and continue on as Jews is questionable. Most probably, even as we adopt empire, Jews will continue to insist that conscience is our guide, because Jewishness cannot be explained outside of conscience. Jews face the daunting challenge of false consciousness, believing that we are innocent when we are not.

We have seen this in the encounters with our Jewish thinkers. During their formative years before and after the Holocaust, they struggled with this emerging dichotomy of empire and conscience. Coming from the underside of European history and experiencing the cycle of violence and atrocity that characterizes the colonial and imperials aspect of empire, they attempted to negotiate the boundaries of empire and conscience so as to chart a path for Jewish survival.

Growing up with this generation of Jewish thinkers as my guide, I admire their complicated and arduous journeys. But as I embarked on my own journey, the contradictions of empire and conscience increased. Especially with the expansion of Israel and the increasing neo-conservative tendencies of Jews in America, the gap between what Jews say about themselves and what Jews do in the world became too great. No doubt this is a failure of these thinkers as thinkers and of Jewishness as it was understood by them. They also underestimated the seductive aspects of power, of how what was initially used for survival would one day become a way of life.

Once empire becomes a way of life, it is difficult to disassociate from its power. The Jewish community's entanglement in the web of empire may be impossible to untangle. The fear is that such disentanglement will land Jews back in the vulnerable position from which we came. Without participating in empire, Jews fear returning to the pre-Holocaust situation of European Jewry. Put bluntly, without empire many Jews feel slated for another Holocaust.

All our Jewish thinkers wrestled with these fears because they knew how important they were to the Jewish future. Only Richard Rubenstein said that Jews simply should do whatever they need to survive. Though he counsels Jews to jettison their assertion of primacy in order to be accepted in the world, he harbors doubts as to whether even then others will accept Jews as ordinary. In other words, there is a mythic status to being Jewish that is so deeply ingrained in the world that, even if Jews renounce their chosenness, the world's definition will remain. Therefore, Jews will always need protection from others who seek to diminish or erase Jewishness from the world.

Rubenstein sees Israel as that place. Either the state exists or Jews will find it difficult to exist. After the Holocaust, morality and ethics are less important than the sheer act of survival, a survival that, for Rubenstein, is still up for grabs.

Though phrased differently, some of our Jewish thinkers thought that after the Holocaust power had to be seized by Jews because power alone could protect us. Some realized that Jews would be changed in the process. Some begged Jews to redefine power, lest we be so changed by the embrace of power that we wouldn't be able to look ourselves in the mirror. Some thought that Jews would have to abandon the Jewish mirror par excellence—the prophetic.

Being Jewish in a Globalized World

When I taught students at Maryknoll, I looked again at the dilemma Jewish thinkers were working through. My students came from outside of America and Europe—China, Hong Kong, Philippines, Indonesia, Kenya, Tanzania,

South Africa, Venezuela, Colombia, Peru, Chile, Nicaragua, El Salvador, Gua-
temala—places where few Jews live but where masses of poor people do. From
there, where Europeans and Americans are looked upon with suspicion as former and present colonialists, I had an outside reference point for the heated
internal Jewish discussion. When I traveled to Israel and Palestine, especially
with Aaron, I had another vantage point as well.

Do Jews ever wonder what the Jewish future looks like from the global perspective? When I visited these countries with my students as guides, I saw and
heard firsthand their version of the world. Through arms shipments and military
assistance, the state of Israel is hardly absent from many of these countries. Often
Israel, like the United States, is on the wrong side of the issues in these countries.

In 2010 I traveled to South Africa to celebrate the twenty-fifth anniversary
of the famous Kairos Document. The Kairos Document is where Christians of
conscience split from the churches that supported apartheid. It was a major
milestone on the way to the new South Africa. It showed that black and white
South Africans could come together around the desire for a world beyond racial
injustice and violence. The Kairos Document classified apartheid as a Christian
heresy. They threw the justice gauntlet down.

The anniversary brought to mind my Jewish and American identities.
Israel played an economic, political, and military role in supporting apartheid
South Africa. When I travel to Central America, I have a similar experience.
Israeli and American arms, aid, and training played a significant role in the
brutal wars against the people of Central America in the 1970s and 1980s.

So as an American but also as a Jew, in both areas of the world I make a
confession. On the American side, the most obvious point is the almost complete turn of American democracy toward empire, this despite our birth in a
struggle against a colonial empire. On the Jewish side, the most obvious point
is the almost complete turn of the victims of empire toward empire. To the
victims of South Africa and Central America it is difficult to argue the benefi-
cence of the American and now Jewish/Israeli empires. Which side are we on?
Which side should we be on? When I confess to the South African and Central
Americans that Jews, too, had been involved on the wrong side of their people's
struggle, I hope to open a window of opportunity for Jews to think again.

Jews have often been a window on life for others. When we close that window on ourselves, it is hard to be a window for others. It is difficult to see how
a Jewish future can unfold without this open window for us and for others. If
history is any guide, Jews will be a window, but for whom and how? What will
others see in our history? Will they see what we say we are? Or will they observe
something different? Often, when others observe something differently than
we do, Jews charge anti-Semitism. When Jews of Conscience make these same
observations, some Jews charge them with Jewish self-hate. The understanding

of Jewish exceptionality and innocence is at stake. This means that there needs to be a sorting out of fact and fiction, myth and reality. Though it is always difficult to do this sorting among competing visions of the world, this is sometimes even more difficult in the case of Jews.

What Jewishness, Jews, and Judaism mean has been a battleground within and outside the Jewish community. If Jews are honest about what we are doing today, and others are honest about their historical sins against Jews, it may be possible that Jews and others can speak and work in an open and committed way.

Our Jewish thinkers would be ambivalent about this possibility, or at least were in their lifetimes. Many Jews continue in this ambivalence, feeling that only empire will protect us from the effects of anti-Semitism. This becomes a twofold internal ambivalence, ambivalence toward others and toward the prophetic essence of the Jewish vocation in the world.

One way of looking at Jews and Jewishness today is through a prism of external and internal warfare. If Jews are at war with the world and among ourselves, it is difficult to see how a peaceful, inclusive, and welcoming Jewish future can come into being. Under some historical circumstances such a future is impossible, and contemplating it is naïve and utopian. At other times such a future seems possible.

Partly because of the recent past, the immediate Jewish future has to be pursued with caution, with outreach toward the outside world and by negotiating between opposing Jewish viewpoints. Then the Jewish future can honor those in the world who accept and seek to embrace the Jewish community. Divisions within the Jewish world might be addressed if each side affirmed the motives of the other side and agreed to discuss and act on mutually accepted goals. Differences would remain but with agreement to understand how both sides have been represented throughout Jewish history and have contributed to Jewish survival and witness in the world.

Based on my encounter with our Jewish thinkers together with my own journey, I propose that the following perspectives are important to explore:

- It is clear that Jews have come through a dark period in history. We ask ourselves as Jews, what is it to be faithful to the memory of those who were systematically murdered in Europe?

- Arguments for the creation of the state of Israel have and continue to be made from a variety of angles. It is wrong to say there is only one way. Israel will remain. The question is what kind of Jewish state it has been, is today, and will be tomorrow.

- Blaming the Palestinians for not accepting Israel as a Jewish state is wrong and misguided. In 1948 there was an ethnic cleansing of Palestinians to create Israel. This needs to be acknowledged if Jews are to understand our history and begin to create a Jewish future closer to what we say we are about. We cannot transgress another people's history, blame those whom we have transgressed, and then pretend that we are innocent.

- No one, including Jews, can have power and remain innocent. No one loves their oppressors, even if oppressors do not think of themselves as such. Martin Buber and Hannah Arendt were right about the Jewish homeland and what would happen to Palestinians, to Israel and Jews if a Jewish state was created. However, no nation-state is fated to be what it was or is today. Jews can create a different future if we face our history. If we do not, then we will become what we loathed about our oppressors—purveyors of violence while pretending we are innocent.

- Our Jewish thinkers were worried about where we as Jews were headed. Levinas especially thought much about Jews taking on the violence of the modern world. In Israel, but also here in America, Jews have done exactly what our Jewish thinkers worried about. In light of the Holocaust, per-haps this was inevitable. Still, as violence becomes normative in the Jewish world, a policing of Jewish thought and dissent has also become norma-tive, as Arendt predicted. Over the years those with power in the Jew-ish community have dismissed or handed over our prophets. In the end, however, we are doomed without our prophets. Jewish life does not make sense without the Jewish prophetic, which today is profoundly alive. The prophetic gnaws at our identity and is not going away. In America and in Israel, Jews of Conscience are everywhere. The accusation of self-hate and anti-Semitism is false. It is also self-defeating. Jews of Conscience carry the essential message of what it means to be Jewish in our time.

- With Jews clearly on both sides of the empire divide, a negotiated settle-ment on the state of Israel is needed. Otherwise, the civil war among Jews will take an even heavier toll on Jewish life than it has. At stake is the continued importance of Holocaust memory and our relations with our Christian and Muslim neighbors. On the ethical side, it is appropri-ate that Christians have offered Jews slack, given how culpable Christian history has been in the cycle of violence and atrocity. Yet it is already difficult to commemorate the Holocaust as if Jews are innocent today. Christians have taken stock of their own culpability in history; Muslims will have to wrestle with theirs. Jews can no longer expect to point an accusing finger outward and not expect it to be pointed back at us.

- Israel's power will not secure Israel or the Jewish future. When Wiesel and Heschel argue Israel's innocence, they are wrong. Such arguments create a deep danger in the Middle East for Israel and the other nations in the region. The Palestinians are the bridge into the Middle East for Israel. Palestinians are not going to invest in a joint future with Israel without a confession of wrong doing and a real Palestinian state with East Jerusalem as its capital. Peace and reconciliation between Israel and Palestine is not going to happen without justice. Until then, we are only one moment away from a catastrophe of unimaginable proportions. In such a catastrophe, Israel might emerge as the victor, but only by inflicting such casualties on the Arab world that the geographic and ethical landscape of the Middle East would be marred forever. Or Israel might be defeated, resulting in a second Holocaust. Jewish leadership is responsible for evading either scenario, which can happen only if a positive and just course is pursued.

- Remaining in a state of denial about Israel's and Jewish culpability allows Jews to change the subject. In changing the subject, we delay the day of reckoning. This occurs when we focus on liturgical reforms, synagogue affiliation, the Jewish birthrate, illiteracy about things Jewish, building more Holocaust memorials, accusing Jews of Conscience of not speaking for the Jewish community or of being self-hating or anti-Semitic. These are attempts to deflect the judgment of history that already has been made. It also delays the inevitable change that has to come. The only question is how much this delay will cost.

- Jews in America and Israel have taken on many of the colonial and imperial qualities of our former oppressors. Like the air we breathe, we don't even notice it. We breathe these qualities as if they were natural and normal. We look at the world through colonial and imperial lenses. Jews or non-Jews who bring this into the open are said to be against Jews, Judaism, the Jewish community, and Israel. They are also labeled as un-American, since more and more of American life is permeated with these same colonial and imperial qualities. As Jews we now see corruption and terrorism everywhere, with misguided leaders, backwardness, barbarism, and darkness surrounding our American and Jewish light. By projecting this outside, we do not see the corruption, terrorism, misguided leaders, backwardness, barbarism, and darkness among us. We Jews, Israelis, and Americans think that we are the light unto the nations of the world. Much of the world has a different opinion.

- The days of public memorialization of the Holocaust are coming to an end. This statement may seem out of place, what with state mandated Holocaust courses and the proliferation of Holocaust memorials throughout the United States and Europe. Nonetheless, there is increasing sentiment that memorials for the Holocaust now function as a way of silencing Jewish and non-Jewish dissent on the question of Israel and the Palestinians. There is also the issue of generational change, with the Holocaust becoming more distant in time and how the Holocaust shapes Jewish particularity. More and more Jewish and non-Jewish voices are demanding a broader attention to historic and contemporary suffering in the world. As well, there is a sense—among some, a fear—that if ever there is a resolution to the Israeli-Palestinian conflict the Holocaust will fade into history. Memorializing the Holocaust increasingly freezes Jewish history at the death camps and Christian history as the persecutors of Jews, almost equating Christianity and Nazism. Yet both Jews and Christians have moved on in significant ways. The interfaith and ecumenical dialogue has evolved into a deal where the Holocaust silences Christian—and Jewish—dissent on Israel and the Palestinians. That deal is now irretrievably broken. Once Christians—and Jews—have the courage to name this ending, we enter into a new relationship. That relationship will not be based on Christian culpability and Jewish innocence but rather on a mutual confession and hope.

■ I teach the Holocaust in a traditional way, combining aspects of all of our Jewish thinkers. I believe that the Holocaust was unique, that Jews were singled out for death, and that the God of history was absent in the death camps. I will hold to these views and teach them for the rest of my life. However, that way of teaching the Holocaust is fated. Historical writings on the Holocaust, like historical writings on the creation of the state of Israel and the catastrophe that befell the Palestinians, insists on a broader, more inclusive, and less Jewish-centric narrative. It is increasingly difficult to justify the teaching of the Holocaust as a form of remembrance and a liturgical rendering of history. World War II saw casualties and slaughter on all fronts with most of the war's victims being caught in between the imperial ambitions of the Soviet Union and Germany. The suffering in World War II was not limited to Jews. Nor were Jews the only singled out people group. As well, the formative need for Jews to make a claim on the West and on Christianity—a claim I support—is no longer credible as we move into the future. In the West and in Christianity, Jews are now included and honored. Often Jews are romanticized. It is now time to assume a more normal telling of the history of that time period.

■ Teaching the Holocaust in a more inclusive way, including highlighting the other victims of the Nazis as of equal importance and seeing the state of Israel as a normal state, with its good points and bad, will *per force* change the way Jews and others view Jewish particularity. As I travel around the world, it is increasingly evident that the time of Jewish ascendancy in discourse and narrative is over. Soon it will be impossible to communicate the specialness of Jewish history and our contribution to the world outside of Europe and the United States. Truth be told, it is becoming increasingly difficult to narrate this legacy in Europe. It is only a matter of time when this becomes the case in the United States. I believe that Jews and Jewish history are special, perhaps uniquely so, but the disjunction between these claims and the way we as Jews live and the policies we support has become too great. When that disjunction is pointed out, the Jewish community usually falls back on the accusation of anti-Semitism. But that tact has become worn and tattered. Having lost the crucial battle of narrating the Jewish story, the Jewish establishment uses power as their lever. As we know from history, power corrupts; it is also destined to change hands. Jews have never been able to go it alone for any length of time and, as a small minority in an increasingly global-ized world, the risks are easy to see. As Arendt called for in Israel and the Diaspora, Jews need an interdependent empowerment to survive and flourish. That will mean humbling ourselves and acknowledging where history and our own decisions have taken us. It will mean taking a new view of the world and recognizing how isolated we have become.

■ The interfaith, ecumenical dialogue is over; it ended decades ago. Main-stream Christianity has moved on into the global sphere of justice and peace concerns. Though for years Christians have held the line on Israel because they recognized their culpability in historic anti-Semitism and the Holocaust, thus supporting and then being silent on Israel as a form of repentance for their history, the movement of their own wit-ness precludes this support/silence in the future. Complimenting their statements of apology for the Holocaust are increasing resolutions of boycott, sanctions, and divestment targeting Israeli policies toward the Palestinians. Though the Jewish establishment has attempted to cir-cumscribe and defeat these efforts, the trend is clear. More and more Jews of Conscience support these actions in their religious and secu-lar forms. Characterizing Israeli policies in Jerusalem and the West Bank as apartheid, as President Jimmy Carter does, is widely accepted throughout the world. Simply decrying this does little but make it more difficult to move toward the next phase of Jewish-Christian dialogue. As well, demanding that Muslims around the world adopt a Jewish establishment understanding on remembering the Holocaust and sup-port of Israel is patronizing and self-defeating. It is an attempt to limit the self-expression of the Islamic community and functions to close down internal critical thought within the Islamic community itself. Regardless, the next phase of Jewish, Christian, and Muslim dialogue is already taking place—outside of the various establishments and on the frontlines where Jews, Christians, and Muslims of conscience struggle together.

■ The Jewish discussion about God is deep and unremitting. The Jewish community has been bold and has much still to share with the world on this issue. Still, other questions about God, including those raised by various Christian liberation theology movements, need to be heard within the Jewish community. As with the state of Israel, Jews should seek a negotiated settlement on the question of God, knowing that the simple affirmation of God's absence or presence in the Holocaust and beyond is too simplistic. Those who identify as Jews have already entered the God discussion to which there is no conclusive answer. With Holocaust theologian Rabbi Irving Greenberg, I think it is best to say that present within every Jew, and perhaps every person, resides theism and atheism side by side. Moreover, a triumphal view that comes from either side of the theism/atheism debate simply encourages the brokenness—and the anger—that is at the heart of contemporary Jewish life. It is more than pop psychology to understand that much of the verbal and physical violence that some Jews use to insist on a certain view of the world comes from that brokenness and anger. What Jews need is a healing. This healing can come only through sharing Israel and Palestine, starting with a shared Jerusalem and a willingness to engage in discussions about forms of spirituality that at least compliment the discussion about God. By looking at the world, ourselves, and God from different perspectives, we may finally end the Holocaust years and the years of oppressing another people.

■ The recent democratic uprisings in the Arab world augur well for the Jewish world, though many Jews are dubious, if not fearful, of this trend. In general, Jewish elites in Israel and America prefer friendly dictatorships that are dependent on the United States and therefore hold the line on criticism against Israel. This might be the final flowering of Arendt's analysis of what a Jewish state would augur for Jewish thought and commitment. Today, the struggle against totalitarian regimes that Jews suffered under is looked upon by many Jews as naïve and utopian. There is a racial and colonial viewpoint here as well. If Arabs in Tunisia and Egypt for example can struggle to establish a democratic framework of governance, the Jewish critique of Palestinians as unable to create a state that lives peacefully alongside Israel is challenged. The next step might be a realization that Jews and Palestinians can create a democracy that encompasses both peoples. In 2011, while the news media was focused on the nonviolent movement for democracy in Cairo's Tahrir Square, some Jews and Palestinians must have thought of establishing such a square in Jerusalem. Clearly, the anxiety of Jews regarding Egypt's movement for democracy has to do with the fate of the Camp David Accords that established a cold peace between Egypt and Israel for more than thirty years, one upheld by the deposed dictator Hosni Mubarak. Should Jews fear a reopening of those accords since a cornerstone of the accords was a positive movement on the Palestinian tract, something that has occurred only in reverse? The demand for democracy in Israel and Palestine coming from a democratic Arab world should be seen as a positive thrust toward breaking the newly found Jewish dependence on empire and dictatorship. Arendt anticipated Jews as the carriers of democracy to the Middle East, though she feared the opposite would be the case. Perhaps that democracy might come from the unexpected Arab source.

These points partly summarize where we as Jews are today. They also pose the question of whether there is a way forward. Though the encounter with our Jewish thinkers seems past, and our own journey in the present continues, the Jewish future can be created only through a fusion of the past and the present. This is why our Jewish thinkers are as relevant today as they were then. Their strengths and weaknesses are both a sign of hope and a warning. They compel us to ask what our strengths and weaknesses are today.

In an increasingly globalized world that interacts with Jews, Judaism, and the state of Israel, and with an increasing presence of that globalized world within the United States, including a growing number of Palestinians, Arabs, and Muslims, Jews now have another window onto the world. Initially this will be disturbing, since the Jewish voice has been ascendant since the close of World War II, primarily through the memory of the Holocaust and the emergence of Israel. Jews held the moral high ground, but this clearly is no longer the case.

Our success in America has also placed the Jewish voice in the elite corners of American society and government. In the next years, other ethnic groups will compete to be there too. If the moral high ground has eroded, if other voices will provide competition, the loud voices and bullying tactics often deployed by some in the Constantinian Jewish establishment seem increasingly out of place. In the years to come they will be counterproductive.

This diminution of Jewish power over the next decades may be as important for the Jewish future as the assumption of that power was after the Holocaust.

Power is the lever that allows the oppressed to find their footing in the world. In the end, though, power functions as a blinder, shielding the powerful from its loss of innocence and its use of power over against others. Power is needed for the liberation of the oppressed. The powerful need to be liberated from the oppression they cause.

The Jewish future will be decided in large part by how and to what effect Jews can renegotiate our place in the world. Though mindful that anti-Semitism remains, we must accept that criticism of Jews and Jewish power is also appropriate. Just as we are aware that there continue to be enemies of Jews and Judaism, we must affirm that there are individuals and communities who are in solidarity with a peaceful and flourishing Jewish future.

The challenge before us is whether as Jews we can once again venture into the world as a witness to ourselves and others. If we can turn yet another historical corner, the Jewish identity of the future will be one of hope and solidarity. Then we can carry elements of Jewishness from the past and transform them to what is needed in the years ahead. Just when many Jews and others think that Jewish life has entered a terminal phase, we might surprise ourselves and others.

Clearly, as our Jewish thinkers testify, Jews have much to share with the world. To create a future worthy of our past, we will have to listen to the world as well. Who knows when the prophetic will once again explode on the world scene? Just when the prophetic fire seems extinguished, it returns. Perhaps it will return to Jerusalem, calling Jews and Palestinians out of the exile in their own shared land.

Notes

CHAPTER 1: ENCOUNTERING THE HOLOCAUST

1. Richard Rubenstein, *After Auschwitz: Radical Theology and Contemporary Judaism* (Indianapolis: Bobbs-Merrill, 1966).

2. For my own work in discussing the formation of Holocaust Theology see *Toward a Jewish Theology of Liberation: The Challenge of the 21st Century*, Third and Expanded Edition (Waco, Tex.: Baylor University Press, 2004), 15–30.

3. Rubenstein, *The Cunning of History: Mass Death and the American Future* (New York: Harper and Row, 1975), 4–5.

4. Ibid., 21.

5. Rubenstein, *The Cunning of History.*

6. Rubenstein, *After Auschwitz*, ix–x.

7. For a history of the development of the museum see Edward Linenthal, *Preserving Memory: The Struggle to Create America's Holocaust Museum* (New York: Columbia University Press, 2001).

8. Elie Wiesel, *A Jew Today* (New York: Random House, 1978), 11.

9. Lucy Dawidowicz, "Thinking about the Six Million: Facts, Figure, Perspectives," in *Holocaust: Religious and Philosophical Implications*, ed. John Roth and Michael Berenbaum (New York: Paragon House, 1989), 61.

10. On the evolution of *Night* see Naomi Seidman, "Elie Wiesel and the Scandal of Jewish Rage," *Jewish Social Studies* 3(Fall 1966): 1–19.

11. Elie Wiesel, *Night* (New York: Hill and Wang, 2006), x–xi.

12. Ibid., 34.

13. Michael Berenbaum, *Elie Wiesel: God, the Holocaust and the Children of Israel* (West Orange, N.J.: Behrman House, 1994), 125–51.

14. Ibid., 127.

15. Elie Wiesel, *The Gates of the Forest* (New York: Holt, Rinehart and Winston, 1966), 197.

16. Ibid., *A Jew Today*, 6.

17. For the 614th Commandment see Emil Fackenheim, *God's Presence in History: Jewish Affirmations and Philosophical Reflections* (New York: New York University Press, 1970), 84.

18. Ibid., 84.

19. For the description of this encounter see "Richard Rubenstein and Elie Wiesel: An Exchange," in *Holocaust,* ed. Roth and Berenbaum, 346–48.

20. Rubenstein, ibid., 355.

21. Ibid., 356.

22. Elie Wiesel, "Israel Twenty Years Later," in *Against Silence: The Voice and Vision of Elie Wiesel*, vol. 2, ed. Irving Abrahamson (New York: Holocaust Library, 1985), 191, 190.

23. Ibid.

24. Ibid., "At the Western Wall," *Hadassah Magazine* (July 1967): 4.

25. Ibid., 7.

26. Ibid., 6.

27. Elie Wiesel, "A Moral Victory," in *Against Silence*, 187.

28. "An Exchange," *Holocaust*, ed. Roth and Berenbaum, 356–57.

29. Ibid., 357.

30. Ibid., 357.

31. Ibid., 367.

32. See Wiesel, *Night*, 24–27.

33. Ibid., 7.

34. Richard Rubenstein, "Elie Wiesel and Primo Levi," *Perspectives on the Holocaust: Essays in Honor of Raul Hilberg*, ed. James Pacy and Alan Wertheimer (Boulder: Westview, 1995), 146, 149.

35. For a critical understanding of Wiesel's moral leadership see Mark Chmiel, *Elie Wiesel and the Politics of Moral Leadership* (Philadelphia: Temple University Press, 2001).

36. Ibid., 150.

37. Norman Finkelstein, *The Holocaust Industry: Reflections on the Exploitation of Jewish Suffering* (London: Verso, 2000), 3–4.

38. Phillip Lopate, "Resistance to the Holocaust," *Tikkun* 4 (1989): 56.

39. Avishai Margalit, "The Kitsch of Israel," *New York Review of Books* 35 (November 24, 1988): 23.

40. www.huffingtnpost(om/2009/06/05obama-buchenwald-speech-t_N-211898.html

CHAPTER 2: ENCOUNTERING THE BIBLE

1. Martin Buber, *I and Thou,* trans. Ronald Gregor Smith (New York: Charles Scribner's Sons, 1970) and Martin Buber, *Israel and the World: Essays in a Time of Crisis* (New York: Schocken, 1963).

2. Elie Wiesel, *All the Rivers Run to the Sea: Memoirs* (New York: Knopf, 1995), 154–55.

3. Ibid., 354–55.

4. Aubrey Hodes, *Martin Buber: An Intimate Portrait* (New York: Viking, 1971), 16.

5. Ibid., 18–19.

6. Quoted in Kenneth Paul Kramer, *Martin Buber's I and Thou: Practicing Living Dialogue* (New York: Paulist, 2003), 5.

7. Charles Hartshorne, "Martin Buber's Metaphysics," *The Philosophy of Martin Buber*, ed. Paul Arthur Schilpp and Maurice Friedman (La Salle, Ill.: Open Court, 1967), 49.

8. Buber," Teaching and Deed," *Israel and the World*, 139, 141, 138, 145.

9. Ibid., 45.

10. Ibid., 45–46.

11. Ibid., 46.

12. Buber, The Two Foci of the Jewish Soul," *Israel and the World*, 28–29.

13. Ibid., 30.

14. Martin Buber, "The Prejudices of Youth," *Israel and the World*, 45.

15. For my discussion of the prophetic voice in the twentieth century see Marc H. Ellis, *Peter Maurin: Prophet in the Twentieth Century* (New York: Paulist, 1980).

16. Buber, *I and Thou*, 70–71.

17. Ibid., 91.

18. Buber, "The Prejudices of Youth," *Israel and the World*, 44.

19. Ibid., 49.

20. Ibid., 50.

21. Ibid., 51, 52.

22. Buber, *I and Thou*, 36.

23. Buber, *I and Thou*, 108.

24. Ibid., 116, 115.

25. Ibid., 120.

26. Ibid., 152.

27. Martin Buber, *On the Bible: Eighteen Studies,* ed. Nahum Glatzer (Syracuse: Syracuse University Press, 2000), 60.

28. For his take on the Ten Commandments see Buber, "What Are We to Do About the Ten Commandments?" *Israel and the World*, 85–88.

29. Martin Buber, "Biblical Leadership," *Israel and the World*, 126–27.

30. Ibid.

31. I write about this experience in *Reading the Torah Out Loud: A Journey of Lament and Hope* (Minneapolis: Fortress Press, 2007).

32. Buber, "The Man of Today and the Jewish Bible," *Israel and the World*, 94.

33. Ibid., 95.

34. Ibid., 95. Also see "The Prejudices of Youth," 49.

35. Martin Buber, "Genuine Conversation and the Possibility of Peace," *Cross Currents* 5 (Fall 1955): 292–93.

CHAPTER 3: ENCOUNTERING GOD *AFTER*

1. Edward Kaplan, *Spiritual Radical: Abraham Joshua Heschel, 1940–1972* (New Haven: Yale University Press, 2007), 225.

2. Ibid., 47.

3. Elie Wiesel, *All Rivers Run to the Sea: Memoirs* (New York: Knopf, 1995), 354.

4. Abraham Joshua Heschel, "No Religion is an Island," *No Religion Is an Island: Abraham Joshua Heschel and Interreligious Dialogue*, ed. Harold Kasimow and Byron Sherwin (Maryknoll, N.Y.: Orbis, 1991), 3.

5. Ibid., 5–6.

6. Ibid., 6.

7. Ibid., 9.

8. Ibid., 13.

9. Kaplan, *Spiritual Radical*, 39–40.

10. Ibid., 40.

11. Richard Rubenstein, *Power Struggle: An Autobiographical Confession* (Lanham, Md.: University Press of America, 1986), 128.

12. Ibid., 184–86.

13. Richard Rubenstein, *After Auschwitz: Radical Theology and Contemporary Judaism* (Indianapolis: Bobbs-Merrill, 1966), ix–x.

14. Abraham Joshua Heschel, *The Sabbath: Its Meaning for Modern Man* (New York: Farrar, Straus and Giroux, 1951).

15. Abraham Joshua Heschel, "The Meaning of This War (World War II)," in *Moral Grandeur and Spiritual Audacity: Essays*, ed. Susannah Heschel (New York: Farrar, Straus and Giroux, 1996), 209–10.

16. Ibid, 211–12.

17. Kaplan, *Spiritual Radical*, 206.

18. Susannah Heschel, "Introduction," *Moral Grandeur*, xxviii–xxix.

19. Ibid., xxix.

20. Martin Buber, *Eclipse of God: Studies in the Relation Between Religion and Philosophy* (Atlantic Highlands, N.J.: Humanities Press, 1979), 129.

21. Abraham Joshua Heschel, *Between God and Man: An Interpretation of Judaism*, ed. Fritz A. Rothschild (New York: Free, 1959), 118, 120.

22. Ibid., 123–24.

23. Rothschild, 110.

24. Ibid., 111–12.

25. Ibid., 112.

26. Ibid., 116–17.

27. Ibid., 125.

28. Ibid., 83.

29. Ibid., 82, 83.

30. Ibid, 82, 83.

31. Ibid., 81–82.

32. Ibid., 59.

33. Ibid., 61–62.

34. Abraham Joshua Heschel, *Israel: An Echo of Eternity* (New York: Farrar, Strauss and Giroux, 1969), 5.

35. Ibid., 5-6.

36. Ibid., 7.

37. Ibid., 17.

38. Susannah Heschel, *Moral Grandeur*, xxv.

39. Heschel, *Israel*, 159.

40. Ibid., 173.

41. Ibid., 174.

42. Ibid., 178–80.

43. Ibid., 180–81.

44. Ibid., 182–83.

45. Ibid., 183–84.

46. Ibid., 187.

47. Ibid., 197.

48. Ibid., 206, 209.

49. Ibid., 202, 214.

50. Heschel, "Existence and Celebration" *Moral Grandeur*, 23.

51. Ibid., 29, 31.

52. Ibid., vii.

53. Kaplan, *Spiritual Radical*, 216.

54. Ibid., 218.

55. Ibid., 225.

56. The event is recalled in Kaplan, *Spiritual Radical*, 324–29.

57. "Carl's Stern Interview with Dr. Heschel," *Moral Grandeur*, 400.

58. Ibid.

59. *Between God and Man*, 82, 84.

60. Kaplan, *Spiritual Radical*, 296–97.

CHAPTER 4: ENCOUNTERING JEWISH POLITICS

1. Maurice Friedman, *Martin Buber's Life and Work: The Later Years, 1945–1965* (Detroit: Wayne State University, 1988), 358, 359.

2. Ibid., 399.

3. Elie Wiesel, *All Rivers Run to the Sea: A Memoir* (New York: Knopf, 1995), 347.

4. Ibid., 347–48.

5. Marc H. Ellis, *Beyond Innocence and Redemption: Confronting the Holocaust and Israeli Power* (San Francisco: Harper & Row, 1990).

6. Ibid., 7–9.

7. Hannah Arendt, *Eichmann in Jerusalem: A Report on the Banality of Evil* (New York: Viking, 1964), 279.

8. " 'Eichmann in Jerusalem': An Exchange of Letters Between Gershom Scholem and Hannah Arendt," in *Hannah Arendt: The Jew as Pariah: Identity and Politics in the Modern Age*, ed. Ron H. Feldman (New York: Grove, 1978), 241–42.

9. Ibid., 246.

10. Ibid.

11. Richard Bernstein, *Hannah Arendt and the Jewish Question* (Cambridge: MIT Press, 1996), 55–56.

12. Hannah Arendt, *The Origins of Totalitarianism* (New York: Harcourt, Brace and Company, 1951), 434.

13. See Rubenstein, *Cunning of History*, 113–31.

14. Ron H. Feldman, "The Jew as Pariah: The Case of Hannah Arendt (1906–1975), *Jew as Pariah*, 15.

15. Elizabeth Young-Bruehl, *Hannah Arendt: For the Love of the World* (New Haven: Yale University Press, 1984), 16.

16. Hannah Arendt, "To Save the Jewish Homeland: There is Still Time," *Jew as Pariah*, 192.

17. Ibid., 42.

18. "Thesis on the Philosophy of History, "*Illuminations: Walter Benjamin: Essays and Reflections*, ed. Hannah Arendt (New York: Schocken, 1969), 253.

19. Ibid., 264.

20. Ibid., 257, 260

21. Hannah Arendt, "Introduction: Walter Benjamin: 1892–1940" *Illuminations*, 27, 36.

22. *Hannah Arendt: The Jewish Writings*, ed. Jerome Kohn and Ron Feldman (New York: Schocken, 2007), 296–97.

23. Ibid., 274.24. Arendt, *Origins*, 436.

25. Ibid., *Jewish Writings*, 264.

26. Ibid., 265, 266.

27. Carter Heyward, Anne Gilson, et al., *Revolutionary Forgiveness: Feminist Reflections on Nicaragua* (Maryknoll, N.Y.: Orbis, 1987).

28. Arendt, *Origins*, 439.

29. Hannah Arendt, *The Human Condition: A Study of the Central Dilemmas Facing Modern Man* (Garden City, N.Y.: Doubleday, 1959), 214–15.

30. Ibid., 218.

31. Ibid., 218.

32. Ibid., 216.

33. Adi Ophir, "Between Eichmann and Kant: Thinking on Evil after Arendt," *History and Memory: Studies in Representation of the Past* 8 (Fall 1996): 96.

34. Ibid., 93.

35. Edna Brocke, "*Big Hannah'—My Aunt,"* in *Jewish Writings*, 516.

36. Ibid., 516.

37. Elizabeth Young-Bruehl, *Love of the World*, 173–80.

38. "The Jewish Army—the Beginning of a Jewish Politics?" in *The Portable Hannah Arendt*, ed., Peter Baehr (New York: Penguin, 2000), 47–48.

39. Arendt, "Jewish Homeland," in *Jewish Writings*, 395.

40. Ibid., 394–95.

41. Baruch Kimmerling, *Politicide: Ariel Sharon's War against the Palestinians* (London: Verso, 2003).

42. Amnon Raz-Krakotzhin, "Bi-nationalism and Jewish Identity: Hannah Arendt and the Question of Palestine," in *Hannah Arendt in Jerusalem*, ed. Steven Aschheim (Berkeley: University of California Press, 2001): 172.

43. Ibid., 170.

44. Ibid., 201.

45. Young-Bruehl, *Love of the World*, 468, 469.

CHAPTER 5: ENCOUNTERING THE JEWISH PROPHETIC

1. Emanuel Levinas, "A Religion for Adults," *Difficult Freedom*: *Essays on Judaism* (Baltimore: Johns Hopkins University Press, 1990), 11.

2. Ibid., 11-12. For an extended and fascinating analysis of Levinas on the political dimensions of Israel see Howard Caygill, *Levinas and the Political* (London: Routledge, 2002): 159–98.

3. Ibid., 12.

4. Richard Rubenstein, *After Auschwitz: Radical Theology and Contemporary Judaism* (Indianapolis: Bobbs-Merrill, 1966), 278.

5. Levinas, "A Religion for Adults," in *Difficult Freedom*, 13.

6. Ibid., 13–14.

7. Ibid., "Loving the Torah More Than God," in *Difficult Freedom*, 143.

8. Ibid., 143.

9. Ibid., "A Religion for Adults," in *Difficult Freedom*, 13.

10. Ibid., 13, 14.

11. Ibid., 15.

12. Ibid., 18.

13. Ibid., 17.

14. Ibid., 17–18.

15. Ibid., 19–20.

16. Ibid., 19–20.

17. Ibid., "Ethics and Spirit," in *Difficult Freedom*, 8–9.

18. Ibid, 5.

19. Ibid., 5–6.

20. Ibid., 6.

21. Ibid., "Judaism and the Present" in *Difficult Freedom*, 213.

22. Ibid., 212.

23. Ibid., "Space Is Not One-dimensional," in *Difficult Freedom*, 263–64.

24. Ibid., 51.

25. Ibid., "Means of Identification," in *Difficult Freedom*, 211.

26. Ibid., "Ethics and Spirit," in *Difficult Freedom*, 5.

27. Ibid., 182–85.

28. Ibid., "Jewish Thought Today," in *Difficult Freeedom*, 165.

29. Ibid., 164.

30. The interview is found in "Ethics and Politics," *The Levinas Reader: Emmanuel Levinas*, ed. Sean Hand (Oxford: Basil Blackwell, 1989), 291, 290, 291, 293.

31. Ibid., 294.

EPILOGUE

1. James E. B. Breslin, *Mark Rothko: A Biography* (Chicago: University of Chicago, 1993), 460.

2. Ibid., 245.

3. Ibid., 473.

4. Ethan Bonner, "Israel Roiled after Chomsky Barred from West Bank," *New York Times*, May 17, 2010.

5. Harry Kreisler, "Activism, Anarchism and Power: Conversations with Noam Chomsky," Institute of International Studies, University of California, Berkeley at http://globetrotter.berkely.edu/people2/Chomsky/chomsky-con1.html

6. Elie Wiesel, "Jerusalem is Above Politics," *New York Times*, April 18, 2010.

7. Yossi Sarid, "For Jerusalem, "A Response to Elie Wiesel," *Haaretz*, April 18, 2010.

8. Assaf Sharon and Avner Inbar, "An Open Letter to Elie Wiesel," *New York Review of Books*, May 27, 2010.

Index